The Cold War in East Asia 1945–1991

COLD WAR
INTERNATIONAL HISTORY
PROJECT SERIES

James G. Hershberg
series editor

Stalin and Togliatti
Italy and the Origins of the Cold War
By Elena Agarossi and Victor Zaslavsky

A Distant Front in the Cold War
The USSR in West Africa and the Congo, 1956–1964
By Sergey Mazov

Connecting Histories
Decolonization and the Cold War in Southeast Asia, 1945–1962
Edited by Christopher E. Goscha and Christian F. Ostermann

Rebellious Satellite
Poland 1956
By Paweł Machewicz

Two Suns in the Heavens
The Sino-Soviet Struggle for Supremacy, 1962–1967
By Sergey Radchenko

The Soviet Union and the June 1967 Six Day War
Edited by Yaacov Ro'i and Boris Morozov

Local Consequences of the Global Cold War
Edited by Jeffrey A. Engel

Behind the Bamboo Curtain
China, Vietnam, and the World beyond Asia
Edited by Priscilla Roberts

Failed Illusions
Moscow, Washington, Budapest, and the 1956 Hungarian Revolt
By Charles Gati

Kim Il Sung in the Khrushchev Era
Soviet-DPRK Relations and the Roots of North Korean Despotism, 1953–1964
By Balázs Szalontai

(*continued on p. 341*)

The Cold War in East Asia 1945–1991

Edited by Tsuyoshi Hasegawa

Woodrow Wilson Center Press
Washington, D.C.

Stanford University Press
Stanford, California

EDITORIAL OFFICES
Woodrow Wilson Center Press
Woodrow Wilson International Center for Scholars
One Woodrow Wilson Plaza
1300 Pennsylvania Avenue, N.W.
Washington, DC 20004-3027
Telephone: 202-691-4029
www.wilsoncenter.org

ORDER FROM
Stanford University Press
Chicago Distribution Center
11030 South Langley Avenue
Chicago, Il 60628
www.sup.org

Telephone: 1-800-621-2736; 773-568-1550

Printed in the United States of America on acid-free paper
2 4 6 8 9 7 5 3 1

Library of Congress Cataloging-in-Publication Data

The cold war in East Asia, 1945–1991 / edited by Tsuyoshi Hasegawa.
p. cm. — (Cold war international history project series)
ISBN 978-0-8047-7331-7 (hardcover)
1. East Asia—Politics and government—20th century. 2. Cold War.
I. Hasegawa, Tsuyoshi, 1941–
DS518.1.C588 2011
950.4′2—dc22

2010048910

The Woodrow Wilson International Center for Scholars is the national, living U.S. memorial honoring President Woodrow Wilson. In providing an essential link between the worlds of ideas and public policy, the Center addresses current and emerging challenges confronting the United States and the world. The Center promotes policy-relevant research and dialogue to increase understanding and enhance the capabilities and knowledge of leaders, citizens, and institutions worldwide. Created by an Act of Congress in 1968, the Center is a nonpartisan institution headquartered in Washington, D.C., and supported by both public and private funds.

The Center is the publisher of *The Wilson Quarterly* and home of Woodrow Wilson Center Press and *dialogue* television and radio. For more information about the Center's activities and publications, including the monthly newsletter *Centerpoint,* please visit us on the web at www.wilsoncenter.org.

The Cold War International History Project

The Cold War International History Project was established by the Woodrow Wilson International Center for Scholars in 1991. The project supports the full and prompt release of historical materials by governments on all sides of the Cold War and seeks to disseminate new information and perspectives on Cold War history emerging from previously inaccessible sources on the "the other side"—the former Communist world—through publications, fellowships, and scholarly meetings and conferences. The project publishes the *Cold War International History Project Bulletin* and a working paper series, and maintains a Web site, http://www.cwihp.org.

At the Woodrow Wilson Center, the project is part of the History and Public Policy Program, directed by Christian F. Ostermann. The project is overseen by an advisory committee chaired by William Taubman, Amherst College, and includes Michael Beschloss; James H. Billington, Librarian of Congress; Warren I. Cohen, University of Maryland at Baltimore; John Lewis Gaddis, Yale University; James G. Hershberg, George Washington University; Samuel F. Wells Jr., Woodrow Wilson Center; and Sharon Wolchik, George Washington University.

The Cold War International History Project has been supported by the Korea Foundation, Seoul; the Leon Levy Foundation, New York; the Henry Luce Foundation, New York; the John D. and Catherine T. MacArthur Foundation, Chicago; and the Smith Richardson Foundation, Westport, CT.

Contents

Acknowledgments

This book originated in three conferences on the Cold War in Asia, 1945–91, which were organized and sponsored by the Center for Cold War Studies of the University of California, Santa Barbara, and held in Santa Barbara in 2005, 2006, and 2007. The first conference was devoted to the period 1945–56, the second to the period 1956–73, and the third to the period 1973–91. After these conferences, Odd Arne Westad and I decided to publish a conference volume focusing on East Asia but excluding Southeast Asia. The most exciting parts of the conferences were the discussions, and we regret that we could not include in this volume a record of the stimulating exchanges at each session. I thank the participants in the conferences, not only the contributors to this volume but also those who presented papers and participated in the discussions, especially Jessica Chapman, Andrew Kuchins, Fredrik Lovegall, Robert McMahon, Christian Ostermann, Tanaka Takahiko, Kathryn Weathersby, and Salim Yaqub.

The three conferences were supported by generous grants from the University of California's (UC's) Institute on Global Conflict and Cooperation (IGCC) and conference grants from the College Council of Deans at UC, Santa Barbara. Peter Cowhey and Susan Shirk, directors of the IGCC, and David Marshall, dean of the College of Arts and Humanities at UC, Santa Barbara, who were ardent and consistent supporters for this project, deserve our thanks. I am also grateful to the Interdisciplinary Humanities Center and the Department of History at UC, Santa Barbara, for extending their support to the conferences in a number of ways.

The graduate student assistants at the Center for Cold War Studies—Paul Baltimore, George Fujii, Moonsil Lee Kim, John Sbardellati (now an assistant professor at the University of Waterloo), Brandon Seto, and Victor Shonagin—worked tirelessly, from writing grant proposals to organizing the logistical details of the conferences.

I am also grateful to Robert McMahon and the anonymous outside reviewer of the book's manuscript, whose valuable comments helped to improve it immensely. Jessica Chapman, Andy Johns, and Kenneth Osgood, our Center for Cold War Studies alumni and now well-established professors, read and commented on the introduction. It was the most delightful privilege as their former teacher to receive their insightful comments. Thanks to them, the introduction was vastly improved.

Joseph Brinley, director of the Woodrow Wilson Center Press, has been most helpful in shepherding the manuscript to publication, and Yamile Kahn did a wonderful job editing the entire book. We also thank Alfred Imhoff for his copyediting skills.

Needless to say, I am the only one responsible for whatever mistakes may occur in the book.

My special thanks go to my colleague and friend, Odd Arne Westad, who has been the inspiration for this entire project, and for all practical purposes, served as the coeditor of the book until he had to withdraw from the technical aspects of the editorial process due to his busy schedule. But even after withdrawing, he was always available for advice.

Finally, I thank my wife, Deborah Steinhoff, who graciously hosted many receptions for the participants at our home, where stimulating discussions continued into the beautiful Santa Barbara evenings. Without her encouragement and support, I would not have taken up the task of editing this book.

A Note on Spelling, Transliteration, and Names

For Chinese names and words, we have used the pinyin system, except for occasional mentions of well-known names such as Chiang Kai-shek (Jiang Jieshi), Mao Tse-tung (Mao Zedong), and Chou En-lai (Zhou Enlai).

For Japanese words, we have adhered to the Hepburn transliteration system with slight modifications. For instance, we use *shinbun* instead of *shimbun*. We omitted macrons in both the text and the notes. Japanese surnames precede given names, except if a Japanese author's publication is in English. For instance, two of the contributors to this volume, Nobuo Shimotomai and Kazuhiko Togo, are introduced with their given names first and family names second; but when we refer to their publications in Japanese, we cite "Shimotomai Nobuo" and "Togo Kazuhiko."

For Korean words, in most cases we have used the McCune-Reischauer Romanization system. In cases where names are commonly referred to using a different spelling or name order, we have adopted the common usage. Examples include Syngman Rhee, Park Chung Hee, Chun Doo Hwan, Roh Tae Woo, Kim Young Sam, and Kim Il Sung.

For Russian names and words, we have used the Library of Congress transliteration system except for well-known names and geographical locations, such as Yalta (rather than Ialta), Mikoyan (rather than Mikoian), and Yakovlev (rather than Iakovlev). Soft signs are generally omitted in the text but are retained in the notes.

The Cold War in East Asia 1945–1991

Introduction: East Asia—the Second Significant Front of the Cold War

Tsuyoshi Hasegawa

The Cold War was a global conflict. First and foremost, it was a dispute between the United States and the Soviet Union, but it was not merely a contest between the two superpowers. The Soviet Union and the United States represented the interests of the socialist camp ("the East") and the democratic-capitalist camp ("the West"), respectively, and the struggle extended to all regions of the globe, involving all states. Some states joined one of the two camps; others, especially in Eastern Europe, were forced to be incorporated into the socialist camp; and still others chose to stay neutral. But none escaped the influence of the Cold War. Of all the world's regions, however, Europe was the most important for the Cold War. The two competing camps were starkly divided in Europe, where they were incorporated into rival military alliances, the North Atlantic Treaty Organization (NATO) and the Warsaw Pact Organization. Especially important was the division of the most important state in Central Europe, Germany, and its capital, Berlin. The superpower conflict had other dimensions in other regions, but there is no question that both the United States and the Soviet Union regarded the defense of their respective spheres of Europe as the most fundamental task of their foreign and security policy. Europe was thus the central front of the Cold War.[1]

The second front of the Cold War was in Asia, where the line that separated the West from the East was drawn differently. Unlike divided Germany, Japan was occupied solely by the United States, serving as the outpost of the U.S. global strategy to counter Communist expansionism. The Communists in China completed the revolution, establishing the People's Republic of China (PRC) in 1949, and they then immediately forged an alliance with the Soviet Union by concluding the Sino-Soviet Treaty of Friendship, Alliance, and

Mutual Assistance in 1950. From then on, the quadrangular relations involving the United States, the Soviet Union, China, and Japan became the major focus of the Cold War in Asia. The developments on the Korean Peninsula further complicated these quadrangular relations. The North Koreans invaded the south in June 1950, initiating the Korean War, the first hot war waged between the United States and the Communist camp. Like the division of Germany, the division of Korea became a permanent fixture of the Cold War (and beyond, in the case of Korea); but this division, unlike that of Germany, reflected more complex interactions of the quadrangular powers.

The conflict in the developing world (or, as it was then known, the Third World) was the third front of the Cold War. Decolonization after World War II would have happened without the Cold War, but the process of decolonization was colored and warped by the Cold War context in Southeast Asia, South Asia, the Middle East, Latin America, and Africa.[2] In this volume, we limit ourselves to East Asia, excluding Southeast Asia and South Asia from our focus of attention. Here, it only needs to be noted that the process of decolonization in East Asia was somewhat different from the process in Southeast Asia and South Asia, because in East Asia the colonial power was defeated Japan, but in the other two regions the colonial powers were Western nations.

Last, the fourth front of the Cold War was fought on the home front in each nation—on both sides. The domestic politics of each nation developed in close connection with the external Cold War, and the Cold War profoundly influenced the media, culture, sports, and people's consciousness.[3]

There is no question that the Cold War conflict was centered on its first front, the East/West conflict in Europe. The Cold War in East Asia constituted only its second front. And yet this second front was by no means insignificant or peripheral. In fact, the Cold War's East Asian front had important implications for its other fronts. Furthermore, it can be argued that it was precisely because Asia constituted only the second front that the United States could afford to resort to military actions there that it could not have undertaken in Europe. Thus in Asia the Cold War did not remain cold but led to two major hot wars—the Korean War in East Asia; and the Vietnam War in Southeast Asia, with which East Asia interacted in important ways.[4]

The Cold War in Asia evolved along a different path from that taken in Europe. In East Asia, the dynamic and changing relations among the major powers created a more complicated situation than in Europe, where the East/West fault line was clearly delineated. During the early phase of the Cold War, when the United States led the anticommunist alliances of Asian nations—thus exhibiting a seemingly similar binary conflict between the two camps—the structure of the Cold War revealed major differences from the Cold War on the first front.

The primary adversary of the United States in Asia in the first phase of the Cold War was China, not the Soviet Union. Whereas in Europe, the East and the West confronted each other at the center of Europe, in divided Germany and in divided Berlin, the divisions in Asia were on the peripheries—Korea and Vietnam. It was against perceived Chinese Communist expansion, though backed by the Soviet Union, that the United States fought the two Asian hot wars and forged its security alliances with Japan and with Japan's former colonies, South Korea and Taiwan.[5] As Ilya Gaiduk argues in chapter 2 of this volume, the Soviet Union preferred to stay in the background, inducing Communist China to stand at the forefront of the Asian Communist movement, a policy that helped China to enhance its prestige and confidence—and ironically to eventually challenge the supremacy of the Soviet Union.[6]

Unlike in Europe—where two military alliances, NATO and the Warsaw Pact Organization, confronted each other—the Soviet Union and the United States did not face each other directly in Asia until well into the 1970s. But at the same time, during the first phase of the Cold War, the United States yielded more power and predominance over its Asian allies than over its European allies, which acted more like partners, albeit junior ones. And also unlike in Europe, where the United States forged a security alliance with liberal democracies, in Asia it created a network of bilateral security alliances with mostly—with the exception of Japan—authoritarian regimes: South Korea, Taiwan, the Philippines, and South Vietnam.[7]

The Beginning of the Cold War in Asia, 1945–56

China provided the crucial factor that separated the Cold War in East Asia from the first front of the Cold War, between the United States in alliance with Western Europe and the Soviet Union. The Chinese Revolution gave the socialist camp tremendous prestige, with the Communist world suddenly stretching across the Eurasian continent, and, coupled with the USSR's possession of atomic bombs, sharply heightened the sense of Communist threat among the members of the Western alliance; directly contributed to the U.S. decision to adopt National Security Council Report 68, known as NSC-68;[8] and provided the major impetus for McCarthyism. The emergence of China under Communism, however, complicated the management of Sino-Soviet relations. Even before the completion of the Revolution in 1949, Mao Zedong's "leaning" on the side of the Communist camp was never in doubt, but the Soviet Union and China were never a monolith. The checkered past of the Chinese Communist Party's relations with Moscow, going back to the 1920s and the Soviet underestimation of the potentialities of the Chinese Revolution after the war, was destined to surface as the Chinese Communists consolidated their power. Although Mao accepted Joseph Stalin's supremacy, the Chinese helmsman had his own Sino-centric vision of revolution colored by the tradition of China's Central Kingdom.[9] Stalin conceded China's leading role in revolutionary and anticolonial movements in Asia, and China assumed the mantle of the socialist leader of the developing world. As such, the PRC was one of the major players at the Bandung Conference of nonaligned nations in 1955, although the PRC's foreign policy could hardly be characterized as nonaligned. It was a matter of time before the two Communist countries diverged in their strategy on how to advance the cause of the socialist camp.[10]

The Korean War is one of the most studied aspects of the Cold War in Asia, although compared with its ugly cousin, the Vietnam War, it has received less attention.[11] The convergence of interests of the three Communist players—Stalin, Mao, and Kim Il Sung—appeared for a long time to lie behind Kim Il Sung's decision to invade the south, in the orthodox interpretation of the origins of the Korean War; and indeed, this understanding was the motivation behind U.S. president Harry S. Truman's decision to intervene in the Korean War. Bruce Cumings, challenging this view, offered a revisionist interpretation that the Korean War had to be understood in the context of the civil war in Korea, blaming equally Syngman Rhee's bellicose intention to unify Korea.[12] However, contrary to Cuming's assertion, recent scholarship (prompted by the opening of archives in Russia and China) indicates that Stalin and Mao were indeed heavily involved in Kim Il Sung's decision to initiate the invasion of the south; but it also shows the differences among the Communist leaders. More than anything else, misperceptions held by both the United States and the Soviet Union were responsible for the outbreak of the Korean War.[13]

The impact of the Korean War on the structure of the Cold War was far-reaching. It determined the division of Korea as a permanent fixture of the Cold War in Asia, and it integrated Japan into the United States' global strategy against Communist expansion. Truman's decision to defend Taiwan to prevent the Chinese Communists from completing their national unification created a thorny Taiwan issue for future U.S.-Chinese relations, ensuring the PRC's isolation from the international community. The Korean War further contributed to the strengthening of the NATO alliance against future Soviet expansion. It also expedited America's transformation into a national security state.[14]

If Korea suffered the brunt of the Cold War conflict, Japan profited from the onset of the Cold War. The democratic phase of the U.S. postwar occupation of Japan yielded to a reverse course. The Japanese conservative powers, headed by Yoshida Shigeru, took advantage of the Cold War and achieved Japan's independence at the San Francisco Peace Conference in 1951 by aligning it closely with the United States in its security arrangement. U.S. military bases in Japan became the center of U.S. operations during the Korean War. And because Japan was protected by the U.S. nuclear umbrella, under Yoshida and his successors it could divert all its energies single-mindedly to economic development, with minimal spending on its Self-Defense Force. Thus Japan's economy received a boon from the Korean War, laying the foundation for the nation's miraculous economic growth in the 1960s.[15]

Yoshida sought the vast market of China as the crucial key to Japan's future economic expansion, but John Foster Dulles, then a special assistant to Truman, forced Japan to conclude a peace treaty with Chiang Kai-shek's (Jiang Jieshi's) Republic of China (Taiwan), foreclosing the possibility that Japan might conclude a peace treaty with the PRC.[16] Although the Soviet Union participated in the San Francisco Peace Conference, the Soviet government did not sign the San Francisco Peace Treaty, thus forfeiting the chance to legalize its occupation of the Kuril Islands, the right and claims for which Japan was forced to renounce. Dulles's masterpiece provision of this treaty, Article 2(c), succeeded in driving a long-lasting wedge between Japan and the Soviet Union, steering Japan's irredentism from Okinawa to the Kurils.[17] Japan's settlements with its former colonies (Taiwan and Korea) and with its enemies (the Soviet Union and the PRC) became entangled with the new Cold War conflict.

The binary Cold War division in Asia (including Southeast Asia) was different from that in Europe. In Asia, decolonization and revolution merged, and China, as the champion of both, stood at the forefront of the Cold War against the United States. The United States, in turn, made Japan its junior partner in its global strategy, a policy that the Japanese conservatives were more than happy to support in order to gain Japan's reintegration with the international community. By providing the economic aid to jump-start Japan's postwar economy, the United States gained permanent military bases on Okinawa and Japan's main islands. In Asia, the Soviet Union receded into the background, though it acquiesced to Kim Il Sung's persistent plea to invade the south and thus to initiate the Korean War. The PRC saved Kim Il Sung's regime from the jaws of defeat by sending "volunteers." China's stature rose, as evidenced in its participation in the Geneva Conference in 1954. But the more influential the PRC became in the Cold War conflict, in either the Korean War or the Vietnam War, the more stubbornly the United States attempted to isolate it from the international community.

Toward Multipolarization, 1956–72

The year 1956 was a fateful one for the Cold War in Asia, as elsewhere. Nikita Khrushchev's secret speech against Stalin's cult of personality at the Twentieth

Party Congress of the Communist Party of the Soviet Union also threatened the power held by Mao Zedong and Kim Il Sung. China played a crucial role in the Soviet handling of the Eastern European revolutions. Mao opposed Soviet intervention in Poland because it might also provide a justification for Soviet interference in China's affairs, but he supported the Soviets' crushing of the Hungarian Revolution because Imre Nagy's dismantling of the Communist Party dictatorship would undermine the Chinese Communist Party's' dictatorial power. Mao weathered the potential criticisms leveled against his own cult of personality, and he launched the Great Leap Forward to consolidate his power. A corresponding radicalism in China's foreign policy, exemplified by the offshore crisis in the Taiwan Strait, was driven by Mao's domestic needs to consolidate his power by exaggerating the danger of U.S. imperialism. Mao's radicalism alarmed Khrushchev, who was pursuing a policy of peaceful coexistence, eventually driving the Soviet leader to withdraw Soviet scientists and engineers from China, including those working on China's nuclear project. The Sino-Soviet conflict began in earnest, to the point that each regarded the other as a major ideological threat.[18]

Mao's Great Leap Forward resulted in economic catastrophe, and opposition from the moderates grew against him. But as Lorenz Lüthi shows in chapter 6, in 1962 Mao succeeded again in channeling China's foreign policy in a radical direction, this time singling out American imperialism and Soviet revisionism as China's major enemies. The Soviet withdrawal of missiles from Cuba and signing of the Partial Test Ban Treaty vindicated Mao's doubts about the Soviet Union as the champion of the international revolutionary movement. The further challenge from the moderates—led by Liu Shaoqi, Deng Xiaoping, and Zhou Enlai—resulted in Mao's extraordinary decision to unleash the Cultural Revolution in 1966, which threw China into utter chaos, isolating it from the world.[19]

Kim Il Sung was also threatened by Khrushchev's secret speech. And because Khrushchev and Mao were concerned with the instability of the North Korean regime under Kim, they sent a joint delegation, headed by Anastas Mikoyan and Peng Dehuai, to depose Kim in August and September 1956. This joint intervention by China and the Soviet Union, as Nobuo Shimotomai argues in chapter 5, served as the decisive starting point from which Kim Il Sung balanced the two Communist neighbors.[20] He established his own dictatorial power by purging both the Soviet and the Chinese factions within the Korean Workers' Party, and developed his own highly dictatorial *chuche* (self-reliance) movement. Turning weakness into leverage for blackmail was a favored tactic for the rulers of weaker states during the Cold War, but Kim Il Sung perfected this method better than any other.

The year 1956 was also a crucial one for Soviet-Japanese relations. The Soviet-Japanese normalization talks that began in 1955 were deadlocked over the territorial dispute about the Kuril Islands. The Soviet Union and Japan were about to reach a compromise solution by splitting the contested four islands into two groups, with the two bigger islands (Etorofu and Kunashiri) remaining with the Soviet Union and Japan gaining the other two islands (Habomai and Shikotan). However, John Foster Dulles, now secretary of state under President Dwight Eisenhower, put strong pressure on Japan not to compromise over the Kurils, with a threat that otherwise the United States would never return Okinawa. Though they were unable to resolve this territorial dispute, the Soviet Union and Japan normalized relations in 1956, merely ratifying the Joint Declaration without a peace treaty.[21] That was the closest that both countries came to resolving the dispute. From then on, the Soviet Union and Japan drifted apart. Rapprochement between the two countries remained elusive throughout the entire Cold War period and beyond—until today. There were fissures of conflict between the United States and Japan. But in contrast to the Communist camp, the United States held its allies of unequal status under firm control. Japan never adopted the equivalent of Willy Brandt's *Ostpolitik* vis-à-vis the Soviet Union.[22]

In 1960, the United States and Japan revised their security treaty. Although this revision corrected many unequal provisions contained in the original treaty, it touched off a massive protest movement. President Eisenhower's visit to Japan was canceled, but Prime Minister Kishi Nobusuke's high-handed parliamentary maneuver succeeded in getting the revised security treaty ratified. This crisis underscored the fragility of the U.S.-Japanese alliance, which concealed the undercurrents of Japan's resentment against U.S. dominance. Seizing this opportunity, Khrushchev annulled the territorial provision of the 1956 Joint Declaration, retracting the promise to return two of the Kuril Islands, Habomai and Shikotan, to Japan in an attempt to decouple Japan from the United States. But this maneuver backfired.

Ikeda Hayato, who succeeded Kishi, concentrated on economic growth. Under his leadership, Japan succeeded in accomplishing double-digit annual growth in the 1960s and creating a trade surplus with the United States. Multipolarization in the capitalist camp in East Asia began within its economic order. As for his approach to the Soviet Union, Ikeda escalated the territorial dispute with the Soviet Union, inventing the term "the Northern Territories" to refer to the four contested Kuril Islands. It was convenient for the Japanese government to have this territorial dispute with the Soviet Union as a way to move Japanese public opinion in the direction of accepting the nation's renewed defense partnership with the United States.[23]

In 1960, student demonstrations in South Korea toppled Syngman Rhee, but the parliamentary democracy that was created was short-lived, giving way to another authoritarian dictatorship by Park Chung Hee the following year. Park concluded a peace treaty with Japan in 1965, prompting South Korea's economic growth with a massive injection of Japanese loans and investment. As Gregg Brazinsky shows in chapter 9, together with Japan's prewar economic modernization, South Korea's success gave rise to the Asian model of economic development, characterized by the crucial role played by the state, authoritarian tutelage, and the oligarchy of economic magnates.[24]

As we will see in more detail below, the escalation of the Vietnam War resulting from Lyndon B. Johnson's decision to Americanize the war in 1965 had far-reaching consequences for the structure of the Cold War beyond the regional conflict in Southeast Asia. The war eroded American prestige and exposed the limits of its influence. It broke the American consensus on the Cold War and polarized domestic public opinion. And with its weakened economy, the United States also lost its unquestioned economic dominance. In addition, the war facilitated the multipolarization of international relations. As we will discuss below, the war's Americanization had serious consequences for the Sino-Soviet conflict. After Khrushchev's ouster, the new Soviet leaders abandoned their predecessor's hands-off policy toward Vietnam and increased Soviet military aid to North Vietnam. This did not lead to a reconciliation of the Soviet Union and the PRC, however; on the contrary, their conflict became more intense.

In 1968, the Soviet Union intervened in Czechoslovakia to suppress the Prague Spring, invoking the "Brezhnev Doctrine." Alarmed by this invasion, the Chinese attacked Soviet troops on the contested Damanskii/Zhenbao Island in the Ussuri River in 1969, provoking a Soviet counterattack in which the Chinese were soundly defeated. After this incident, the Soviets hinted at a possible preemptive nuclear attack against the Chinese. The Sino-Soviet dispute was no longer limited to ideology but was now expanded to state-to-state military conflict.[25] Mao and Zhou Enlai sensed the danger of continuing the Cultural Revolution, and they began exploring the possibility of achieving rapprochement with their archenemy, the United States. Richard Nixon and Henry Kissinger, for their part, were desperately looking for a way to end the Vietnam War and lure the Soviet Union into accepting the arms control treaty, to arrest what seemed to be an insatiable appetite for strategic weapons. U.S.-Chinese hostility, which had dominated the Cold War in Asia since 1950, was about to end.[26]

Détente and East Asia, 1973–79

Three factors that emerged during the 1970s made the structure of the Cold War in East Asia fundamentally different from that in Europe.[27] First and foremost, U.S.-Chinese rapprochement raised the prestige of China. The PRC now became a pivotal third power between the two superpowers. China and the United States began strategic cooperation against the Soviet Union, and in the developing world, China supported anti-Soviet forces, often in cooperation with the United States. Second, the United States' defeat in the Vietnam War seriously eroded its prestige and revealed the limits of its power in its commitment to Asia. Together, these factors led to a situation in which a strategic triangle replaced the bipolarity of the first phase of the Cold War. In the Communist camp, China—which had once been the junior partner of the Soviet Union and which had stood at the camp's forefront against the United States—became an independent strategic player to be courted by the United States to counter the Soviet threat; and this in turn gave China an opportunity to enter the international system as a great power. Under Deng Xiaoping's leadership, China launched four modernizations. To carry out these modernizations, China's opening to capitalist countries was a sine qua non.[28]

The strategic triangle heightened the Soviet sense of insecurity, because Moscow now had to deal with two different rivals. It began to deploy more than fifty divisions along the Chinese border and in Mongolia to counter the Chinese threat. At the same time, the Soviets began to modernize their strategic forces in the Far East as part of the strategic arms race with the United States. The Soviet military adopted a bastion strategy, turning the Sea of Okhotsk into the Soviet inland sea, where it deployed its newly modernized nuclear submarine forces capable of reaching the United States, and also strategically deploying Backfire bombers in the Soviet Far East. For the first time since 1945, the Soviet strategic forces directly confronted their U.S. counterparts in Asia.[29]

China was not the only rising star. During this decade, Japan attained the status of an economic great power, which gave it growing confidence as an independent player in its foreign policy. Although the U.S.-Japanese security alliance continued to be the anchor of Japan's foreign policy, the United States was no longer in a position to dictate its will to Japan, as it had done during the early phase of the Cold War. Tensions and conflicts also emerged in U.S.-Japanese bilateral economic relations.[30] Furthermore, the Asian economy attained unprecedented vitality, with Japan leading the pack, followed by the four Asian tigers of South Korea, Hong Kong, Taiwan, and Singapore.[31] In contrast, the Soviet Union entered a period of stagnation, missing the boat of structural reform and integration with the international economic system, which was undergoing revolutionary transformation. Instead of becoming the window to Asia and the Pacific, the highly militarized Soviet Far East was closing its doors ever more tightly, cutting itself off from interactions with the vibrant Asia-Pacific economic community. As Gregg Brazinsky shows in chapter 9, although South Korea accomplished spectacular economic modernization under the authoritarian rule of Park Chung Hee, North Korea, isolated from the global international economy, became more and more dependent on Soviet and Chinese assistance. South Korea's economic development, however, was not accompanied by liberal and democratic political reforms. Park Chung Hee instituted the Yushin Constitution in 1972, installing himself as the permanent president, but the success of his economic policy created a large number of middle-class citizens, who became interested in voicing their political opinions. In October 1979, Park was assassinated, but another army dictator, Chun Don Hwan, took his place.[32]

The New Cold War in Asia, 1979–85

From a global perspective, the phase of the Cold War from 1979 to 1985 can be characterized as one of intensifying U.S-Soviet confrontation. This new phase began with the Soviet invasion of Afghanistan and the collapse of the détente process. Following the election of Ronald Reagan, the crisis was further escalated with the intermediate nuclear forces crisis, the abrogation of the second round of Strategic Arms Limitation Talks (SALT II), and economic sanctions against the Soviet Union.[33] In the Asian context, two contradictory trends were discernible. First, Japan's position underwent significant change. As Kazuhiko Togo and Tsuyoshi Hasegawa argue in chapters 7 and 8, respectively, Japan had attempted to steer an equidistant policy between Moscow and Beijing throughout the early 1970s, but it had then decisively tilted toward China, having concluded the Sino-Japanese Treaty of Peace and Friendship in 1978. After the Soviet invasion of Afghanistan, Japan closed ranks with the United States, raising the two nations' level of security cooperation to a higher level. With the increasing strategic importance of the Northern Territories for the Soviet bastion strategy, the territorial conflict between the Soviet Union and Japan further intensified, making it impossible for them to achieve rapprochement.[34]

However, there was also a subtle change in Sino-Soviet relations during this period. Leonid Brezhnev's olive branch calling for Sino-Soviet rapprochement in his Tashkent speech in 1982 was received warmly by Deng Xiaoping. Sino-Soviet border negotiations were resumed, and trade between the two countries increased. Clearly, having attained great power status, China was now recoiling from full membership in the anti-Soviet alliance engineered by the United

States, although it made no concrete moves toward normalization of relations with Moscow by imposing three "obstacles" as the precondition for full normalization with the Soviet Union.[35]

Gorbachev's Perestroika, 1985–91

East Asia also injected discordant notes into the general process of East-West rapprochement in the closing years of the Cold War, 1985–91.[36] As Vladislav Zubok argues in chapter 10, despite Mikhail Gorbachev's Vladivostok speech, which signaled his intention to initiate a new Asian policy, he proposed no "common Asian house," though he referred to Europe as the "common European house." Sino-Soviet rapprochement was achieved in 1989 with the Gorbachev–Deng Xiaoping summit, but as soon as rapprochement was achieved, the Tiananmen Square incident nullified its historic significance. While Communism collapsed in Eastern Europe in 1989 and then the Soviet Union itself ended in 1991, the Communist regimes persisted in China and North Korea in East Asia, and in Vietnam and Laos in Southeast Asia.

In the meantime, while other major states in the West achieved different forms of rapprochement with Gorbachev's Soviet Union, Japan held firm in resisting reconciliation with the Soviet Union, insisting that the Cold War was not over in Asia, because Gorbachev continued to reject Japan's demand for the return of the Northern Territories. Japan refused to lend its full-scale economic and financial assistance to restructuring the Soviet economy, thus contributing to the demise of the Soviet Union.[37]

While the two Germanys were reunited, the two Koreas remained divided. South Korea, now having achieved democratization as well as economic prosperity, normalized its relations with the Soviet Union and China. But, as Sergey Radchenko shows in chapter 11, North Korea, having been abandoned by its two Communist patrons, became isolated and marginalized. The end of the Cold War left the Korean Peninsula more unstable.[38]

It is thus difficult to say that the Cold War in East Asia ended in 1991. It is probably more accurate to say that East Asia gradually entered a post–Cold War era, with most of the key regional conflicts remaining unresolved, thereby leaving many dangerous legacies for our own time.

An Overview of This Book

In the last few years, access to historical materials on the Cold War in East Asia has vastly expanded. As a result, scholarship on the Cold War in the region has greatly advanced. Yet even with this marked scholarly progress, there is still no single volume that synthesizes the state of our knowledge on the East Asian Cold War across the entire region.

The present volume is a collection of overviews that examine various aspects of the Cold War in Asia based on the new evidence. The chapters included in this volume were selected from the papers presented at three conferences on the Cold War in Asia organized by the Center for Cold War Studies at the University of California, Santa Barbara, in 2005, 2006, and 2007.

This volume has two distinct features. First, its chapters have been written by the foremost authorities in the field. Second, each chapter, while delving into specific topics with the use of new materials, also provides an overview of the broader framework of the Cold War in East Asia. The book therefore stresses the uniqueness of the region's historical experience, while explaining the background of some of the key conflicts in East Asia today.

Chapter 1, by Odd Arne Westad, examines state building by the PRC during the golden years of the Sino-Soviet alliance in the 1940s and the 1950s, when the Chinese leaders attempted to build a new state that would reject both their former Western imperialist exploiters and the corrupt Chinese traditions. By focusing on four key areas—military organization, education, urban planning, and minority policies—Westad delineates the PRC's struggle for modernity. He argues that while Mao and the Chinese leaders took the Soviet experience as the model for China's own modernity, the Soviet model served dual, often contradictory purposes—both "plan" and "leap." One the one hand, "Moscow was seen as standing for planning, procedure, and gradualism"; but on the other hand, "Soviet campaigns, purges, and acts of will" inspired the Chinese to take a "leap." The "plan" and the "leap" increasingly clashed with each other in 1950s, foreshadowing the cataclysm of the Great Leap Forward and the Cultural Revolution.

In chapter 2, Ilya Gaiduk asserts that Moscow's major attention during the first phase of the Cold War, from 1945 to 1956, was focused on Europe, with little energy and interest in Asia. The only exception was China, but here all the decisions were made by Stalin himself. Moscow was not interested in the rest of Asia, including Vietnam. Furthermore, Moscow was anxious to avoid unnecessary conflict with the West in Asia and to maintain the Yalta framework. Even after the successful Chinese Revolution, Stalin cautioned the other Communists in the region not to imitate the Chinese example. After the Korean War, Stalin conceded to China the leadership of the Communist movement in Asia. Although Khrushchev began to see the importance of the developing world, the pattern established by Stalin did not significantly change. Gaiduk concludes: "Thus, in 1956, as in the late 1940s, Asia seemed to continue occupying a secondary place on the list of Soviet foreign policy priorities."

In chapter 3, Chen Jian argues that the Chinese Revolution represented a defining moment for the global Cold War structure. He postulates that the Korean War happened in the context of the victory of the Chinese Communist Revolution and that China entered the Korean War primarily because it was a "revolutionary country." During the Korean War, Beijing's decisionmaking structure was Mao centered, and China's alliance with the Soviet Union was a "cornerstone" of its war efforts. China's relationship with North Korea was substantial yet never harmonious. After the Korean War, Mao established his supremacy, consolidated his power, and moved both China's foreign and domestic policy in a revolutionary direction. Mao's policy made the Cold War more ideological, excluding the possibility of realpolitik. The Korean War also made the management of the Communist alliance more difficult. Chen Jian concludes: "China's 'Korean War–centered' early Cold War experience . . . changed the two superpowers' basic perceptions of the scope and perimeter of the escalating confrontation between them, turning East Asia into the new focus of the global Cold War."

In chapter 4, Steven Hugh Lee views South Korean history in the decade after 1945 in the context of an extended American military occupation. He contrasts the first phase of the occupation, from 1945 to 1948, with the second phase, from 1950 to 1954, which was necessitated by the Korean War and its aftermath. In the occupation's first phase, Major General John Hodge and the American military forces dismantled the Korean People's Republic that had emerged after Japan's defeat, and worked closely with conservatives who had in many cases collaborated with Japan during the colonial period. At the same time, the Americans had an uneasy relationship with the anti-Japanese conservative political leader Syngman Rhee, largely because Rhee refused to cooperate with the occupation policy regarding trusteeship. The second phase of the occupation followed up on many activities started during the first phase, especially in its efforts to bring modernity to Korea through electrification, education reform, and vaccinations against disease. The second phase, however, accomplished something the first phase had only begun, and was characterized by the creation of a grassroots anticommunist Korean-American partnership.

Lee places American occupation policy in the larger framework of the U.S. approach to military occupation since the end of the nineteenth century, and he contrasts American policy with formal colonial rule. Finally, he discusses a change in U.S. policy after the Korean War. In 1947, Korea was peripheral to American strategic thinking, but "by 1953, Korea was a frontline state in the containment strategy of the United States, and by 1958, the United States had stationed atomic weapons on the Korean Peninsula." The pre-1950 "defensive perimeter" strategy gave way to the containment of the Sino-Soviet alliance, with a determination to defend parts of continental Asia. Lee argues that in this sense, U.S. intervention in the Korean conflict created a precedent for America's involvement in Vietnam.

On the basis of the extensive use of hitherto unused Russian and Eastern European archives, in chapter 5 Nobuo Shimotomai examines how North Korean leader Kim Il Sung exploited the emerging Sino-Soviet conflict to steer an independent foreign policy and to consolidate his power by purging his real and potential political enemies. His formative experience was the August-September 1956 incident, engineered by the joint Soviet-Chinese team dispatched to Pyongyang, that almost ousted him from the leadership position. By turning his weakness into leverage to gain the support of Moscow or Beijing without totally committing to one side, Kim played a masterful balancing act. He was forced to pay lip service to the idea of peaceful unification by forming a "confederation" with South Korea in 1954, 1960, and 1972 that was only superficially in conformity with the Soviet foreign policy line, but he never abandoned his goal of forceful unification. Shimotomai also offers his unique interpretation of Kim's simultaneous signing of the treaties of alliance with Moscow and with Beijing in 1961: This was not evidence of Kim's equidistance with Moscow and Beijing, but rather a sign of his definite leaning toward the PRC at the expense of the Soviet Union.

Chapter 6, by Lorenz Lüthi, examines the trajectory of Chinese foreign policy from that of a pariah nation before 1960 to a respected world power in 1979. Instead of focusing on changes in the context of the Sino-Soviet-American triangle, he analyzes this process through the prism of ideology and modernization, emphasizing the domestic sources of China's foreign policy changes. The chapter explores the conflict between revolutionary and modernizing impulses that led the country to international political isolation and global economic integration by the first years of the Cultural Revolution. The chapter also covers China's rapid emergence in international relations from 1968 to 1972, triggered by internal and external causes. Finally, the chapter addresses the success of the moderate line of modernization. Lüthi makes extensive use of a wide array of Swiss, East German, British, and American archival materials to supplement Chinese-language sources.

The next two chapters examine Japan's quest to achieve rapprochement with the PRC and the Soviet Union. Chapter 7, by Kazuhiko Togo, examines Japan's policy under Sato Eisaku and Tanaka Kakuei. Togo reevaluates Sato's intention to seek rapprochement with Japan's two Communist neighbors, despite China's hostility toward him. As for Japan's Soviet policy, Sato missed the opportunity to exploit the Soviet approach to settle the territorial dispute on the basis of the 1956 Joint Declaration, because Sato's major attention was focused on the Okinawa reversion, leaving little time to attend to other issues. Nixon and Kissinger's rapprochement with Beijing without consultation with the Japanese government greatly shocked the Japanese, and propelled Tanaka Kakuei to seek an assertive foreign policy, independent of the United States. In 1972, Japan normalized its relations with the PRC by resolving two thorny issues: the status of Taiwan and the U.S.-Japanese Security Treaty. Tanaka then went to Moscow, but the negotiations with Brezhnev did not resolve the territorial question. Although the Joint Communiqué issued at the summit in 1973 referred to the need to resolve the unsettled questions left after World War II, there was no written agreement. From then on, whether the "unsettled questions" included the territorial question remained a contentious issue between the two countries.

In chapter 8, using Japan's foreign policy in 1977–78 as a pivot, Tsuyoshi Hasegawa examines the quadrangular relations of the four East Asian powers —the United States, Japan, China, and the Soviet Union—using the Sino-Japanese Treaty of Peace and Friendship (PFT) as the focus of analysis. With extensive use of U.S. archival materials made available by the National Security Archive, Hasegawa argues that Fukuda Takeo's omnidirectional foreign policy toward the Soviet Union and the PRC reflected Japan's reaction to the U.S. retrenchment from its commitment to Asia. The change in President Jimmy Carter's policy toward China had a significant influence on Fukuda's policy, prompting Japan to conclude the PFT with the PRC in 1978 by accepting the anti-hegemony clause. Soviet policy toward Japan seeking to forestall Japan's rapprochement with China fell short, because the Soviets never entertained the resolution of the territorial dispute in a way that would have satisfied Japan's demand. With the conclusion of the PFT, Japan established the foundations for further expansion of economic relations with the PRC. Nevertheless, by accepting the anti-hegemony clause, it failed to maintain an omnidirectional foreign policy, tilting decidedly toward entente with China against the Soviet Union and contributing to the crisis of détente. Given the nature of quadrangular strategic positions, however, Hasegawa argues that Japan would have no other alternatives than the course it chose.

In chapter 9, Gregg Brazinsky examines how North Korea and South Korea, which in 1972 were at approximately the same stage of economic development, with similarly authoritarian/totalitarian repressive political systems, ended up fifteen years later as two starkly different countries. South Korea had become a global economic powerhouse, an important player in the international community, and a full-fledged democracy, while North Korea was suffering from economic stagnation, had isolated itself from the international community, and had become one of the most repressive totalitarian states. Brazinsky explains these different outcomes as stemming from the way each Korea reacted to the new situations that developed in the 1970s. The period of détente, which ended the superpowers' indulgence toward the two Koreas, prompted both Koreas to seek centralized political power by eliminating dissent. In South Korea, Park Chung Hee established one-man rule by instituting the Yusin Constitution. In North Korea, Kim Il Sung engaged in political repression through the "Three Revolutions" movement while promoting his son, Kim Jong Il, as his successor.

But the big difference was how the two Koreas reacted to the economic challenge of the 1970s. Taking advantage of Japanese credit and capital, South Korea aggressively took advantage of the new global capitalism and adopted an effective development strategy favoring *chaebol,* South Korean business conglomerates. North Korea maintained its independence by taking advantage of the Sino-Soviet conflict, but it chose not to interact with the global economic system. South Korea's economic development led to its greater political interaction with the international community, even including its own erstwhile adversary, the PRC. Eventually, it engendered a political force that challenged the authoritarian regime and brought democracy to South Korea. The South Korean model of economic development also repudiated the Communist development model, contributing to the economic downfall of Communism in Asia and the developing world.

The last two chapters are devoted to Soviet policy toward East Asia during the period 1985–91 under Gorbachev. In chapter 10, Vladislav Zubok argues that Gorbachev's policy toward Asia remained only a secondary priority compared with the primary priority given to his policy toward the United States and Western Europe. In comparison with his policy toward the West, which was often driven by grandiose and unrealistic goals, Gorbachev's approach to Asia was cautious, gradualist, and conservative, reflecting realities rather than exalted expectations. Because he was motivated by the economic necessities of cutting defense costs, he was primarily concerned with security interests in Asia, and he succeeded in achieving rapprochement with China, thus ending the Sino-Soviet conflict that had been a permanent fixture of the Cold War in Asia since the 1960s. In contrast, he failed to accomplish reconciliation with Japan, despite the obvious economic gains he could have derived from it, because he refused to make concessions on the territorial issue that would satisfy Japan's demand. In Zubok's view, this failure stemmed not from Gorbachev's underestimation of Japan but rather from the Japanese government's unrealistic intransigence. Despite the failure to achieve rapprochement with Japan, however, Zubok views Gorbachev's policy toward Asia as, overall, "impressive and lasting."

In chapter 11, Sergey Radchenko examines Soviet policy toward the two Koreas during the perestroika period. He argues that Gorbachev's Korea policy suffered from "contradictions, frequent reversals, and uncertainty." Although relations with North Korea actually improved during Gorbachev's early years in power, ideas of the new thinking and the changing strategic equation in Asia eroded Soviet interest in North Korea. In contrast, Soviet interests in South Korea began to grow in 1988, especially after the Soviet economy faced an unprecedented crisis. Gorbachev's liberal-minded advisers advocated a new approach to South Korea, but this policy was opposed by the Foreign Ministry, headed by Eduard Shevardnadze, along with the military and the KGB, which counseled against abandoning Moscow's support for North Korea. In Radchenko's view, it is wrong to characterize the conservatives' view as ideological dogmatism. They accepted the imperative of recognizing Seoul but advocated a more balanced approach that would not involve burning bridges to Pyongyang. The economic imperative in the end trumped other considerations, and Moscow and Seoul achieved rapprochement, establishing full diplomatic relations. This provoked Pyongyang's strong reaction—it warned that it "would be free to develop its own defense against the U.S. nuclear weapons in South Korea by pulling out from the Nuclear Non-Proliferation Treaty." Overnight, Soviet influence in North Korea was reduced to nothing.

These chapters represent the state of the art for current scholarship on the Cold War in East Asia. However, two crucial issues are not sufficiently covered elsewhere in this volume: first, the U.S. role in the Cold War in East Asia; and second, the relationship between the Vietnam War and the East Asian Cold War. It is therefore necessary and helpful to add here these two missing pieces to the book's overview of the Cold War in East Asia.

The United States and the Cold War in East Asia

U.S. policy toward Asia can be reduced to one question: How did the United States balance its policies toward the Soviet Union and toward China? Its policies toward Japan, South Korea and North Korea, and Southeast Asia, including Vietnam, were mainly derived from this overarching question.

It is sometimes contended that until Nixon and Kissinger initiated the policy to achieve rapprochement with China, U.S. policy toward Asia was founded on its erroneous perception that the Communist Bloc was a monolith, with China faithfully following Moscow's directions. Certainly, this perception provided the framework for NSC-68. Truman said that the Communist government in China "was Russian and nothing else."[39] John Foster Dulles declared in 1951: "By the test of conception, birth, nurture and obedience, the Mao Tse-tung regime is a creature of the Moscow Politburo, . . . a puppet regime."[40]

This does not mean, however, that the United States was totally oblivious to the differences between the Soviet Union and the PRC until the early 1970s.

In fact, as Gordon Chang argues, American policymakers were well aware of the differences between China and the Soviet Union, and were eager to exploit the discord to advance U.S. interests. In other words, the "strategic triangle" had been the policy of the United States from the inception of the Cold War. Before the Korean War, the secretary of state, Dean Acheson, had attempted to implement a "wedge" policy designed to turn China into Asia's Yugoslavia. Despite its rigid anticommunism, the Eisenhower administration also was well aware of the Sino-Soviet differences. Unlike Acheson's wedge policy, however, Dulles's policy was to take a hard line against China—a "closed door" policy—so that Beijing would have no choice but to seek help from the Soviet Union, which, Dulles was convinced, would not be able to deliver. Eisenhower's atomic diplomacy aimed at China can be interpreted in this context.[41] Toward the end of the 1950s, the Eisenhower administration began to respond to Moscow's initiative for peaceful coexistence, in part to isolate Beijing. By the end of the 1950s, after Mao had displayed his aggressive domestic and foreign policy, the United States' most dangerous Asian enemy, which had been the Soviet Union under the Truman administration, had now become China.

John F. Kennedy went further by attempting to conclude an entente with the Soviet Union. Although he failed to gain Khrushchev's support to stop China's nuclear program, Kennedy's policy further facilitated the Sino-Soviet split. Mao concluded that the Soviet Union, which had made substantial concessions to the United States in the Cuban Missile Crisis and agreed to conclude the Partial Test-Ban Treaty, was a revisionist power that had abandoned its revolutionary mission as the head of the international Communist movement. The United States viewed China's increasingly revolutionary rhetoric and actions with alarm. Viewing North Vietnam as China's proxy, the Johnson administration turned the Vietnam War into an American war with a massive military buildup and extensive bombing of North Vietnam. But it should be noted that the shift toward an "open door" policy toward China had begun under Johnson, as he called for reconciliation with China in his speech "The Essentials for Peace in Asia" in 1966.[42]

By the time Richard Nixon became president, however, the prestige of the United States had been greatly diminished by the protracted Vietnam War, while the Soviet Union had managed to achieve strategic parity with the United States in the nuclear arms race. The major threat to the United States had now again shifted from China to the Soviet Union. Nixon and Kissinger's playing of the "China card" was motivated by their larger strategic need to counter the Soviet threat at a time when U.S. leverage was diminishing. President Jimmy Carter and his national security adviser, Zbigniew Brzezinski, pushing their China policy a step farther than Nixon and Kissinger's equidistance, sought a quasi-military entente with China against the Soviet Union, but there was little difference in their motivation to seek the means to counter Soviet expansionism. Reagan's initial pro-Taiwan policy set off China's equidistance policy from the two superpowers by gingerly accepting Brezhnev's call for reconciliation. Nevertheless, Reagan clearly viewed the Soviet Union as the most dangerous "evil empire," and therefore the policy of accommodation with China naturally followed.

Gorbachev's perestroika posed a new challenge to the United States. It is to the credit of the anticommunist presidents Reagan and George H. W. Bush that they embraced Gorbachev's perestroika to end the Cold War. Nevertheless, there was a fundamental disconnect between U.S. policy toward the Soviet Union from the Atlantic in the European context and its policy toward the Soviet Union from the Pacific as an Asian power. After the Tiananmen Square incident in 1989, the occupant of the category of favorite Communist regime again shifted to the Soviet Union from China. But arms control in the Pacific generally remained untouched by the overall arms control agreements.[43] The Northern Territories dispute between Japan and the Soviet Union, which the United States had encouraged during the Cold War, came to serve as a major stumbling block to accomplishing rapprochement between Japan and the Soviet Union. Finally, the United States' refusal to agree with Gorbachev's call for de-nuclearization on the Korean Peninsula and in the Pacific eventually led the North Koreans to develop their own nuclear weapons. In Asia, the Cold War did not end well—or it is not clear if the Cold War ended at all.

Various issues—including the importance of domestic politics and alliance politics, among others—can be raised with respect to the U.S. policy seeking to balance the Soviet Union and China. But in the context of the Cold War in Asia, one fundamental point must be noted: The United States consistently underestimated the importance of the nationalism that drove China's policy. China's embrace of communism was partly an aspect of nationalism that aspired to achieve national unification and modernization and to recapture the central role of China in the world.[44] Mao Zedong and Chiang Kai-shek were united in their uncompromising One-China Principle. In this respect, Truman's decision to defend Taiwan was a decisive moment in U.S.-Chinese relations. Had the Truman administration recognized the PRC and refrained from defending Taiwan, which was well within the realm of possibility, as Thomas Christensen argues, U.S.-Chinese relations would have traveled along a different trajectory.[45] There was no chance that the United States' two-Chinas policy would have been accepted by the PRC, and thus the Taiwan issue proved to be the most difficult one for the successive administrations after Nixon in their attempts to improve relations with China.

This brief outline underscores the decisive role that the United States played in the Cold War in East Asia. Its policy toward China determined its shape and course in a fundamental way. The United States figures prominently in chapters 4, 7, 8, and 9, and, although its role is not a central issue, it also casts a long shadow in the rest of the chapters.

Vietnam and the Cold War in East Asia: U.S. Involvement in Vietnam

Another missing link in this volume is the relationship between the Vietnam War and the Cold War in East Asia. Although Southeast Asia is outside the scope of this volume, the issue of Vietnam—not only the war but also its aftermath—had a tremendous impact on the dynamics of the Cold War in Asia.[46]

The impact of Vietnam on the Cold War in East Asia must start with U.S. involvement in Vietnam and with one question: How did the United States place its role in Vietnam in the overall context of the Cold War in East Asia and its global strategy? I must stress at the outset that U.S. policy toward Vietnam was never directed at Vietnam itself but always toward the larger Cold War contest beyond Vietnam. In fact, without the Cold War, it is unlikely that the United States would have interjected its vast power and resources in a remote corner of Indochina.

The Truman administration's decision to support the return of the European colonial powers in Southeast Asia was initially derived from its need to support the Western European powers in the contest against the Soviet Union. Britain, the Netherlands, and especially France needed their colonies for economic survival as well as prestige. But the U.S. involvement in Vietnam intensified even after this justification disappeared, when Western Europe achieved economic recovery by the middle of 1950s. Why?[47]

First and foremost, the American thinking behind the nation's involvement in Vietnam was dominated by the "domino" theory: Unless the United States prevented the Communist takeover in Vietnam, the Communists would inevitably expand to other countries in Southeast Asia, eventually threatening Japan and beyond. Closely connected to the domino theory was the fear of losing U.S. credibility. Unless the United States as the champion of the Free World took a strong stand to defend Vietnam, Western European allies and other noncommunist allies in Asia would not believe the U.S. commitment to defend them against Communism. Maintaining credibility was the foundation of U.S. global strategy. Successive administrations, from Truman to Johnson, subscribed to the twin fears of the domino effect and a loss of credibility.[48]

There was another key factor: the realm of domestic politics. And this factor intersects with the key focus of this volume, East Asia, in that the domestic political imperative that drove successive U.S. presidents to get involved in Vietnam had a great deal to do with the debilitating "who lost China" debate. Truman got dragged through the mud of "losing China," and no successive president, and especially no Democrat, wanted to endure another "who lost China" debate.[49]

The twin fears of the domino theory and a loss of credibility raise a fundamental question about what the successive American administrations perceived to be the limits of U.S. involvement in Vietnam, or whether they even raised the question of the limits of the American involvement in Vietnam at all. Robert McMahon best expresses this question: "If Southeast Asia was so vital that its loss to Communism would severely compromise American national security, how could the United States accept *any* limits on its actions?"[50] What, indeed, were the limits of its actions? Could the defense of Vietnam be equated with the defense of Western Europe or Japan? In the hierarchy of the escalation ladder, how far should the United States be prepared to go to defend Vietnam?

The history of U.S. involvement in the Vietnam War indicates that successive administrations did not confront the issue of the limits of involvement as they climbed rungs on the ladder of escalation. The goal of preserving a noncommunist, independent South Vietnam became divorced from larger strategic goals, producing the circular justification for American involvement, in which the only conceivable alternative to de-escalation was escalation. American leaders were trapped by their own rhetoric into escalating the war, dictated more by domestic political circumstances than by geostrategic considerations. Despite the changes in the Cold War that made Vietnam less strategically important to Americans in the period 1964–68 than in 1950–54, they could not shake off the heavy weight of the twin fears. By 1968, the number of U.S. troops in Vietnam had mushroomed to 535,100. The domino theory and the fear of losing credibility so firmly gripped each successive administration's mindset that the question of the limits of intervention was never seriously considered—until the Tet Offensive, that is.

Although the Tet Offensive undertaken by the Viet Cong and the North Vietnamese in 1968 was a resounding military failure, it nonetheless demonstrated the capacity to attack anywhere in South Vietnam, including the U.S. Embassy compound in Saigon.[51] If the war had been escalated to maintain the credibility of the United States, it was precisely this credibility that was now being destroyed. President Johnson refused the military's request to add 206,000 more troops. Vietnam was not worth expanding the commitment to three quarters of a million American soldiers without an end in sight. But if not, how important was Vietnam to the security of the United States? For the first time, the question of the limits of intervention was asked and answered.

Nixon recognized the limits of intervention. To preserve U.S. power and prestige, Nixon and Kissinger believed, the United States had to disengage from Vietnam. But how? The policy of "Vietnamization" was their answer. But if the Americanization of the war had been necessary precisely because the South Vietnamese were not capable of carrying out the war, then how could the South Vietnamese army be expected to take over the war without the Americans? The real truth of Vietnamization, despite Nixon's gimmick of allowing a "decent interval" before the ultimate end of the conflict, was thus its implicit acceptance of the United States' ultimate defeat in the war and the Communist takeover of all Vietnam.[52] The rest of the operations in the war were nothing but a charade for domestic consumption, though immensely costly and tragic, to effect the ultimate form of this truth. The United States and North Vietnam concluded a peace agreement in January 1973. By the end of March, all the U.S. troops had been withdrawn from Vietnam. In two years, the Saigon government fell. The Communists finally succeeded in unifying Vietnam under their control, the outcome that the United States had sought to prevent at the cost of 58,220 American soldiers killed in action and 153,303 wounded, along with the killing of a quarter million South Vietnamese soldiers and 1.1 million North Vietnamese soldiers and Viet Cong.[53]

Why did the successive U.S. administrations cling so tenaciously to the twin fears of the domino effect and losing credibility? To answer this question, in addition to considering the domestic political pressure mentioned above, two further questions must be answered. First, were the domino effect and credibility loss a correct assessment of reality? And second, what if Vietnam fell into the hands of the Communists?

It must be noted that recent unclassified documents reveal how deeply the Chinese were involved in the Vietnam War, especially in the First Indochina War. Mao definitely supported his Vietnamese comrades, primarily as part of their overall international struggle against Western imperialism in Southeast Asia and beyond.[54] To that extent, the United States' subscribing to the domino theory can be vindicated as far as this theory referred to Mao's *intentions*. Mao encouraged, and instigated where possible, national liberation movements in Southeast Asia. Nevertheless, his intentions were far from China's capabilities, and his policy had unintended consequences that he of course did not foresee. Even at the height of the close collaboration between China and Vietnam, Sino-Vietnamese relations were hardly a monolith, and the Chinese and the Vietnamese thus had different visions and pursued different goals for the struggle in Vietnam.

The corollary of the domino theory was the underestimation of indigenous nationalism in Southeast Asia, and more generally a lack of understanding of the complexity and diversity of Southeast Asian politics, society, culture, and history. Nationalism in one part of the region was different in its origins, goals, and methods from nationalism in other parts, and nationalists thus did not necessarily speak a common language. The Communists in Southeast Asia espoused Marxist-Leninism, and some of them advocated its Maoist version. We should not ignore their ideological commitments and categorize all these Communists as a different branch of nationalism. Nonetheless, these Communists were also inspired by their national aspirations. The United States, however, had a proclivity to view all forms of nationalism and Communism in this region as the same. For example, in his cable to the U.S. consul in Hanoi in 1949, Acheson declared: "Question [whether] Ho as much nationalist as Commie is irrelevant. All Stalinists in colonial areas are nationalists."[55] This myopia made it exceedingly difficult for the United States to find a noncommunist nationalist leader willing to challenge the Communists and channel the national aspirations of his people into noncommunist nation building. The United States' support for Ngo Dinh Diem and its subsequent approval of the generals' coup against him, when Diem moved to negotiate with the Viet Cong, demonstrated the American dilemma in promoting a noncommunist leader who could receive indigenous support.

Essentially, the domino theory was an utterly simplistic shorthand for an extremely complex reality. Neither Moscow nor Beijing was ever in a position to dictate local situations in Southeast Asia. The implicit assumption was that Vietnam was a proxy of the international Communist movement directed by Beijing and/or Moscow. The absurdity of this assumption was revealed when Nixon achieved rapprochement with Beijing; as McMahon writes: "This lifelong anticommunist was *inviting* China to assume a major role in Southeast Asian politics, the very thing that every U.S. policy initiative in the region had, since the Truman administration, been designed to prevent."[56] If the United States managed to learn to live with the PRC, could it not have accommodated itself to Ho Chi Minh's Vietnam without the costly war?

It is now clear that the United States' involvement in Vietnam itself was responsible for the erosion of U.S. credibility, the weakening of the U.S. economy, and the destruction of the domestic consensus. Domino effects never occurred. The powerful Indonesian Communist Party (known as the PKI) was destroyed by Suharto's coup in 1966, causing a major setback for the Communist camp. The Communists came to power in Vietnam, Laos, and Cambodia, but Vietnam invaded Cambodia in 1977, and China invaded Vietnam in 1979. This was hardly the monolithic communism imagined by American officials. The reality was more complex and unexpected than had ever been predicted by those who espoused the domino theory. As for the fear of credibility, "if U.S.

credibility was on the line in Vietnam," as Campbell Craig and Fredrik Logevall argue, "it was only because successive administrations had put it there, with their constant public affirmations of the struggle's importance. They, not their adversaries, made Vietnam a 'test case' of American resolve."[57]

The most important impact of the Vietnam War on the Cold War in East Asia was the United States' rapprochement with China. This diplomatic revolution fundamentally changed the dynamics of the Cold War in East Asia. After the Communist victory in 1975, Vietnam no longer occupied the central place in U.S. foreign policy, as it should never have.

The Vietnam War and Sino-Soviet Relations

U.S. involvement was merely one side of the coin of the Vietnam War. The other side was its impact on China and the Soviet Union.[58]

Documents now available clearly demonstrate China's predominant influence on Vietnam, especially in the period before the Americanization of the war in 1965. It was partly a function of Moscow's lack of interest in Vietnam. Because Moscow was preoccupied with Europe, it was willing to concede to China the leadership of national revolutionary movements in Asia.[59] But China's predominant influence on Vietnam was not merely a function of the division of labor. It was also partly derived from its security needs and, more important, it stemmed from Mao Zedong's notion of China's leading role in national liberation movements in Asia and beyond. This vision of world revolution through national liberation movements meant that China aimed to challenge the capitalist-imperialist order, and, as such, it contradicted Khrushchev's policy of peaceful coexistence. This difference became one of the fundamental causes of the Sino-Soviet conflict.[60]

One of the most interesting discoveries in the documents that have recently become available is the extent to which China was involved in all aspects of the First Indochina War, including the decisive campaign against Dien Bien Phu in 1954. But the Vietnamese Communists were never China's puppet. China's predominance should not be mistaken for Vietnam's subservience. We must keep two fundamental facts in mind when considering the history of the Vietnam War. First, the Vietnamese Communists consistently and unswervingly pursued their ultimate goal: the unification of Vietnam under their control. Second, they were keenly aware that they could not accomplish this goal without the support of China and the Soviet Union. Thus, while single-mindedly pursuing their ultimate goal, they skillfully manipulated their two Big Brothers to maximize their military and financial aid to carry out their struggle.

The Geneva Conference in 1954 exposed differences among China, the Soviet Union, and Vietnam. The Soviets, who were more preoccupied with European affairs, were anxious to settle the Vietnam conflict with the division of Vietnam. The Chinese, who needed a respite for domestic reconstruction, were also interested in a peaceful settlement to prevent U.S. intervention in the conflict. The Vietnamese, pressured by the Soviet Union and China, reluctantly accepted the settlement of a divided Vietnam. The Geneva Accord, which the Vietnamese considered a betrayal of their cause, helped to implant their determination that they would never again let their Big Brothers dictate the outcome of their struggle.

From this time on, there was a two-way race. While North Vietnam searched for a Big Brother to provide better military and financial support in its struggle for unification, the Chinese and the Soviets competed with each other to gain its support. From 1954 to 1963, neither Moscow nor Beijing supported North Vietnam's eagerness to wage an armed struggle in the south. Despite his own radical foreign policy in the Second Taiwan Strait Crisis, Mao told the Vietnamese comrades to concentrate on socialist construction in the north. The Soviets saw the Vietnamese armed struggle as obstructing their policy of peaceful coexistence.

But Beijing's policy toward Vietnam took a sudden radical turn in 1963. China extended extensive military aid to North Vietnam, and it pledged that if the United States expanded the war into the north, the Chinese would cross the border into North Vietnam to fight the Americans.[61] China's radical turn can be explained by the combination of two factors: first, Mao's political agenda to recover his authority, which had been discredited by the failure of the Great Leap Forward; and second, the intensifying Sino-Soviet conflict. Khrushchev's pro-Indian attitude in the China-India border conflict, his retreat in the Cuban Missile Crisis, and above all his signing of the Partial Test-Ban Treaty when the Chinese were developing their own nuclear weapons led Mao to conclude that the Soviet Union had become an irredeemable revisionist power that had abandoned the revolutionary mission. In the contest for the leadership of true revolutionary movements, assistance to Vietnam became a litmus test.[62] As China actively endorsed Hanoi's decision to wage an armed struggle in the south, North Vietnam, which had remained neutral in the Sino-Soviet dispute, began to "lean" toward the side of China.

Johnson's decision to Americanize the Vietnam War in 1965 changed the dynamics of the tripartite relations among Hanoi, Beijing, and Moscow. It created a dilemma for China, because the war might be escalated into China. Faced with this danger, China made the decision to provide military aid and logistical support to North Vietnam. It also made it clear that the Chinese would send in their ground troops only when American land forces invaded North Vietnam.[63] After Khrushchev's ouster, the new Kremlin leadership was also confronted with contradictory foreign policy tasks. U.S. bombing of the north was a direct challenge to Moscow's authority as the leader of the socialist camp and destroyed its hope of preventing the internationalization of the conflict. The Soviet government for the first time decided to extend substantial military aid to North Vietnam.[64]

Despite North Vietnam's wish that Moscow and Beijing would coordinate their aid to North Vietnam, Mao scornfully rejected Soviet premier Aleksei Kosygin's proposal to end polemics and coordinate their joint support for Vietnam. China refused to let Soviet arms be transported overland through China. As the war went on, frictions and confrontations between the Vietnamese and the Chinese on the ground increased. The Cultural Revolution that Mao initiated in 1966 further alienated Hanoi. As Sino-Vietnamese relations deteriorated, Moscow increased its aid to North Vietnam. By 1968, North Vietnam began to "lean" toward Moscow.

The Soviet invasion of Czechoslovakia in 1968 and the Sino-Soviet border clash on Damanskii/Zhenbao Island in 1969 changed the dynamics of Soviet-Chinese-Vietnamese triangular relations. Mao came to consider the Soviet Union the most serious threat to China's security, and he explored the possibility of rapprochement with the United States. North Vietnam viewed China's rapprochement with the United States as a betrayal, and it demanded the cancellation of Nixon's trip to Beijing. Mao refused.[65] China, which had opposed the negotiated settlement of the Vietnam War in 1968, now favored an "early conclusion of the Vietnam War in order to preserve American power and contain Soviet influence."[66] Although China attempted to finesse the basic contradictions between rapprochement with the United States and support of the Vietnamese struggle against the United States, clearly China's national interest took precedence over Vietnam's.

The Vietnam War also presented a dilemma for Brezhnev's policy to seek détente with the United States.[67] A serious crisis in Soviet-Vietnamese relations arose over Nixon's scheduled visit to Moscow in May 1972 for a summit. In early May, Nixon ordered the bombing of Hanoi and mining of Haiphong. With its ally being attacked, the Soviet Politburo was divided over whether Moscow should cancel the summit. In the end, overruling the objections of the hard-liners, Brezhnev decided to invite Nixon to Moscow for the summit. "The winning argument was," Vladislav Zubok states, "that the North Vietnamese should not be allowed to exercise a veto over Soviet relations with the United States."[68] National interests also trumped solidarity for the Vietnamese with respect to the Soviets. After Nixon's visit to Moscow, Soviet-Vietnamese relations experienced their most difficult period, which coincided with North Vietnam's Easter Offensive, about which Moscow had no prior knowledge.[69] Nevertheless, Moscow managed to weather the crisis. As Gaiduk argues, the

Soviet Union consistently used a low-key, passive policy in the conflict in Indochina, and, in contrast to the Chinese, scrupulously avoided interjecting its influence into the negotiating process.[70] In the end, North Vietnam perceived China's rapprochement with the United States, not Soviet détente with the United States, as more "treacherous."[71] After 1973, North Vietnam decisively tilted toward the Soviet side.

By then, however, Vietnam was no longer the dominant issue. "The emergence of friendly ties between Beijing and Washington," Qiang Zhai states, "suddenly marginalized and trivialized the Vietnam conflict, which had been the central focus of international politics. The new great power triangle of Beijing, Washington, and Moscow replaced the Vietnam War in dominating the international system."[72]

Yet even though Vietnam was now marginalized and the war over it had ended, it still cast its shadow on the Cold War in East Asia. After Hanoi unified Vietnam in 1975, its relations with China deteriorated precipitously. The two countries quarreled over the contested Parcel and Spratley islands in the Gulf of Tonkin. They bitterly disagreed over their policies toward the Khmer Rouge in Cambodia, and the Chinese resented Vietnam's treatment of ethnic Chinese in Vietnam. Beijing finally cut off all aid to Vietnam in 1978. In the meantime, the Soviets developed closer relations with Hanoi, financing Vietnam's first post-reunification Five-Year Plan and concluding many other agreements. In 1978, Vietnam joined Comecon. Finally, Vietnam and the Soviet Union signed a Treaty of Friendship and Cooperation in November 1978, in response to the Sino-Japanese Treaty of Peace and Friendship signed in August. The United States and China normalized relations in December. The Soviets acquired the right to use the bases at Danang and Cam Ranh Bay. For the first time since it had withdrawn from Port Arthur, the Soviet Union acquired military bases outside its own territory and Eastern Europe. The line was now clearly drawn between the Soviet-Vietnamese alliance and the U.S.-Chinese-Japanese entente. Vietnam, with the Soviets' backing, invaded Cambodia in 1978, and China invaded Vietnam to "teach Vietnam a lesson" in February 1979. The end of the Vietnam War did not bring stability to Indochina. The Vietnamese sought to take the revolutionary lead, supplanting China as the hegemonic power in Indonesia, and giving the Soviets an advantage in the region that China considered its domain.[73]

The task of nation building after the ravages of the war was an exceedingly difficult one for Vietnam. Heavily relying on aid from the Soviet Union and Comecon, Vietnamese leaders embarked on an economic modernization initiative based on the Soviet economic model, precisely at the time when the efficacy of the socialist command economy was being discredited. This was when the four Asian tigers and the countries belonging to the Association of Southeast Asian Nations (ASEAN) were experiencing unprecedented economic growth, and even China under Deng Xiaoping was embarking on economic modernization. Vietnam's catastrophic economic failure, coupled with its costly invasion of Cambodia, threw it deeper and deeper into dependency on Soviet economic aid. Then, when Gorbachev launched perestroika, the continued Soviet financial bailout of Vietnam became impossible. The transition from socialism and a command economy was thrust on Vietnam. Unlike North Korea, however, Vietnam launched its *doi-moi* policy, abandoning rigid centralization, nationalization, and collectivization, and seeking a market-oriented economy that was open to the outside world. This Vietnamese version of perestroika changed Vietnam's relations with capitalist countries and with ASEAN. Vietnam was finally being integrated into the regional and world economies, but for that outcome to be achieved, the Cold War in Asia had to undergo fundamental change.

Contributions of This Volume and the Future Agenda

Historians have recognized the importance of the Cold War in Asia, and they have produced an impressive array of valuable monographs. But these monographs have tended to focus on specific topics such as the Chinese Revolution, the Korean War, the Sino-Soviet conflict, U.S.-Japanese relations, the territorial dispute between the Soviet Union and Japan, the strategic triangle, and the Vietnam War. It is not an exaggeration to state that there is no authoritative interpretation that integrates the fruits of these monographs into a comprehensive synthesis, characterizing the uniqueness of the Cold War in Asia as a whole, as distinguished from its other fronts, and assessing the influence that the Cold War in Asia exerted on its other fronts.

To achieve such a synthesis, a series of four tasks must be placed on our research agenda. First, we must pay more attention to Japan and Korea beyond specific issues such as the origins of the Korean War, the conclusion and the evolution of the U.S.-Japan security treaty, the Okinawa reversion, the Northern Territories dispute, and U.S.-Japanese trade friction. It is necessary to place these issues in a broader international context and to consider their interconnections. The present volume includes four chapters dealing with Korea and two chapters dealing with Japan. This is a step in the right direction, but we recognize that it is merely the first step.

Second, the Soviet Union must be fully integrated into the study of the Cold War in East Asia. How did the Soviet leaders balance their policies toward the West and toward Asia? Did they have a comprehensive strategy toward Asia encompassing China, Japan, and Korea? In the present volume, these questions are addressed by chapters 2, 5, 7, 8, 10, and 11, by, respectively, Gaiduk, Shimotomai, Togo, Hasegawa, Zubok, and Radchenko. Although there is no consensus among these authors, they all recognize that to advance our knowledge of the role of the Soviet Union, the further opening of Russian archives is an essential prerequisite.

Third, the role of the United States should also be reintegrated in the broader international context. Did the United States have a comprehensive policy toward the Cold War in Europe and in Asia? How did it try to balance the two? How were U.S. policies toward China, Japan, the Soviet Union, and the two Koreas connected? Although we give a brief outline of the U.S. role in the Cold War in East Asia, we recognize that this is not sufficient.

Fourth and finally, it is important to call our attention more to the uniqueness of the Cold War in East Asia as an intersection between revolution and national liberation. As Westad and Shimotomai point out in chapters 1 and 5, respectively, Stalinist socialism served as a model for modernity for China and North Korea, but Mao Zedong Thought and Kim Il Sung's *chuche* movement were based on their intense nationalism seeking to attain independence from foreign domination. Furthermore, the legacy of colonialism and the economic imperative were intertwined in a contradictory manner in China's and South Korea's relationships with Japan.

Thus, we face a formidable challenge. We hope this volume begins to meet it.

Notes

1. The bibliography on the Cold War is so extensive that there is no need to give a comprehensive list here. I merely list a few most important recent books: John Lewis Gaddis, *The Cold War: A New History* (New York: Penguin Books, 2006); Melvin Leffler, *For the Soul of Mankind: The United States, the Soviet Union, and the Cold War* (New York: Hill and Wang, 2007); Vladislav Zubok, *A Failed Empire: The Soviet Union in the Cold War from Stalin to Gorbachev* (Chapel Hill: University of North Carolina Press, 2008); Campbell Craig and Fredrik Logevall, *America's Cold War: The Politics of Insecurity* (Cambridge, Mass.: Belknap Press of Harvard University Press, 2009); and Melvin Leffler and Odd Arne Westad, eds., *The Cambridge History of the Cold War,* 3 vols. (Cambridge: Cambridge University Press, 2010).

2. See Odd Arne Westad, *The Global Cold War: Third World Interventions and the Making of Our Times* (Cambridge: Cambridge University Press, 2006).

3. It is important to note that not everything that happened from 1945 to 1991 was connected with the Cold War. Decolonization and the Israeli-Palestinian conflict, for instance, would have happened without the Cold War, but the Cold War influenced the course of developments of these instances. Another important feature in the international system during this period is the fundamental change in the international economic system. Nevertheless, the change in the international economic system cannot entirely be divorced from the Cold War. The economic growth in Western Europe and

Japan contributed to the multipolarization of the liberal-democratic powers. The choice between liberal economic order and the socialist command economy was a crucial factor for development strategies for developing nations. Finally, the failure of the socialist command economy to compete with the liberal market economy spelled the doom of the socialist camp.

4. The third hot war, the Soviet-Afghan War, also took place in Asia, and the same principle that the Soviet intervention was possible without the risk of provoking the direct East/West military conflict can be applied. South Asia, however, is beyond the scope of this book.

5. For U.S.-Chinese relations, see Gordon H. Chang, *Friends and Enemies: The United States, China, and the Soviet Union, 1948–1972* (Stanford, Calif.: Stanford University Press, 1990); and Odd Arne Westad, *Decisive Encounters: The Chinese Civil War, 1946–1950* (Stanford, Calif.: Stanford University Press, 2003).

6. See chapter 2 in this volume, by Ilya Gaiduk.

7. For U.S. policy toward Southeast Asia, see Robert McMahon, *The Limits of Empire: The United States and Southeast Asia since World War II* (New York: Columbia University Press, 1999).

8. In NSC-68, Paul H. Nitze, the head of the State Department's Policy Planning Staff, defined the Cold War as "a basic conflict between the idea of freedom under a government of laws, and the idea of slavery under the grim oligarchy of the Kremlin."

9. See Chen Jian, *Mao's China and the Cold War* (Chapel Hill: University of North Carolina Press, 2001).

10. Odd Arne Westad, ed., *Brothers in Arms: The Rise and Fall of the Sino-Soviet Alliance, 1945–1953* (Washington, D.C., and Stanford, Calif.: Woodrow Wilson Center Press and Stanford University Press, 1998); Lorenz M. Lüthi, *The Sino-Soviet Split: Cold War in the Communist World* (Princeton, N.J.: Princeton University Press, 2008).

11. The most recent literature on the Korea War includes Sergei N. Goncharov, John W. Lewis, and Litai Xue, *Uncertain Partners: Stalin, Mao and the Korean War* (Stanford, Calif.: Stanford University Press, 1993); Chen Jian, *China's Road to the Korean War: The Making of the Sino-American Confrontation* (New York: Columbia University Press, 1994); William W. Stueck Jr., *The Korean War: An International History* (Princeton, N.J.: Princeton University Press, 1995); Michael Sheng, *Battling Western Imperialism: Mao, Stalin, and the United States* (Princeton, N.J.: Princeton University Press, 1997); Zhang Shuguang, *Mao's Military Romanticism: China and the Korean War, 1950–1953* (Lawrence: University Press of Kansas, 1995); and William Stueck Jr., *Rethinking the Korean War: A New Diplomatic and Strategic History* (Princeton, N.J.: Princeton University Press, 2002). Also see Zhu Jianrong [Shu Kenei], *Mo Takuto no chosen senso* [Mao Zedong's Korean War] (Tokyo: Iwanami shoten, 1991); Wada Haruki, *Chosen senso* [The Korean War] (Tokyo: Iwanami shoten, 1995), and Wada Haruki, *Chosen senso zenshi* [A comprehensive history of the Korean War] (Tokyo: Iwanami shoten, 2002).

12. Bruce Cumings, *The Origins of the Korean War: The Roaring of the Cataract, 1947–1950* (Princeton, N.J.: Princeton University Press, 1990).

13. Kathryn Weathersby, *Soviet Aims in Korea and the Origins of the Korean War, 1945–1950: New Evidence from Russian Archives,* Cold War International History Project Working Paper 89 (Washington, D.C.: Cold War International History Project, Woodrow Wilson International Center for Scholars, 1993); Evgenii Bajanov, "Assess-

ing the Politics of the Korean War, 1949–51," *Cold War International History Project Bulletin,* issue 6–7 (1995): 54, 87–90.

14. See Melvin P. Leffler, *A Preponderance of Power: National Security, the Truman Administration, and the Cold War* (Stanford, Calif.: Stanford University Press, 1992), chap. 9; and Arnold A. Offner, *Another Such Victory: President Truman and the Cold War, 1945–1953* (Stanford, Calif.: Stanford University Press, 2002), chaps. 13–15.

15. See Hosoya Chihiro, *Sanfuranshisuko kowa eno michi* [Road to the San Francisco peace] (Tokyo: Chuokoronsha, 1984); Igarashi Takeshi, *Tainichi kowa to reisen: Sengo nichibei kankei no keisei* [The peace settlement with Japan and the Cold War: Formation of postwar Japanese-U.S. relations] (Tokyo: Tokyo daigaku suppankai, 1986); and Takeshi Igarashi, *Formation of Post-WWII U.S.-Japanese Relations* (Tokyo: Kodansha, 1995).

16. See Tanaka Akihiko, *Nicchukankei, 1945–1990* [Sino-Japanese relations, 1945–1990] (Tokyo: Tokyo Daigaku shuppankai, 1991).

17. For the Soviet Union and the San Francisco Peace Conference, see Tsuyoshi Hasegawa, *The Northern Territories Dispute and Russo-Japanese Relations,* vol. 1, *Between War and Peace, 1697–1985* (Berkeley: International and Area Studies, University of California, 1998), 74–105. For the history of the Northern Territories dispute, see also Hiroshi Kimura, *The Kurillian Knot: A History of Japanese-Russian Border Negotiations* (Stanford, Calif.: Stanford University Press, 2008); Wada Haruki, *Hopporyodo mondai* [The Northern Territories problem] (Tokyo: Asahi sensho, 1999); and Gilbert Rozman, ed., *Japan and Russia: The Tortuous Path to Normalization, 1949–1999* (New York: St. Martin's Press, 2000).

18. See Chen Jian, *Mao's China and the Cold War;* and Lüthi, *Sino-Soviet Split.*

19. See Chen Jian, *Mao's China and the Cold War;* and chapter 6 in this volume, by Lorenz Lüthi.

20. See chapter 5 in this volume, by Nobuo Shimotomai. Also see Shimotomai Nobuo, *Mosukuwa to Kin Nissei* [Moscow and Kim Il Sung] (Tokyo: Iwanami shoten, 2006); A. Lankov, *From Stalin to Kim Il Sung: The Formation of North Korea 1945–1960* (New Brunswick, N.J.: Rutgers University Press, 2002); A. Lankov, *Crisis in North Korea: The Failure of De-Stalinization* (Honolulu: University of Hawaii Press, 2005); and Szalontai Balazs, *Kim Il Sung in the Khrushchev Era: Soviet-DPRK Relations and the Roots of North Korean Despotism, 1953–1964* (Stanford, Calif.: Stanford University Press, 2005).

21. See Hasegawa, *Northern Territories Dispute,* 106–41; Tanaka Takahiko, *Nisso kokko kaifuku no shiteki kenkyu* [Historical analysis of Japan-Soviet normalization] (Tokyo: Yuhikaku, 1993).

22. For U.S.-Japanese relations since the Occupation, see Michael Schaller, *Altered States: The United States and Japan since the Occupation* (New York: Oxford University Press, 1997).

23. See note 17 above.

24. See Gregg Brazinsky, *Nation Building in South Korea: Koreans, Americans, and the Making of a Democracy* (Chapel Hill: University of North Carolina Press, 2007).

25. See Jian Rongji [Shu Kenei], *Mo Takuso no betonamu senso: Chugoku gaiko no daitenkan to Bunka daikakumei no kigen* [Mao Zedong's Vietnam War: The great change in China's foreign policy and the origins of the great Cultural Revolution] (Tokyo: Tokyo daigaku shppankai, 2001). See also, Qiang Zhai, *China and the Viet-*

nam Wars, 1950–1975 (Chapel Hill: University of North Carolina Press, 2000); Chen Jian, *Mao's China and the Cold War,* chap. 8; Lüthi, *Sino-Soviet Split,* chap. 10. For Soviet policy toward the Vietnam War, see Ilya Gaiduk, *Confronting Vietnam: Soviet Policy toward the Indochina Conflict, 1954–1963* (Washington, DC: Woodrow Wilson International Center for Scholars; and Stanford: Stanford University Press, 2003); Ilya Gaiduk, *The Soviet Union and the Vietnam War* (Chicago: Ivan Dee, 1996).

26. See Chang, *Friends and Enemies;* Robert S. Ross, *Negotiating Cooperation: The United States and China, 1969–1989* (Stanford, Calif.: Stanford University Press, 1995); Evelyn Goh, *Constructing the U.S. Rapprochement with China, 1961–1974: From "Red Menace" to "Tacit Ally"* (New York: Cambridge University Press, 2005).

27. For a comprehensive view of the détente period, see Raymond Garthoff, *Détente and Confrontation: American-Soviet Relations for Nixon and Reagan,* rev. ed. (Washington, D.C.: Brookings Institution Press, 1994). For the Nixon years, see Fredrik Logevall and Andrew Preston, eds., *Nixon and the World: American Foreign Relations, 1969–1977* (New York: Oxford University Press, 2008). For Kissinger's policy, see Jussi M. Hanhimaki, *The Flawed Architect: Henry Kissinger and American Foreign Policy* (New York: Oxford University Press, 2004); and Walter Isaacson, *Kissinger* (New York: Simon & Schuster, 2005).

28. For U.S.-Chinese relations during the 1970s, see Harry Harding, *A Fragile Relationship: The United States and China since 1972* (Washington, D.C.: Brookings Institution Press, 1992). For U.S. foreign policy under Jimmy Carter, see Scott Kaufman, *Plans Unraveled: The Foreign Policy of the Carter Administration* (De Kalb: Northern Illinois University Press, 2008).

29. See Richard Solomon and Masataka Kosaka, eds., *The Soviet Far East Military Buildup: Nuclear Dilemmas and Asian Security* (Dover, Mass.: Auburn House, 1986); and Derek da Cunha, *Soviet Naval Power in the Pacific* (Boulder, Colo.: Lynne Rienner, 1990).

30. See Stephen D. Cohen, *An Ocean Apart: Explaining Three Decades of U.S.-Japan Trade Friction* (Greenwood, Conn.: Praeger, 1998).

31. Keun Lee, *New East Asian Economic Development: The Interaction of Capitalism and Socialism* (Armonk, N.Y.: M. E. Sharpe, 1997); Eun Mea Kim, *The Four Asian Tigers: Economic Development & the Global Political Economy* (London: Academic Press, 1999).

32. See Brazinsky, *Nation Building in South Korea.*

33. For Reagan's foreign policy, see Kenneth B. Oye, Robert J. Lieber, and Donald Rothchild, eds., *Eagle Resurgent: The Reagan Era in American Foreign Policy* (Boston: Little, Brown, 1987).

34. Tsuyoshi Hasegawa, "The Soviet Factor in U.S-Japanese Defense Cooperation, 1978–1985," *Journal of Cold War Studies,* forthcoming.

35. Gerald Segal, *The Soviet Union and the Pacific* (London: Royal Institute of International Affairs, 1990).

36. For Gorbachev's foreign policy, see Vladislav Zubok, *A Failed Empire: The Soviet Union in the Cold War from Stalin to Gorbachev* (Chapel Hill: University of North Carolina Press, 2008), chap. 10.

37. For Soviet-Japanese relations, see note 17 above.

38. See chapter 11 in this volume, by Sergey Radchenko.

39. Leffler, *Preponderance of Power,* 400.

40. Quoted by Chang, *Friends and Enemies,* 83.

41. For atomic diplomacy, see Craig and Logeval, *America's Cold War,* 147–53, 179–83.

42. Ibid., 271, 273.

43. See Tsuyoshi Hasegawa, "Soviet Arms Control Policy in Asia and the U.S.-Japan Alliance," *Japan Review of International Affairs* 2, no. 2 (Fall–Winter 1988): 204–30.

44. See chapter 1 in this volume, by Odd Arne Westad.

45. See Thomas J. Christensen, *Useful Adversaries: Grand Strategy, Domestic Mobilization, and Sino-American Conflict, 1947–1958* (Princeton, N.J.: Princeton University Press, 1996). For the counterargument, see Chen Jian, *Mao's China and the Cold War,* 48; Chen Jian, "The Myth of American 'Lost Chance' in China: A Chinese Perspective in Light of New Evidence," *Diplomatic History* 21 (Winter 1977): 77–86.

46. For a comprehensive bibliography on the Vietnam War, see David L. Anderson, *Columbia Guide to the Vietnam War* (New York: Columbia University Press, 2004); Marilyn B. Young and Robert Buzanco, eds., *A Companion to the Vietnam War* (Malden, MA: Blackwell, 2002); Edwin E. Moïse, "Vietnam War Bibliography," http://www.clemson.edu/coah/history/facultypages/edmoise/bibliography.htm.

47. See McMahon, *Limits of Empire,* chap. 2. For early U.S. involvement in Vietnam, see Mark Atwood Lawrence, *Assuming the Burden: Europe and the American Commitment to War in Vietnam* (Berkeley: University of California Press, 2005); and Mark Philip Bradley, *Imagining Vietnam and America: The Making of Postcolonial Vietnam, 1919–1950* (Chapel Hill: University of North Carolina Press, 2000). Lawrence argues that Britain and France angled in the 1940s to convince the United States that Indochina was an important Cold War battleground, and that this laid the groundwork for Truman to make a solid commitment to aid France and South Vietnam once Mao emerged victorious in China, and especially after the outbreak of the Korean War.

48. Numerous books refer to the domino theory and the fear of loss of credibility. For a cogent analysis of this topic, see Craig and Logevall, *America's Cold War,* 220–23, 226–40, 276–78. The domino effect and the fear of credibility loss were connected, but how they were connected over time must be examined carefully. In 1963–64, when Vietnam became less strategically important, and hence the domino effect lost its significance, the credibility issue became more important. Furthermore, as Logevall argues, under Lyndon Johnson, the credibility of the nation was superseded by Johnson's personal credibility. See Fredrik Logevall, *Choosing War: The Lost Chance for Peace and the Escalation of War in Vietnam* (Berkeley: University of California Press, 2001).

49. See Craig and Logevall, *America's Cold War,* chaps. 6 and 7.

50. McMahon, *Limits of Empire,* 62.

51. Don Oberdorfer, *Tet: The Turning Point in the Vietnam War* (Baltimore: Johns Hopkins University Press, 2001).

52. See H-Net discussion, "Politics of Troop Withdrawl," by Lloyd Gardners, Robert Jervis, Jeffrey Kimball, and Marilyn Young, net.org/reviews/showrev.cgi?path=31585950218853.

53. The number of American soldiers killed and wounded is from Congressional Research Service, "American War and Military Operation Casualties: Lists and Statistics (February 26, 2010), p. 11 (http://www.fas.org/sgp/crs/natsec/RL32492.pdf). According to the National Archive the number of American soldiers killed was 58,193,

http://www.archives.gov/research/vietnam-war/casualty-statistics.html#branch. The number of South Vietnamese soldiers killed is from R. R. Rommel, table 6,1A in Statistics of Democide, chap. 6, Statistics of Vietnamese Democides, Estimates, Calculations, Sources (http://www.hawaii.edu/powerkills/SOD.Chap6HTM). The number of North Vietnamese soldiers and Vietcong killed was given by the North Vietnamese government in a press release to Agence France Presse in April 1995.

54. Westad, *Global Cold War,* 180.

55. Quoted by Young, *Vietnam Wars,* 20.

56. McMahon, *Limits of Empire,* 166.

57. Craig and Logevall, *America's Cold War,* 276.

58. See Jian Rongji [Shu Kenei], *Mo Takuso no betonamu senso: Chugoku gaiko no daitenkan to Bunka daikakumei no kigen* [Mao Zedong's Vietnam War: The great change in China's foreign policy and the origins of the Great Cultural Revolution] (Tokyo: Tokyo daigaku shppankai, 2001. See also Qiang Zhai, *China and the Vietnam Wars, 1950–1975* (Chapel Hill: University of North Carolina Press, 2000); Chen Jian, *Mao's China and the Cold War,* chap. 8; and Lüthi, *Sino-Soviet Split,* chap. 10. For Soviet policy toward the Vietnam War, see Ilya Gaiduk, *Confronting Vietnam: Soviet Policy toward the Indochina Conflict, 1954–1963* (Stanford, Calif.: Stanford University Press, 2003); and Ilya Gaiduk, *The Soviet Union and the Vietnam War* (Chicago: Ivan Dee, 1996).

59. See Gaiduk, *Confronting Vietnam;* and Gaiduk, *Soviet Union and the Vietnam War.* See also chapter 2 in this volume, by Gaiduk.

60. See Chen Jian, *Mao's China and the Cold War.*

61. Ibid., 208–9.

62. Ibid., 211.

63. Ibid., 221.

64. Zubok, *Failed Empire,* 198–99; Gaiduk, *Soviet Union and the Vietnam War,* 27–51.

65. See Qiang Zhai, *China and the Vietnam Wars,* chap. 9.

66. Ibid., 197. See also Chen Jian, "China, the Vietnam War, and the Sino-American Rapprochement," in *The Third Indochina War: Conflict between China, Vietnam, and Cambodia, 1972–73,* ed. Odd Arne Westad and Sophie Quinn-Judge (New York: Routledge, 2006), 33–64; and Lien-Hang T. Nguyen, "The Sino-Vietnamese Split and the Indochina War, 1968–1975," in ibid., 12–32.

67. For Soviet policy toward Vietnam in the 1970s, see Gaiduk, *Soviet Union and the Vietnam War;* and Stephen J. Morris, *The Soviet-Chinese-Vietnamese Triangle in the 1970s: The View from Moscow,* Cold War International History Project Working Paper 25 (Washington, D.C.: Cold War International History Project, Woodrow Wilson International Center for Scholars, 1999).

68. Zubok, *Failed Empire,* 220.

69. Morris, "Soviet-Chinese-Vietnamese Triangle," 19.

70. Gaiduk, *Soviet Union and the Vietnam War,* 247–49.

71. Morris, "Soviet-Chinese-Vietnamese Triangle," 17; Qiang Zhai, *China and the Vietnam Wars,* 202.

72. Qiang Zhai, *China and the Vietnam Wars,* 201–2.

73. Christopher E. Goscha, "Vietnam, the Third Indochina War, and the Meltdown of Asian Internationalism," in *Third Indochina War,* ed. Westad and Quinn-Judge, 152–86.

1. Struggles for Modernity: The Golden Years of the Sino-Soviet Alliance

Odd Arne Westad

The alliance between the Soviet Union and China, which in terms of its diplomatic significance lasted from 1945 up to some point in the mid-1960s, was a key element in both countries' search for a modernity of their own. From the Soviet perspective, the alliance with China established Moscow as the center of a global anti-hegemonic system of states and confirmed the attractiveness of its social and political model for countries outside Europe. For many Chinese, the alliance was about finding a pattern for building a modern state that was neither derived from their grotesque images of Western imperialist countries nor inherently exploitative in Chinese terms. This chapter briefly discusses key aspects of China's state-building exercise in the 1940s and 1950s in light of Sino-Soviet cooperation, and thereby attempts to address some of the questions about the alliance that have been asked but never fully answered, through a focus on foreign policy or strategy, such as what motivated the relationship, what were the roles of ideologies and common concerns, and—especially—what was the function of that most amorphous of concepts, "Chinese nationalism."

To seek out the links between the international and the domestic in the struggles for modernity during the golden years of Sino-Soviet cooperation, in this chapter I concentrate on four areas of government activity that were underlined in importance on both the Chinese and Soviet sides and in central as well as local affairs. First, I look at concepts of war and warfare, and how these were influenced by Soviet theory and practice. I am particularly interested in military organization, the area where experience (especially of Chinese Communist soldiers coming up through the ranks) met the ideals of planning. Second, I discuss some of the main debates in China within the field of education, showing how the new government wanted to plan for a modern, educated, urban society of workers, creating many "Moscows of the East," as the leaders put it. Third, following on from the Communists' educational ideals, I give a brief overview of the curious debates on city planning in China in the 1950s, especially as they relate to Beijing. Fourth and finally, I consider how Chinese minority policies developed during the later phase of the civil war and the new state's infancy.

The main argument of the chapter is straightforward. From the mid-1940s to the late 1950s, the concepts of modernity in the Chinese Communist Party (CCP) and, to some extent, among nonparty elites, were increasingly oriented toward the experience of the Soviet Union. But Chinese perceptions of the Soviet Union were dual. One the one hand, Moscow was seen as standing for planning, procedure, and gradualism. On the other hand, Soviet campaigns, purges, and acts of will (in both its Stalin and Khrushchev variations) inspired those within the CCP who detested contemplating a lengthy wait until Communism appeared on the horizon. These two directions—the Plan and the Leap—increasingly clashed with each other in 1950s China, with both directions appealing for legitimacy through a reading of the Soviet experience. Indeed, one could say that the political showdown between these tendencies contributed decisively to the cataclysm that China went through in the decade that followed the disintegration of the Soviet alliance, during the Great Leap Forward and the Cultural Revolution.

Historical Background: The 1920s to 1940s

The CCP was founded in the early 1920s with Soviet aid, drawing on the inspiration that the Russian Revolution provided for many Chinese intellectuals of the May 4th era. The concepts of (Western) modernity that were inherent in the new Bolshevik state appealed to the members of a Chinese generation who feared for the very survival of their country, confronted as it was by foreign imperialism and domestic "backwardness." Lenin's adaptation of Marxism for Russian purposes promised a state that was both modern and just, that would give the Chinese—upon their implementation of the model—a purpose within China and in the world. This sense of *both* saving one's country *and* being part of an alternative global movement that would eventually rule the world was the driving force behind the tremendous appeal that Communism had across continents in the 1920s and 1930s. In China, it created a significant group (although a tiny portion of the total population) that was dedicated to the construction of a socialist state.[1]

Many historians have insisted that a creative adaptation of Leninist Marxism for Chinese purposes started almost immediately after the CCP was organized. Significant figures within the party, it is argued, realized that the Soviet model had to be adjusted to Chinese realities if it was to be a realistic program for attaining power. There is obviously much to this argument. Not only were the major CCP figures of the founding period aware of the differences between Russia and China, but they were also insistent that Chinese experiences would have to be taken into consideration when forming political programs. Indeed, the Soviets and the Comintern themselves encouraged studying local conditions and adapting universal Marxist principles to "Chinese realities" (even though Moscow, of course, believed it had the final word in deciding what those "realities" were).

However, the more I look at texts from the 1920s and—especially—the early 1930s, the more I am struck by how much of the CCP's approach was determined not by deliberate adaptation but by what anthropologists call "creative misunderstandings." From the very beginning in 1920–21, and increasingly as the isolation of the party took hold after 1927–28, many party members began building on their version of Soviet Communism, with relatively little actual information about conditions north of the border, not to mention in European Russia. Instead, they read the Soviet Union in a way that made sense for their own visions of China's future and based on experiences the CCP cadre could understand. In many CCP texts about the Soviet Union, what appears is a modern China, with technology, education, and a righteous state, but with values and procedures that are culturally as well as historically Chinese.[2]

An interesting text in this regard is the writer Qu Qiubai's notes on Moscow in 1924, which were written for his CCP comrades back in China. Qu, who was later to become the leader of the party—only to have his life ended by a Guomindang firing squad in 1935—presents the Soviet capital as the center of an enormous machine that is the Soviet Union. It is a productive city, with factories spreading far and wide, but first and foremost it is the head of the socialist body, from where instructions to Communists in Russia and all around the world are sent out. It attracts the best and the brightest, and it defines how to organize a just society for the future. While Qu describes the Soviet capital in terms many Confucians would hail as ideal, for him Moscow is the image to which modern China—leaving its past behind—ought to aspire.[3]

What had attracted many Chinese to the Soviet experiment in the first place was the combination of personal resolve and historical necessity that was supposed to bring forth socialism. The former appealed to a generation of youth who were still steeped in Confucian ideals of self-control and strength of character. The latter promised to give a socialist China a place of prominence in a new and modern world. But as the real world for Chinese Communists in the

1930s became darker and darker, both those who had experienced the Soviet Union firsthand (who were a tiny minority) and those who "saw" Stalin's socialism through Chinese writings and the power of imagination came to emphasize the personal aspects of building a party and a new state over those of Marxist determinism. To some degree, this is of course parallel to the 1930s' developments in the USSR, where a highly voluntaristic discourse came to replace much of the Marxism that had been left in Lenin's party as Bolshevism took hold. As David Apter and Tony Saich point out, the new logocentric CCP of the Yan'an period therefore became a party whose key texts stressed individual sacrifice, dedication to party norms, and devotion to the party's leaders as recipes for success (or at least survival).[4] Of the powerful mix of will and inevitability in Bolshevism, by the 1940s most Chinese Communists had come—consciously or not—to underline the former.

Building an Army

A central element of modernity was having a well-organized, well-trained, well-equipped, and well-disciplined army, eventually to be supplemented by a full-fledged navy and air force. As Michael Adas has pointed out, many of the key concepts of modernity on a global scale were connected to the regimentation and molding of men for which armies and war offered the opportunity.[5] The remaking of a society and the creation of the fundamentals of a new state were made much easier, "founding fathers" from Bonaparte, via Lenin and Ataturk, to Mao Zedong believed, by linking a large percentage of the male population to a mass army. The army was not only there to protect the state (or those who held power in it); it was also an important force for shaping society in the form the power holders wanted to see. As Charles Tilly was fond of pointing out, armies and wars could make states as well as break them, and in some cases it was the prospects for militarization (in sociological terms) of both state and society that attracted leaders as much as victories on the battlefields.[6]

The visions of a future military machine were also a significant component of the contests over the future of China among reformers from Zeng Guofan in the nineteenth century to Sun Yatsen and Mao Zedong in the twentieth. In spite of their widely differing political beliefs, these leaders all saw something more in the creation of a modern army than just the force to resist foreign aggression. The dream of the Chinese army was to possess an instrument that could transform society through changing values and allegiances as much as through winning wars. In the early part of the twentieth century, when the people who created the People's Republic formed their political views, many Chinese admired Japan's leap into modernity. But they had particular admiration for the Meiji Army, which, according to one keen Chinese observer, the reformer Liang Qichao, had "reconstituted the Japanese nation."[7]

After May 4, many Chinese turned their gaze toward the Red Army of the Soviet Union as an object of emulation. Not only were the Soviets confronting foreign intervention successfully, but many Chinese leaders (and by no means only the Marxists) also believed that the Red Army was the most regimented and dedicated army possible. It served the state (but in no way controlled it), gave political as well as general education to its men, and emphasized technology and mobility. First and foremost, the Soviet army served as an instrument for integrating peasants into the new state; they entered the army with a peasant mentality, Stalin famously said, but left it with a proletarian mentality.[8]

Nothing would have pleased the young CCP leaders more than being able to import a tool for making peasants into proletarians. Unfortunately for them (but possibly as a stroke of good luck for the peasants), the political conditions of China in the 1920s did not allow for the creation of a nationwide Red Army. Instead it was the CCP's enemies, the Guomindang, that came to set up its anticommunist army based to a large extent on Soviet advice from the first United Front period, when some of the key Soviet military theorists served in China. From the late 1920s on, the CCP was condemned to a period of defensive warfare, in which survival was the objective. Naturally, this favored small and highly mobile units over the ideal of massive conventional forces. Contrary to the CCP's own well-beloved myths, the guerrilla tactics of the 1930s and the anti-Japanese war were the products not of choice but of necessity. With the dream of the Chinese army intact, Mao and his colleagues would have to survive the onslaught of their enemies on lesser dreams.

The year 1945 changed all that. With the Red Army in Manchuria and the Japanese Empire in ruins, the CCP, for the first time in its history, began building a modern army. Though the party's military experiences from the previous fifteen years obviously formed the backdrop for what became the People's Liberation Army (PLA), the inspiration for its organization, as well as its strategy, were explicitly Soviet. More than 1,500 young Chinese officers got their training in Soviet military academies *before* the People's Republic was set up, and more were trained by Soviet instructors in Manchuria between 1947 and 1949. After 1949, the most cited figure is one of 9,000 trained in the Soviet Union. The number trained inside China must have been many times that. The result was a modern Chinese army that looked increasingly like the Red Army that served the same purposes internally and fought wars more or less in the same way.[9]

The organization of the new PLA was consciously and directly modeled on that of the Soviet Red Army. The units, the ranks, the weaponry, the tactics, and even the uniforms were taken from Soviet textbooks or from advice given by Red Army instructors. The new army was the pride of the CCP's leaders and seen—with some right—as an impressive combination of battle skills learned in the Chinese civil war and in the war against Japan, on the one hand, and "Soviet learning," on the other. Even though some Chinese officers found it hard to give up the much more improvised and flexible approach to military affairs propagated before the last offensives of the civil war in 1948 and 1949, they too were easily won over by the increased status that their modern hardware (not to mention their shiny new uniforms) gave them. By 1955, this Sovietization of the PLA was more or less complete, though the concept of fourteen military ranks was somewhat difficult for the egalitarian-minded Chinese soldiers to swallow.[10] The *People's Daily* [*Renmin ribao*] had to argue hard for the reforms:

> Why must the PLA adopt the system of military ranks at present? This is because with [conscription], the modern equipment of the armed forces requires that the training and activities of servicemen should follow strict systems and regulations. The ranking and relationship of officers should be clearly defined, and the organization and discipline of the armed forces should be consolidated. . . . All officers must wear badges and insignia of their ranks so that there will be clear distinction between officers and other ranks. . . . Only in this way would the units of the armed forces be able to carry out successfully their task of defending the country in a changing situation and under the new conditions of complex equipment, speed of movement, and joint action of the different branches.[11]

The concept of a conscript army—entirely new to China—was another Soviet-inspired PLA invention, which—as in the Soviet Union—was intended to serve many purposes besides military power. The transition was made during the Korean War, when the Chinese soldiery—in spite of its propagandistic name of "the Chinese People's Volunteer Army"—went from being a professional army of sorts (such as had been assembled during conditions of war) to a full-fledged conscript force. As Bruce Elleman argues convincingly, it was the civil war that created the framework for the new Chinese army, but the Korean War that trained its personnel to match the structure.[12] What came out of the war in Korea was the material of which the new army was to be built.

The new PLA served three major purposes. First, it was intended to be an effective fighting force, trained in the latest Soviet military doctrines and equipped with the best weapons that the Soviets and Eastern Europeans were willing to offer. Second, it was to be a laboratory for educating young Chinese men to serve in a new world of socialism. And third, it was intended to help build China's civilian development projects, at least in the most intensive phase on construction, which most leaders expected China to undertake starting in the mid-1950s.[13] Though often cited as coming out of the Chinese Communist experience of the 1930s and 1940s—and being at variance with the highly professionalized Soviet model—one key inspiration for the military links to construction campaigns was Stalin's Soviet Union, in which millions of servicemen had participated in grand projects, from dam building to cultivating new land.[14] China's new military forces were therefore a key element both in terms of the construction and the socialization needed to create a modern state.

Even though only a limited portion of each yearly cohort ended up serving in the new conscript force (there were exemptions to be had for most things, from study to farming), the reduced army did become a school for socialism and perhaps China's most effective instrument for mass education and social betterment. The roughly eight hundred thousand youngsters who were conscripted each year for two to three years of service came mostly from the countryside. In the army they were educated, they traveled, and they learned about their country (as seen by the CCP) and about the new creeds of socialism and nationalism. Though the PRC spent a very high proportion of its annual budget—an average of 30 percent in the 1950s—on military affairs, at least the part that went into training officers and soldiery was later paid back, because many of these men came to play key parts in China's overall development projects.

The latter is particularly true for China's technological development. The patents, models, and training received from the Soviets in the military field in the 1950s were crucial to China for two decades to come. Much of the Soviet technology was intentionally dual-purpose; it could be used in the military as well as in the civilian sector. Whereas the Chinese navy and air force developed according to Soviet models, the technologies taught in China's military academies became crucial for China's capacity in other fields as well, such as in its nuclear programs (civilian as well as military), its aircraft industry, and much of its heavy machine building. The first Chinese-built aircraft in common use, the Y-5 (Yunshu-5, or Yun-5), was a Chinese copy of the Russian Antonov An-2 light cargo biplane designed in the 1940s. Although an extraordinarily slow plane, it was well suited to China's needs because of its versatility and low operating costs. The factory in Nanchang, the capital of then-dirt-poor Jiangxi Province, produced the first aircraft with Soviet assistance in 1957, making the production site almost sacred ground for Chinese modernization enthusiasts.[15]

What the military example shows is that—at least for a while—the virtues of planning and improvisation could go together. An army, of course, lends itself particularly well to planning (the main thing, it could be said, that armies are not able to plan for is war). But in the Chinese case, the strains between the two aspects of the Soviet model (or how the Soviet model was understood) became quite clear by the late 1950s, when army planners (e.g., Peng Dehuai, the Korean War commander, and Zhang Aiping, who played key roles in building the navy and the air force, as well as the atomic bomb) confronted those who emphasized "creative" or "mass" solutions to military challenges. The latter group—which is often linked to Lin Biao but in reality was headed by generals such as Chen Geng, who had led the PLA expedition to Vietnam in 1950, and Chen Xilian, who commanded the artillery attacks on Jinmen in 1958 and later was to be in charge of the attacks on the Soviet army along the Manchurian border in 1969—did not consciously deviate from the Soviet model in the 1950s, but rather stressed the tactical skills of the Red Army over the strategic lessons Soviet advisers tried to imprint on them.[16]

As in the case of military technologies, the Soviet war-fighting model contained both the Plan and the Leap. It is clear from the evidence we now have that the debates and divergences on the approach to military development in the 1950s did not favor one over the other until Chinese politics, driven by Mao Zedong's visions, began presenting the Leap as "Chinese" and the Plan, at least in its most restrictive form, as somehow "Soviet." As has been shown by Chen Jian and Yang Kuisong, the military in general was among those who had benefited the most from the Soviet link, and therefore needed to be jolted into a more autarchic vision of development through the Great Leap Forward and the purges that accompanied it.[17] But, as they had been trained to do as part of the modernization project, the Chinese military in the end followed the political authorities on their journey through many disasters, until in 1976 they finally could take no more.

Education

The emphasis on educational reform that the CCP introduced to the areas it occupied and, after 1949, by the PRC is not new in Chinese history. During processes of political change in Imperial China and during the Republican Era, much of the same emphasis had emerged. But never before—or at least not since the early Tang Dynasty, in the seventh century A.D.—had Chinese education been wholly remade according to a foreign model. The CCP deliberately patterned its educational policies at all levels on the Soviet experience in ways that would come to have a fateful impact on two generations of Chinese students.[18]

Just as with military affairs, Chinese higher education policies also drew from both the Plan and the Leap aspects of Soviet methods. At the higher level of tertiary education, the Plan certainly dominated all the way up to the Cultural Revolution, except for short, intense purges aimed at bourgeois elements in the universities. The key to development was technical and science education, and the state set the aims of how many engineers, chemists, and other specialized groups were needed every year. The candidates for entry were selected according to political, class, and achievement criteria; they had to be both bright and Red. The Education Ministry underlined the need to be able to predict the numbers of people who would be available to send to work in plants and mines every year—just as in the Soviet Union in the 1930s, students were often given a specific future work assignment as early as their second year in college (even though the authorities rarely found it necessary to inform the students themselves of what lay in store).[19]

Even though the implementation of the Soviet model started in earnest after 1945, there was much to build on in China—even outside the CCP—in terms of admiration for Soviet higher education and teaching methods. Much of this resonance went back to the May 4th era, but the wartime Chinese People's Anti-Japanese Military and Political University and Yan'an University introduced Soviet pedagogical methods on a much grander scale. During the civil war from 1946 to 1950, the lessons of the Yan'an period were infused with much more direct contact with Soviet educational and technical advisers, especially in the Northeast. The First National Higher Education Conference in June 1950—the first of the normative conferences on changes in education—advocated a complete rebuilding of the Chinese higher education system according to a Soviet model. All universities and colleges were to be placed directly under the Education Ministry, young teachers were to be sent to the Soviet Union or Soviet-staffed training colleges in China for instruction in pedagogical methods, and a massive program of translating Soviet textbooks was inaugurated. Simultaneously, the conference decreed the abolition of the system of individual teachers being responsible for training students; from now on, there should be full-fledged departments that taught students collectively and were jointly responsible for the political content of their teaching.[20]

But before these socialist visions could be realized, the CCP concluded—probably correctly—that it would have to overcome the resistance to the new curricula and teaching methods among intellectuals. A significant part of the antibourgeois campaigns of 1951–53 was directed against this group, with purges of many of those who resisted or were suspected of resisting as a result. The purge (conducted, again, fully according to Soviet standards) was generally effective from the CCP's point of view: Not only did one get rid of "enemies," but—more important—the brutal methods that were used frightened remaining skeptics into silence and obedience. For the majority of intellectuals, who embraced the new regime's educational policies mostly for patriotic reasons, the purges could be deemed acceptable because they served the greater national purpose. "Thought reform"—*xi'nao,* literally, "brainwashing"—may not have been popular, but it was often seen as serving the needs of national as well as personal reconstruction.[21]

The purges of the early 1950s delayed the full implementation of the 1950 program for higher education until the academic year 1952–53, in which all institutions were supposed to be fully restructured. In the capital, for instance, the new Beijing University was created by adding departments from Yanjing University and Qinghua University. Most important of all was the creation of People's University in Beijing, a new institution that taught politics and social sciences and prepared students for further study in the Soviet Union (in the same way that, two generations earlier, nearby Qinghua University had been set up to prepare students for further study in the United States).[22]

The wholesale importing of curricula and pedagogies led to much enthusiasm and not a little confusion.[23] In some cases, newly translated Soviet textbooks replaced U.S. or European ones that were far better informed on the subject (and a whole generation of Chinese technicians paid the price). In others, students were trained for technologies that did not yet exist in China, or that required skills in other fields that were not taught in Chinese universities. The CCP's insistence that work skills were as important as study skills led to the entry of large numbers of unqualified students into the universities for "political" reasons. The needs of the First Five-Year Plan, introduced in 1953, meant that enormous pressure was put on the universities and colleges to produce high numbers of personnel for industry and—in many cases—that standards were slipping because of the need to educate more people. There was a fair share of claims of unrealistic attainment, leading to a need to falsify results.[24]

No other area of cooperation attracted as many Soviet advisers as education. Generally, they were left unimpressed by what they saw as piecemeal Chinese attempts to reform the educational system. Education in China was hopelessly backward, as they saw it. By the mid-1950s, there were still far too much deference toward teachers and far too little emphasis on political education. Some of the Soviet advisers placed in the central bureaucracy advocated large-scale campaigns directed primarily against illiteracy in the countryside; they thought that too much in terms of resources was being spent in the cities and on higher education. The models, as they saw them, were the methods developed in Soviet Central Asia and in Mongolia in the 1930s. Progress in this area could be, and ought to be, faster than the First Five-Year Plan envisaged.[25]

As in agriculture, 1955 became the year of reckoning in Chinese education. One the one hand, criticism of the universities for slipping standards and not providing personnel with the skills needed to fulfill the Plan was on the rise. The programs for adult education—to turn workers into students, as the Soviets did in their *rabfaks*—were criticized for being unrealistic and expensive (and in effect were abolished at year's end). On the other hand, those at the CCP center—and probably Chairman Mao himself—were increasingly impatient with the educational sector, but for different reasons. Their sense was that reform in education was moving too slowly to catch up with the country's needs, and they wrote this inertia down to a lack of political motivation. At the same time, there was an increasing sense (shared by the Soviets, as we have seen) that the countryside was being left behind. The so-called Little Leap, launched by Mao in the spring of 1956, was intended to correct these tendencies.[26]

The beginning of the divergence of approaches to education in China and the Soviet Union cannot simply be explained by the CCP's perceived need to "Sinify" or "radicalize" its policies starting in about 1956. Soviet advisers criticized the Chinese planners of the early 1950s in a manner that shared many of Chairman Mao's concerns, especially with regard to incrementalism and the lack of rural development. The "Leap" approach was as much a Soviet as Chinese invention; when turning to more "fundamental" methods to force change, Mao and his associates turned as much to "high Stalinism" in the Soviet Union in the mid-1930s as to their own Yan'an experience. An April 1957 article in *Jiaoshibao,* quoted by Suzanne Pepper, traces the origins of the Little Leap to Stalin's methods in 1929–30.[27] The lessons given by Soviet advisers, in other words, were neither unitary nor extrinsic—ideological elements happily crossed any national divide.

Urban Planning

Besides land reform and education, perhaps the most important transformative policy of the new regime was in the field of urban planning. In spite of its Marxist origins, the CCP had grown up as a party deeply skeptical of life in the cities, to the extent that its chairman, Mao Zedong, famously refused at first to move to Beijing after the city fell to the Communists in the spring of 1949, preferring to stay with the troops on its periphery. Having had to conquer the cities from the outside, the Chinese Communists expected little support there—even from among the much-lauded "proletariat"—and generally regarded China's major urban centers as dungeons of vice and counterrevolution. In 1950, there had even been a heated debate in the Politburo on a proposal from one of the senior leaders—the head of the Manchurian party Gao Gang—to abolish

Shanghai altogether and send all its prerevolutionary inhabitants for "rectification" in the countryside.[28]

The little experience the CCP had with urban administration came from its work in Manchuria, and it was not positive. From the beginning, the CCP leaders felt, large numbers of urban inhabitants had conspired against them after they had taken control of the region in 1947 and 1948. It took a major effort from the Soviet advisers to make the CCP units look more favorably on their immediate potential in the cities. But even after the transformative framework for building socialism in the Manchurian cities had been explained to them by the Soviets, the emphasis as understood by the CCP cadre was on transcendence rather than transformation—that is, only by being reborn in a socialist image could Shenyang, Harbin, and Jilin be of use to New China. In a cultural sense, it was of course particularly problematic that much of the "bourgeois dirt" and "bad egg exploiters" had their roots in the region's Russian colonial past. But just as Russia had been reborn as the anti-imperialist Soviet Union, now China's ally, the Manchurian cities could eventually become Chinese socialist cities, based on planning and people's needs.[29]

The idea of urban planning in China had been developed among a few Western-trained intellectuals in the 1920s and 1930s. People who had been educated in Europe or America had taken with them the Western admiration for Soviet urban planning principles based on the "general plan," the idea that all aspects of city life could be organized to serve society as a whole, as well as the improvement of all its inhabitants. Though the early industrial cities were pockets of filth and vice—created, of course, in the Soviet view by capitalist exploitation—the "new" cities would be built to serve the people, both the working class that already lived in them and the peasant masses who would enter them to be transformed into industrial workers.[30]

In the early 1950s in China, there was a striking meeting of minds between the leaders of the new regime, who first of all wanted to regulate so as to keep control, and the noncommunist intellectuals, who believed in urban planning to improve living conditions. Both sides distrusted all the elements of what they liked to call "old China," including the urban environments of cities such as Beijing, Tianjin, and Wuhan. Their problem was whether—or if so, how—these cities could be quickly transformed from a parasitic to a productive part of society. The urban crisis that the CCP had inherited from the Guomindang—refugees, unemployment, inflation, scarcity of goods—contributed to the urgency; output in the cities continued to fall during the first two years of Communist rule.[31]

Their minds met in Soviet urban planning theory, developed in the 1930s and embodied in its most complete form in the 1935 General Plan for Moscow.[32]

By the mid-1930s, Stalin had decided to transform the structure of the Soviet capital to make it a fitting symbol of socialism, to make it more productive, and to make it more secure for the Communist elite. First and foremost, the city needed more central regulation and more immediate functionality so it could serve as a showcase for advanced socialism. The haphazard destruction of old Moscow that had taken place in the 1920s was no longer enough. There had to be a centralized *plan* for both destruction and construction, not the experimental and individual or group-based architectural projects of the early Communist period.[33]

The early 1930s saw two very different approaches to urban planning in the Soviet Union. Those of the radicals who had survived (physically, if not politically) the initial purges tried to make their ideas fit into the new Stalinist intellectual landscape. Two of them were particularly important for events in China (almost a decade after their deaths, as it happened). One was Nikolai Aleksandrovich Ladovskii, who was accused by his enemies of being a "closet constructivist" in the early 1930s, after having proposed the pattern of alternating functions of zones and sectors within the radiating ring segments that became the basis for the Moscow General Plan in the 1920s. The other was Nikolai Vasil'evich Dokuchaev, who had been accused of being a "rationalist" in the 1920s, and who developed much of the Soviet concept of urban planning, devising methods and measures for viewing human urban society as a machine. Though Dokuchaev was prevented from having his own designs implemented, his main influence was as a teacher of future generations of Soviet architects and planners, including many of those who would go to China in the 1950s.[34]

But Stalin's favored urban planners were not these two "wild men" of the 1920s. On the contrary, he preferred those architects and designers who had been displaced from their central position in Russian intellectual life by the Bolshevik Revolution, neoclassicists such as Aleksei Viktorovich Shchusev and Ivan Vladislavovich Zholtovskii.[35] Given Stalin's own constant search for legitimacy in a Russian context—and his rather petit bourgeois tastes in general—this particular predilection is not surprising: He attempted to link his own rule with that of the great reformers of the past, and especially, of course, with that great Russian builder Tsar Peter I and Saint Petersburg, the new capital he had built on the Neva River. No wonder Stalin found as his favorite architect the former church builder Shchusev, who in the 1920s, when his neoclassical form was strictly out of vogue, had mostly been limited to designing workers' sanatoria and *kolkhoz* headquarters.[36] By the early 1930s, Shchusev and his friends were back with a vengeance, now priding themselves on having become "social-realists." The final word on the "Great" Moscow Plan of

1935 was Shchusev's, as was the immediate responsibility for the destruction of the old city that followed (although—thankfully, some would say—most of his designs, e.g., the Palace of Soviets, were never erected). We know that Zholtovskii's great idea—the "historical" link between revolutionary Moscow and the Italian Renaissance, exemplified in his own "Palladian" designs—deeply impressed Chinese visitors to Moscow.[37] The style of the Plan, so to say, when transplanted to China, was a celebratory, historicist version of Western development.

Paradoxically, it was Chinese noncommunist intellectuals who introduced the CCP cadre to the specific Soviet ideas of urban planning, in part as preparation for receiving larger numbers of advisers from Moscow. The more the party faithful understood these principles, the more they liked them. For a leadership that distrusted their city populations, however much they lauded the virtues of the "proletariat," Soviet urban planning ideas were eminently practical, as well as theoretically correct. Broad avenues and big urban squares facilitated the mobility of workers from home to the factory and back, but they also could come in handy in case the PLA needed to enter a city center to crush a counterrevolutionary rebellion. But first and foremost, it seems, the CCP leaders were convinced by the glory of it all. By transforming their cities in the Soviet image, China would for the first time have urban centers that were celebrations of the modern form—planned, functional, and productive, rather than haphazard, dysfunctional, and consumptive, as they believed the cities of "Old China" to have been.[38]

Beijing—the Chinese city I know best—symbolized this development during the 1950s. It was exceptional in many ways because it had been designated the capital (even though this decision was not made final until the late spring of 1949), and it also became a pattern and showcase for Communist China's urban planning. When the work on transforming the capital started—well before the People's Republic was declared in October 1949—the 1935 Moscow Plan was immediately taken as the model. The first Soviet planning team that arrived in Beijing, in September 1949, helped this process along, even though there were disagreements within the joint teams that were set up to work toward a General Plan for Beijing.[39]

One of these disagreements was about where to place the headquarters of the CCP and the new government. Some Chinese architects and planners, such as Liang Sicheng, the U.S.-educated son of the famous Chinese reformer Liang Qichao, proposed erecting a completely new administrative center *outside* the old city, in the western parts of Beijing. According to many Chinese works on urban planning—and in Beijing popular lore—Liang and his colleagues wanted to rescue the Ming and Qing city from destruction by locating a new center away from the Forbidden City and the old imperial quarters. Judging from his notes at the time, his view seems to have been more driven by a wish to start building the new modern—and architecturally modernist—Beijing in a location away from the clutter and complications of the old city.[40] His son remembers that Liang Sicheng "believed that the time had come for mapping out a real scientific, reasonable plan for the city, because under socialism all the urban land is owned by the country and all the architectural activities are brought under a unified management."[41] Whatever Liang's own motives may have been, the planners close to the CCP leaders had another motive for their insistence on a new location: They argued that these leaders simply would not be safe enough in the center of a city that was still "unreconstructed" and where "old elements" were roaming freely.[42]

The Soviet advisers, conversely, claimed that the relocation argument was theoretically unsafe—the Red government had to take possession of the capital and show, symbolically as well as functionally, that it was the master of the place. To remake Beijing as a Red City and China as a Red Country, the Communists had to be at the center of it, not hiding away on the outskirts. They were supported by a clear majority of those who were providing planning and architectural advice to the new regime, including the Japanese-educated Zhao Dongri (who later designed the Great Hall of the People) and the French-educated architect Hua Lanhong, who was close to Le Corbusier.

Even though he did not contribute to the final design for the renovated city center that won the day (for that, Zhao collaborated with Zhu Zhaoxue, one of the few architects who was actually a Communist), Hua Lanhong was by far the most influential architect to participate in the battles over the fate of old Beijing. Léon Hoa, as he is known as in France, grew up in Paris, where his father, Hua Nangui, had been the first Chinese student at the prestigious École Nationale des Travaux Publics de l'État at the beginning of the twentieth century. Léon graduated from the same college as his father in 1936, and went on to study at the École Nationale Supérieure des Beaux-Arts, where he got his doctorate in 1942. He first practiced as an architect in France, holding several positions in the post-1944 planning committee for the Paris region. In 1949, he left for China and was immediately appointed to the number two position in the Urban Planning Committee for Beijing.[43]

Hua's argument was both aesthetic and practical: Beijing needed a new city center to symbolize New China. Examples of the old should be integrated with the new, but only to prove the progress that China had made from its dynastic, dysfunctional, and disease-ridden past to the internationalist, functional, and hygienic present. In a report he and Zhu Zhaoxue completed in April 1950, the emphasis was on creating a new capital: The massive city walls should be torn down and new highways constructed through the old center. The ceremonial focus of Beijing should be turned away from the Forbidden City and toward a new gigantic square to be constructed between the Gate of Heavenly Peace and the Front Gate. Hua's view was that the Communist takeover represented a golden opportunity, not to be missed, to modernize and rationalize old Beijing.[44]

In rather typical fashion for Communist China, both Liang and Hua were attacked during the purges in the late 1950s. First, Liang condemned Hua and his associates during the Hundred Flowers campaign in 1957, and then Liang himself was attacked—much more seriously—during the antibourgeois campaign of 1958 and later during the Cultural Revolution. Liang Sicheng died, still writing his mandatory self-criticism, in 1972.[45] Hua Lanhong fared somewhat better. In a wonderful twist of fate, his daughter, the French architect Hua Xinmin, has now emerged as a key defender of what is left of old Beijing after the ravages of the plan her father helped implement in the 1950s.

As so often happened with the founding of the PRC, Mao Zedong sided with the Soviets and their supporters on the issue of where to place the administrative center. Given the vagaries of his thirty-year revolutionary career, he had had enough of hiding on the outskirts. "Apparently, emperors can live in Beijing, but I cannot," the chairman is said to have exclaimed angrily as he rejected Liang Sicheng's plan.[46] But it is also likely that Mao and the Politburo found that whatever their own preferences were, they would have to lead from the inside in the transformation of China's cities. If the Soviet Union had created socialist cities, China could do so as well. And Beijing would be the key example. In the work toward the first draft of the General Plan for Beijing, finally published in the spring of 1953, Dokuchaev would have had no problem in recognizing the discourse: The whole city was to be reconstructed on a grid system according to strict zoning principles, with the factory as the overall model. Key to the plan was that Beijing should become not just a capital but also an industrial center to serve the whole country. The population should be relocated to new housing complexes near their places of work. There should be complete equality of services among different groups of the population, and the bulk of these services—education excepted—should be provided through their work units, with the city government being in charge of overall planning.[47]

The Preliminary Version of the General Plan for Beijing, from 1957, and the plan itself (promulgated in June 1958, but never fully implemented because of the chaos of the Great Leap Forward), were even more closely patterned on the Soviet plan than the 1953 version had been. Beijing would fully adopt the model of zoning in circles radiating from the city center (which was also the center of government).[48] The center itself would be rebuilt, with the massively enlarged central square at its heart (now known as Tiananmen Square) and massive building complexes representing the new government (the Great Hall of the People and the Revolutionary Museum) overlooking the square. A massive new avenue for military parades—called, with some irony, the Avenue of Eternal Peace—would bisect the old city. In Beijing as a whole, 1 million old houses should be destroyed each year, and 2 million new ones should be built. The city should aim for the same population density as Moscow, with the majority of its inhabitants being industrial workers (a group that had been only 4 percent of the workforce in 1949).[49]

The basic elements of the General Plan for Beijing—elements that stayed in place up to the 1990s—epitomized the need to control and improve the urban population.[50] The whole Soviet and PRC urban planning system was based on these principles: There were to be three hierarchical administrative levels—small district, residential district, and "district"—with the functions of each sharply defined in terms of services and political surveillance. The local CCP organization and the police shared the responsibility for keeping a network of informers at all levels.[51] In addition, in Beijing, as in Moscow, the population was divided into "basic" and "nonbasic" elements, with essential services reserved for only the former when the imperialist attack came. Other cities all over China were planned and organized according to the same model. For Beijing, it meant the end of a city that had existed since the mid–fifteenth century. Over time, at least, the rationality of planning delivered little with which to replace it. As Victor Sit observes, the Beijing planners often achieved the opposite of the modernity that their plans called for, because "dysfunctioning the price mechanism meant grossly inefficient use of urban land, and a homogeneous city of prefabricated housing with poor services."[52]

Although it is tempting for those who look back at it today to blame the first Communist leaders—or their Soviet advisers—for the destruction of old Beijing, the story of what actually happened is more variegated and more problematic. The old city could not survive the needs of a modern city that was to be superimposed on it. The extensive use of Soviet models, ill suited as they were for a Chinese city, carried its part of the blame. But the main reason why the old city fell was the link between Western-trained modernizing intellectuals, who admired the Soviet version of city planning, and the rough balance between rapid development needs and long-term goals that the new government sought. Though prerevolutionary Moscow had been seen by some as the third Rome, Beijing was going to be the second Moscow, even bigger and more modern than the Soviet capital. And though the Plan would secure the result, the Leap—symbolized by the 1958–59 construction of the Great Hall of the People in less than ten months—would reduce the wait to a minimum.

Minorities

Policy toward minorities or "nationalities" was probably the field of social engineering in which Chinese approaches were most closely modeled on the Soviet experience. There were many reasons for this. Soviet nationalities policy was regarded as highly successful, not just by the Chinese—dealing with ethnic minorities was something Moscow was considered good at, in an international and Western comparison. Besides, the Chinese knew that policy toward minorities was a particular area of interest for the "main master" himself; Joseph Stalin, Georgian by birth, had served as commissar for nationalities in the early 1920s and had written extensively on the topic.[53] Also, old China, like old Russia, had been an imperial state with many different ethnic groups, and the Soviet solutions could therefore produce a practical blueprint for New China.

Already, in the first conversations that the CCP's top leaders had with the Soviets after coming to power, the nationalities issue loomed large. There was a need, the new Chinese government argued, for a new minorities policy as soon as possible, because the problems were urgent. Much of the reason for this urgency may be found in the CCP's rediscovery of China's ethnic minorities during the civil war, when the party had come into contact with a far larger segment of the country's ethnic minority population than ever before. The CCP rank and file observed the oppression and terrible social conditions under which many of these groups lived and sympathized with their predicament. They also noticed how difficult it was to develop real alliances within these groups, because centuries of suspicion against Han Chinese stood in the way. "Liberating" the minorities was therefore an urgent task, and it could only be done by convincing them that New China, unlike governments of the past, truly represented *all* those who lived within the state. It was to be, as the CCP was fond of pointing out, a new type of central government.[54]

While improving the conditions for national minorities, the CCP leaders were insistent that New China was to be a unitary and not a federal state. Their whole political genesis dictated this aim: The CCP had been born as a reaction against perceived imperialist designs to break up China. The party leaders believed firmly that with the right kind of policy, everyone who lived within Chinese territory could be made to feel and think Chinese, as part of a Chinese socialist state. The resistance and distrust with which the party was met as it tried to penetrate regions that in effect had been self-governing for more than two generations—Tibet, Qinghai, Xinjiang, and parts of the Southwest—convinced the CCP leaders even further that Soviet advice was urgently needed. The Chinese party had to get the theory right, and it found—correctly, to some extent—that Marxism possessed a reservoir of thinking on nationalities issues that could be of relevance to China's concerns. Winning the minorities for socialism, while curbing Han chauvinism and the majority's lack of sensitivity toward "less developed" peoples' national needs, were the tasks that the CCP leaders hailed as keys to creating New China.[55]

The Soviet advisers on nationalities issues who came to China in December 1949 did not expect much in terms of understanding from the Chinese side of the "advanced principles of Marxism" in handling national minorities. Because many of the most important minority groups—Mongols, Koreans, and the peoples of the Northwest—all lived in the Sino-Soviet borderlands, some of these Soviet experts had been able to observe Chinese relations with the minorities firsthand before coming to the PRC, and their experiences had prepared them for the worst. There were conflicts in 1950–51; in some cases, Soviet experts misinterpreted Chinese eagerness to learn as testimony to the low level of Marxist schooling from which they started out. In other cases, the Chinese suspected that the Soviets wanted to keep their own influence among minority peoples even after the PRC had been set up. But overall, the Chinese leaders viewed the Soviet Union as holding the solution to one of China's major problems, and insisted that the CCP cadre should learn from Soviet advisers and study Marxist literature on the topic extensively.[56]

This is not the place to review the complexities of PRC nationalities policies in its early years, but several of the singularities that came out of the Sino-Soviet interaction are worth noting. First, both Chinese Communists and Soviets were driven by a desire to categorize and label, to count and register, alongside the mission to civilize and transform. Each minority had to be discovered again—the ways ethnicity had been seen in the past were not suited for a socialist state. The debates in the 1950s on which groups should have the status of recognized minorities on a national scale was therefore fierce and deeply ideological, centering on what constituted a "people" in socialist terms. The debate was even more heated because all sides appealed directly to the views personally expressed by the great Stalin in his 1914 *Marxism and the National Question.*

Second, as Chen Yongfa has pointed out, the CCP's own past visions of China's different minorities clearly played a major role in the policies it recommended.[57] The CCP's relationship with Tibetans and Muslims had not been easy in the 1930s and 1940s, and many Communist leaders saw the traditional leaders of the communities as sworn enemies of their political project. Their preferred policy—supported by many Chinese ethnographers—was to carry out revolutions *within* these groups, by finding and empowering their oppressed peasants, landless workers, and slaves. Soviet advisers generally supported this policy, but urged caution and stressed the need for long-term planning in carrying it out. In some cases, there were clashes early on (e.g., 1951–52), in which Chinese leaders—including quite a few with at least some experience working in minority areas—argued that the Soviets themselves had not shown much caution in carrying out revolution within minority areas in the 1920s and 1930s. The Soviets, on their side, suspected some of the Chinese Communists of being "Han" chauvinists, who wanted to subsume all minorities within a greater "Han" Chinese people.[58]

Third, the preexisting links between the Soviets and some of the groups on China's border areas complicated the encounter between Soviet and Chinese nationalities policies. The Chinese political leaders at the center were from the very beginning of their rule torn between the perceived need to learn from Soviet political and academic theory on these thorny questions and the desire to underline Chinese, and not Soviet, predominance inside China's borders. Reading through the archival records of top-level conversations on questions of nationality, I have the sense that the Chinese interlocutors often consciously replaced examples from minorities along the Soviet border with those from minorities of the interior (or other borders, e.g., the Tibetans) when discussing policy with the Soviets. But while sometimes embarrassing to both sides—and often inconvenient—the Soviets in China understood the CCP's sensitivities with regard to the border issues and underlined their desire to help the Uighurs, Kazakhs, and Mongols living in China find their place within the new Chinese community of peoples.[59]

Although both Chinese and Soviet ethnographers operated within Stalinist paradigms up to the end of the 1950s and beyond, in practice (both theoretical and applied) they had to rely on "creative thinking" to come up with solutions that fit their subjects. The fascinating work on the 1954 PRC Ethnic Classification Project (*minzu shibie*) done recently by Thomas Mullaney and others is certainly right in pointing out how Chinese ethnographers consistently thought outside the Stalinist confines and also how influenced they and their political masters were by Chinese conceptual schemes originating in the Qing and Republican eras.[60] But it is a misunderstanding to claim that this "creativity" was necessarily in opposition to the views of their Soviet advisers. Because it had been rather obvious to any ethnographer—whether they came out of Chinese conceptual schemes or European training—that Stalin's most dogmatic definitions were not applicable in practice (except at great cost to the modernizing project itself), Communist experts on minority issues had worked around them both in an academic and a practical context ever since the founding of the Soviet state. The defeats incurred by a mechanical application of Stalin's faith in stages of development had been very visible in the Soviet Union in the late 1920s and early 1930s, and the Soviet ethnographers who came to China in the

1950s were not intent on repeating that experience. Though they of course had to stay within the Stalinist political framework and the Soviet ethnographic lexicon, coming to China also meant that they were further away from their own political controls than they had been at home, and therefore freer to set their own agendas.[61]

The CCP's insistence on "recataloging" its inventory of ethnic groups, combined with the unprecedented period of regional and local autonomy created by the wars of the early twentieth century, made for unexpected results in the 1950s. In the great counting of peoples, local agency sometimes combined with the intricacies of Stalinist theory to give opportunities for assertion to groups that had never before had such opportunities. Even though the breakdown into fifty-six nationalities that resulted was haphazard and, in some cases, a mere product of decisions made in Beijing rather than regionally, it still meant that some groups that had never had their own institutions recognized suddenly found themselves to be one of China's peoples, with representation all the way up to the National People's Congress (China's parliament). Though Communist political repression could hit anyone within China's borders, recognition as a separate nationality gave some degree of protection from the most vicious aspects of PRC political campaigns, at least until the Cultural Revolution began in 1966.[62]

In some cases, the Chinese search for a nationalities policy that closely mirrored the Soviet one led to minorities being defined as such even somewhat against their own will. The cases of the Zhuang in Guangxi, as described by Katherine Palmer Kaup, or the Hui or Chinese Muslims, show that the adaptation of the Soviet approach provided opportunities for self-definitions and redefinitions among the peoples on China's periphery (and sometimes even its center, in the case of Muslims) that they had never had before in Imperial or Republican China.[63] In some of these cases, the Soviet input was more political than theoretical; just as the Soviet Tatars had been defined as a nationality so they could be better managed, the Chinese Muslims went the same way for the same reasons. The Zhuang seem to have been a particular case, in which Soviet ethnographers chose to set an example to their Chinese colleagues of what constituted a nationality, even if many Chinese (even among those defined as Zhuang) had difficulties envisaging its defining qualities. The Soviets played a very significant role in establishing the new Guangxi Zhuang Autonomous Region in the 1950s, even to the point that Soviet linguists developed a unique romanized Zhuang writing system that is still in use in parts of the province.[64]

The complex history of the 1950s encounter between Soviet and Chinese ethnography—and the nationalities policies with which they were intertwined—

will be a rich field for research in the future. Though there are few areas in which Soviet influence did more to establish the form of the contemporary Chinese state, we are, as we have seen, in no way dealing with a one-sided cause-and-effect pattern. Chinese attitudes—local, from the past, and from European training—helped shape policies and outcomes. In many cases, the meeting of minds between Soviet and Chinese ethnographers went far beyond what were called for by the extraordinarily simplistic Stalinist theories of the time. The contemporary opportunities for research in both Russian and Chinese archives should help us establish a clearer view of their interaction in defining China, and take us away from the dichotomies of past definitions concerning the Sino-Soviet relationship.

Toward a New Understanding of the Alliance

My main aim in this chapter has been to argue against the "Chinese versus Soviet" approach to studying China's international history in the mid–twentieth century. The opening of large amounts of Russian material, and some Chinese, since the early 1990s has moved scholars to focus on understanding the diplomatic processes that led to the breakdown of the Sino-Soviet alliance in the late 1950s and early 1960s. Though the research that deals with these issues is both impressive and necessary, it does unavoidably center on conflicts and crises, and—in some cases—comes very close to reading history backwards: Because we know that the breakdown in relations happened, what we must search for in the past are its causes, at least going back to the 1950 alliance treaty, if not to the unequal treaties of the late nineteenth century.

The approach I suggest here is different, both in terms of perspective and research agenda. For most of the 1950s, it is wrong to think in terms of Soviets versus Chinese in China's struggle for a socialist modernity. In all four areas briefly surveyed here, the indications in the literature we have so far are that cooperation within the largest international development project the world has ever seen was not held back because of strict national differences in concepts, methods, or aims. On the contrary, the approaches to China's development chosen by Chinese and Soviet experts were remarkably similar, and often there was as much debate within each group as between them. On some key issues, such as urban planning and education, there seems to have been more disagreement across a wide spectrum of Chinese opinion—even within the Communist Party—than between Chinese and Soviet experts.

Choosing a development perspective, rather than a diplomatic or political one, also calls for broadening the existing research agenda on the Sino-Soviet alliance. By studying dam builders, ethnographers, and educators, we get a better picture of what motivated the alliance and the ideas that drove it forward. We also, I think, get a clearer image of the limitations of the political theories according to which they attempted to operate, and how these limitations drove both sides to improvise in ways that put increasing strains on their alliance. As Chen Jian and Yang Kuisong have both pointed out, it was the search for a model that could overcome the gradualism of Stalinist planning that in the end did more than anything else to destroy the Sino-Soviet relationship.[65] The Great Leap Forward, it could be said, was one leap too far for the alliance to survive.

The research agenda proposed here borrows heavily from recent historical studies of transnational issues arising from noncommunist concepts of development. By adding the transnational to the international, new vistas of the Sino-Soviet alliance open up that help "normalize" the study of this particular period. The people involved in the massive development program that was the centerpiece of the alliance tried to find socialist and modern solutions to problems they believed had been created by generations of underdevelopment. Soviet and Chinese experts wanted a future for China that in all its forms was more easily recognizable in Paris or Los Angeles than in any part of the PRC of the 1950s. In technical and organizational (not to mention aesthetic) terms, the solutions discussed came out of the transnational debates of the 1920s and 1930s, which—at least to some degree—formed all the Soviet and Chinese teachers, engineers, and architects. The Sino-Soviet elite that commanded China's struggle for modernity in the first decade of the People's Republic was not driven apart by ethnocentrism or cultural differences but by the remarkable inability of Communist dictatorships to mediate political diversity even between the closest of allies.

Notes

1. See Hans J. Van de Ven, *From Friend to Comrade: The Founding of the Chinese Communist Party, 1920–1927* (Berkeley: University of California Press, 1991); and Arif Dirlik, *The Origins of Chinese Communism* (Oxford: Oxford University Press, 1989). On Shanghai, see S. A. Smith, *A Road Is Made: Communism in Shanghai, 1920–1927* (London: Curzon, 2000).

2. Karin-Irene Eiermann gives a fascinating overview of the hopes and fears of female Chinese Communists in the Soviet Union. Karin-Irene Eiermann, "'When I Entered Middle School, I Was a Great Pessimist': The Autobiographies of Chinese Communist Women in Moscow during the 1920s," *Twentieth-Century China* 33, no. 2 (2007): 4–28.

3. Qu Qiubai, "Chidu xinshi" [Impressions of the Red Capital], in *Qu Qiubai wenji* [Collected works of Qu Qiubai], vol. 1 (Beijing: Renmin wenxue, 1985).

4. David E. Apter and Tony Saich, *Revolutionary Discourse in Mao's Republic* (Cambridge, Mass.: Harvard University Press, 1994).

5. Michael Adas, *Machines as the Measure of Men: Science, Technology, and the Ideologies of Western Dominance* (Ithaca, N.Y.: Cornell University Press, 1989).

6. For a good, critical discussion of Tilly's views, see "Symposium: Tilly's Explanation of the *Longue Durée* of State Formation," *Contemporary Sociology* 20, no. 2 (1991): 176–79; or, in a form even more applicable to China, Charles Tilly, "War-Making and State Making as Organized Crime," in *Bringing the State Back In,* ed. Peter Evans, Dietrich Rueschemeyer, and Theda Skocpol (Cambridge: Cambridge University Press, 1985), 169–91.

7. For Liang Qichao's views on Japan's armies, see his articles in *Yinbingshi heji* [Books from an ice-drinker's studio] (Shanghai, 1917), vol. 1. For an excellent summary of Liang's views, see Yang Xiao, "Liang Qichao's Political and Social Philosophy," in *Contemporary Chinese Philosophy,* ed. Chung-Ying Cheng and Nicholas Bunnin, online version, http://www3.interscience.wiley.com/cgi-bin/bookhome/117866979/.

8. See Joseph Stalin, "The Political Tasks of the University of the Peoples of the East," May 18, 1925, in *Sochineniia* [Works], vol. 7 (Moscow, 1946), 137–38.

9. Sergei Goncharenko, "Sino-Soviet Military Cooperation," in *Brothers in Arms: The Rise and Fall of the Sino-Soviet Alliance, 1945–63,* ed. Odd Arne Westad (Washington, D.C., and Stanford, Calif.: Woodrow Wilson Center Press and Stanford University Press, 1998); Shen Zhihua, *Sulian zhua jia zai Zhongguo, 1948–1960* [Soviet advisers in China, 1948–1960] (Beijing: Zhongguo guoji guangbo, 2003).

10. On the 1955 reforms, see Ouyang Qing, *1955 Gongheguo jiang shuai da shouxian* [The 1955 presentation of rank to the republic's generals and marshals] (Jinan: Huanghe, 2008), esp. 20–48.

11. *Renmin ribao,* September 28, 1955.

12. Bruce Elleman, *Modern Chinese Warfare, 1795–1989* (London: Routledge, 2001), 252.

13. For an overview of the civilian-military link, see Xu Yan, *Zhongguo guofang daolun* [An introduction to Chinese defense] (Beijing: Guofang daxue, 2006).

14. See Mark von Hagen, *Soldiers in the Proletarian Dictatorship: The Red Army and the Soviet Socialist State, 1917–1930* (Ithaca, N.Y.: Cornell University Press, 1990), 308–25; or, for a more critical view of the campaigns, see Roger R. Reese, *Stalin's Reluctant Soldiers: A Social History of the Red Army* (Lawrence: University Press of Kansas, 1996).

15. The Y-5 was produced by Shijiazhuang Aircraft Industries well into the 1990s and is, remarkably enough, still flying.

16. The views of Chen Geng are particularly interesting here; see Chen Geng, *Chen Geng junshi wenxuan* [Chen Geng's selected works on military affairs] (Beijing: Jiefangjun, 2007).

17. Chen Jian and Yang Kuisong, "Chinese Politics and the Collapse of the Sino-Soviet Alliance," in *Brothers in Arms,* ed. Westad.

18. An excellent overview is given by Chen Xuexun, ed., *Zhongguo jiaoyushi yanjiu: Xiandai fenjuan* [Research on the history of Chinese education: The contemporary period] (Shanghai: Huadong shifan daxue, 1994); but also see Liu Shaoxue, *Zhongguo daxue jiaoyu shi* [The history of Chinese university education] (Taiyuan: Shanxi jiaoyu, 2007). In English, the best introduction is the magisterial book by Suzanne Pepper, *Radicalism and Education Reform in Twentieth-Century China: The Search for an Ideal Development Model* (Cambridge: Cambridge University Press, 1996).

19. Rui Yang, "Tensions between the Global and the Local: A Comparative Illustration of the Reorganisation of China's Higher Education in the 1950s and 1990s," *Higher Education* 39 (2000): 319–37.

20. For Shanghai, see Li Dehong, ed., *Shanghai shi zhongxue jiaoshi yundong shiliao xuan* [Selected materials on the secondary school teachers' movement in Shanghai] (Shanghai: Shanghai jiaoyu, 1997).

21. See Julian Chang, "The Mechanics of State Propaganda: The People's Republic of China and the Soviet Union in the 1950s," in *New Perspectives on State Socialism in China,* ed. Timothy Cheek and Tony Saich (Armonk, N.Y.: M. E. Sharpe, 1997).

22. See the fascinating book by Cui Xiaolin, *Chongsu yu sikao: 1951 nian qianhou gao xiao zhishifenzi sixiang gaizao yundong yanjiu* [Remolding and rethinking: A study of the movement to transform the thinking of intellectuals in colleges and universities around 1951] (Beijing: Zhonggong dangshi, 2005). For Renmin Daxue, see Douglas A. Stiffler, "Building Socialism at Chinese People's University: Chinese Cadres and Soviet Experts in the People's Republic of China, 1949–1957," PhD dissertation, University of California, San Diego, 2002.

23. Having observed firsthand the same mixture at the (re)introduction of American curricula and teaching methods in China in the 1980s, I can only sympathize with the students on whom all of this was tested out.

24. Eddy U, "The Making of *Zhishifenzi:* The Critical Impact of the Registration of Unemployed Intellectuals in the Early PRC," *China Quarterly* 173 (2003): 100–121; and Eddy U, "The Hiring of Rejects: Teacher Recruitment and Crises of Socialism in the Early PRC Years," *Modern China* 30, no. 1 (2004): 46–80.

25. See, e.g., the record of a conversation between Mao Zedong and Soviet ambassador Iudin, December 21, 1955, Arkhiv Vneshnei Politiki Rossiiskoi Federatsii (AVP RF, Russian Foreign Ministry Archive), Moscow, fond (f.) 0100, opis' (op.) 49, papka (p.) 410, delo (d.) 9, listy (ll.) 11–19.

26. See Stiffler, "Building Socialism at Chinese People's University."

27. Pepper, *Radicalism and Education Reform in Twentieth-Century China,* 224.

28. O. A. Westad, *Decisive Encounters: The Chinese Civil War, 1946–1950* (Stanford, Calif.: Stanford University Press, 2003), 274–76.

29. See Wang Xiaodong, "Cold War in Manchuria: Sino-Soviet-United States Relations, 1948–1953," PhD dissertation, University of North Carolina at Chapel Hill, 2004; and Steven Levine, *Anvil of Victory: The Communist Revolution in Manchuria, 1945–1948* (New York: Columbia University Press, 1987). Jeremy Brown discusses the CCP's policies on urban issues in depth; see Jeremy Brown, "Crossing the Rural/Urban Divide in Twentieth-Century China," PhD dissertation, University of California, San Diego, 2008. Also see Jeremy Brown and Paul Pickowicz, eds., *Dilemmas of Victory: The Early Years of the People's Republic of China* (Cambridge, Mass.: Harvard University Press, 2008).

30. For an overview, see Zhang Jinggan, *Beijing guihua jianshe wushinian* [Fifty years of city planning in Beijing] (Beijing: Zhongguo shudian, 2001); see also Lu Duanfang, "Architecture and Global Imaginations in China," *Journal of Architecture* 12, no. 2 (2007): 123–45.

31. See, e.g., James Gao, *The Communist Takeover of Hangzhou: The Transformation of City and Cadre, 1949–1954* (Honolulu: University of Hawaii Press, 2004); for

CCP attitudes to Beijing, see Wang Jun's controversial *Cheng ji* [Records of the city] (Beijing: Sanlian shudian, 2003).

32. Barbara Kreis, *Moskau 1917–35: Vom Wohnungsbau zum Städtebau* [Moscow 1917–35: From Living Quarters to City Buildings] (Düsseldorf: Edition Marzona, 1985); Alessandra Latur, ed., *Rozhdenie metropolii: Moskva, 1930–1955—vospominaniia i obrazy* [Birth of a metropolis: Moscow, 1930–1955—recollections and images] (Moscow: Iskusstvo-XXI vek, 2005); R. A. French, *Plans, Pragmatism and People: The Legacy of Soviet Planning for Today's Cities* (London: UCL Press, 1995).

33. For an excellent critical review of urban planning as a "modernist movement," see Peter Hall, *Cities of Tomorrow: An Intellectual History of Urban Planning and Design in the Twentieth Century,* 3rd ed. (London: Blackwell, 2003).

34. On both Ladovskii and Dokuchaev, see Selim O. Kahn-Magomedov, *Vhutemas: Moscou 1920–1930,* 2 vols. (Paris: Éditions du Regard, 1990). See also W. C. Brumfield, *The Origins of Modernism in Russian Architecture* (Berkeley: University of California Press, 1981); and C. Cooke, *Russian Avant-Garde: Theories of Art, Architecture and the City* (London: Academy Editions, 1995).

35. For the effects of Stalinist planning on today's urban environment in Russia, see John W. Neill, "Tomsk and Vladivostok: A Comparative Study in Historical Urban Development," paper for presentation at the Fourth International Seminar on Urban Form, University of Birmingham, Birmingham, July 18–21, 1997, http://www.geocities.com/CollegePark/Library/4722/; and A. Eshtokin, *Liubimyi gorod: 125 let Vladivostoka* [Beloved city: Vladivostok at 125 years] (Vladivostok: Dal'nevostochnoe knizhnoe, 1985).

36. Shchusev had survived the 1920s as an architect because the party leadership—exasperated by the avant-gardist designs for Lenin's mausoleum—had turned to him for outlining a suitably respectful monument. Given his significance for Moscow's urban landscape, there is remarkably little written on Shchusev; the latest full biography is by K. N. Afanas'ev, *A. V. Shchusev* (Moscow, 1978).

37. E.g., Zholtovskii's apartment house (1933–34) on Mokhovaiia Street, Moscow, is an enlarged version of the Loggia del Capitaniano (1570s), Vicenza, by Palladio.

38. Wu Hung, *Remaking Beijing: Tiananmen Square and the Creation of a Political Space* (Chicago: University of Chicago Press, 2005), provides an original and entertaining view of CCP attitudes toward the city.

39. Several of the reports on Soviet advice, as well as material relating to some of the early CCP discussions, can be found in *Jianguo yilai de Beijing chengshi jianshe ziliao: Di yi juan—Chengshi guihua* [Materials on the urban construction of Beijing since the founding of the PRC: Book 1—Urban planning], internal publication (Beijing: Beijing jianshe shishu bianji weiyuanhui bianjibu, 1987). The following paragraphs build in part on all seven volumes of this important series.

40. See his writings in *Liang Sicheng quanji* [Collected works of Liang Sicheng], vol. 6 (Beijing: Zhongguo jianzhu gongye, 2001).

41. Quoted in *China Daily,* October 1, 1999.

42. Wang Jun, *Cheng ji,* is excellent on this, esp. 22–65.

43. Hua later returned to France, where he published his memoirs in 1981; Léon Hoa, *Reconstruire la Chine: Trente ans d'urbanisme, 1949–1979* [Reconstructing China: Thirty years of urbanism] (Paris: Moniteur, 1981).

44. Zhu Zhaoxue's and Hua Lanhong's memorandum is in *Jianguo yilai de Beijing chengshi jianshe ziliao: Di yi juan.*

45. For a rather prettified picture of Liang's life, see Wilma Fairbank, *Liang and Lin: Partners in Exploring China's Architectural Past* (Philadelphia: University of Pennsylvania Press, 1994). See also Peter G. Rowe and Seng Kuan, *Architectural Encounters with Essence and Form in Modern China* (Cambridge, Mass.: MIT Press, 2002).

46. Wang Jun, "1950 niandai: Dui Liang-Chen fangan de lishi kaocha [1950s: A historical investigation of the Liang-Chen proposal], available at http://www.cc.org.cn.

47. See *Jianguo yilai de Beijing chengshi jianshe ziliao: Di yi juan.*

48. The only major difference was that in Beijing the main academic institutions would be spread out, rather than clustered (as demanded by the Moscow Plan); the purpose probably being to avoid academic troublemakers gathering together.

49. See Shuishan Yu, "Redefining the Axis of Beijing: Revolution and Nostalgia in the Planning of the PRC Capital," *Journal of Urban History* 34, no. 4 (2008): 571–608. See also the very useful piece by Chang-tai Hung, "Mao's Parades: State Spectacles in China in the 1950s," *China Quarterly* 190 (June 2007): 411–31.

50. The two post–Cultural Revolution General Plans for Beijing, from 1982 and 1992, are remarkably similar in shape to the 1957 draft plan, even though some of the key planning functions have been removed; see Zhang Jinggan, *Beijing guihua jianshe wushinian.*

51. On the essentials of Chinese urban policing, see Børge Bakken, *The Exemplary Society: Human Improvement, Social Control, and the Dangers of Modernity in China* (Oxford: Oxford University Press, 2000), 211–314.

52. Victor Sit, *Beijing: The Nature and Planning of a Chinese Capital City* (New York: John Wiley & Sons, 1995), 86.

53. Stalin, *Marxism and the Nationalities Question,* first published in *Prosveshchenie,* nos. 3–5, March–May 1913.

54. An excellent overview of the development of CCP attitudes is given by Xiaoyuan Liu, *Reins of Liberation: An Entangled History of Mongolian Independence, Chinese Territoriality, and Great Power Hegemony* (Washington, D.C., and Stanford, Calif.: Woodrow Wilson Center Press and Stanford University Press, 2006).

55. The key documents from the late 1940s and 1950s can be found in *Minzu wenti wenxian huibian* [A collection of documents on the nationalities question], internal circulation (Beijing: Zhonggong zhongyang dangxiao, 1991).

56. I do not have a percentage figure on how much of the Soviet theoretical literature that was translated up to 1955 dealt with minorities' issues, but a rough guess would be as much as 30 percent; see Greg Guldin, "Anthropology by Other Names: The Impact of Sino-Soviet Friendship on the Anthropological Sciences," *Australian Journal of Chinese Affairs* 27 (1992): 133–49.

57. For this, see Chen Yongfa, *Zhongguo gongchan geming 70 nian* [Seventy years of Chinese Communist revolution], 2nd ed., vol. 1 (Taipei: Lianjing, 2001).

58. See the undated Soviet Embassy report (early 1954), AVP RF, f. 0100, op. 417, p. 379, d. 7, ll. 25–35.

59. For a view from the time when the People's Republic was being constructed, see the record of a conversation between Zhou Enlai and Soviet ambassador N. V. Roshchin, November 15, 1949, AVP RF, f. 7, op. 22, p. 36, d. 220, ll. 57–66.

60. E.g., see Thomas S. Mullaney, "Coming to Terms with the Nation: Ethnic Classification and Scientific Statecraft in Modern China, 1928–1954," PhD dissertation, Columbia University, 2006.

61. On developments in the Soviet Union, see, first and foremost, Francine Hirsch, *Empire of Nations: Ethnographic Knowledge and the Making of the Soviet Union* (Ithaca, N.Y.: Cornell University Press, 2005); but also Wim van Meurs, "Sovetskaia etnografiia: Okhotniki ili sobirateli?" *Ab Imperio,* no. 3 (2001): 26–33; Peter Skalnik, "Soviet etnografiia and the national(ities) question," *Cahiers du monde russe et soviétique* 31, nos. 2–3 (1990): 183–93; and Sergei V. Sokolovskii, "Men'shinstva v rossiiskikh regionakh: Otechestvennaia etnografiia i politicheskaia praktika" [Minorities in the Russian regions: Patriotic ethnography and political practice], *Etnometodologiia,* no. 4 (1997): 82–100. See also Sergei Kan, "My Old Friend in a Dead-End of Empiricism and Skepticism: Bogoras, Boas, and the Politics of Soviet Anthropology of the Late 1920s–Early 1930s," in *History of Anthropology Annual,* ed. Regna Darnell and Frederic W. Gleach (Lincoln: University of Nebraska Press, 2007).

62. This is a reason why one of my ethnic minority friends likes to quip about China's political history representing "Han's cruelty to Han."

63. See Katherine Palmer Kaup, *Creating the Zhuang: Ethnic Politics in China* (Boulder, Colo.: Lynne Rienner, 2000). For another key case, see Almaz Khan, "Who Are the Mongols? State, Ethnicity, and the Politics of Representation in the PRC," in *Negotiating Ethnicities in China and Taiwan,* ed. Melissa J. Brown (Berkeley: Institute for Asian Studies, University of California, 1996).

64. Adams B. Bodomo and Pan Yanqin, *A Proficiency Course in Zhuang: Fieldwork Documentation and Revitalization of a Language and Culture of Southwestern China* (Hong Kong: Linguistic Society of Hong Kong, 2001).

65. Chen and Yang, "Chinese Politics."

2. The Second Front of the Soviet Cold War: Asia in the System of Moscow's Foreign Policy Priorities, 1945–1956

Ilya V. Gaiduk

In their attempt to make generalizations concerning the past, historians encounter two opposing situations: either an abundance of sources, from which they have to pick the most important and illustrative documents to support their conclusions; or a lack, or even scarcity, of primary materials, which requires them to complement the picture with their own hypotheses and speculations. It is hard to say which situation is more favorable to researchers, for in both cases there remain doubts about their approaches and opportunities for colleagues to challenge their conclusions.

The Origins and Evolution of Postwar Soviet Foreign Policy toward Asia

It is in the latter situation, a scarcity of primary research materials, in which one finds oneself if one tries to reconstruct the system of Soviet foreign policy priorities in the first years after the end of World War II. In coping with this difficulty, researchers must admit that, unfortunately, the available sources do not allow them to give definitive answers to many of their questions. There is always a risk that any newly available document may shatter, if not demolish, any edifice that they create. Moreover, in such a situation historians tend to exaggerate the importance of every single document they discover, and thus to make on its basis unjustified or doubtful conclusions, especially if they analyze it in isolation from the overall context of known historical events and developments.

It is not always possible to positively resolve many issues related to the Soviet leaders' attitudes toward the role of Asian countries in the Cold War confrontation, including factors that influenced these attitudes, and their development over time. There is also a difference of opinion among historians regarding the flashpoints of this confrontation and the place that Asia occupies in it. For instance, historians disagree on the question of when the great powers, primarily the Soviet Union and the United States, started the Cold War in Asia and how the Asian Cold War contest directly affected their national security interests. It seems that everybody does agree that the birthplace of the Cold War was Europe, despite the fact that one of the first post–World War II crises between the wartime allies took place in Iran in 1946. Also, it was obvious to most contemporary observers that it was not Soviet policy toward Iran about which the West was most concerned but Moscow's actions in Central and Eastern Europe aimed at the consolidation of Soviet-style regimes in those countries. Also of concern were Soviet plans with respect to Germany, France, Italy, and other Western European powers as possible targets of invasion by the Red Army, or at least of subversion with the help of local Communist parties.

Besides, most of Asia, in the immediate aftermath of World War II, was in a state of colonial dependence. Japan and China were among the few exceptions. But the West was less preoccupied with the situation in Asia. In Japan, the United States' preponderant positions were unchallenged due to its leading role in the war in the Pacific, whereas in China a compromise seemed possible between Chiang Kai-shek and Mao Zedong that could lead to Communist participation in the Chinese government, a half measure that could possibly satisfy the West.

Soviet attention was likewise concentrated on Europe. Historically, the most dangerous threat to Russian, and later Soviet, integrity and independence came from Western Europe. Polish kings, Lithuanian princes, German knights, and Swedish sailors again and again invaded the territory of Russia, craving to conquer or occupy it and to enslave the Russian population. After the establishment of the Communist regime in the country, from 1918 to the early 1920s the newly created Soviet nation became the object of Western powers' intervention, and in 1941 the victim of Nazi Germany's aggression. Not surprisingly, Joseph Stalin's conception of security envisaged not so much territorial gains for the Soviet Union as establishing along his country's European borders a system of dependent states with a neutral Germany, which twice in the twentieth century had acted as an aggressor against Russia. As for Asia, Stalin was initially satisfied with the concessions promised to him at the Yalta Conference: port and railroad rights in Manchuria, the southern half of Sakhalin Island, and all the Kuril Islands.[1]

Thus, it seems that during the first post-1945 years, Asia remained outside the immediate concerns of the two opposing Cold War blocs, which were quickly going through the process of formation over issues bearing, at first glance, no direct relation to the situation in Asia. Two questions arise in this respect. First, what factors led to this neglect? And second, when did this situation change in favor of the great powers' active involvement in Asian events? As far as the Soviet Union is concerned, one factor already mentioned is Soviet preoccupation with the situation in Europe, where Moscow was trying to consolidate its sphere of influence and attain a favorable position from which to deal with the West. That this task consumed much of the Soviet leaders' energy and time is beyond question. To see this, it is enough to look through the lists of meetings and contacts of various Soviet officials with foreign leaders and diplomats in those years.

The only exception to this unconcern with Asia was, probably China,[2] where the struggle between the Guomindang and the Chinese Communist Party (CCP) attracted, from time to time, Moscow's attention. However, this attention was incomparably smaller than that devoted to Europe. The foreign policy apparatus' involvement in the decisionmaking process in this area was minimal, which also comes as a proof of Asian affairs occupying a lower status in Soviet foreign activities. All contacts between Moscow and the CCP were concentrated in the hands of Stalin and his closest subordinates in the Politburo and in military intelligence. The Soviet Embassy in China was virtually excluded from handling any sensitive diplomatic tasks and was strongly instructed to avoid any demonstration of sympathy to either of the rivals in the civil war. Even the Foreign Ministry was often unaware of developments in Soviet policy toward China. This was the result of the two-track policy toward China pursued by Stalin, who had strong reservations about Mao Zedong and his party's prospects of success, and accordingly did not want to antagonize Chiang Kai-shek and his allies in the West. According to Andrei M. Ledovskii, a Soviet diplomat who was at that time an official in the Soviet Embassy in China,

> when, at the height of the civil war, an active correspondence took place between Stalin and Mao Zedong, we in the Soviet Embassy continued to follow instructions prohibiting our interference in domestic Chinese affairs, in relations between the CCP and Guomindang; more exactly, it was suggested that we demonstrate maximum flexibility, seemingly defending Chinese Communists, but without providing a formal pretext for accusations of interference in conflicts between the [Guomindang] and CCP on the side

> of the Communists. The same flexibility was also suggested to be demonstrated in the sphere of relations with the Chiang Kai-shek government, as well as with the Americans and British, while at the same time combining this diplomatic flexibility with the display of firmness in defending the interests of the Soviet Union.

In support of his words, Ledovskii cited (almost in full) the Soviet Politburo's directives to the Soviet Embassy in China in May 1948.[3]

In all other cases, the Soviet Union remained a detached, though perhaps sympathetic, onlooker of events in the countries where, after the war, forces of national liberation were waging wars against colonial powers and local magnates—as in Burma, Malaya, Indonesia, and the Philippines. At least, there is so far no firm evidence of Soviet direct support or of any kind of involvement in these conflicts. Moreover, Moscow sometimes took no immediate notice of the events that were to have strong repercussions on Soviet policy in the future, as happened with Vietnam's August Revolution, which aroused no discernible reaction from Moscow.[4]

Closely intertwined with the Soviet preoccupation with European affairs was Moscow's desire to avoid unnecessary aggravation of its relations with the United States and its allies. In the first postwar years, this desire stemmed from Stalin's hope for maintaining the USSR's World War II alliance with the Western countries after V-E Day. Even after this hope had passed, the Soviet leadership was not prepared to risk an open clash with the United States over issues of minor importance to state security. Undoubtedly, these issues mostly concerned Asia. If, in Europe, the Soviets could resort to bold measures to defend their sphere of influence or to probe Western attitudes, as during the First Berlin Crisis in 1948–49, in the East they usually kept a low profile, trying not to reveal their sympathies prematurely and avoiding drastic measures that could endanger their own interests. Even at the height of the Cold War, while discussing with Mao Zedong the issue of concluding a new treaty between the Soviet Union and China, Stalin pondered how it could be possible to avoid giving a pretext to the United States and Great Britain to revise the Yalta Agreement, especially in the parts that dealt with the Kuril Islands and Sakhalin Island.[5]

This also explains why the Kremlin tried to keep all its contacts with representatives of the national liberation movement in Asia strictly secret, so that even Soviet diplomats were unaware of what was transpiring in the sphere of Soviet policy toward Asia. Soviet–Communist Chinese contacts in those years have already been mentioned. A similar situation seems to have prevailed in Soviet dealings with the Vietminh and its leader, Ho Chi Minh. All correspondence between Ho Chi Minh and Moscow went through the Kremlin. It is noteworthy that not long before the Vietnamese leader's visit to Moscow in January 1950, the Soviet Foreign Ministry, preparing an overview of the Vietminh's activities abroad, had to state openly: "On the question of Ho Chi Minh's government policy toward the USSR, as well as its position concerning the North Atlantic Pact and some other documents, . . . the Southeast Asia Department [of the Foreign Ministry] does not possess any evidence."[6] Ho's visit to Moscow in January 1950 took place in secret, which of course was per the Vietnamese leader's own request but also fully corresponded to the interests of his Soviet hosts. According to Nikita Khrushchev, however, when Ho, who had already been to Moscow, changed his mind about the secret character of his visit and asked Stalin to stage an official airport welcoming reception for him to reveal his arrival in Moscow, Stalin laughed this away.[7] Apparently, in addition to the Soviet desire to avoid unnecessarily aggravating the USSR's relations with the West, this secrecy helped Moscow minimize the damage to Soviet interests in case of the Vietnamese Communists' failure to achieve success in their struggle.

This aspect was especially important, considering Stalin's lack of belief in the success of the Communist revolution in Asia and his distrust of local Communist leaders. The Soviet leader's attitude toward Mao Zedong and Ho Chi Minh is well known. He called the former, according to Khrushchev, a "cave-dweller-like Marxist,"[8] implying that his views were primitive and outdated. Stalin also did not trust Ho Chi Minh and did not believe in the success of the Vietminh's struggle against the French. This was probably the main reason why he complained that the decision to recognize the Democratic Republic of Vietnam in 1950 had been premature.[9] Besides, Moscow could not forget Ho's overtures to the West. The Soviet Foreign Ministry noted "some ambiguity" in statements Ho made to foreign correspondents. For instance, the Soviets did not like his answer to a Thai journalist's question: "Which of the two countries, the United States or the Soviet Union, will you cooperate with for the purpose to secure peace in the world?" Ho was evasive: "Vietnam will cooperate with any country, which will be ready to maintain a sincere cooperation on equal basis. The country could remain neutral between the two powers, like, for example, Switzerland." The ministry also observed that Ho kept silent about "the imperialistic substance of the North Atlantic Pact and U.S. attempts to establish a reactionary Pacific bloc as a branch of this pact."[10] Such a reticence on the part of a Communist leader naturally seemed suspicious to Soviet policymakers.

As a matter of fact, the neutralism of most Asian leaders might have served as another obstacle to the Soviets in their approach toward the region as a source of support in their confrontation with the West. This went back to the tenets of Lenin's theory that in the struggle between the working class and the bourgeoisie, there should not be a middle way. Moscow felt that eventually the neutrals would have to choose the side with which they wanted to align themselves. Nevertheless, as the Cold War developed, Stalin and his followers modified their attitude toward the neutrality of Asian leaders, and came to prefer it to outright alignment with the West. At least, in his conversation with the representatives of the Indian Communist Party, in February 1951, Stalin refused to consider Nehru's government a "puppet" of American imperialists: "I cannot consider Nehru's government a puppet. It still has roots among the population. This is not Bao Dai's government. . . . Bao Dai is a puppet, indeed."[11]

Finally, when analyzing the factors that influenced the Soviet attitude toward Asia during the early years of the Cold War, one should keep in mind the limited nature of Soviet resources and power, which forced Moscow to concentrate on the one direction that it saw as of vital importance in its competition with the West. The war damage in the Soviet Union was especially severe. During the first years after World War II, the Soviet leadership had to undertake tremendous efforts to restore the Soviet economy, to rebuild cities and factories, and to support agriculture. All that was left was channeled into supporting the Communist regimes in Europe, which also needed to recover from the war.

Therefore, during the first several years after World War II, Asia was not even the second front of Soviet confrontation with the West. It remained outside this confrontation, which was possible because the United States also did not pay much attention to that part of the world.

Asia Becomes a Cold War Battleground

If this was the case, a question arises: When did this situation change, and what triggered this change? Historians have come to a more or less common view, identifying the years 1948–50 as the starting point of the Asian region's transformation into a battleground of the Cold War. Akira Iriye is convinced that before 1950 Southeast Asia, for example, did not seem to have fallen within either the American or the Soviet sphere of influence. It was the possible penetration of Southeast Asia by Communist China that upset the U.S.-Soviet balance of power in this region.[12] John Gaddis agrees with this opinion and also regards the Communist victory in China as a powerful factor that changed the overall situation in Asia: "Prior to 1949, the Cold War had barely touched the Asian mainland. . . . By 1950, or so it seemed a fundamental shift in the balance of power had taken place: Nearly overnight the Communist world appeared almost to have doubled its extent."[13] Another event that Gaddis regards as a turning point of the Cold War in Asia was the Korean War, which greatly intensified U.S.-Soviet confrontation.[14] Although Vojtech Mastny also regards the years 1948–50 as a crucial period for the reorientation of Soviet policy toward Asia, he considers this turnover a result of Stalin's "setbacks" in Europe.[15]

Although all these arguments are convincing in explaining the spread of the Cold War in Asia, it seems that it was primarily the United States that started approaching the region from a position of confrontation with the Soviet Union. As for Moscow, there are remarkably few signs of any significant change in its policy in the region in those years. True, with the victory of the Chinese Communists, the Soviets acquired a powerful ally in Asia. However, the Soviets contributed little to this victory, and it would be some time before they realized what advantages they could gain for their policy in the region by obtaining such a partner. The Korean War may testify to a more aggressive Soviet policy, but again, as is now known, Moscow was not the initiator of this war and Stalin was initially reluctant to give his blessing to Kim Il Sung's invasion of South Korea. In addition, although the USSR lent its support and assistance to North Korea and China, it was not directly involved in the hostilities, and its role in the war remained passive at best. Furthermore, both China and the Korean Peninsula were in the immediate proximity of the Soviet borders, so the factor of "geographical security" played a more powerful role in the Kremlin's considerations.[16] As far as the more remote countries of the Asian continent were concerned, Soviet involvement remained virtually absent.

Had Stalin followed the conception of world revolution in conformity with the domino theory, he would have urged Asian Communists in India and Indonesia, the second-largest countries on the continent, to accelerate their preparations for the overthrow of their local governments and for the establishment of Communist regimes, as had happened in China. However, quite to the contrary, in writing and conversing with local Communists, the Soviet leader advised patience, taking on "practical molecular 'dirty' work on the question of the everyday needs of workers, peasants and working intelligentsia."[17] He warned against a blind copying of the Chinese experience, repeating that the "Chinese path was good for China," but not for other countries, where it was necessary to take into account local conditions.[18]

It remains an open question how familiar Stalin was with those conditions and to what extent he kept in mind Soviet interests, while giving recommendations and advice, which foreign Communists regarded as "instructions." Of course, he thoroughly read materials concerning the respective countries prepared for him by the party apparatus and possessed some basic knowledge of the situation there.[19] But a comparison of at least two documents containing his recommendations to Asian Communists (in India and Indonesia) made almost at the same time leaves the impression that the Soviet leader adhered strictly to Marxist-Leninist dogma, meaning that he considered advanced industrial countries as best prepared for socialist revolutions. It also leaves the impression that he was more concerned with the interests of the Soviet Union as a great power involved in the precarious balance of forces in the international arena than with the real aspirations and demands of his Asian Communist comrades.

In any case, an analysis of Soviet policy toward Asia after 1948 hardly substantiates the conclusion that it underwent radical transformation in comparison with the previous period. Some changes did take place, but they were mostly of an ideological nature. In fact, although Moscow did little to render effective support to the national liberation movement in Asia, it had to display its sympathy for and solidarity with the Asian struggle against Western colonialism and American imperialism. This was a requirement of the position of the Soviet Union as the vanguard of the world Communist movement and the exponent of aspirations of oppressed peoples. Moscow was eager to uphold this image if it cost nothing in terms of geopolitical interests. To fulfill this task, the Soviets used, in particular, various public forums as well as international organizations. Andrei Zhdanov devoted some space to the situation in the developing world in his report titled "On the International Situation," which he presented at the constituent meeting of the Communist parties in September 1947 that led to the establishment of the Cominform. He drew attention to the crisis of the world colonial system resulting from World War II, a crisis that expressed itself in the significant development of national liberation movements in Western colonies and dependent countries. Speaking about the division of the world in two camps, he declared: "Anti-imperialist and antifascist forces form the other camp. The basis of this camp is the USSR and the new democracies. . . . Indonesia and Vietnam adjoin the anti-imperialist camp; India, Egypt and Syria sympathize with it."[20]

It is in this light that we should consider the international youth conference in Calcutta in February 1948. Some scholars are inclined to regard its role as similar to that of the Cominform in Europe, linking it with the uprising that followed in Southeast Asia in 1948.[21] However, others, like Ruth McVey, strongly question the validity of such a linkage.[22] Although the final resolution of this problem should await the opening of the pertinent documents in Russian archives, the format of the forum (a youth conference) and the level of representation of the countries (nobody from the highest echelons from the Soviet Union, China, or any other countries) make it improbable that the conference played the role traditionally ascribed to it. Rather, it served as a demonstration of Soviet adherence to the ideas of anticolonial struggle in the developing world.

Another public place where the Soviets demonstrated their support for this struggle was the United Nations. For instance, considering the question of whether Moscow should agree on participation in the activities of the UN Trusteeship Council, Soviet Foreign Ministry officials recommended such participation as a venue for expressing Moscow's criticism of the colonial policies and practices of the British, Americans, French, and other colonialists "from advantageous positions." Undoubtedly, this would create, among other things, a favorable impression of the Soviet Union in the colonies as a staunch supporter of their struggle for liberation. But Moscow had something else in mind: "The main line of behavior" of the Soviet representative at this council, stated the Foreign Ministry official, should be aimed at "putting an obstacle in the way of the formation of a colonial empire by the United States and helping the disintegration of the old colonial empires, primarily those of England, France, and Belgium."[23] That is, while displaying concern for the situation of the oppressed peoples in Western colonial possessions, Moscow could try to gain scores in the struggle with its principal rivals by affecting their positions in the colonies.

Nevertheless, Asian revolutionaries expected from the Soviet Union more than Moscow's moral and ideological support. However, their expectations turned to disappointment, for except for "advice" and "recommendations," the Stalin regime's leadership provided them with almost nothing substantial. Not surprisingly, as the prospects for a Communist victory in China became more assured, representatives of the Asian national liberation movement turned toward Beijing in the hope that the new Chinese leadership would prove itself more receptive to their needs and aspirations. The following report of a meeting in Prague in June 1949 illustrates these feelings.

On June 26, 1949, the head of the Chinese delegation to the Third World Congress of Trade Unions hosted a reception in the Czech capital for delegations of Asian countries to the congress, which was to be held in Italy. The Soviet ambassador in Czechoslovakia, Mikhail Silin, was invited along with delegates from Mongolia, India, Vietnam, and Indonesia. Liu Ninyi, the Chinese representative, touched upon the prospects for the struggle of the people in Asia in his introductory remarks, pointing out the two paths open before the national liberation movement: "Chiang Kai-shek's path, and the path of a democratic revolution which has been shown by the Chinese Communist Party under the leadership of Mao Zedong." "Only the latter path," he declared, "means liberation from the oppression of imperialism. The victory of the democratic forces in China is a guarantee of future victories of democrats in all countries in Asia."[24]

This statement received enthusiastic responses from almost all present. As the Soviet ambassador wrote in his report, delegates from India, Vietnam, and

Indonesia declared that "the working class and all the people" of their countries "regard China as a shining example for themselves." Each of them raised a toast to Mao Zedong, while the Vietnamese delegate affirmed "the CCP's victories raised the spirits of the Vietnamese people and strengthened their belief in near victory over the French imperialists."[25]

Only the Mongolian speaker drew attention to the great importance of his country's friendship with the USSR and its aid to Mongolia. His statement seemed to remind those present of the necessity to pay tribute to their "Big Brother." Liu Ninyi again took the podium to repair the neglect and to clarify his country's attitude toward the Soviet role in the national liberation movement in Asia. According to him, there were two groups of countries. On the one hand, in the Asian part of the USSR, in the Mongolian People's Republic, North Korea, and in the liberated regions of China, the construction of a new society was under way with the help of the Soviet Union. On the other hand, the peoples of China, Vietnam, Indonesia, Burma, and other countries were waging armed and other forms of struggle for their liberation. "All the peoples of Asia constantly feel behind them the support from the great Soviet Union and wise leadership of great Stalin," he declared. And according to Silin, "all those present heartily joined the toast to Comrade Stalin."[26]

Asian revolutionaries praised Mao Zedong first, and Stalin second. This was not accidental. It reflected, among other things, the almost negligible role of the Soviet Union in developments in Asia before 1950. It is possible, however, that the positive reports about the national liberation movement in Asian countries may have resulted from Stalin's conversations with Asian Communists, who, like the Indians, did not conceal their admiration for the CCP's success. And their desire to emulate it suggests that the Soviet leadership came to adopt the idea of some sort of "division of labor" between Moscow and Beijing, especially after the proclamation of the People's Republic of China on October 1, 1949.[27] At least Stalin freely talked about such a division during his conversation with Zhou Enlai in September 1952. After having raised the issue of the Peace Congress, scheduled to be held in Beijing in late September of that year, the Soviet leader asked whether delegations from India and Pakistan were going to attend. He then stated that "now it is necessary to follow the line toward China's playing the leading role, because (1) the initiative to rally the Congress belongs to China; [and] (2) that way is better, since the USSR is only partly in Asia, while the whole of China is in Asia, the leading role must belong to it."

On the basis of this conversation and other evidence, some among Soviet diplomats came to the conclusion that "Stalin, it seems to us, while keeping for the USSR the leading role at the global level, was encouraging the CCP leadership to play the principal role in the sphere of issues of international relations in the Asian region."[28] After Stalin's death, Khrushchev and the new Soviet leadership inherited this principle. Referring to his first visit to China in 1954 on the occasion of the celebration of the fifth anniversary of the People's Republic of China, Khrushchev wrote in his memoirs: "Our other conversations in Beijing dealt directly with issues of the world Communist movement. We thought it expedient to realize a certain 'division of labor' in the sphere of relations with communist parties of nonsocialist countries. Since the CCP achieved victory in China, we believed it would be better if it was to maintain closer ties with fraternal communist parties in the countries of Asia and Africa. Besides, according to the level of industrial development and the standard of living, China stood closer to the peoples of such countries as India, Pakistan, and Indonesia. As far as we were concerned, it was these countries that we kept in mind in the first place [when we thought of the Asian Communists]. And we wanted to leave for ourselves the strengthening of relations with communist parties in the West, primarily European and in the USA."[29]

Nevertheless, the Soviet leaders were not going to completely abandon the developing world, leaving it entirely to the Chinese. It was in the early 1950s when Soviet policy toward Asia started undergoing some transformations in favor of a more active posture vis-à-vis the rapid development of the national liberation movements in the colonial world. The first signs of the new Soviet posture were already visible in the last months of Stalin's reign. At an economic conference held in Moscow in April 1952, the president of the Soviet Chamber of Commerce stated that the Soviet government wanted to increase its trade relations with the developing nations, which was an indication that there were officials in the Soviet Union who wished to increase contacts with the developing world. One Western researcher saw the reasons for this change in the realization "that the states which had obtained their independence since the end of World War II were areas of potential Soviet influence but that the rigid and hostile policy which the Soviet government had followed since 1947 had actually isolated it from these areas."[30]

Although no reversal of Soviet policy had occurred before Stalin's death, the new Soviet leadership announced its accession to power with the revision not only of Soviet foreign policy priorities in the sphere of relations with the West, where they proclaimed the policy of détente, but also of Moscow's attitude toward developing nations. In July 1953, the Soviet representative to the United Nation Economic and Social Council announced that the USSR would contribute 4 million rubles to the UN program of technical assistance to underdeveloped nations. "This reversed a long history of opposition of the program and signaled the beginning of a major effort to court the Third World."[31] The new tendency with respect to the developing world also manifested itself in the Soviet attitude toward the admission of new members to the UN. Whereas in previous years the Soviets had insisted on voting for every single candidate to this international organization, in 1952 they recommended voting for the admission of fourteen new countries simultaneously as a countermeasure to "the policy of discrimination and favoritism pursued by the powers of the Atlantic Union with regard to the admission to the UN of new members."[32] The result of this decision was that along with Soviet allies—such as Albania, Bulgaria, Romania, and Hungary—and those of the Western powers (Italy, Portugal, Austria, Ireland), in 1955 several Afro-Asian states became UN members, including Ceylon, Nepal, Libya, and Jordan. This led Western analysts to suspect that the Soviet Union had changed its previous uncompromising stance on the issue of UN admission out of a realization that a growth in membership could add "if not Soviet allies, at least states whose history made them naturally unsympathetic to the West. In Soviet eyes, the UN was becoming less of an appendage of Western foreign policy as new states, dominated by the 'nationalist bourgeoisies' instead of by 'bourgeois imperialists,' entered."[33] If this was the Soviet intention, these hopes were realized in later years, when in the second half of the 1950s the admission of the newly independent states of Africa and Asia led to the establishment of an anticolonial consensus in the UN.

The most dramatic sign of the Soviet reconsideration of relations with developing nations in Asia was the trip of Khrushchev and Nikolai Bulganin throughout South and Southeast Asia in 1955. For the Soviet leaders, this trip became virtually a discovery of Asia. To prove this, it is sufficient to read Khrushchev's memoirs. Each chapter on the countries he visited at the beginning of his rule opens with an almost identical phrase. "What had we known about India before?" he started a section on India. "I am talking here about myself and Bulganin. Perhaps, very little." And further: "Our knowledge about India was, frankly speaking, not only superficial, but primitive."[34] The next stop was Burma: "About Burma we knew even less than about India."[35] The Soviet leadership's knowledge about Indonesia, which at the time became the birthplace of the nonalignment movement, was not much better: "We knew about Indonesia very little and did not display any special interest toward it. . . . For the first time we began talking about Indonesia at the level of the CPSU [Communist Party of the Soviet Union] CC [Central Committee] Presidium (Politburo) in 1955 at the time the Bandung declaration was signed."[36] One would hardly suspect Khrushchev of excessive modesty. Of course, he might have been inclined to underline the shift in Soviet policy toward the developing world under his rule. But he was obviously not far from the truth in writing about the Soviet leadership's lack of knowledge about the Asian countries.

Khrushchev's introduction of the concept of the zone of peace at the Twentieth Congress of the CPSU in 1956 had been regarded in the West as a justification for this shift. He spoke of "the emergence in the world arena of a group of peace-loving European and Asian states which have proclaimed nonparticipation in blocs as a principle of their foreign policy." The nonaligned states, together with the socialist countries, formed "a vast peace zone." He emphasized the significance of decolonization for Soviet foreign policy and Soviet willingness to contribute to it: "The very fact that the Soviet Union and other countries of the socialist camp exist, that they are ready to help the underdeveloped nations with their industrial development on terms of equality and mutual benefit, is a major stumbling bloc to colonial policy."[37]

Yet before 1956, all these Soviet declarations and statements had remained no more than good intentions. It is true that by the time of Stalin's death, the Soviet Union had strengthened its positions in the international arena. The most acute phase of the Cold War seemed to have passed with the cease-fire negotiations in Korea, as well as with the settlement of the situation in Berlin and the stabilization of the pro-Soviet regimes in Eastern Europe. The announcement of the policy of détente by the new leadership opened prospects for the normalization of East-West relations. Furthermore, with the end of the period of recovery after World War II, the Soviet Union had received an opportunity to channel more economic resources not only to its allies in Europe but also for the support of newly independent countries in the developing world, especially in Asia. However, the Soviets' attention would again soon be consumed by developments in Europe. The uprisings in East Germany in 1953, the unrest in Poland, and the Hungarian crisis in 1956 prevented Moscow from paying much attention to Asia and from undertaking practical steps to translate words into actual closer cooperation with the national liberation movements in the region. Besides, the Soviet Union's interest in developing relations with the United States and other Western countries made it more cautious in putting forward initiatives that might jeopardize the precarious equilibrium in the East/West confrontation. Soviet leaders were generally more complacent, and more easily agreeable, vis-à-vis Western positions on the issues related to the situation in Asia. The Soviet behavior at the 1955 Geneva summit could serve as a good illustration of this.

Considering the questions that could be the subject of discussion at the summit, Moscow attached importance to some issues in Asia and the Far East. Among the issues the Soviets planned to raise was the question of China's admission to the UN, the Taiwan question, and the situation in Indochina, where an all-Vietnamese election was to be held.[38] In the initial versions of the directives to the Soviet delegation, a proposal had also been included about the convocation of a conference on peace and security in Asia and the Far East sometime during 1955. Not only was this proposal thrown out by Viacheslav Molotov from the final version of the directives (apparently as a result of deliberations at the CPSU CC Presidium), but the Soviets failed to press their Western counterparts about a plenary discussion of all the other issues related to Asia. Moscow gave the following explanation for this omission in its telegram to Beijing sent in the summit's aftermath to inform Mao Zedong about its results: "The representatives of the three Western powers refused to discuss the problems of Asia and the Far East, on which the Soviet delegation insisted. We, in our turn, rejected an attempt to put forward as a subject of discussion at the Conference the question about the situation in East European countries and about 'world Communism.'"[39]

Again, Moscow had traded off Asian problems for what it considered more vital questions related to Eastern Europe. Instead, the Soviets had to confine themselves to raising these issues during private conversations with Western leaders. "Naturally," as Moscow emphasized in its telegram to Mao, "the main attention from our part was paid to the question of Taiwan and the [People's Republic of China's] rights in the UN." The Soviet leaders also discussed at their meetings with the French the issue of the election in Vietnam.[40] As a result, the summit was almost completely devoted to Europe, with Asia playing the role of a sideshow, without any effect on the fate of Asian peoples.

Conclusion

Despite the clear shift in Soviet foreign policy toward a more active policy in Asia after 1953, the Kremlin seemed all too ready, as it had under Stalin, to place the main burden of responsibility in the region on Chinese shoulders. Even in the sphere of their relations with North Vietnam, which after the 1954 Geneva Conference on Indochina should have been regarded as part of the socialist camp, the Soviets were reluctant to assume any obligations to help the Democratic Republic of Vietnam without China's participation. Soviet premier Georgii Malenkov made this clear to Pham Van Dong in 1954 during their meeting in the immediate aftermath of the Geneva Conference on Indochina. He explained at length that it was beyond the capacity of the Soviet Union to support all the people's democracies in the world. Therefore, according to the Soviet leader, it would be expedient to divide functions between Moscow and Beijing. The Soviet Union would take care of socialism and democracy in Europe, while China would be concerned with Southeast Asia.[41]

Thus, in 1956, as in the late 1940s, Asia seemed to continue to occupy a secondary place on the list of Soviet foreign policy priorities. Except for some instances of Moscow's active posturing in certain situations in specific regions of Asia (like the Middle East), and despite certain signs of the shift in Soviet attitude toward that part of the world (Soviet leaders' visits to South and Southeast Asia, their desire to keep the leading Asian representatives informed about some Soviet foreign policy issues,[42] their increasing cooperation with Asian allies in the economic sphere, and their defense of newly independent nations in the UN), there was no significant change in the usual Soviet orientation toward Europe and in Moscow's emphasis on its relations with the West. Obviously, still to come was the era of Moscow's systematic and large-scale intervention in the developing world, its open alignment with one of the opposing forces, and its demand for allegiance from those whom it supported and backed.

Notes

1. There is an abundant literature on the Western and Soviet allies' postwar aims and actions and their contribution to the beginning of the Cold War. See, e.g., John Lewis Gaddis, *We Now Know: Rethinking Cold War History* (Oxford: Clarendon Press, 1997); and Vojtech Mastny, *The Cold War and Soviet Insecurity: The Stalin Years* (New York: Oxford University Press, 1996). Among the books published in Russia, one worth citing is by I. V. Gaiduk, N. I. Egorova, A. O. Chubarian, eds., *Stalinskoe desiatiletie kholodnoi voiny: Fakty i gipotezy* [Stalin's decade of the Cold War: Facts and hypotheses] (Moscow: Nauka, 1999).

2. North Korea, where Soviet troops were stationed in 1945, was a special case, and later, after the withdrawal of Soviet military units, it was firmly tied to the Soviet Communist Bloc.

3. A. M. Ledovskii, *SSSR i Stalin v sud'bakh Kitaia: Dokumenty i svidetel'stva uchastnika sobytii 1937–1952* [The USSR and Stalin in the fortunes of China: Documents and testimonies of a participant of the events 1937–1952] (Moscow: PIM, 1999), 48–50.

4. See Christopher E. Goscha, "La survie diplomatique de la RDVN: Le doute soviétique effacé par la confiance chinoise (1945–1950)?" [The diplomatic survival of the RDVN: The Soviet doubt removed by Chinese confidence (1945–1950)?], *Approches-Asie* (Pedone, France), no. 18 (2003): 23.

5. Ledovskii, *SSSR i Stalin,* 122.

6. Brief memorandum, "Viet-Nam Government's (Ho Chi Minh) Missions Abroad (Paris, Bangkok, Prague)," November 1949, Arkhiv vneshnei politiki Rossiiskoi Federatsii (hereafter AVP RF), fond (f.) 079, opis' (op.) 3, papka (p.) 2, delo (d.) 5, list (l.) 127.

7. Nikita S. Khrushchev, *Vremia, Liudi, Vlast': Vospominaniia v 4-kh knigakh* [Time, People, Power: Memoirs in four books], vol. 3 (Moscow: Moscow News, 1999), 114. For some of the details of Ho's 1950 visit to Moscow and the ensuing development of Soviet-Vietnamese relations, see Ilya V. Gaiduk, *Confronting Vietnam: Soviet Policy toward the Indochina Conflict, 1954–1963* (Washington, D.C., and Stanford, Calif.: Woodrow Wilson Center Press and Stanford University Press, 2003), 5–11.

8. Khrushchev, *Vremia, Liudi, Vlast',* 23.

9. Ibid., 114.

10. Memorandum, "Democratic Republic of Viet-Nam," January 14, 1950, AVP RF, f. 079, op. 4, p. 2, d. 7, ll. 12, 13.

11. Memorandum of Conversation between Stalin and Representatives of the CC of the Communist Party of India Rao, Dange, Gosh, and Punaya, February 9, 1951, Rossiiskii gosudarstvennyi arkhiv sotzial'no-politicheskoi istorii (hereafter RGASPI), f. 558, op. 11, d. 310, ll. 80–81.

12. See Akira Iriye, *The Cold War in Asia: A Historical Introduction* (Englewood Cliffs, N.J.: Prentice Hall, 1974).

13. Gaddis, *We Now Know,* 55.

14. Ibid., 82–84.

15. "In trying to offset its setbacks in Europe, Moscow encouraged Communist advance in parts of the world where the West had been retreating. It provided political direction, though precious little material support, to its followers participating in the anticolonial movements in Indonesia, Indochina, Malaya, Burma, and the Philippines." Mastny, *Cold War and Soviet Insecurity,* 55.

16. Natalia Egorova, "Evropeiskaia bezopasnost' i 'ugroza' NATO v otsenkakh stalinskogo rukovodstva" [European security and the "threat" of NATO in the Stalin leadership's estimates], in *Stalinskoe desiatiletie,* ed. Gaiduk, Egorova, and Chubarian, 60.

17. Stalin's handwritten letter to Liu Shaoqi, February 2, 1951, RGASPI, f. 558, op. 11, d. 313, l. 61. See also Larisa M. Efimova, "Stalin and the Renewal of the Cold War in Indonesia," *Cold War History* 5, no. 1 (February 2005): 116.

18. Memorandum of Conversation between Stalin and the Representatives of the CC of the Communist Party of India, RGASPI, f. 558, op. 11, d. 310, l. 80.

19. However, the Indonesian Communists dared to challenge the correctness of Stalin's analysis of the situation in their countries and insisted that they should combine their struggle against the Dutch colonialists with the resistance to American imperialism, about which Stalin warned them. See "Memorandum on Documents Concerning the Question of the Communist Party of Indonesia," n.d., RGASPI, f. 558, op. 11, d. 315, ll. 16–18.

20. Federal'naia Arkhivnaia sluzhba Rossii [Federal Archival Service of Russia], *Soveshchaniia Kominforma, 1947, 1948, 1949: Dokumenty i materialy* [The Conferences of the Cominform, 1947, 1948, 1949: Documents and materials] (Moscow: Rosspen, 1998), 154, 157.

21. "At the international youth conference it sponsored in Calcutta in February 1948, it imposed a similar turnabout as that which the Cominform had required the Western European Communists to perform the previous September—with similarly disappointing results." Mastny, *Cold War and Soviet Insecurity,* 55.

22. McVey dismisses the thesis that the 1948 uprisings in Southeast Asia were in accordance with the instructions given them at the Calcutta Conference. Rather, she insists, the uprisings were the reaction of the Communist parties to their respective local conditions. Ruth McVey, *The Calcutta Conference and the Southeast Asian Uprisings* (Ithaca, N.Y.: Cornell University Press, 1958).

23. A. A. Sobolev to Viacheslav Molotov, July 21, 1947, AVP RF, f. 07, op. 12a, p. 41, d. 1, ll. 2–3.

24. M. A. Silin to Soviet foreign minister Andrei Vyshinskii, June 28, 1949, AVP RF, f. 0138, op. 30, p. 159, d. 6, l. 52.

25. Ibid., l. 53.

26. Ibid., l. 54.

27. Stalin could notice these feelings when he read materials from the Communist Party of India (CPI) about the situation within the party on the eve of his meeting with the Indian Communists in February 1951. For instance, he did not overlook the fact that the principal issue of discussions in the CPI CC was whether the "Chinese path" could be followed by the Indian Communists. During a preliminary conversation with the members of the Soviet Politburo, the representatives of the CPI drew the attention of their Soviet comrades to the fact that the discord was about an interpretation of the Chinese path. "Some people held the opinion that it is necessary to follow the Chinese path, especially after Liu Shaoqi's speech at the Beijing conference [of trade unions of Asian countries], in which he put forward armed struggle as the principal form of struggle. Many believed that we are now following the Chinese path and in all cases put emphasis on armed struggle, while all other forms are being ignored"; see memorandum of conversation of the members of the VKP(b) CC Commission with the representatives of the CPI CC on February 4 and 6, 1951, Top Secret: Special Dossier, RGASPI, f. 558, op. 11, d. 310, ll. 17, 18. Others tried to prove that the CPI did not possess the resources necessary for unfolding armed struggle and that this form could not be considered principal for the party; see G. Malenkov, M. Suslov, V. Grigorian, and P. Iudin to Stalin, February 8, 1951, ibid., l. 4.

28. Ledovskii, *SSSR i Stalin,* 171, 175.

29. Khrushchev, *Vremia, Liudi, Vlast',* 44–45.

30. Roger E. Kanet, "Soviet Attitudes toward Developing Nations Since Stalin," in *The Soviet Union and the Developing Nations,* ed. Roger E. Kanet (Baltimore: Johns Hopkins University Press, 1974), 27.

31. Bruce D. Porter, *The USSR in Third World Conflicts: Soviet Arms and Diplomacy in Local Wars, 1945–1980* (Cambridge: Cambridge University Press, 1984), 16.

32. Directives to the USSR delegation at the Seventh Session of the UN General Assembly, adopted by the Politburo on September 29, 1952, AVP RF, f. 047, op. 7-v, p. 42, d. 1, l. 80.

33. Richard W. Mansbach, "The Soviet Union, the United Nations, and the Developing States," in *The Soviet Union and the Developing Nations,* ed. Kanet, 253.

34. Khrushchev, *Vremia, Liudi, Vlast',* 317.

35. Ibid., 339.

36. Ibid., 369.

37. *Pravda,* February 15, 1956.

38. See "Directives for the USSR Delegation at the Conference of the Heads of Governments of the Four Powers," draft, n.d., top secret, AVP RF, f. 06, op. 14, p. 3, d. 43, ll. 120–38.

39. Telegram to the Soviet ambassador in Beijing, top secret, July 30, 1955, ibid., d. 44, l. 31.

40. Ibid., ll. 36–37.

41. For this episode, as well as for other examples of the realization of the principle

of the "division of responsibilities" as applied to Vietnam, see Gaiduk, *Confronting Vietnam,* chap. 4.

42. E.g., the CPSU CC Presidium decided to send Nehru information about the CPSU's Twentieth Congress; it kept the Indian president informed about developments around Suez and in Hungary in 1956. See Federal Archival Service of Russia et al., *Prezidium TsK KPSS 1954–1963* [The Presidium of the CPSU CC 1954–1963], vol. 1: *Chernovye protokol'nye zapisi zasedanii—Stenogrammy* [Draft minutes of the meetings—Verbatim reports] (Moscow: Rosspen, 2003), 115, 203, 207.

3. Reorienting the Cold War: The Implications of China's Early Cold War Experience, Taking Korea as a Central Test Case

Chen Jian

The global Cold War was characterized by the confrontation between the United States and the Soviet Union, and also between the two contending blocs led by these two superpowers. Yet, in several key senses, China's position in the Cold War was not peripheral but central. China's early Cold War experience not only played a crucial role in shaping the Cold War's specific course in Asia but also, and more important, helped create the conditions whereby the Cold War remained "cold." In this chapter, I take China's Korean War experience as a central test case for addressing several broader issues in order to pursue a deeper understanding of China's early Cold War experience and its impact on how the global Cold War—and the Cold War in Asia, in particular—was shaped and reoriented in the late 1940s and early 1950s. This understanding takes shape first through five key findings, and then through five implications, which I explore in turn.

Five Key Findings

The first finding is that the Korean War happened in the context of the victory of the Chinese Communist Revolution. This simple and straightforward statement is rich with comprehensive and complex meanings. In the development of the global Cold War, the establishment of the People's Republic of China (PRC) in 1949 represented a defining moment. Although the Chinese Communist Party's (CCP's) victory over the Guomindang (GMD, or the Nationalist Party) primarily originated in the profound political, social, and cultural crises that China had encountered in modern times, and was facilitated by the GMD's political, economic, and military failures, the emerging Cold War provided a crucial condition for the CCP to wage and, finally, win its war with the GMD. As revealed in studies by scholars like Odd Arne Westad, Yang Kuisong, Michael Sheng, and myself, the intensifying confrontation between Moscow and Washington played a pivotal role in pushing the Soviet leader Joseph Stalin to choose to support the CCP's military operations (especially those in China's Northeast, or Manchuria) against the GMD government, thus dramatically enhancing the CCP's capacity in the war. In turn, with the CCP eventually emerging as the winner in the Chinese civil war, the Soviet-American Yalta Agreement on China and East Asia was virtually nullified.[1] Consequently, the Soviet Union's influence and power position in East Asia became greatly strengthened in the late 1940s and early 1950s.

When Mao Zedong and his CCP comrades seized power in China in 1949, the Cold War in Asia also reached a critical juncture. The victory of the Chinese Communist Revolution enhanced the perception on the part of Communists in various East Asian countries that history indeed was on their side, making them (including Kim Il Sung in Korea and Ho Chi Minh in Indochina) believe that what had happened in China—the collapse of the "old regime" in the face of the challenges of this violent Communist Revolution—could also happen in their own countries.[2] Furthermore, the fact that the United States had failed to intervene in China on behalf of Chiang Kai-shek and the GMD government convinced Communists in China and other East Asian countries—and probably Stalin in Moscow as well—that Washington lacked the will and capacity to involve the United States in suppressing revolutions in East Asia, at least for the foreseeable future.[3] All this not only encouraged the North Korean Communist leader Kim Il Sung to repeatedly put forward plans for unifying Korea through a revolutionary war in 1949 and early 1950 but also eventually led Stalin to approve Kim's plans to attack South Korea.[4] Mao and his fellow CCP leaders, despite their own plans to "liberate" Taiwan and unify China, also provided Kim and the Korean Communists with a virtual green light to wage a revolutionary war on the Korean Peninsula.[5] In the summer of 1949 and spring of 1950, the CCP agreed to send about seventy thousand ethnic Korean soldiers enlisted in the Chinese People's Liberation Army (PLA), with weapons, back to Korea. With these troops (some of the PLA's best units) being incorporated into the Korean People's Army, the North Korean Communist forces significantly expanded their offensive capacity, thus allowing Kim and his comrades to implement their plans to attack the reactionary South.[6] In all these senses, it is probably safe to conclude that if there had not been victory in the Chinese Communist Revolution, the Korean War would never have happened.

The second finding is that China entered the Korean War primarily because it was a "revolutionary country." Mao's China was a revolutionary country from the time of its formation. Like other typical revolutionary countries in world history, it had its own language and theory, and would only follow its own values and codes of behavior in international affairs. But unlike many other revolutionary countries, China's international revolutionary behavior had been profoundly conditioned by a unique "Chinese victim mentality," epitomized by its people's deep frustration caused by the sharp contrast between their conviction of China's glorious tradition as the "Central Kingdom" and their collective memory of China's humiliating modern experience as the "sick man in the East." Challenging and, in the final analysis, overturning the existing international order dominated by the Western powers thus became a crucial, or even central, element in legitimizing Mao's grand enterprise of "continuous revolution," which, in his own expressions, was designed to transform China into a land of universal justice and equality, as well as to revive China's *central* (but not *dominant*) position in the world. All this was essential for comprehending Mao's and the CCP leadership's decision to enter the Korean War.

When Mao and his fellow CCP leaders decided to dispatch Chinese troops to Korea, they intended to pursue a glorious victory over the "U.S. imperialists."[7] Underlying this approach was the CCP leaders' desire—and, in particular, Mao's desire—to transform the challenges brought about by the Korean crisis into the dynamics for enhancing the CCP's control of China's state and society, as well as to promote China's international prestige and influence. Mao meant to use the management of the Korean crisis to create new sources of extensive domestic mobilization, so that the Chinese Revolution would not lose its momentum after its nationwide victory.[8]

A brief survey of China's Korean War experience helps make this point clearer. In July 1950, only two weeks after the outbreak of the Korean War (and long before the war had caused a direct threat to China's border security), Mao and the CCP leadership began preparations to enter the war by ordering the "formation of the Northeast Border Defense Army."[9] Accompanying the military mobilization was a nationwide mass mobilization campaign, the "Great Movement to Resist America and Assist Korea," aimed at revolutionizing China's state, society, and population.[10] On August 5 and 18, 1950, almost one month before the Inchon landing, Mao twice set the deadline—first at the end of August, and then at the end of September—for the Chinese troops to complete preparations for military operations in Korea.[11] After the Chinese troops pushed the U.S.-UN forces back to areas south of the 38th Parallel in December

1950 and occupied Seoul early in 1951, the PRC government repeatedly refused to accept an armistice on the battlefield until after the Americans had been "kicked into the Pacific Ocean."[12] Then, during the armistice negotiations from July 1951 to July 1953, Mao's and the CCP leadership's primary criteria for judging whether the terms for an armistice were acceptable was how they might influence the development of the "Great Movement to Resist America and Assist Korea."[13] Therefore, it is clear that for Mao and his fellow CCP leaders, China's intervention in Korea, among other concerns, was—most important of all—an integral component of Mao's "continuous revolution."

The third finding is that Beijing's decisionmaking structure was Mao-centered. As revealed by newly available Chinese documentation, Mao was the single most important policymaker in the CCP's and PRC's policymaking structure. He dictated policy principles and often participated in defining policy details, especially when he believed that the details would decisively determine to what extent the principles would be realized. These important features made the CCP's and PRC's policymaking structure unconventional—the making and implementation of policy decisions were tightly controlled and supervised by Mao himself; and the whole bureaucratic apparatus of the CCP and PRC seemed overwhelmed by his superior authority. As a result, the usual checks and balances produced by different levels and sections of the bureaucratic structure gave way to Mao's paramount and monolithic leadership role.

Indeed, Mao played a crucial role at almost every important stage of Beijing's management of the Korean crisis. When top CCP leaders were considering whether China should enter the Korean conflict in early October 1950, Mao, despite the different opinions held by many of his colleagues, used both his wisdom and authority to convince them that intervention was the only right choice.[14] During the war years, he continuously exerted tight control over Chinese policies and strategies toward Korea, especially when the situation on the Korean Peninsula was facing crucial changes.[15] If there had been no Mao, the history of China's intervention in the Korean War could have been significantly different.

The fourth finding is that China's alliance with the Soviet Union was a cornerstone of its war efforts. The treaty of strategic alliance and mutual assistance that the PRC signed with the Soviet Union in February 1950 symbolized a high level of cooperation between Beijing and Moscow. Among the terms of the treaty, most noteworthy is that it resulted in Moscow's major commitments to supplying military and other support to the PRC if threatened by "hostile imperialist forces."[16]

However, Beijing's alliance with Moscow was not without limits. This was clearly revealed in October 1950, when the issue of whether the Soviet Union would provide direct air support for Chinese ground forces in Korea became a hurdle for Beijing in executing the decision on intervention. As early as July 1950, when Chinese leaders consulted with Stalin about the decision to establish the Northeast Border Defense Army, the Soviet leader not only supported the plan but also offered that if Chinese troops were indeed to begin operations in Korea, Moscow would "provide air cover for these units."[17] In July and August 1950, Moscow dispatched a Soviet Air Force division, with 122 MiG-15 fighters, to China's Northeast to help strengthen its air defense.[18]

Stalin's attitude toward the issue of Soviet air cover for Chinese troops in Korea, however, became ambivalent after the Inchon landing and, especially, in early October 1950, when Mao and his comrades were engaged in crucial deliberations concerning whether to send Chinese troops to Korea. In a series of communications with Beijing's leaders, Stalin urged the Chinese to enter the war, but he failed to clarify what military support—and the air cover for Chinese ground forces, in particular—Moscow would provide if Beijing decided to do so.[19] Only after a tortuous process of negotiations did Stalin agree that Moscow would take the responsibility for defending China's own airspace, that it would provide Beijing with sufficient weapons and military equipment, and that it would use the Soviet Air Force in operation in Korea "two to two and a half months" after Chinese troops had entered the war.[20] Stalin's ambivalent attitude toward this key issue clearly revealed that for him the interest of the Soviet Union (and avoiding a direct military confrontation with the United States over Korea was a top-priority concern for him at that time) was always more important than the interest of the Sino-Soviet alliance. Stalin's lack of a clear and firm commitment on Soviet air support in Korea certainly disappointed Mao and his fellow CCP leaders. But the Soviet leader's promise to deliver sufficient military equipment as well as provide limited and conditional air support to China also allowed Mao to tell other top CCP leaders that intervention was feasible.[21]

During the war years, the relationship between Beijing and Moscow became increasingly closer. Mao consulted with Stalin on almost all important decisions. In December 1950 and January 1951, when Mao and his comrades made the decision to order Chinese troops to cross the 38th Parallel, Beijing maintained daily communication with Moscow and received Stalin's unfailing support.[22] In May and June 1951, when Beijing's leaders were considering adopting a new strategy to end the war, one that would shift their policy emphasis from fighting to negotiations, they had extensive exchanges of opinions with Stalin, and they did not make the decision until the new strategy received

Moscow's complete endorsement.[23] During the early stage of the armistice negotiations, Beijing maintained daily telegraphic communication with Moscow. After 1952, when the armistice negotiations at Panmunjom hit a deadlock on the issue of prisoners of war, Beijing consulted with Moscow and concluded that the Chinese and North Korean side would not compromise on this issue until its political and military position had improved.[24] Consequently, China's Korean War experience in an overall sense made Beijing's alliance with Moscow more substantial and consolidated than ever before. Therefore, we must regard the Sino-Soviet alliance as the cornerstone of China's intervention in Korea.

After Chinese troops entered the war, the Soviet Union also provided China with large amounts of ammunition and military equipment. Units of the Soviet Air Force, with China's Northeast as the base, began to engage in defense of the transportation lines across the Chinese-Korean border as early as November 1950, and began operations over the northern part of North Korea in January 1951.[25] In the meantime, Stalin became more willing than before to commit Soviet financial and technological resources to China's economic reconstruction—and as a consequence, the Soviet Union's share of China's foreign trade increased from 30 percent in 1950 to 56 percent in 1953.[26] The "Stalin model," as a result of the Chinese experience in Korea, thus gained a powerful position to dominate China's "socialist revolution and reconstruction" after the war ended in July 1953.

The fifth finding is that China's relationship with North Korea was substantial yet never harmonious. The CCP's relationship with the North Korean Communists was close before the Korean War. During China's civil war, from 1946 to 1949, the Korean Communists offered their CCP comrades in China's Northeast substantial support, which allowed the Chinese Communists to occupy a favorable position in their life-and-death confrontation with the Chinese Nationalists.[27] From the summer of 1949 until the spring of 1950, as mentioned above, the CCP decided to send about seventy thousand ethnic Korean soldiers enlisted in the Chinese PLA to Korea, and these troops would play a crucial role in North Korea's invasion of South Korea.[28] However, problems existed between the Chinese and North Korean Communists. Kim Il Sung, in planning the war, did not visit Beijing to consult with Mao and the CCP leadership about his plans to attack South Korea until mid-May 1950. Even more seriously, as revealed by Chinese and Russian sources, Kim failed to inform Beijing's leaders of the exact schedule of the invasion, let alone to involve China in the implementation of the plan to attack South Korea.[29]

That the outbreak of the Korean War on June 25, 1950, was not the result of the CCP's planning reflected the very complicated relationships between Beijing, Pyongyang, and Moscow at that time. It is now well known that the Chinese and Soviet Communist parties reached a "division of labor" agreement in the summer of 1949 during the visit to the Soviet Union of the CCP's second in command, Liu Shaoqi. According to this agreement, though the Soviet Union would remain the center of the international Communist movement, China's primary duty would be the promotion of revolutions in East Asia.[30] However, it seems that Korea was an exception in this general design for "revolutions in the East." Largely because the northern part of the Korean Peninsula had been under Soviet military occupation, Korea was continuously designated as Moscow's—rather than Beijing's—area of responsibility.

During the early stage of the Korean War, when the North Korean Communist forces were marching toward the southern tip of the peninsula, Beijing's leaders made the decision to establish the Northeast Border Defense Army and set the deadline for Chinese troops to get ready to begin operations in Korea. One main reason for the Chinese troops' failure to enter the war before the Inchon landing lay in the fact that Kim Il Sung never extended an invitation for Chinese intervention. Although Mao repeatedly conveyed his concerns to Kim that the U.S.-UN forces might conduct landing operations to the rear of the Korean People's Army, the North Korean leader paid little attention to Mao's warnings.[31]

After Chinese troops entered the war to rescue Kim's regime in October 1950, China's relations with the North Korean Communists seemed closer than before, but problems continued between the two sides. According to Chinese sources that became available in the past decade, China and North Korea experienced at least four major disputes during the Korean War years. First, in January 1951, when Chinese troops had pushed the battle line from areas close to the Yalu River to areas south of the 38th Parallel, PLA commanders believed that their troops were not in a position to continue the offensive, but Kim insisted upon bringing the war further south. Second, in the spring of 1951, when U.S. forces had begun a counteroffensive on the battlefield, the Chinese commanders carried out a strategy of "positive defense" to win time and space to reorganize their troops, but Kim again pushed the Chinese to use a counteroffensive to cope with the American offensive. Third, after the armistice talks began in July 1951, the Chinese found it necessary for them to continue controlling North Korea's railway transportation system so that military needs would be treated as the top priorities, but Kim endeavored to resume Pyongyang's direct control of the railway system. Fourth, in June and July 1953, after South Korean leader Syngman Rhee ordered the release of more than 25,000 anticommunist North Korean prisoners, the Chinese believed it necessary to give the enemy "another bitter strike" before reaching an armistice, but

Kim opposed the plan and argued that it was better for military operations on the battlefield to stop immediately.[32]

Although these differences can be regarded as discrepancies in strategies and tactics that usually would emerge in any alliance relationship, it was more serious from a Chinese perspective when Kim Il Sung purged several prominent members (including Pak Il-yu and Mu Chong, the highest-ranking PLA commanders in the Korean People's Army) of the "Yan'an faction" within the Korean Workers' Party.[33] While doing so, Kim demonstrated an extraordinary ability to manipulate the situation under the circumstances that his own regime's very survival was at the mercy of the 1.35 million Chinese troops who were fighting a war in Korea on his behalf. Ostensibly Kim was able to use Mao Zedong's promise that the Chinese troops in Korea would under no circumstances interfere with Korea's internal affairs to keep the Chinese out of these intraparty purges. In essence, however, Kim's success epitomized a more general pattern in Beijing's mentality—one that had been profoundly penetrated by the Chinese sense of moral superiority in dealing with its subordinate neighbors (e.g., Korea and Vietnam)—in perceiving and handling relations with Kim and North Korea. Indeed, Mao believed that to send Chinese troops to Korea was not for such an "inferior" purpose as pursuing China's direct political and economic control over North Korea but was for the purpose of, among other aims, achieving the Korean Communists' inner acceptance of China's morally superior position in directing the "revolutions in the East." In turn, Beijing's self-imposed principle on not interfering in North Korea's internal affairs provided Kim with the much-needed space to consolidate his control of the Korean Workers' Party and regime. This pattern of alliance between China and North Korea, as demonstrated by the "lips and teeth" rhetoric related to the alliance, formed an interesting yet underresearched aspect of China's early Cold War experience. More study on this important issue is in order.

Five Implications

The first implication is that Mao became more central in China's decision-making structure. When Chinese troops entered the Korean War in October 1950, the U.S.-UN forces were approaching the Chinese-Korean border; but when the war ended with an armistice in July 1953, the Chinese troops successfully stabilized the demarcation line along the 38th Parallel. In the meantime, China's state and society had experienced significant changes in accordance with Mao's and the CCP's plans. These "victories" significantly enhanced Mao's leading position in the CCP and in China, making the Chinese chairman almost unchallengeable in a practical political sense. If many of Mao's comrades in the CCP leadership had previously experienced doubts about his determination to involve China in a confrontation against an international coalition headed by the strongest nation in the world and composed of almost all the major Western industrial powers, they were forced to recognize at the conclusion of the war that Mao possessed a much broader vision than they did. When his decision to enter the Korean War was widely praised as "brilliant," and when his name became more tightly linked with "truth" and "correctness," an enhanced pattern emerged in Chinese politics: China's state building and societal transformation became increasingly entangled with the development of his personal cult. Because he now enjoyed political power with fewer checks and balances, he was in a more powerful position to carry out his utopian plans to transform China's state, society, population, and international outlook. Thus, with almost unlimited power at his disposal, he would finally lead China toward such disastrous "continuous revolution" experiments as the "Great Leap Forward" and the "Great Proletarian Cultural Revolution." Indeed, during the Cold War era, few other cases besides that of Mao more fully exposed the huge impact of personality or human agency upon politics.

The second implication is that China became more revolutionary, both domestically and internationally. Related to Mao's dramatically increased impact as the result of China's participation in the Korean War was the continuous rise of the "new China" as a revolutionary country. During the Korean War years, a series of political and social revolutions swept across China's cities and countryside. In the wake of China's entrance into the war, Mao's Communist regime found itself in a powerful position to penetrate almost every area of Chinese society through an intensive mass mobilization under the banner of "Resisting America and Assisting Korea." During the war years, several nationwide campaigns swept through China's countryside and cities: the movement to suppress counterrevolutionaries, the land reform movement, the "thought transformation" campaign (mainly taking the intellectuals as its target), and the "Three Antis" and "Five Antis" movements.[34] When the war ended in July 1953, China's society and political landscape had been altered—organized resistance to the new regime had been destroyed, land in the countryside had been redistributed and the landlord class had been eliminated, the national bourgeoisie was under the tight control of the Communist state, and the petit bourgeois intellectuals had experienced the first round of Communist reeducation. Consequently, the CCP effectively extended and deepened its organizational control over Chinese society and dramatically promoted its authority and legitimacy in the minds of the Chinese people.

In a theoretical sense, all the above-mentioned points offer the potential for scholars to reach a more sophisticated comprehension of the relationship between a nation's domestic politics and its external policies, a question that has been widely considered and debated by scholars of international relations. Simply put, though China's changing domestic politics certainly played a crucial role in shaping the orientation of its external policies, it would be an oversimplification to claim that the latter was the extension (or a reflection) of the former. To relate this issue to the need to reconsider the interplay between "power" and ideology and between ideology and culture, we may find that the key here is probably to reexamine the traditional understanding of the boundaries and interconnections between "domestic" and "external."

As a matter of fact, Mao never drew a clear boundary between "domestic" and "external" issues in his management of China's international affairs. Indeed, within the framework of his "continuous revolution," which aimed to bring about a total transformation simultaneously of China's state, society, and international outlook, "domestic" and "external" issues were interrelated in the sense that they were both integral components of his grand enterprise of "continuous revolution." A term he frequently used in describing the space in which the "continuous revolution" should be carried out was *tian xia* (all under heaven), a concept that can only be properly understood when one digs into its historical and cultural roots. Because the Chinese during traditional times were deeply convinced that Chinese civilization and the Chinese way of life were the most superior in the known universe, they had only a vague imagination of the "world," and they would feel more comfortable using the concept *tian xia,* which implied that the "Central Kingdom" was the only civilized land in the known universe—that, in effect, China was civilization in toto.[35]

Thus Mao's particular use of language suggests that the CCP's foreign policy, no matter how revolutionary its appearance, had a hidden yet profound origin in the Chinese tradition that the Communist revolution had promised to destroy. The vagueness involved in the boundary between "domestic" and "external," as indicated by Mao's use of *tian xia,* should push scholars to reconsider the definition of these two space-related concepts (i.e., "domestic" and "external") in broader theoretical terms.

The third implication is that Communist alliance politics became more difficult to handle. China's early Cold War experience in general and its Korean experience in particular allow scholars to better understand patterns of alliance among Communist actors. There exists no ground for scholars to return to the interpretation of the "traditional school," which emphasized that there was a monolithic "Soviet Bloc" threat to international peace in the early Cold War period. The actual situation was much more complicated. On the one hand, as reflected in Beijing's handling of the Korean crisis, what underlay Beijing's policy was a strong sense of unity based on the belief that the revolutionary changes in both China and Korea had been an integral part of a great cause of radical revolutions emerging in East Asia. Although the most profound origins of these radical revolutions lay in the social, political, and economic developments within each East Asian country, as a whole they challenged the international order dominated by the Western imperialist powers in East Asia. Therefore, although each revolution had its own priorities and specific aims because of special local, national, and regional conditions, it shared a position in a common struggle against the global reign of capitalism-imperialism.

On the other hand, however, China's "proletarian internationalism" was from the beginning conditioned by Chinese revolutionary nationalism, along with the Maoist notion of reviving China's big power status through the promotion of an "Eastern Revolution" following the Chinese model. This notion, according to its own logic, inevitably posed potential challenges to Moscow's dominance of the international Communist movement. Consequently, Communist alliance politics became more difficult to handle for both Moscow and Beijing in the wake of the Korean War. It is here that one finds one of the deeper causes of the later collapse of the Sino-Soviet alliance.

The fourth implication is that the Cold War became more ideological. China's Korean War–centered early Cold War experience played a crucial role in changing the "essence" of the Cold War. Indeed, the revolutionary discourses pursued by Mao's China made the global Cold War more ideological in orientation and less "conventional" in development.

The study of international history and international relations has long been dominated by realpolitik-driven approaches. Scholars of international relations have paid attention to the role played by ideology, but they have often regarded this role as more one of justifying already-existing policy decisions than of shaping them at deeper levels or as deeper causes.[36] The Chinese documents newly available to us, many of which concern the internal discussions between CCP leaders and thus reflect their deliberations and calculations during the process of policymaking, put forward serious challenges to such approaches. What we can see from these documents is that Mao and his comrades not only often used ideological terms to defend their policy decisions but also widely referred to their beliefs in Communist ideology as *the* basic reason to make and legitimize critical policy decisions.

When the Chinese Communist leadership made the decision to enter the Korean War in October 1950, the newly established People's Republic of China was only one year old. While making the decision, Mao and his comrades did repeatedly point out that otherwise the Chinese-Korean border would face serious and direct threats from the U.S.-UN forces rapidly marching toward the

Yalu River. But what Mao most emphasized was the impact that such a decision might have on maintaining and enhancing the momentum of the Chinese Communist Revolution, as well as on the fate of the "Eastern Revolution" (in which, according to Mao and his comrades, the Chinese Revolution should occupy a central position). In actuality, Mao defined the People's Republic's "national security interests" in highly ideological terms, making it clear that China had to enter the Korean War because of both revolutionary commitments and security concerns—and that these two aspects in his conceptual world were closely interrelated.

If we are to acknowledge that ideology indeed has played a more basic role in international relations than has been perceived by realpolitik-centered scholars, we also face the challenge of redefining "ideology." Among other things, this means that we should reconsider the relationship between "power" and ideology and redefine the interconnections between ideology and culture. We still have a very long way to go in coming up with more comprehensive and persuasive theses on these important themes.

The fifth implication is that the Cold War became more likely to remain "cold." Most important of all, China's "Korean War–centered" early Cold War experience challenged and, as a result, changed the two superpowers' basic perceptions of the scope and perimeter of the escalating confrontation between them, turning East Asia into a new focus of the global Cold War.

In retrospect, there were many possible alternative paths when the global Cold War was being shaped in the late 1940s. That the Cold War would remain "cold" throughout its history was by no means predetermined. Indeed, until the late 1940s, when the Cold War gradually emerged, it had been a common phenomenon in modern history that confrontations between big powers—and particularly between the contending alliances they formed—all in one way or another eventually led to "hot" wars. Compared with the political and military complexities that history had witnessed in previous prewar situations, the tensions between the United States and the Soviet Union—along with the two contending blocs they led—seemed even more complicated and potentially explosive. In addition to conflicts over political, economic, and security interests, the confrontation between the United States and the Soviet Union was also characterized by fundamental differences in ideologies, and in visions and designs of social systems and forms of government. Each side not only challenged the political and strategic interests of the other side but also, and more important, questioned the very legitimacy of the other side's political institutions, social systems, and even ways of life. Given the profoundness of these conflicts between the two sides, it would have seemed quite logical for the confrontations between the United States and the Soviet Union, and also between the two blocs they headed, to have inevitably resulted in major hot wars.

Yet the global Cold War never evolved into a worldwide "hot" war. Why? An important reason lay in the fact that China's early Cold War experience created some of the key conditions that, in hindsight, would help the Cold War remain "cold." The Korean War erupted at a time when the development of the global Cold War was facing a crucial juncture. Two important events—the 1948–49 Berlin blockade, and the Soviet Union's first successful test of an atomic bomb in August 1949—combined to pose a serious challenge to the two superpowers. If either tried to gain a strategic upper hand against the other—and if a showdown were to occur in Europe, where the dividing line between the two contending camps had already been drawn in a definitive manner—the Cold War could have escalated into a global catastrophe, one that might have involved the use of nuclear weapons. Against this backdrop, both Moscow (by entering a "division of labor" agreement with Beijing and providing support to Pyongyang) and Washington (by developing and implementing National Security Council Report 68, known as NSC-68) gave more strategic attention to East Asia. This shift in the two superpowers' global strategies represented one of the most important factors in the making of the international environment in which the Korean War had been shaped.

Largely because of Stalin's caution—which was echoed by the caution of President Harry S. Truman, as demonstrated in the controversy between Truman and General Douglas MacArthur in the spring of 1951—the Korean War did not evolve into a direct military confrontation between the two superpowers. Yet the Chinese-American war in Korea had already turned East Asia into the main battlefield of the Cold War. Even after the Korean War armistice was reached in 1953, East Asia continued to be a main focus of the Cold War's international confrontations throughout the 1950s and 1960s. While China played a central role in the two Taiwan Strait crises (in 1954–55 and 1958) and in the Vietnam War (the longest "hot" war during the Cold War), the strategic attention of the United States, following the assumption that China was a more daring enemy than the Soviet Union, became increasingly fixed on East Asia.

Ironically and unexpectedly, however, Beijing's active role in East Asia turned this main Cold War battlefield into a strange "buffer" between Washington and Moscow; with China and East Asia standing in the middle, it was less likely that the United States and the Soviet Union would become involved in a direct military confrontation. The situation would remain like this until the early 1970s, when Sino-American rapprochement finally ended the total confrontation between China and the United States. In the meantime, détente began to redefine the rules for U.S.-Soviet confrontation, decisively reducing the possibility of a nuclear showdown between the two superpowers. In this sense, we may claim that China's "Korean War–centered" early Cold War experience played a role in helping the Cold War remain "cold"—although Washington, Beijing, and Moscow had not planned for this outcome.

Notes

1. See the discussions by Odd Arne Westad, *Cold War and Revolution: Soviet-American Rivalry and the Origins of the Chinese Civil War* (New York: Columbia University Press, 1993), especially the concluding chapter; Yang Kuisong, *Zhonggong yu mosiko de guanxi, 1920–1960* [The CCP's relations with Moscow, 1920–1960] (Taipei: Dongda tushu, 1997), 520–71; Michael M. Sheng, *Battling Western Imperialism: Mao, Stalin, and the United States* (Princeton, N.J.: Princeton University Press, 1997); and Chen Jian, *Mao's China and the Cold War* (Chapel Hill: University of North Carolina Press, 2001), chap. 1.

2. See, e.g., the ciphered telegram from Shtykov to Vyshinskii, January 19, 1950, Arkhiv Vneshnei Politiki Possiiskoi Federatsii (hereafter AVP RF), fond (f.) 059a, opis' (op.) 5a, delo (d.) 3, papka (p.) 11, listy (ll.) 87–91; and telegram, Liu Shaoqi to Mao Zedong, concerning the issue of supporting Vietnam, December 24, 1949, in *Jianguo yilai Liu Shaoqi wengao* [Liu Shaoqi's manuscripts since the formation of the People's Republic] (Beijing: Zhongyang wenxian, 2005), vol. 1, 226–27.

3. For a discussion, see Chen Jian, *China's Road to the Korean War: The Making of the Chinese-American Confrontation* (New York: Columbia University Press, 1994), chap. 4.

4. See, e.g., Kathryn Weathersby, "Korea: 1949–1950: To Attack, or Not to Attack? Stalin, Kim Il-sung, and the Prelude to War," *Cold War International History Project Bulletin,* no. 5 (Spring 1995): 1, 2–9.

5. For a more extensive discussion, see Chen Jian, "In the Name of Revolution: China's Road to the Korean War Revisited," in *The Korean War in World History,* ed. William Stueck (Lexington: University Press of Kentucky, 2004), 99–101.

6. See Chen Jian, *China's Road to the Korean War,* 106–11; and Bruce Cumings, *The Origins of the Korean War* (Princeton, N.J.: Princeton University Press, 1990), vol. 2, chap. 11.

7. See the discussions given by Chen Jian, *China's Road to the Korean War,* 178–79.

8. See, e.g., Zhou Enlai's speech at the national defense conference, August 26, 1950, *Zhou Enlai junshi wenxuan* [Selected military papers of Zhou Enlai], vol. 4, 43–50.

9. See, e.g., letter from Mao Zedong to Nie Rongzhen, July 7, 1950, in *Jianguo yilai Mao Zedong wengao* [Mao Zedong's manuscripts since the formation of the People's Republic] (Beijing: Zhongyang wenxian, 1987), vol. 1, 428.

10. For a more detailed discussion, see Chen Jian, *China's Road to the Korean War,* 137–41, 190–94.

11. See telegram, Mao Zedong to Gao Gang, August 5 and 18 1950, in *Jianguo yilai Mao Zedong wengao,* vol. 1, 454, 469; and Zhou Enlai's speech at the national defense conference, August 26, 1950, in *Zhou Enlai junshi wenxuan,* vol. 4, 43–50.

12. See, e.g., telegrams, Mao Zedong to Peng Dehuai, December 13 and 21, 1950, in *Jianguo yilai Mao Zedong wengao,* vol. 1, 722,731–32; and telegram, Mao Zedong to Peng Dehui and Kim Il Sung, January 14, 1951, in *Zhongguo renmin zhiyuanjun kangmei yuanchao zhanshi* [A history of the Chinese People's Volunteers in the War of Resisting America and Assisting Korea], ed. Shen Zonghong and Meng Zhaohui et al. (Beijing: Junshi kexue, 1987), 67. Also see *Cold War International History Project Bulletin,* nos. 6–7 (Winter 1995–96): 55–56.

13. See, e.g., instruction, the CCP Central Committee, "On Further Promoting the Movement to Resist America and Assist Korea among All Walks in the Country," February 1, 1951, in *Zhonggong dangshi jiaoxue cankao ziliao* [Reference materials on teaching and studying CCP history] (Beijing: Guofang daxue, n.d.), vol. 19, 242–43.

14. See the discussion given by Chen Jian, *China's Road to the Korean War,* chap. 6.

15. See Chen Jian, *Mao's China and the Cold War,* chap. 4.

16. For a plausible discussion, see Sergei N. Goncharov, John W. Lewis, and Xue Litai, *Uncertain Partners: Stalin, Mao and the Korean War* (Stanford, Calif.: Stanford University Press, 1993), chaps. 3 and 4; and Shi Zhe, *Zai lishi juren shenbian: Shi Zhe huiyilu* [On the side of historical giants: Shi Zhe's memoirs], rev. ed. (Beijing: Zhonggong zhongyang dangxiao, 1998), 353–84.

17. See, e.g., telegram, Stalin to N. V. Roshchin, Soviet ambassador to China, with message for Zhou Enlai, July 5, 1950, *Cold War International History Project Bulletin,* nos. 6–7 (Winter 1995–96): 43.

18. See the discussion given by Chen Jian, *China's Road to the Korean War,* 156; and telegram, Filippov (Stalin) to Zhou Enlai, August 27, 1950, *Cold War International History Project Bulletin,* nos. 6–7 (Winter 1995–96): 45.

19. See, e.g., telegram, Stalin to Mao Zedong and Zhou Enlai, October 1, 1950, *Cold War International History Project Bulletin,* nos. 6–7 (Winter 1995–96), 114; and the discussion given by Shen Zhihua, *Mao Zedong, Sidalin he hanzhan* [Mao Zedong, Stalin and the Korean War] (Hong Kong: Tiandi tushu, 1998), 236–37.

20. See Shi Zhe, *Zai lishi juren shenbian,* 442–49; telegram, Stalin and Zhou Enlai to Soviet Embassy in Beijing and conveyed to Mao Zedong, October 11, 1950, Rossiiskii gosudarstvennyi arkhiv sotzial'no-politicheskoi istorii, f. 558, op. 11, d., 334, ll. 134–35; and *Novaia i noveishaia istoriia,* no. 5 (2005): 108–9. See also Chen Jian, *China's Road to the Korean War,* 197–200.

21. Telegram, Mao Zedong to Zhou Enlai, October 13, 1950, in *Mao Zedong wenji,* vol. 6, 103–4. See also Chen Jian, *China's Road to the Korean War,* 202–3; and Chen Jian, *Mao's China and the Cold War,* 56–61.

22. See Kathryn Weathersby, trans. and ed., "New Russian Documents on the Korean War," *Cold War International History Project Bulletin,* nos. 6–7 (Winter 1995–96): 47–53.

23. See Chen Jian, *Mao's China and the Korean War,* 97–99; and Weathersby, "New Russian Documents," 59–66.

24. See Shi Zhe, *Zai lishi juren shenbian,* 455–58; and "Stalin's Conversations with Chinese Leaders," *Cold War International History Project Bulletin,* nos. 6–7 (Winter 1995–96): 10–20.

25. When and how the Soviet Air Force entered operations in Korea has been a confusing question for scholars in recent years. Though some scholars, basing their discussion on information provided by Russian recollections and documents, believe

that this occurred as early as November 1950, others, following the insights gained from Chinese sources, argue that the Soviet Air Force began operations in Korea in January 1951. I believe that the key here is to make a distinction between operations for the purpose of defending China's Northeast and the transportation lines across the Chinese-Korean border, especially the bridge over the Yalu River, and operations designed for supporting Chinese–North Korean land forces fighting in Korean territory. Though the former did happen as early as November 1950 (as an inevitable extension of defending the airspace of China's Northeast), the latter did not occur until January 1951.

26. Xue Mouhong, *Dangdai zhongguo waijiao* [Contemporary Chinese diplomacy] (Beijing: Zhongguo shehui kexue, 1988), 28–30; Pei Jianzhang, *Zhonghua renmin gongheguo waijiao shi, 1949–1956* [A diplomatic history of the People's Republic of China, 1949–1956] (Beijing: Zhongguo shehui kexue, 1994), 40–41.

27. See Chen Jian, *China's Road to the Korean War,* 106–9; see also Bruce Cumings, *The Origins of the Korean War* (Princeton, N.J.: Princeton University Press, 1990), vol. 2, chap. 11.

28. Chen Jian, *China's Road to the Korean War,* 110–12; Kim Donggil, "A New Study on the Returning of Ethnic Korean Soldiers of the PLA to North Korea," *Lishi yanjiu* [Historical Research], no. 6 (2006): 103–14.

29. Mao complained in a telegram drafted for Stalin (but that was not sent) that "before the outbreak of the war [in Korea], Comrade Kim Il Sung did not inform us of the exact schedule of the attack, keeping us in the dark." The original handwritten draft of the telegram, Mao Zedong to Stalin, October 2, 1950, is kept at the CCP Central Archives in Beijing. See also Pang Xianzhi and Li Jie, *Mao Zedong yu Kangmei yuanchao*[Mao Zedong and resisting America and assisting Korea] (Beijing: Zhongyang wenxian, 2000), 12–13. In the published version of the telegram (*Jianguo yilai Mao Zedong wengao,* vol. 1, 550–52), the sentence quoted above is not included.

30. Shi Zhe, "With Mao and Stalin: Liu Shaoqi in Moscow," *Chinese Historians* 6, no. 1 (Spring 1993): 84–85.

31. Shi Zhe, *Zai lishi juren shenbia,* 492. Mao Zedong later complained to Stalin about Kim Il Sung's failure to listen to Beijing's advice on the possibility of U.S.-UN forces landing operation at the Inchon area. Telegram, Mao Zedong to Stalin, October 2, 1950, cited by Pang Xianzhi and Li Jie, *Mao Zedong yu kangmei yuanchao,* 12–13.

32. See Peng Dehuai, *Peng Dehuai zishu* [Peng Dehuai's autobiography], internal ed., n.d., n.p., 349–52; and discussions given by Shen Zhihua, "Sino-North Korean Conflict and its Resolution during the Korean War," *Cold War International History Project Bulletin,* nos. 14–15 (Winter 2003–Spring 2004): 9–24.

33. For a recent and plausible study on this issue, see Yu Weimin, "The Rise and Demise of the 'Yanan Faction' of the Korean Revolution," paper presented to an international conference on "Limits of the 'Lips and Teeth' Alliance: The Antinomies of the Chinese-North Korean Relationship," Cornell University, Ithaca, N.Y., September 2006.

34. The "Three Antis" movement was designed to oppose corrupt Communist cadres; the "Five Antis" movement was aimed at the national bourgeoisie class, "who should not be destroyed at this stage but who needed to be tightly controlled by the power of the people's state."

35. For a more extended discussion of the complicated and interactive relationship

between Mao's worldview and the age-old "Central Kingdom" mentality, see Chen Jian, *Mao's China and the Cold War,* 7–8.

36. What we see here is the predominant impact of Hans Morgenthau, author of the highly influential classic *Politics of Nations: The Struggle for Power and Peace* (New York: Alfred A. Knopf, 1948), and other influential "realist" theorists, e.g., George Kennan. For a critical review emphasizing the failure of various schools of international relations theory in predicting the development of the Cold War, see John Lewis Gaddis, "International Relations Theory and the End of the Cold War," *International Security* 17 (Winter 1992–93): 5–58.

4. Military Occupation and Empire Building in Cold War Asia: The United States and Korea, 1945–1955

Steven Hugh Lee

The American occupation of Korea between 1945 and 1948 has been the subject of a number of dissertations, books, articles, and book chapters over the past several decades. Most authors have examined the occupation either as a self-contained era of Korean history and Korean-American relations or as part of the wider story of the origins of the Korean War.[1] This chapter examines the history of the occupation in a new light. In particular, the 1945–55 period is treated as an extended, though interrupted, American occupation of southern Korea. There are no works that explore the U.S. role in Korea in this framework, mainly because South Korea gained formal sovereignty in 1948 and U.S. military forces left the Korean Peninsula in 1949. They returned to counter the North Korean attack in June 1950. The historical discontinuity of the 1948–50 era has impeded historians from seeing the broader continuities of military occupation during the period as a whole. Additionally, most historians have been preoccupied with the political and big power dimensions of the Korean conflict; although U.S. civil affairs teams returned to Korea in 1950 and took up many of the same duties they had exercised during the earlier occupation, historians more interested in the international dimensions of the war have tended to ignore these aspects of Korean-American relations during the period. As a result, they have favored the political and diplomatic history of the war over its social and economic history. An examination of the interplay between Ko-

The author thanks Chen Jian, Tsuyoshi Hasegawa, and Christian Ostermann for their valuable comments on this chapter, and Alexa Eun Bok Kim for research assistance with Korean sources.

rea and the United States within a wider framework of extended occupation offers us an excellent opportunity to analyze how Cold War dynamics affected Koreans and Americans, and how, in turn, the diplomacy of these two states shaped the broader parameters of the conflict in East Asia.

Studying the history of the American occupations of Korea between 1945 and 1948 and in the Korean War era also leads us to explore the relationship between the particular and the general in the history of American foreign policy, for these occupations should be viewed in light of the wider history of American military interventions in the modern era. Indeed, it is useful to remind ourselves that the history of American occupations over the last one hundred years or so takes us beyond the study of Asia and into the realm of understanding America's perceived global mission. Military occupations have been a defining feature of the United States' foreign policy since the Spanish-American-Cuban-Filipino War. In many respects, they have been *the* defining element of the American empire since the United States undertook a global expansionist role in the late nineteenth century. Although it is beyond the scope of this chapter to discuss the history of the American military as an occupying power around the world, the U.S. occupations of the Philippines, Cuba, Puerto Rico, the Rhineland, Haiti, and the Dominican Republic in the 1898–1945 era did leave a legacy for post–World War II American military governments in places like Germany, Japan, Korea, Okinawa, Vietnam, and, ultimately, Iraq and Afghanistan today.[2]

The earlier U.S. occupations, which theoretically were designed to establish forms of "modern" American-style democratic governance, failed dismally in their efforts, as the continued U.S. interventions in places like Cuba, Haiti, and the Dominican Republic in the pre-1945 and postwar eras demonstrated. These interventions, however, did establish an informal operational blueprint for occupation that would be followed in the post-1945 world; that is, American military occupation in most of these areas involved the creation of a provisional government, the establishment of an internal security force, the overseeing of the formation of an "independent" government, and the eventual withdrawal of American troops. Occupation, in short, was designed as a temporary, although at times extended, period of U.S. rule. It differed from traditional colonialism in that American troops were not meant to stay in the country indefinitely.[3]

The departure of American troops from Haiti in 1934, and the articulation of what became known as the "Good Neighbor" policy, did not end the U.S. experiment in occupational diplomacy; but neither did it result in the creation of a formal occupation strategy by the U.S. military. Before World War II, there was no central coordinating document that outlined American military objectives during an occupation. It was not until after the start of the war in Europe that the U.S. government authorities formally articulated the theory and practice of American military government. World War II thus had a significant impact on the evolution of U.S. thinking about military governance.

The first major effort to define a formal U.S. policy for dealing with occupied territories occurred in 1940, under the auspices of the army's Judge Advocate General's Office. The office produced a manual titled *Military Government,* often referred to as *FM* [*Field Manual*] *27-5.*[4] This manual built on some of the ideas discussed in an earlier manual, *The Rules of Land Warfare,* published in October 1939, which contained a chapter devoted to military occupation. Soon after the publication of the first edition of *FM 27-5,* military officials began to point out that the manual placed too much emphasis on the liberal treatment of the occupied.[5] In 1943, the army published a new version of the manual, titled the *United States Army and Navy Manual of Military Government and Civil Affairs,* which laid the policy foundations for subsequent American occupations after World War II.[6] In effect, the manual represented an American version of Lord Lugard's policies of "indirect rule." It stated that though occupation often required the purging of high-ranking enemy officials, "so far as practicable, subordinate officials and employees of the local government should be retained in their offices and made responsible for the proper discharge of their duties."[7] Furthermore, it was important, especially in cases where local populations were under the domination of another power, to train "native" personnel. Overall, the U.S. military should as much as possible "deal with the inhabitants of the local government through such officers and employees of the local government as are retained or appointed." The corollary to this was that local laws and practices were to remain in place, except where the military government decided otherwise. It was important that no existing political party or prominent politician be given any say in the determination of occupation policies; civil affairs soldiers "would avoid any commitments to, or negotiations with, any local political elements except by directions from higher authority."[8] In short, the military government was to retain control over the territory until such time as it saw fit to hand over power to local elites. To sustain law and order in the occupied area, "local civil police forces or constabularies . . . shall be used to the maximum extent."[9] Many of these policies would be applied to Korea and other areas occupied by the United States after the war. Although military officials were critical of leftist ideologies, they did not articulate in the document an explicitly antileftist or anticommunist stance. This was a major difference between American occupations before 1945 and those that occurred after the beginning of overt competition for global spheres of influence between the United States and the Soviet Union.

The American Occupation of Korea, 1945–48

My analysis now turns to a study of the significance of the first American occupation of Korea, which lasted from the fall of 1945 through to the creation of the Republic of Korea in August 1948.[10] It is useful to begin with a global and comparative understanding of the occupation of the area south of the 38th Parallel because it shares some general features with the American occupations of Japan and Germany. Korea, like Germany, though less so, underwent a degree of political decentralization during the initial phases of the occupation. The imperatives in Korea of containing the perceived threat from the left, however, quickly resulted in policies that led to a more centralized form of governance than had existed under Japanese colonialism.[11] The occupation of Korea differed significantly from those of Japan and Germany in another important respect: Some 400,000 Germans and 200,000 Japanese were "purged" from office in the American zone in western Germany and in Japan.[12] But relatively few Koreans were removed from office as a result of their collaboration with the Japanese authorities during the war. In fact, those who had collaborated with the Japanese were generally favored over others who now demanded major changes in postcolonial Korean society. There was thus no "liberal" phase of the American occupation of Korea, largely because of Lieutenant General John Hodge's concerns about leftist influence and "Communism" immediately from the time of his arrival in Pusan in the summer of 1945. The occupation of Korea was also unique in the sense that Korea was a dependent colonial territory of the Japanese Empire, and not a formal belligerent of the United States. Thus, though there were some general similarities in all three areas, specific occupation policies varied according to local political and economic considerations.

In both Korea and Japan, the occupation authorities tended to work more through the existing local government than they did in Germany, where officials were sensitive to the population's ties with the country's Nazi past. The Potsdam Declaration, issued on July 26, 1945, stated that "the *Japanese Government* shall remove all obstacles to the revival and strengthening of democratic tendencies among the Japanese people. Freedom of speech, of religion, and of thought, as well as respect for the fundamental human rights shall be established" (emphasis added). This was basically the approach taken with Korea, and it reflected the premises of *FM 27-5*. Yet, as Howard Schonberger has written, the instructions given to MacArthur for the occupation of Japan contained contradictions: "On the one hand, these basic directives called for a remarkably progressive set of reforms of Japan's entire social structure but, on the other hand, directed that these reforms be implemented through the emperor of Japan and officials of the Japanese government whose interest was generally opposed to the democratization program."[13] These policies contrasted with the initial American strategy for dealing with defeated Germany, which was articulated in September 1944 in a draft of Joint Chiefs of Staff Directive 1067, a major planning document defining American objectives toward Germany, which stated that the American military would create a "stern all-powerful military administration of a conquered country, based on [Germany's] unconditional surrender, impressing the Germans with their military defeat and the futility of any further aggression."[14] These goals were often compromised during the occupation itself. Carolyn Eisenberg has pointed to the perceived need to work with German businessmen to rehabilitate the economy, as well as American concerns about the influence of the left in postwar Germany.[15] Comparatively speaking, however, the American military government in Korea took a lenient policy toward officials in power, insofar as Korean bureaucrats were retained in positions of authority.

The influence of Japan in American thinking about Korea emerged from the beginning of the occupation; the Twenty-fourth Army, which was assigned the task of occupying the area south of the 38th Parallel, was originally supposed to occupy Japan. But the Soviet Union's rapid entry into the war dramatically changed those plans.[16] The orders for the army were revised in light of the September 1945 American-Soviet agreement on spheres of influence, which divided the Korean Peninsula into Soviet and American zones. Although the U.S. troops that occupied Korea were inadequately trained for the task—for example, few knew the Korean language—some soldiers viewed the experience of preparing for the occupation of Japan as beneficial for their new duties. As the history of the Korean Bureau of Domestic Commerce pointed out, civil affairs officials in Korea relied on their knowledge of Japan. Although there was little planning for the administration of domestic commerce south of the 38th Parallel, "considerable time and energy [were] spent by some Military Government officers on Japanese methods of operation. Conditions which existed in South Korea on 10 September 1945, when the Military Government officially took over from the Japanese at the Capitol in Seoul, were notably parallel to the Japanese structure."[17]

Korea before the American Occupation, August-September 1945

The Americans arriving in Korea in 1945 were ill prepared for the political ferment that rapidly transformed the politics of the former Japanese colony. A nascent civil society, freed from the wartime associations the colonial regime had required the population to join, began to fill the political and social vacuum created by the final collapse of Japanese power. Several million peasants established their own moderate and radical unions; one sociologist estimated that one person in every peasant family joined such unions.[18] Korean workers formed labor unions and established workers' self-management committees collectively to operate factories and create profit-sharing schemes for employees. Labor unions, which had previously been prohibited under the Japanese, began to reconstitute themselves, and many linked up with the newly created political structures of the Committee for the Preparation of Korean Independence and, after September, the Korean (Chosŏn) People's Republic, which initially represented politicians from a wide range of political ideologies. Labor organizers, freed from prison, began to build nationwide unions. Laborers took over factories and schools that had been run by the Japanese. Local people's committees worked with the peasants and workers to end the vestiges of the colonial system. The new structures marginalized the landlords, many of whom were criticized for the injustices that accompanied the rise of colonial rule. The largely nonviolent revolutionary forces from below thus dismantled existing colonial structures and enacted fundamental political and social change. The authorities lacked the coercive power and legitimacy to oppose these efforts. As Jun Sang-In has remarked, the colonial regime collapsed in 1945, leaving "Korean landlords who had been supported by colonial powers . . . deprived of political backing."[19]

Colonial Legacies and the American Occupation

On a number of fundamental levels, these efforts conflicted with American occupation goals. One of the keys to understanding the American occupation of Korea was the ways in which American concepts and forms of political and socioeconomic modernity shaped the structures of power that were established in southern Korea. There was, in effect, a kind of clash of modernity in the southern zone of the country during the occupation. In part, this conflict can be understood as the difference between late colonial Japan's "Japanization" policies and America's postwar "Koreanization" strategy, both of which produced suffering for the Korean people, though in different ways and for different reasons. These respective sociopolitical projects were meant to make formal and informal rule over Korea compatible with Japanese and American domestic political and social models.

The late colonial "Japanization" of Korea involved indoctrinating Koreans into an ideology of empire that promoted the unity of subjects under the Japanese emperor, social controls implemented through the powers of the colonial police system, and the promulgation of legislation designed to assimilate Koreans into Japanese culture. The colonial regime passed public health and hygiene laws enforced by local police; initiated education projects designed to inculcate Japanese culture, language, and history in Korean schools; fostered the Shinto religion; ordered communications censorship and the proscription of the articulation of certain kinds of ideas, especially Korean nationalism and criticism of the emperor; and integrated elite-assimilated Koreans into regional and global networks of Japanese power, including the military, business, trade, and culture-sports.[20]

The American military government's "Koreanization" program sought to overturn not only Japan's authoritarian legacies but also the new bases of indigenous political power linked to local people's committees and the Korean People's Republic, which had been established in September 1945. The Americans imposed their own vision of modernity on southern Korea, one based in theory on inculcating democratic principles, promoting Korean culture and nationalist ideology, and, most important, establishing a Korean political system compatible with the pursuit of America's international objectives.

Politically, appeals to American ideals of liberty and justice were meant to legitimize the military government, to Americans as well as Koreans. Lieutenant General Hodge's occupation forces followed the general outlines for occupation laid down in *FM 27-5,* but also underlined something that was taken for granted in the planning document: that peoples everywhere wanted liberty, and on American terms. As provided for in the manual of military government, Hodge issued a series of proclamations and announcements to the Korean population after his forces arrived in the fall of 1945. Some of these followed upon regulations being promulgated in Tokyo. For example, the Office of the Supreme Commander Allied Powers issued a directive on October 4, 1945, that prohibited discrimination on the basis of race, nationality, religion, and political orientation. Twelve days later, in calling upon Koreans to support the military government, Hodge proclaimed that the U.S. authorities in Korea were "guided by democratic principles and not by the politics of pressure groups." The southern population was "guaranteed freedom of speech, freedom of thought, freedom of the press, freedom of worship, and freedom from official discrimination because of race, color, or creed."[21] These liberal freedoms were meant in part to address the discrimination Koreans had experienced during the colonial era. In abstract terms, politically minded Koreans associated with the Korean People's Republic may have agreed with these ideals. However, they conflicted with the reality that Hodge and the military circumscribed the rights of Koreans by denying the legitimacy of the Korean People's Republic and by saying that the only authorized government in the country was the one brought about under American auspices. In October, Hodge told the Korean people that "political parties who have the interest of Korea and its inhabitants at heart must give first support to establishment of government and a sound economy by United States forces. After that is established comes the time for personal groupings, and opinions to be expressed in the formation of political parties."[22] By this point, his troops had begun to dismantle and contain the Korean People's Republic.

The reality on the ground was that Hodge and American officials were following the advice of a narrow group of Koreans who had represented the elite under Japanese rule. The prominent Koreans with whom the military government worked tended to come from the elite circles of the colonial era. The political adviser in Korea, H. Merrill Benninghoff, recognized that Koreans wanted radical changes in the country's sociopolitical structure. He reported to Secretary of State James Byrnes on September 15 that the southern part of the country was a "powder keg" and that Korea was "completely ripe for agitators." Nevertheless, "the single most encouraging factor in the political situation is the presence in Seoul of several hundred conservatives among the older and better-educated Koreans. Although many of them have served with the Japanese, that stigma ought eventually to disappear."[23]

This is not to say that Americans did not reform the existing political or economic system. They did. News releases in the initial months of the occupation are replete with information about how many Japanese were being removed from positions of power in the bureaucracy, factories, businesses, and the educational system. In announcing the takeover of the Oriental Developmental Company, for example, the establishment's new director, Major Wayne J. Estes, proclaimed that 600 Japanese workers had been removed from their jobs. The Japanese management, the major asserted, had used its ¥1 billion in assets "to crush the Korean people and control the economy of Korea."[24] Such statements, though reflecting sympathy with the plight of Koreans under Japanese colonialism, did not meet the demands of most Koreans at the time, because control of the major assets of Japanese colonialism was now in the hands of the new occupying power working with many of the former Korean colonial elite. It is in this sense that the legacies of colonialism continued into the postwar era through U.S. military occupation policies. And this was precisely what many Koreans objected to in the early years of the occupation.

To facilitate the consolidation of U.S. authority in southern Korea, the military government established an Advisory Council made up of members of the conservative elite who had worked closely with the Japanese colonial administration, and who were members of, or intimately affiliated with, the Korea Democratic Party. The chairperson of the council, Kim Sŏng-su, had looked to the Meiji statesman Okuma Shigenobu (1838–1922) as a model, and had held a prominent position within the Japanese Central Council during World War II.[25] Thus, even though Japanese administrators were purged from power, they were replaced by Koreans who had had some affiliation with the colonial regime or some connection with the Korea Democratic Party. Such was the case with the first American-appointed mayor of Seoul, Yi (Lee) Pŏm-sŭng, a legal studies graduate of Kyoto Imperial University, whom Military Governor Archibald Arnold appointed with the advice of Korean conservatives in the fall of 1945. When the president of the Seoul Citizens' Committee, Ch'oe Wŏn-t'aek, protested that the new mayor had collaborated with the Japanese and did not have the confidence of the general public, the military government ordered Ch'oe to submit evidence of his accusation. He refused, and was twice sentenced to perform hard labor for violating the order and failing to substantiate his accusations, which were printed in the leftist newspaper *Chosŏn inmin-bo.* The military regime increased his initial sentence of two months of hard labor to eleven months, and ordered him to pay a fine of ¥12,000.[26] The occupation perpetuated important vestiges of colonialism; the military government removed Japanese representatives of colonial rule while maintaining a significant degree of its Korean core. By late 1945, those prosecuted by the American military government for political reasons had protested policies reinforcing the legacies of colonial rule. By contrast, the occupying authorities worked through or protected many Koreans who had collaborated with the Japanese.

This was perhaps nowhere more true than with the police force. Military officials strengthened the pre-1945 national police system, changing what had been a somewhat decentralized structure into one that had a nationwide coordinated base of operations. This was done so that the police could deal more effectively with the "disorder" associated with the occupation. Only about 15 percent of the Korean police who had served the Japanese remained outside the American-sponsored police system.[27] In November 1945, the military government placed the police under the authority of the newly created Office of the Director of National Defense. Symbolically, the Americans did ask a Korean to redesign the old Japanese police uniform, and the new style resembled uniforms worn by police in New York State. But the black cloth used to make the uniform came from the presurrender era; the symbols of American power and modernity took the place of deeper political change, something recognized by Koreans at the time. The explosion of violence during the autumn 1946 urban and peasant uprisings occurred in part because of these policies pursued by the American military government. During the tumultuous months of September and October, police were often targets of vicious attacks by Koreans acting in response to the repression and violence meted out by the police in colonial and postcolonial times.

Legacies of Occupation: Modernity's "Ization"

The colonial past and the theme of collaboration were very important issues during the U.S. occupation, for both Koreans and Americans.[28] But these issues went beyond Korea itself, and together they embodied one of the central dilemmas of American foreign policy in the early Cold War: how the imperatives of containment resulted in compromises with processes associated with decolonization and independence. Ironically, by late 1947, high-ranking American officials like Lieutenant General Albert C. Wedemeyer were criticizing the Korean police as "another obstacle to the attainment of American objectives" in southern Korea.[29] In his September 1947 report to President Harry S. Truman on the Korean political situation, he wrote that "so long as there is no reform of the present police system and police brutality and partisanship continue, there seems to be little hope that a government can be established fully representative of the freely expressed will of the Korean people in South Korea." The central problem, he argued, was the dearth of Koreans to replace those who had worked for the Japanese colonial administration. The Korean police were "increasing the shift of Korean political thinking to the left," and this had "an important effect both on the attainment of American objectives in Korea and on the prestige of the United States."[30] Here, in microcosm, was a contradiction that was already afflicting the American Cold War strategy in other parts of the world, and especially in Indochina: how to contain the left in areas where the local security forces were associated with repressive colonial rule. In Korea, Americans supported the colonial police, and in Indochina they provided for the French colonial army. Yet the difference between Korea and Vietnam was that in Korea, the American military forced the colonizer out of the occupied territory. Had they not done this, the security situation in Korea would have been far worse, and the left in the north and south would have been even more successful in gaining the support of the population. One of the key failures of the United States in Vietnam was its support of French forces in the colony. The decision to back the French compromised America's efforts to roll back Communism in Southeast Asia from the start. The Japanese colonizers left Korea as a result of an American war with Japan; in Vietnam, it was the Communist armies that defeated the French. The United States thus went into Vietnam not as victor over colonialism but as the successor to French colonialism, and it proceeded to supplant one form of colonial domination with another variant of empire. The United States maintained its own informal empire in Korea, but under different circumstances and with dissimilar consequences.[31]

Wedemeyer's report to Truman came at an important transition period in the U.S. occupation, one associated with efforts by the United States to create a provisional government. Wedemeyer wrote in the aftermath of the Truman Doctrine, the launching of the Marshall Plan, and the United States' introduction of the "Korean Question" to the United Nations General Assembly. His letter thus followed major efforts to rehabilitate the global capitalist economy and to contain international Communism. The United States' strategy now keyed on the establishment of a separate South Korean state. By this time, as though in anticipation of the future, American occupation officials commonly referred to southern Korea as "South Korea." A preliminary step toward creating a provisional government had been taken in November 1946, when the military authorities created an interim National Assembly. In the context of these events, officials paid lip service to concepts of political modernity and to the ideals of Western-style democracy. In fact, however, the elections for the Assembly were held under terms consistent with colonial electoral laws and political culture—what Hodge himself referred to as "the old Korean system of election." The general pointed out that the system could "only produce a Rightist group," because "family heads get together and select a couple of delegates to vote in the next higher echelon, etc., up for three echelons to get the final representatives for the Legislature."[32] Hodge's statement may have reflected a limited degree of disappointment with the process of establishing a new government for the south, because the military government had hoped to include anticommunist moderates in the new Korean political structure.

Below the surface of rhetoric, officials came to focus on what they called "Koreanization." As General Wedemeyer wrote, "Culturally, as well as politically, efforts have been made to carry out a process of 'Koreanization' looking toward a free and independent Korea."[33] If we consider the ending "ization" as a process of becoming something or making into, we can see that this particular U.S. version of modernization was associated with a specific developmental project that was political in character. "Koreanization" thus was a reference to ensuring that the Koreans who led an "independent" government would further the political containment objectives introduced by the occupying forces on the Korean Peninsula. Lieutenant General Hodge made this point in a speech in November 1946, when he argued that the new Korean Assembly was "a truly democratic agency that should be welcomed by all Koreans with democratic ideas." Those who opposed the Assembly were a minority of the population, "vicious agitators who seek to establish a reign of terror and destruction in the beautiful 'Land of the Morning Calm.'"[34] The "ization," in other words, was a kind of code for a proxy partner in a given political project. In October 1947, Hodge told Undersecretary of War William Draper that the military government had "gradually worked out what we called the Koreanization Program to where we have a situation now where the Koreans are nominally the head of the various departments, bureaus, and sections, and are governors, mayors of the cities, etc., and the Americans act as advisors. In some cases that is actual; in other cases the American still has to handle it himself to a great extent."[35] The implication of this statement was that once the "ization" process was completed, American forces would be permitted to leave the territory, confident that their mission had achieved its goals.

The "ization" process is particularly well suited to America's own version of empire—the occupation—and that the term has a historical genealogy. In the early 1930s, U.S. officials associated with the occupation of Haiti spoke of "Haitianization" when they referred to the need to create a government that could take over from the occupying army. Similarly, Americans spoke of "Vietnamization" in the early 1970s in the aftermath of President Richard Nixon's decision to pull American troops out of Indochina. In other words, the "ization" process was introduced at critical junctures of occupation and conflict, and thus represented an effort to resolve some sort of specific crisis associated with occupation. "Ization" emerged when a policy to deal with the crisis had been formulated, and when policymakers thought there was some success in achieving it.

Furthermore, though the transformative powers of "ization" have important implications for our understanding of U.S. policy in the Cold War in Asia, the use of the term more generally suggests that we should, in approaching the Cold War in Asia, also understand it from perspectives that reach beyond the regional history of Asia and engage aspects of global history and America's world mission since the late nineteenth century. That the term seems to have been used only in the context of occupations in the developing world also is significant, for it illustrates that the perceived "status" of the territory being politically transformed shaped the rhetoric and policy of the occupiers. That is, "ization" cases were meant to be or possibly remain at a particular level of socioeconomic development. Germany and Japan, conversely, were not "ization" cases, and so "ization" was targeted only for the developing world, and for states that would retain a subordinate status within a global capitalist framework.

Modernity in Occupied Korea

The military government was involved in a full range of government activities, from establishing policies for the post office and road building to commerce and cultural exchanges. The "modernity" that the American military government introduced to Korea, however, was mediated and shaped by colonial legacies. This was true in endeavors outside purely security-related functions. Public health and education were also targeted for reform by the military government.

The military, for example, attempted to legitimize the occupation through its work in medical and scientific fields. Vaccines were imported from America, and people were inoculated for diseases like typhoid. Soldiers also introduced modern forestry methods and seed-planting techniques to the south; they talked about problems associated with soil erosion and fuel—all part of the program to revamp the colonial era and to introduce a new version of "scientific" modernity and progress to the Korean people. The military government also emphasized training. Korean doctors were sent to the United States, and American educators came to Korea to make recommendations about reforming the educational curriculum and teaching. The U.S. military did make important structural changes in how the state dealt with education. As Gregg Brazinsky has argued, "Americans and Koreans agreed on the urgency of increasing educational opportunities for all South Koreans and expunging Japanese influence over their schools."[36] Under the occupation, almost a million more children were able to attend primary school, compared with the numbers during the colonial era. The newly evolving state structure did allow greater access to education, and instruction placed emphasis on the ideology of democratic governance and the importance of modern science and technology for contemporary society.[37] Even in these fields, however, U.S. efforts were influenced by colonial trajectories. Na-mi Yi (Lee), for example, has argued that in the field of education, Americans recruited Korean collaborators, and that their main goal was not to educate the population but to create passive and obedient citizens who supported the anticommunist cause in the Cold War.[38]

Social expressions of modernity under the American occupation also included forms of entertainment such as sports and radio broadcasting. As a means of encouraging exercise, getting Korean support for the military government, and perhaps most significantly, fostering a sense of pride in the emerging Korean nation-state, American officials organized sporting events for the Koreans, including boxing, baseball, and basketball matches. The military also eliminated Japanese news programs from the radio waves of the Radio Corporation of Chosŏn. Some news, however, continued to be broadcast in Japanese.[39]

The promotion of sports events and entertainment was part of a broader effort to inculcate feelings of Korean nationalism and identity. In the cultural sphere, the American military government overturned Japanese legislation that had required Koreans to use Japanese names, and legalized the use of Korean names in property transactions and legal documents. The occupation authorities also supported the propagation of Korean mythological history. In October 1946, for example, the government set aside a special holiday called the National Foundation Day for Tangun, a mythical being associated with the beginnings of Korean "civilization." To publicize the event, schoolchildren were encouraged to participate in celebrations.[40]

These activities were accompanied by some strained efforts to promote democracy in Korea. In his examination of postwar United States–Korea relations, Brazinsky has underlined the roles that Americans and Koreans have played in shaping the character of modern Korean democracy. In the period under study, he argues that the pursuit of America's hegemonic objectives in Korea led to an emphasis on security issues that undermined efforts to pursue democratization.[41] Concepts of empire, however, are absent from his analysis. American policy in Korea was not only hegemonic but also intimately linked to the evolution of the longue durée of America's informal global empire; additionally, the American decision to occupy Korea must be viewed in the framework of the tremendous violence and suffering that occurred in Korea and other parts of Northeast Asia in the decade following World War II.

The Korean War and the Second Occupation of Korea, 1950–55

The Republic of Korea was established in August 1948, but the country's new president, Syngman Rhee, a conservative and anti-Japanese nationalist, did not welcome the departure of American troops from Korea in mid-1949. Rhee had had a troubled and conflicted relationship with the occupation authorities, particularly Lieutenant General John Hodge, largely because of Rhee's opposition to the 1945 Moscow agreement and trusteeship for Korea.

The logic of containment had led to an American commitment to the Rhee regime, partly through the signing in December 1948 of a bilateral economic aid package. But Rhee wanted a formal U.S. commitment to the Korean Peninsula, and he continued his efforts to get American support for a military-backed, South Korean–led unification of the peninsula. The northern attack in June 1950 and the decision by the United States to enter the conflict constituted a momentous event in the history of southern Korea, for without American support the state would have ceased to exist. The U.S. intervention also brought with it another occupation, once again under the auspices of the American military—this time the U.S. Eighth Army—and various civil affairs teams. The literature on the war generally does not view the conflict in the context of an occupation. Histories of the fighting have been more concerned with the war's origins, with the conflict's impact on rearmament, and, more recently, with Stalin's and Mao's roles in wartime diplomacy. The political and great power dimensions of the war have thus taken precedence over its social meanings. Approaching the Korean War from the point of view of occupation reverses this priority and makes possible an understanding of the impact of the struggle from the point of view of Korean civilians and their interactions with American military officials and soldiers. It leads, in other words, to a better understanding of how the Cold War in Asia shaped the lives of Koreans.

The context of the second occupation was very different from that of the first. In 1945, U.S. soldiers took their positions in Seoul and in the southern provinces at a time when no formal fighting was going on. The second occupation, particularly in its initial phases, occurred in the chaos of war, with the massive movements of refugees and rapidly changing front lines. The goals of the occupation were also different. The United States had in 1948 recognized South Korea as a sovereign state, though in practice the wartime emergency significantly curtailed the Republic of Korea's authority, and an agreement between President Rhee and the United Nations Command early in the war left strategic control of the Korean armed forces with the United States–UN Command officers.

In 1950, Korea became a protectorate of the United States. Although a successful counteroffensive against Communist forces in 1950 would have led to detailed policies regarding the establishment of a new government for all Korea, the intervention of the Chinese in the late fall prevented U.S. officials from implementing a long-term strategy for the occupation of the north and linking it to the southern regime. However, during the short period when the United Nations' forces did occupy North Korea, the United States refused to recognize the area as constitutionally part of the Republic of Korea, and this led to conflict with President Rhee, who declared that it was part of the southern government's sovereign territory. The role of the United Nations in the Korean War also distinguished it from the first American occupation. Formally, civil affairs teams were supposed to be made up of the armies of the United Nations, and the civil affairs command in the second occupation was referred to as the United Nations Civil Assistance Command, Korea (UNCACK). In reality, however, this was effectively a designation for the American Eighth Army, and civil affairs teams were overwhelmingly made up of American soldiers from the 8,201st unit of that army.

Suffering Modernity: Wartime Korea

Recent research on Korean modernization has stressed the significance of the New Deal in shaping the history of American development projects around the world. As David Ekbladh has pointed out, this was true for Korea in the 1950s.[42] In fact, "modernization" was a central concern of the American military during both occupations. In Korea, one of the projects with which the military was closely associated was the production of electrical power. The lack of electricity in southern Korea was a legacy of the first occupation, and the issue was closely tied to the rivalry between the two Koreas in the late occupation period. Kim Il Sung had played a prominent role in cutting off the northern supply of electricity to the south in 1948. Within the broader context of the second occupation of the Korean Peninsula, the American military conceived of its modernization project in terms of the need to overcome the legacies of the Japanese developmental project in Korea, and planners viewed electrical power in this light. A report prepared in 1951 by the UN Command pointed out that one "aspect of Japan's industrial development of Korea which subsequently has had great significance in view of the division of the country at the 38th Parallel is that eighty-five percent of the heavy industry is in the North and seventy-five percent of the light industry is in the South." Although northern Korea had initially provided power to the south after 1945, the flow was cut in May 1948, several months before the official creation of the South Korean regime. As the report noted, "Without electricity, the economy of South Korea cannot function." The author then underlined the role of the UN Command in rehabilitating the South Korean economy and the important job that civil assistance played in that project. The section concluded on an optimistic note, saying that despite the many difficulties involved, "the outlook for 1952 is encouraging."[43]

There were many such developmental projects in Korea during the war and afterward. Between 1951 and 1955, many were planned and implemented by UNCACK. They included the rebuilding of schools, the repair of factories, the provision of food, preventive medical care, and monitoring of working and labor conditions in various businesses.[44] The goal was to restore some sort of normalcy to an abnormal and debilitating human environment. But the UN Command's public reports on these activities commonly downplayed the social dislocation and devastating psychological impact of the conflict on Koreans. Reports cited many facts and figures associated with health care, DDT spraying, inoculations, and fertilizer use, but they did not talk directly about the war's impact on the population.[45] The kind of modernity that the army projected onto Korea thus emphasized science, technology, and economic reconstruction, while denying the substantial suffering caused by the war. Reports affirmed the role of the military as provider of modern facilities, sanitation stations, vaccinations against epidemics, and housing for refugees. Though it may seem absurd in retrospect, refugees were often seen as a problem for civil affairs teams. Because civil affairs doctrine emphasized the importance of the supporting role of civil affairs in fighting a war, when refugees moved around, there was a general fear that they might hide the movements of enemy troops, or that guerrillas might be disguised as refugees. Thus a booklet titled *Civil Assistance in Korea* stated in its opening paragraph that refugees presented "a constant problem to civil assistance."[46] In the course of my research, I came across a warning sign prepared by a civil affairs team that stated refugees crossing a certain local boundary marker would be shot. This sets a context for the terrible treatment of refugees by some soldiers in the conflict, including the events of late July 1950 associated with the village of No Gun Ri, where U.S. troops killed up to four hundred South Korean refugees. The South Korean Truth and Reconciliation Commission is currently investigating more than two hundred cases where Korean civilians were attacked and killed by American forces during the Korean War.[47]

Voluntary Organizations and Christian Aid Groups in Korea

On a number of levels, the second occupation of the Korean Peninsula had a more significant psychological impact on the population than did the first. This was largely a function of the wartime context in which the occupation occurred. Between 1950 and 1955, the activities of the military and civil affairs teams paralleled, and in many cases exceeded, the efforts of the first occupation. But that impact did not come so much directly from the work of the civil affairs economic and rehabilitation teams in the field of "modernization" as from the nongovernmental organizations working with the American military and the Korean population.

The participation of nongovernmental organizations working with the American military authorities in Korea began during the first occupation. Here, then, is an important element of continuity over the 1945–55 era as a whole. Organizations that were involved in projects during the initial occupation included the Ford Foundation, which participated in educational projects, and various religious groups, which were active in numerous refugee and welfare programs.[48] The operations of nongovernmental organizations, however, expanded tremendously as a result of the conflict. The war found many more Koreans in dire need of assistance. By mid-1951, there were an estimated 4.4 million refugees in South Korea, out of a population of about 21 million. More than one year later, there were still approximately 2.7 million refugees throughout the country. In fact, the dislocation caused by the war took several decades to overcome, and its psychological effects remain powerfully embedded today in both Koreas.[49]

Groups that played a role in relief activities before the signing of the armistice in July 1953 included the Red Cross Society, the Church World Service, the Lutheran World Relief Agency, the Oriental Missionary Society, the

Cooperative for Assistance and Relief Everywhere (CARE), the Australian Presbyterian Mission, the Christian Children's Fund, the Young Women's Christian Association (YWCA), the National Catholic Welfare Conference, Save the Children Federation, the Korean Gospel Mission, the Korean Union of Seventh-Day Adventists, the Salvation Army, and the Methodist Mission. The number of agencies increased over time. Even after the armistice, more entered the Korean field. Between July 1953 and the end of June 1954, twenty-two private voluntary organizations signed up with the military civil assistance authority, now designated the Korean Civil Assistance Command. Of these twenty-two organizations, sixteen were explicitly religious in character.[50]

Given this background, a major reason why Korea today has a relatively large Christian population is explained by this wartime context for aid and conversion. The spread of Christianity and Western values in Korea was directly related to the role that voluntary aid groups and Christian missionaries played in providing direct aid to suffering Koreans during and immediately after the war. Such voluntary work carried with it a number of other ideological assumptions and predispositions, so to some extent the war appears to have done what the first occupation failed to do: establish a stronger sense of an American-Korean, or, more generally, a Korean-Western partnership at the grassroots level. The increased numbers of Korean conversions to Christianity would attest, for example, to greater belief in Cold War ideology and democracy, which was supposed to have been established by the American military government by 1948.

Korean Christian ministers played an important role in these conversions. In the modern era, Koreans had been trained by Western missionaries as church leaders since the late nineteenth century, and during the Korean conflict Koreans associated with various church groups became involved in refugee relief activities, for example, by establishing refugee stations or children's homes to provide aid and to attempt to convert those being cared for. One Korean Pastor, Yi (Lee) Chŏng-ho, who was originally from northern Korea, wrote to his benefactors in the United States that he and the 398 orphans under his care "have experienced how Communism is cruel. So that I have been teaching the orphans that the democracy can bring happiness and freedom to the human being. And I have been doing my best to make these orphans faithful Christians."[51]

After the Korean War, private relief agencies and nongovernmental organizations continued to play a major role in the civil affairs activities of the U.S. Army. This was true, for example, in the Vietnam War. Today, civil affairs teams establish close links with voluntary organizations in the areas where they operate. In this way, the Korean War shaped the longer-term evolution of U.S.

policies in the Cold War in Asia, and more generally in occupied areas around the world.

The Significance of the American Commitment to Korea for the Cold War in Asia

When U.S. troops left Korea in 1949, planners at the Department of Defense believed that Korea would be a peripheral part of any wider conflict with the Soviet Union. As a result of the experience during the Korean War, American strategic thinking about Korea's place in the international system changed radically. By 1953, Korea was a frontline state in the containment strategy of the United States; and by 1958, the United States had stationed atomic weapons on the Korean Peninsula.

This newfound commitment also had significant implications for the subsequent history of the Cold War in Asia, for it changed the trajectory of the pre-1950 "defensive perimeter" strategy. After 1953, policymakers in the United States did not approach Northeastern Asia from the strategic point of view of an island chain in the Pacific based on Japan, the Ryukyus, Taiwan, and Indonesia. Rather, their policies were intricately tied up in the containment of the Sino-Soviet alliance in Eurasia. For the first time, the United States formally and publicly committed its prestige to defend parts of continental Asia. In this sense, U.S. intervention in the Korean conflict created a precedent for American involvement in Vietnam, for it was in the aftermath of the Korean War that U.S. bureaucrats and politicians turned their attention to Southeast Asia. The lessons of that war were very much in mind as they did so, and their experiences in Korea played a vital role in how they approached Vietnam for the next three decades.

The conflict also had a significant impact on South Korean concepts of rollback and containment, and on its diplomacy in Asia as a whole. Syngman Rhee, now prevented by the UN Command from initiating a second Korean War, looked to Vietnam and Taiwan as possible alternative sites where he might be able to play out his own rollback strategies in Asia. Though he held periodic meetings with Chiang Kai-shek, his preferred strategy by 1953 was to focus on Vietnam. In April 1954, in the context of the opening of the Geneva discussions on Korea and Indochina, he offered the U.S. government Korean troops for the conflict in Southeast Asia. In July, he offered the American ambassador in Seoul three Korean divisions, saying that "Koreans cannot survive in Communist-dominated Asia."[52] Although the Dwight Eisenhower administration rejected this offer, it served as a precedent for South Korea's substantial participation in the Vietnam conflict in the 1960s.

Conclusion

This chapter has underlined new ways to approach the study of the Cold War in Asia. It has argued that the United States did not occupy Korea once but twice in a period of ten years, and that Korea was thus unique in experiencing a dual occupation. The second occupation, which occurred in traumatic circumstances, was crucial in shaping Koreans' worldview and their attitudes about the Cold War. It was only in the aftermath of the Korean War that something more closely resembling a Cold War consensus appeared in the Republic of Korea. The chapter has also uncovered some of the neglected aspects of the social history of Korea's Cold War. As Frederick Cooper has recently commented, "Empires were big and had long communications routes; they depended on a range of agents, on missionaries, settlers, and fortune-seekers and on local elites who could find an interest in imperial circuits of commerce and power."[53] I would add military officials to his list of agents. Indeed, the two American occupations of Korea between 1945 and 1955 highlight important aspects of this social history of empire, particularly the role that the U.S. Army and nongovernmental organizations played in influencing Koreans' daily lives. If we consider these early occupations in light of the U.S. military presence in South Korea today, we could make a strong case that no country in Asia has been more affected by American soldiers than South Korea. This chapter has also shown how the United States' policy toward the Korean Peninsula after 1945 established some of the foundations for America's longer-term regional containment strategies for Northeast as well as Southeast Asia. Finally, it suggests that examining the post-1945 history of Asia alone is not a fully adequate way of understanding the broader dimensions of the Cold War in that region of the world. The dynamics of global history also affected the trajectory of the superpower conflict for spheres of influence, and the pre-1945 history of the American empire also needs to be considered in our evaluation of how U.S. policymakers reacted to and shaped the momentous events in Asia in the first postwar decade.

Notes

1. See, e.g., Bruce Cumings, *The Origins of the Korean War, Liberation and the Emergence of Separate Regimes 1945–1947* (Princeton, N.J.: Princeton University Press, 1981); James Matray, *The Reluctant Crusade: American Foreign Policy in Korea, 1941–1950* (Honolulu: University of Hawaii Press, 1985); Jun Sang-In, "State-Making in South Korea, 1945–48: U.S. Occupation and Korean Development," PhD thesis, Brown University, 1991; Hyung-kook Kim, *The Division of Korea and the Alliance-Making Process: Internationalization of Internal Conflict and Internalization of International Struggle, 1945–1948* (Lanham, Md.: University Press of America,

1995); Han Hung-su et al., *Han'guk hyondaesa ui chae insik 1: haebang chongguk kwa Mi-So kunjong* [Rethinking modern Korean history 1: The political situation of Korea shortly after its liberation vis-à-vis the U.S. and Soviet governments] (Seoul: Han'guk chongsin munhwa yon'guwon, 1998); Han Hung-su et al., *Han'guk hyondaesa ui chae insik 2: chongbu surip kwa chehon kukhoe* [Rethinking modern Korean history 2: The establishment of Korea and the Constituent National Assembly] (Seoul: Han'guk chongsin munhwa yon'guwon, 1998); Steven Hugh Lee, *The Korean War* (London: Longman, 2001); and Bonnie Oh, ed., *Korea under the American Military Government, 1945–1948* (Westport, Conn.: Praeger, 2002).

2. For a sampling of the historiography on American occupations prior to 1945, see Louis A. Perez, *Cuba between Empires, 1878–1902* (Pittsburgh: University of Pittsburgh Press, 1998); Jose Trias Monge, *Puerto Rico: The Trials of the Oldest Colony in the World* (New Haven, Conn.: Yale University Press, 1997); Bruce J. Calder, *The Impact of Intervention: The Dominican Republic during the U.S. Occupation of 1916–1924* (Austin: University of Texas Press, 1984); and Hans Schmidt, *The United States Occupation of Haiti, 1915–1934* (New Brunswick, N.J.: Rutgers University Press, 1995). For an overview of the American occupation of Beijing during the Boxer Rebellion, see Michael Hunt, "The Forgotten Occupation: Peking, 1900–1901," *Pacific Historical Review,* November 1979, 501–29.

3. The American occupations of Puerto Rico, Guam, and Tutuila (in American Samoa) were different in this respect, because they did not lead to independence for these territories.

4. "*FM*" stands for "*Field Manual,*" and "*27*" is an arbitrary number associated with issues of military law. The manual was thus meant to establish a legal framework for occupation.

5. E.g., Section 9b spoke of the need for "just, considerate and mild treatment of the governed by the occupying army," because such a policy would "convert enemies into friends." See Carl J. Friedrich, "Military Government as a Step toward Self-Rule," *Public Opinion Quarterly,* Winter 1943, 528 n. 1.

6. The military phased out the *FM 27-5* series in the early Cold War era, replacing it in 1954 with a new number designation, *FM 41,* which dealt specifically with "civil affairs" issues in occupied territory. The new manual provided a detailed description of the role of civil affairs, but it lacked the broad frame for occupation policy that was discussed in the *FM 27-5* series. Those themes are now dealt with in national security memos, but the key underlying assumptions underpinning occupation strategy remain the same. A recent edition of the civil affairs field manual is *FM 3-05.401* (2003); it has been revised in light of American occupation experiences in the 1990s and early 2000s, and is called "Civil Affairs Tactics, Techniques, and Procedures."

7. *United States Army and Navy Manual of Military Government,* December 22, 1943, 9.

8. Ibid., 10.

9. Ibid., 36.

10. U.S. troops remained in South Korea until June 1949, but after August 1948 formal sovereignty rested with the Republic of Korea.

11. For a discussion of Korea, see Jun, "State-Making in South Korea," 182–85. The military government began to appoint American provincial governors in southern Korea in late October 1945.

12. See Holger H. Herwig, *Hammer or Anvil? Modern Germany 1648–Present* (Lexington, Mass.: D.C. Heath, 1994), 361; and Richard B. Finn, *Winners in Peace: MacArthur, Yoshida, and Postwar Japan* (Berkeley: University of California Press, 1992), 83. In December 1945, there were about 100,000 Germans in American military prisons in western Germany. The purge in Germany was much more thorough, at least before 1947, than that undertaken in Japan; we must also take into account that the U.S. zone of Germany had a population of about 17 million, whereas Japan had 72 million.

13. Howard B. Schonberger, *Aftermath of War: Americans and the Remaking of Japan, 1945–1952* (Kent, Ohio: Kent State University Press, 1989), 48.

14. Earl F. Zeimke. *The U.S. Army in the Occupation of Germany* (Washington, D.C.: Center of Military History, U.S. Army, 1990), 103.

15. Carolyn Eisenberg, *Drawing the Line: The American Decision to Divide Germany, 1944–1949* (Cambridge: Cambridge University Press, 1996), chap. 3.

16. Military commanders chose the Twenty-fourth Army Corps because of its close proximity to Korea—it was stationed in the Ryukyu Islands at the time.

17. "Outline History of the Department of Commerce, 1945–1948," n.d., RG 332, box 13, National Archives and Records Administration (hereafter NARA).

18. Gi-Wook Shin, *Peasant Protest and Social Change in Colonial Korea* (Seattle: University of Washington Press, 1996), 145.

19. Jun, "State-Making in South Korea," chap. 4; the quotation is on 127.

20. For discussions of Korea's colonial modernity, see Gi-Wook Shin and Michael Robinson, eds., *Colonial Modernity in Korea* (Cambridge, Mass.: Harvard University Asia Center, 1999); Michael E. Robinson, "Colonial Publication Policy and the Korean Nationalist Movement," in *The Japanese Colonial Empire, 1895–1945,* ed. Ramon Myers and Mark R. Peattie (Princeton, N.J.: Princeton University Press, 1984), 312–46; and Theodore Jun Yoo, *The Politics of Gender in Colonial Korea: Education, Labor, and Health, 1910–1945* (Berkeley: University of California Press, 2008).

21. "Historical Journal, Press Release, October 16, 1945," RG 332, box 27, NARA.

22. Ibid.

23. U.S. Department of State, *Foreign Relations of the United States* (hereafter *FRUS*), vol. VI (Washington, D.C.: U.S. Government Printing Office, 1969), 1049–50.

24. "Historical Journal, Press Release, October 18, 1945," RG 332, box 27, NARA.

25. Carter J. Eckert, *Offspring of Empire: The Koch'ang Kims and the Colonial Origins of Korean Capitalism, 1876–1945* (Seattle: University of Washington Press, 1991), 36; Jun, "State-Making in South Korea," 148–49.

26. "Historical Journal, Press Release, November 10, 1945," RG 332, box 27, NARA. Lee had worked with the colonial regime in forestry and agriculture and had been appointed commissioner of Hwang Hae Province in the 1920s before resigning his position. In September 1945, he became chief of police of Yang Ju County. Interestingly, the current Web site for mayors of Seoul does not list him as a former mayor; see http://english.seoul.go.kr/gover/office/office_06suc.htm. This is because the military government recognized Seoul as an independent city with provincial status only on September 28, 1946, the date linked to the start of the tenure of the first formal postwar mayor of the city, Kim Hyong-min. The controversy associated with Mayor Lee, however, has subsequently been erased from the official historical record.

27. Jun, "State-Making in South Korea," 191.

28. For another discussion of the relationship between modernity and "ization," see Frederick Cooper, *Colonialism in Question: Theory, Knowledge, History* (Berkeley: University of California Press, 2005), 117–19. This chapter, however, was written before I read Cooper's book.

29. *FRUS,* 1947, VI, 798.

30. Ibid.

31. For more on the character of the American empire in Korea and Vietnam, see Steven Hugh Lee, *Outposts of Empire: Korea, Vietnam, and the Origins of the Cold War in Asia, 1949–1954* (Montreal: McGill–Queen's University Press, 1995).

32. Records of Provisional Government, "Orientation for Undersecretary of the Army," September 23, 1947, RG 332, box 29, NARA.

33. *FRUS,* 1947, VI, 800.

34. Special Press Releases, 1946, "Statement by Lieutenant General John R. Hodge," November 11, 1946, RG 332, box 24, NARA.

35. Records of Provisional Government, "Orientation for Undersecretary of the Army," RG332, box 29, NARA.

36. Gregg Brazinsky, *Nation Building in South Korea: Koreans, Americans, and the Making of a Democracy* (Chapel Hill: University of North Carolina Press, 2007), 42.

37. See David Ekbladh, "A Workshop for the World: Modernization as a Tool of U.S. Foreign Relations in Asia, 1914–1973," PhD dissertation, Columbia University, 2003, 179–84.

38. Na-mi Yi (Lee), "Migunchonggi ui minjujuui kyoyuk: Ilche sigi wa ui Yonsok-song ul chungsimuro" [The American military government's education in Korea: With a focus on prolongation of Japanese colonialism], *Tongyang chongch'i sasangsa* [Asian Political Thought] 3, no. 1 (2004): 197–220.

39. Ibid. This was a "national" station, with local affiliates and transmitters in Seoul, Pusan, Kwangju, Masan, Chunchon, Chongju, Taegu, Mokp'o, and other cities. Japanese news generally followed broadcasts in Korean. News in Korean and in Japanese was given equal radio time.

40. General Headquarters, Commander-in-Chief, U.S. Army Forces, Pacific, *United States Military Government Activities in Korea,* Summation 13, October 1946, 79.

41. See Brazinsky, *Nation Building in South Korea,* chap. 1, "Security Over Democracy."

42. See Ekbladh, "Workshop for the World." For a discussion of the role of the New Deal in shaping America's foreign policy goals during World War II, see Elizabeth Borgwardt, *A New Deal for the World: America's Vision for Human Rights* (Cambridge, Mass.: Harvard University Press, 2005).

43. United Nations Command, "Civilian Relief and Economic Aid—Korea," July 7, 1950–September 30, 1951, RG 59, box 6498, National Archives of Canada.

44. For a study of UNCACK-KCAC activities in public health during the war, see Ho Un, "1950 nyondae chonban Miguk ui 'saengch'e chongch'i' wa Han'guk sahoe hegemoni kuch'uk—Chuhan Migun minsagiku ui hwaldong kwa songkyok" [The bio-politics practiced by the United States during the early 1950s and the establishment of its hegemony over Korean society—With a special focus on the activities and characteristics of the Korean Civil Assistance Command] *Han'guksa yon'gu* [Journal of Korean history], 2006, 175–210.

45. Ibid.

46. *Civil Assistance in Korea,* n.d. (but published around the summer or fall of 1951), RG 407, box 1214, NARA.

47. See Truth and Reconciliation Commission, Republic of Korea, "1,222 Incidents Classified as Genocides," http://www.jinsil.go.kr/English/Information/general/news_01/old_05.asp.

48. The first shipment of 60,000 Bibles printed in Hangul, the Korean alphabet, arrived in Korea in May 1947. Shortages of paper and printing facilities prevented them from being published in Korea, and they were published in the United States by the American Bible Society, a nondenominational organization. U.S. Military Government in Korea, Press Release, May 27, 1947, RG 332, box 24, NARA.

49. "Civil Assistance in Korea"; and United Nations Command, "United Nations Civil Affairs Activities in Korea," October 1952, 66, RG 407, box 1407, NARA.

50. United Nations Command, "Civil Assistance and Economic Affairs–Korea," July 1, 1953–June 30, 1954, RG 469, box 21, NARA.

51. Yi (Lee) Chong-ho to Sigma Club, Ohio State University, February 17, 1954, CARE Collection, New York Public Library. His "presents" were sent to him through agents of CARE in Korea.

52. Donald Stone Macdonald, *U.S.-Korean Relations from Liberation to Self-Reliance: The Twenty-Year Record* (Boulder, Colo.: Westview Press, 1992), 109.

53. Cooper, *Colonialism in Question,* 200–201. His book tends to discuss the theme of empire in relation to Europe, and he concludes that "the most important fact about empires is that they are gone," a point with which this chapter would not agree.

5. Kim Il Sung's Balancing Act between Moscow and Beijing, 1956–1972

Nobuo Shimotomai

The year 1956 was a decisive turning point in Cold War history. Nikita Khrushchev's famous denunciation of Joseph Stalin at the Twentieth Party Congress of the Communist Party of the Soviet Union (CPSU) triggered a chain reaction all over the world, especially in many Communist countries, and the Democratic People's Republic of Korea (DPRK) was no exception. However, the extent to which a campaign against Kim Il Sung's "cult of personality" was organized in response to Khrushchev's de-Stalinization has not been well studied until recently.[1]

At the August 1956 Plenum of the Korean Workers' Party (KWP), a group of high-ranking officials headed by vice prime ministers Pak Ch'ang-ok and Choe Ch'ang-ik organized a movement against the cult of Kim, but they were immediately purged from the leadership. Four officials fled to the People's Republic of China (PRC). This event apparently frightened officials in both Beijing and Moscow, because this was the first upheaval in Asia following the Eastern European political turmoil caused by the de-Stalinization campaign. Worried about this situation, both the Soviet and Chinese Communist parties organized a joint delegation, headed by Anastas Mikoyan and Peng Dehuai, which arrived in Pyongyang on September 23. Under their pressure, at the September Plenum of the KWP, Kim Il Sung reluctantly had to accept his Big Brothers' advice and restore party membership to Pak and Choe. It seems that Kim's foreign "friends" might have contemplated more drastic measures, including a purge of Kim himself. In fact, he came very close to being ousted from power. The events of August and September 1956 proved to have a decisive influence on Kim's relationship with the Soviet Union and China for years to come.

It was the Eastern European democratization movement of October and November 1956 that saved the North Korean dictator. The Hungarian and Polish revolts in October became the main concerns of both Moscow and Beijing. The CPSU subsequently declared that Communist parties all over the world were autonomous, and thus lessened the pressure on Pyongyang, eventually saving Kim's political life.

The August-September incident traumatized Kim Il Sung, and after September 1956 he began to exercise greater autonomy and independence vis-à-vis his "brother" countries. In the domestic arena, the intervention propelled him to establish a heavily authoritarian political system, purging all kinds of "deviationists" and potential rivals from leadership positions. This was not limited to the elite; society as a whole was subjugated to Kim's will and mobilized to promote his cause. As a result, the ideology of *chuche,* roughly meaning "autonomy," emerged by the late 1950s and 1960s.

This chapter examines how Kim Il Sung maneuvered between Moscow and Beijing, exploiting the emerging Sino-Soviet conflict, in order to consolidate his power and pursue his own foreign policy. For Pyongyang, the Soviet Union represented the model socialist system, the liberator of 1945, and the source of economic and military assistance. Moreover, the PRC had a special, "lips and teeth" relationship with the DPRK, which had been sealed by the dispatching of the million-strong Chinese volunteer army to fight for North Korea in the hard winter of 1950. The DPRK had little know-how and resources with which to build a socialist society, and thus it had to rely heavily on the resources and expertise of its socialist neighbors. It is hard to overstate how badly Kim's regime needed food and technological assistance from China and the USSR.

The August-September 1956 incident, however, represented a defining moment for Kim Il Sung. The survival of his regime depended on North Korea's relations with its socialist neighbors, but he never forgot that they almost ousted him. He thus pursued a policy of engaging his Big Brothers without totally committing to either one of them, skillfully exploiting their widening conflict. He leaned toward one side at the expense of the other, depending on the circumstances, while domestically consolidating his power by systematically removing real and potential opponents, and regimenting the entire society under the umbrella of *chuche* thought. Because he was motivated by intense nationalism, he was determined to maintain independence by turning his position of weakness into leverage.

Although no reliable North Korean historical sources are accessible, in recent years some Russian and Eastern European sources have become available that can help us examine North Korea's relations with the Soviet Union and the PRC from 1956 to 1972. I also hope to shed light on some lesser-known but crucial background information that will help us understand this period in East Asia.

Kim Il Sung and the New Soviet Leadership before the August-September Crisis

The emerging chasm between Moscow and Pyongyang was not entirely due to Khrushchev's denunciation of Stalin's cult of personality in his February 1956 address at the Twentieth Congress of the CPSU. It originated in the immediate post-Stalin era, with Stalin's death in March 1953, when the collective leadership in Moscow decided to try a fresh approach to foreign policy. The new Kremlin leaders wanted to guide their policy with the principle of "peaceful coexistence."[2] The adoption of this new approach implied that the socialist camp no longer considered war with the "capitalist" countries inevitable, and that it could, in fact, coexist with them.

Generally speaking, Khrushchev's peaceful coexistence was unpopular among the Asian Communist countries. Both the DPRK and the PRC still had not completed their goals of national unification: all of South Korea for the DPRK, and Taiwan for the PRC, with American influence predominating in both these places. Thus, it is not surprising that Khrushchev's new approach of "peaceful coexistence" with Western capitalist countries, led by the United States, was unwelcome in Pyongyang and Beijing.

Meanwhile, as soon as the fighting in Korea had stopped, Kim Il Sung began to pursue radical domestic policies, against the wishes of Moscow and Beijing. Rather than returning to normalcy after the war, Kim intended to continue the wartime national mobilization, and he wanted to carry out rapid industrialization and collectivize agriculture along the Stalinist model in the 1930s. Alarmed by this new development, Soviet advisers recommended a somewhat moderate set of domestic policies. Even the Stalinist Viacheslav Molotov had advised Nam Il, the DPRK's foreign minister, in April 1954 that the Koreans should pay more attention to the material needs of the population.[3] However, Kim rejected the Soviet adviser's recommendations. By August 1953, he had already purged from the leadership all possible rivals who had voiced opposition to his radical policies—Pak Hŏn yŏng from the Southern faction, Hŏ Kă-ŭi from the Soviet-Koreans, and Pak Il-u from the Chinese faction. Having consolidated his power within the KWP, Kim proceeded to carry out his radical domestic policies, which resulted in the near famine of 1955. But despite these calamitous consequences of his ill-advised policies, he still wanted to adopt a program for the KWP that would put the emphasis on strengthening the "socialist base of the North" in order to liberate the "southern part of the peninsula."[4]

These initiatives were unwelcome news in Moscow, which was pursuing a policy of peaceful coexistence with Western and Asian capitalist nations. Mutual suspicions had emerged between Moscow and Pyongyang by the beginning of 1955. Khrushchev was critical of Kim Il Sung's policy of rapid industrialization and his draft KWP program, which advocated the unification of Korea, if necessary by force. Above all, the Soviet leader was alarmed by Kim's monopoly of power. Moscow advised Kim to limit his "cult of personality" and share power with other politicians, just like in Moscow, where "collective leadership" was the rule. Moscow wanted Pyongyang to adopt a new policy of "peaceful coexistence" with South Korea. Despite Moscow's advice, however, Kim adamantly clung to his hard-line policy and rejected the idea of reconciling with South Korea, as Ambassador Lim Ha told Vice Foreign Minister Nikolai Fedorenko in April 1955.[5]

A serious and widening gap had opened between the two countries, and Khrushchev urged Kim to come to Moscow in April 1955 to consult with Soviet leaders on the KWP program, as well as economic and foreign policy. Kim had advanced a draft of the new KWP program, which aimed to have socialism adopted in a united Korea by the end of 1955.[6] However, because Korea was not united, Moscow was skeptical and bluntly advised Kim to forget about adopting a new KWP program.[7] In effect, Moscow tacitly urged Kim to abandon the radical idea of "unification by force," a principle that Kim was reluctant to give up.

Another concern for Moscow was Kim's poorly executed agricultural policy of collectivization, which caused a semi-famine in rural North Korea. Moscow considered Kim's proposed Five-Year Plan (for 1957–61) too ambitious. Heavy pressure on the peasants to implement this plan resulted in a sharp decline of yields across the country, where agricultural products were always in short supply. Kim was simply copying the Stalinist strategy of rapid industrialization based on heavy industry and implemented through collectivization via highly coercive methods, which the post-Stalin Soviet leadership was encouraging Kim to discontinue.

Furthermore, the Soviet leaders were concerned about Kim's "cult of personality" and asked Kim to officially separate his government duties from his position as KWP chairman by the end of 1955. Under Moscow's heavy pressure, Kim was forced to bow to this criticism. Moscow then sent a new ambassador to Pyongyang, Vladimir Ivanov, a Leningrad CPSU apparatchik, to oversee how Kim would implement the policies recommended by Moscow.[8]

However, Moscow found it difficult to manipulate Kim. By the end of 1955, after coming back to Pyongyang, Kim began to adopt a policy of self-reliance with heavy nationalist overtones. In fact, at the December Plenum of the KWP,

Soviet-Korean intellectuals like Chŏng Lyul and Ki Sŏk-pok were harshly criticized for their alleged dismissive attitude toward Korean writers. Kim's real objective was to purge the Soviet-Koreans from leadership positions, especially from the KWP, which had largely been molded and developed by the Soviet-Korean faction. Kim criticized and reprimanded Vice Premier Pak Ch'ang-ok.[9] Of special concern was the central party apparatus, which the Soviet-Koreans had turned into a power base. Hŏ Ka-ŭi had been pushed to commit suicide in July 1953, but his successor, Pak Yŏn-bin, was another Soviet-Korean, who also had influence over personnel appointments. Pak Yŏn-bin was dismissed in April 1955. Ch'oe Yong-gŏn, an old guard partisan and Kim loyalist, who had been the nominal leader of the Democratic Party—a "fraternal party" that was controlled by the KWP—was appointed vice premier and vice chairman of the KWP in December 1955. This was a part of Kim's challenge to the Soviet-Koreans within the leadership. As Kim purged the Soviet-Koreans in the 1955 December Plenum, he brought pro-Chinese elements to the political foreground. What eventually became the famous ideology of *chuche* started as a tool used to eliminate Soviet influence on DPRK ideology and education, although the term *chuche* itself was not clearly defined until the end of the 1950s.[10]

Foreign Influence in the KWP

Khrushchev's criticism of the cult of Stalin in his speech at the Twentieth Congress of the CPSU took place against this background, and the speech dealt a devastating blow to Kim Il Sung's new course in both domestic and foreign policy. The most important issue that faced Kim's regime was the role of "foreign" elements inside the DPRK and in KWP politics. It goes without saying that China and the Soviet Union exercised considerable influence over North Korean political life. Historical ties going back to national liberation, geopolitics, and ethnic and economic considerations were all invoked by the two major powers, which used their influence to put pressure on the DPRK's domestic and foreign policies through various channels. During the initial stage of state building, the elite class of North Korea was essentially composed of people recruited from the Korean communities of the Soviet Union or China, although some South Koreans also came to North Korea between 1945 and 1948. Some 470 Soviet-Koreans played leading roles in Pyongyang, especially in creating the KWP and the organs of state power. They also had a hand in creating the North Korean military.

Also, according to Li Sang-jo, the DPRK's ambassador to Moscow in 1956, some five hundred ethnic Korean Communists came from China.[11] Chinese influence appeared strongest in the Korean Army, especially after Mao Zedong decided to intervene in the Korean War to save Kim Il Sung's regime in October 1950. In addition, more than a hundred thousand South Koreans were working in the DPRK, though they were more strictly controlled after 1953, when Pak Hŏn-yŏng, leader of the South Workers' Party and the DPRK's foreign minister, was condemned as "an American spy."[12]

Thus, foreign influence predominated in the KWP's politics at the initial stage of its life. Ho Ka-ŭi, a Soviet-Korean who had been nicknamed the "Party Doctor" because he had introduced the Soviet model of party construction, was eliminated from the KWP leadership. The next KWP secretary was again a Soviet-Korean, Pak En Bin. Soviet influence on Pyongyang's decisionmaking process seemed natural, because of the dominance of Soviet models in the realms of party organization and the economy. Also, Moscow provided all kinds of aid, including textbooks and manuals on institution building, the military, the large-scale construction of public works like the subway, and even food. North Korea was always short of food, so Soviet aid, especially staples like rice, was indispensable.

In the Shadow of 1956

It is not necessary to describe the August-September 1956 incident in detail, because it is widely known, but several key points must be noted here.[13] First, the fall of the Soviet-Korean faction by the beginning of 1956, especially its loss of control over the official ideology and the KWP, was accompanied by the gradual rise of Chinese-Korean elements within the leadership. Ch'oe Yong-gun, Kim Il Sung's comrade in arms in their guerrilla days in the 1930s, was also a member of the Chinese-Korean faction as early as August-October 1956.[14] As we have seen, this delegation, or at least the Chinese Communist Party, was inclined to try to remove Kim from power. The Chinese-Korean Communists were so deeply embedded in Pyongyang's politics, in fact, that they largely remained hidden even from the Soviet and other socialist nations' ambassadors. Many prominent Koreans, such as Kim Ch'ang-man and Lim Ha, were known for their leaning toward Beijing. The influence of the Chinese-Koreans within the KWP thus was another potential threat to Kim Il Sung's power.

Second, Khrushchev also wanted to strengthen his power among both his domestic and foreign supporters, and he was thus inclined to compromise with the Korean mini-dictator by 1957. He was perhaps motivated to restore the harmony of the Communist camp, for it had been shaken by the anti-Stalin campaign of the previous year. For his part, Kim Il Sung was not confident about his grip on the North Korean leadership. The Soviet ambassador, Aleksandr

Puzanov, who had replaced the anti-Kim Ivanov, was informed in May 1957 that Kim was still prepared to separate his role as the party chairman from that of the prime minister, as the Soviets had recommended. Kim Il, the vice premier, was supposed to be appointed premier, with Kim Il Sung remaining as KWP leader, a move apparently modeled on the Soviet separation of the party (Khrushchev) from the government (Nikolai Bulganin).[15]

However, it was Khrushchev himself who concentrated both governmental and party positions in one person by eliminating the "antiparty group" of Malenkov, Molotov, and Bulganin in June 1957. Kim Il Sung seized this opportunity to follow Khrushchev's model of power concentration. After this dramatic turn, the fortieth anniversary of the October Revolution was to be commemorated in Moscow, and Mao Zedong and Kim Il Sung were both invited to the Moscow World Communist–Workers' Party Meeting in November 1957.

Mao, for his part, sacrificed Peng Dehuai by blaming him and his personal intervention for messing up the internal affairs of the KWP in August and September 1956. Mao no longer had leverage to engage in DPRK affairs. Also, in 1956 his agenda for domestic affairs shifted from reluctant anti-Stalinism to expulsion of "right-wing elements" that were critical of the Chinese Communist Party. Thus, Mao was attempting to reach rapprochement with Kim Il Sung by using Peng as a scapegoat. After this, Ambassador Puzanov was informed by Kim that Mao had considered Peng's behavior in September 1956 an "intervention in the domestic affairs of the KWP" and that "we decided we should no longer rely on such action."[16] Iurii Andropov, then the CPSU secretary for socialist countries, assured the DPRK's ambassador that "factionists" like the former North Korean ambassador to the Soviet Union, Li Sang-jo, would be removed from Moscow to a remote city.[17] Yi, a Chinese-Korean by origin, had been an adversary of Kim in the summer of 1956. Thus, both Moscow and Beijing were anxious to conciliate Kim Il Sung by denouncing the PRC-Soviet collective pressure in the August-September events on Kim. Neither Moscow nor Beijing was interested in continuing a destabilizing de-Stalinization campaign.

All these developments gave Kim the green light to consolidate his power by 1958. Khrushchev, as we have seen, had also consolidated power in his hands by 1958, and thus he had a personal motivation not to criticize Kim's efforts to establish his sole rule. Kim eventually dismissed all potential rivals from the leadership, including Chinese-Koreans like Kim Tu-bong, by the first KWP Conference in March 1958. This timing was well chosen, for the Chinese had decided to withdraw their half-million volunteer army from the Korean Peninsula. Zhou Enlai came to Pyongyang in February 1958 to announce the withdrawal.[18] This was significant because Kim had not been very confident of his grasp on power until then, because pro-Chinese elements had been strong within the Korean Army. The withdrawal of Chinese troops meant the removal of the Chinese-Koreans' influence, which contributed to Kim's growing power.

Kim cleverly and brutally exploited the emerging tensions between Moscow and Beijing. Even such prominent elites as the chairman of the Supreme Congress, Kim Tu-bong, and the vice premier, Pak Yi-hwan, pro-Soviets who were not directly involved in the "August-September incident," became targets of attacks at the March 1958 Conference of the KWP, where they were criticized as "revisionists."[19] Those who were skeptical of Kim's abilities were regarded as "factionalists" and "revisionists," and were branded as "enemies." According to the report by Iurii Andropov to the Twenty-first CPSU Congress in January 1959, altogether 3,912 party officials were purged and eliminated.[20] This action provoked covert criticism among North Korean elites, who distributed "antiregime" leaflets, which were collected by the Soviet Embassy.[21]

Following the withdrawal of the Chinese volunteer army in November 1958, Kim strengthened his grip over the party. Interior Minister Pang Hak-se, a Soviet-Korean and Kim loyalist, informed the Soviet Embassy that prominent oppositionist figures of both Chinese and Soviet origin were arrested in November 1958.[22] Pang reported that some ten thousand elites were under investigation. By then, all the pro-Chinese and pro-Soviet elites were suspected as being a "fifth column," along with some hundred thousand southerners residing in the DPRK.[23]

All the while, antiforeign attitudes were becoming entrenched in North Korea. Almost all North Korean students who had been dispatched to socialist countries were called back home in 1958. In Moscow, some students refused to return, and so eleven students were stripped of their Korean citizenship.[24] DPRK security officials used force to capture and repatriate an unwilling student, Li San-gyu, in November 1959. Soviet foreign minister Andrei Gromyko severely criticized these actions. Upon Moscow's protest, DPRK ambassador Li Sin-p'al was immediately recalled to Pyongyang. Kim had to personally apologize to Ambassador Puzanov on December 19, telling him "that was unfortunate."[25]

The Sino-Soviet Split

An ever-deepening split between Moscow and Beijing toward the end of the 1950s was the crucial factor in Kim Il Sung's balancing act between the two Big Brothers, China and the USSR. By 1960, the Sino-Soviet conflict had become more obvious and open. And the more Moscow and Beijing clashed, the more each wanted to draw Kim's government into its camp. By 1959, however,

Kim had concluded that Mao's commitment to the "people's communes" seemed too adventurous. The "Great Leap Forward" was a catastrophic failure, forcing some Chinese-Koreans to flee to the DPRK illegally to escape hunger in China. The economic disaster in China in turn strengthened Moscow's position in Pyongyang.

Kim's leaning toward Moscow was also necessitated by North Korea's need for Soviet economic assistance. Despite his antiforeign campaign, Kim Il Sung definitely needed Soviet technology and resources as he pursued his Five-Year Plan (1957–61). Pyongyang's top priority was industrialization. The September 1958 reorganization of the KWP's apparatus was aimed at strengthening its leadership's control over the economy, particularly in heavy industry.[26] From this point of view, Soviet technological expertise, especially in the development of nuclear weapons, was highly prized. In fact, Pyongyang intended to introduce Soviet nuclear technology to North Korea by 1958. On April 28, Yi Sin Pkhar submitted an earnest request to Gromyko that the USSR aid the DPRK in the peaceful utilization of nuclear technology.[27]

Kim was too sly and unscrupulous, however, to simply become Moscow's faithful follower. Between 1958 and 1961, Kim's three visits to Moscow were always preceded by visits to Beijing. During his visit to Moscow in January 1959, he let it be known that the DPRK was interested in inviting Khrushchev to Pyongyang. Apparently this was motivated by Kim's long-standing desire to conclude a Treaty of Alliance with Moscow, and inviting Khrushchev to Pyongyang to conclude this treaty became a top priority for Kim.[28]

Soviet leaders had been skeptical of any alliance with the DPRK, despite the fact that the United States had concluded the Mutual Defense Treaty with the Republic of Korea (ROK) in October 1953. Khrushchev might have had an optimistic view of the viability of "peaceful coexistence" in this region. Nevertheless, he did at least reply affirmatively to the conclusion of a joint defense agreement against an ROK "surprise attack."[29] From Kim's point of view, the Chinese volunteer army had withdrawn and some measures had to be taken. By May 1959, Kim's government began to prepare for the visit of the Soviet delegation.

However, events in 1959 turned out to have grave effects on Kim's position. The harvest was disastrous, and the country only produced 3.2 million tons of grain out of the targeted 5 million. The food shortage was further exacerbated by China's simultaneous famine resulting from the Great Leap Forward. The Sino-Soviet conflict entered its worst phase, as Kim Il Sung himself saw in October 1959, during his visit to Beijing for the tenth anniversary of the founding of the PRC. The Chinese leaders and Khrushchev clashed over the Taiwan Strait issue. Kim was reported to have expressed his sympathy for the Soviet position, but the details of Kim's meeting with Khrushchev are not known. What we know is that the expected visit of Khrushchev to Pyongyang following his visit to Beijing was canceled for "political reasons," although Moscow had agreed on the general text of the proposed alliance.[30] Kim's prestige was closely tied to Khrushchev's visit. Kim was deeply offended by Khrushchev's unwillingness to come to Pyongyang. The real reason for recalling the DPRK's ambassador may have been Li Sin-p'al's failure to secure Khrushchev's visit to Pyongyang.[31]

The worsening Sino-Soviet conflict allowed Kim to embark on a new round of power consolidation in the DPRK regime. The DPRK authorities even tightened controls over the activities of its embassies in the Eastern European "fraternal" countries. Its ambassador to the USSR, Li Sin-p'ai, was recalled to Pyongyang in December 1959. The second wave of the *chuche* campaign, organized by the vice chairman of the KWP, Kim Ch'ang-man, and others, was intensified by the end of 1959. The notorious "people's neighborhood" decree was issued at that time, which sought to persuade neighbors to spy on each other. Kim told the Soviet ambassador that this was introduced to defend the "social order" of the North Korean regime.[32] A Soviet citizen residing in Pyongyang informed the Soviet Embassy that these neighborhood associations held closed seminars and meetings where the values of autonomy and autarchy were extolled. For instance, at these meetings, it was claimed that "all goods made in the DPRK are better than foreign goods." The Soviet-Koreans again faced hardships. Their dual citizenship status was revoked, especially among the elites, and all "foreign" citizens were advised to leave the DPRK, including the vice foreign minister, Pak Kil-lyong, who had trouble with the authorities and finally was allowed to leave for Moscow due to the intervention of the CPSU.[33] The *chuche* campaign, first organized in December 1955 and again in 1959, was related to the food shortage, and targeted foreign (i.e., Soviet and Chinese) influence. This campaign was designed to divert citizens' attention from the food shortage by getting them to work against this influence.

By the time of the purge of 1958–59, the Soviet-Koreans, who had formerly dominated the foreign services, had lost much of their influence. Nam Il, a Soviet-Korean foreign minister, among others, was dismissed in November 1959 and replaced by Pak Son-ch'ol. Nam's departure was also related to his repeated failures to secure Khrushchev's visit. Pak was Kim's loyal supporter from the Chinese faction inside the KWP, whom the Soviet Foreign Ministry characterized as a "supporter of Chinese foreign concepts (orientations)."[34] In fact, Nam as vice premier was deprived of his ability to act independently, and his access to the Soviet ambassador became severely restricted before he was finally purged in 1960s.[35]

While suppressing the Soviet-Koreans at home, Kim still had no choice but to follow the Soviet model of industrialization. Technological and financial aid from Moscow was vital, especially when the Chinese were undergoing a domestic crisis. As Vice Premier Chŏn-Il-lyong told the Soviet ambassador, next to industrialization, the second priority at the December 1959 Plenum of the KWP was given to the building of the metropolis, by which Pyongyang was to be transformed into a modern city of a million people.[36] Clearly the North Koreans had adopted the Soviet model, not the Chinese "Leap," to bring modernity to Korea.

Kim's then pro-Soviet position was fully revealed in 1960, when he revised his Five-Year Plan to become a Seven-Year Plan, following the Khrushchev model. In March 1959, the DPRK government had originally planned a Second Five-Year Plan from 1961 to 1965, but following Khrushchev's sudden adoption of a Seven-Year Plan, Kim followed the Soviet example in May 1960 and set the new time frame as 1961–67.[37]

Important events that took place in Asia in 1960 influenced Pyongyang politics. Japan's decision to renew the security treaty with the United States alarmed Kim, and pushed him closer to the USSR. The downfall of the ROK dictator Syngman Rhee in April 1960 and the unstable situation in South Korea forced the KWP to adopt a new policy to extend its influence toward the south. Yet Kim faced a dilemma: Soviet aid was vital, but China was too close to neglect. Thus he visited Beijing in May 1960, just before his planned visit to Moscow. Pang Hak-se, the interior minister of Soviet origin, later stated to the Soviet ambassador that Kim was satisfied with the results of the Beijing visit, though the contents of the talks with Mao are not known.[38] Kim was likely to have assured Mao that his visit to Moscow was not intended to damage the DPRK-China relationship.

Kim traveled to Moscow unofficially on June 13 and stayed until June 18. There he discussed economic issues, but the major topic on the table was Soviet-Chinese relations, especially the interpretation of the August-September 1956 incident in this context. Frol Kozrov, secretary of the CPSU, informed Kim of Mao's conversation with Soviet ambassador Pavel F. Iudin in November 1956, just after the "August factional activities." During the conversation with Iudin, Mao had harshly criticized Kim. Deputy Minister Anastas Mikoyan also explained to Kim his personal involvement in the events of September 1956, and handed over to Kim the record of the conversation with Peng Dehuai, insinuating that the real initiative to oust Kim came from Beijing. He thus shifted all the blame to the Chinese side.[39] Kim realized that the Chinese had wanted him to become another "Imre Nagy," in the sense that he would have been ousted from power like the Hungarian prime minister. Kim was so stunned to hear the Soviet interpretation of the 1956 events that he remained speechless.

After returning to Pyongyang, Kim severely condemned Mao at the July Plenum of the KWP, accusing him of having the audacity to "compare himself to Marx, Engels, Lenin and Stalin." He also claimed that China wanted the DPRK to become a "colony of the PRC."[40] He even sided with the Soviets on the nuclear issue when he said that Mao wanted to use the Soviet experts as if they were "Chinese." Khrushchev rewarded Kim by sending a confirmation letter on July 1960 to start the flow of aid.[41]

Nevertheless, a widening gap between Moscow and Pyongyang was soon revealed when Moscow pushed North Korea to adopt a "peaceful coexistence" strategy with the South Koreans. There had been a long-established running debate between Moscow and Pyongyang on whether or not the ROK should be treated as a state. Once, at the Geneva Conference in 1954, the DPRK had recognized the ROK as a state. With the exception of this incident, however, Kim had consistently refused to acknowledge that the ROK was an independent sovereign state, as was noted by Nam Il.[42]

At the fifteenth anniversary of the liberation of Korea on August 15, 1960, Kim Il Sung proposed to the South Koreans that a "confederation" should become the model for Korean unification, an idea that Moscow had long wanted him to suggest. Was Kim sincere about this proposal? The East German ambassador had hinted that this idea of confederation came from Moscow, not from Kim, and in fact, Khrushchev endorsed this idea as soon as Kim proposed it. Khrushchev's idea was coupled with his idealistic vision of total and comprehensive disarmament, proposed on June 2, 1960. Presumably, this total and comprehensive disarmament also extended to the Korean Peninsula. Pyongyang nominally supported this, but in my view Kim Il Sung was, in fact, against any such move. While endorsing Khrushchev's idea, he was vigorously campaigning against the supposed intensification of the "Washington-Tokyo" security framework, which North Korean officials felt was intended to squash the inevitable "democratization, which would follow in the wake of the downfall of Syngman Rhee's regime." Ambassador Puzanov reported to Moscow that, contrary to Kim's pledge to support the idea of a confederation, the DPRK government was saying that "people of the whole world must heighten their caution against the Imperialists."[43] It is safe to conclude that Kim's proposal for a confederation was meant to pay lip service to Khrushchev without really changing his past policy of unifying Korea by force.

Meanwhile, Kim again invited Khrushchev to visit Pyongyang by October 1960. He told the Soviet ambassador that the text of the alliance treaty needed to be confirmed.[44] To Kim's great disappointment, however, Khrushchev again canceled his trip to Pyongyang as late as October 8, with a simple explanation that the "international situation" made it impossible for him to visit North Korea before the end of the year. Again, Kim had been snubbed. Kim understood that U.S.-USSR issues were behind Khrushchev's cancellation of the scheduled visit to Pyongyang. Later in 1963, Kim Il Sung confided to the Romanian ambassador that he twice invited Khrushchev to Pyongyang, but the Soviet leader never came. Thus, Kim took Khrushchev's unwillingness to come to Pyongyang as a sign that Moscow's attitude toward him was insincere.

In the meantime, Beijing never missed a chance to take the initiative to shore up the Chinese-DPRK relationship. In October 1960, on the tenth anniversary of the intervention of the Chinese volunteer army, China sent a high-ranking delegation to North Korea, headed by Marshal and Vice Premier He Long. The DPRK began to drift once more toward China. According to Puzanov's diary, Kim did not go to Moscow and did not even come to the Soviet Embassy in Pyongyang that November to commemorate the anniversary of the 1917 Revolution because of "health reasons."[45] In fact, Vice Premier Chŏn Il-lyong, who attended the October Revolution anniversary observance, harshly criticized the "revisionist tendency" (code words for criticism of the Soviet Union) within the socialist movement, instead stressing the validity of *chuche* ideology. These circumstances influenced Kim's position on the pending Treaty of Alliance with the Soviet Union. The more Khrushchev moved toward reconciliation with the United States, the more skeptical Kim's stance toward the alliance became.

Treaties of Alliance with Moscow and with Beijing

By 1961, things had again swung in China's favor. On January 4, Kim Il Sung told the Soviet ambassador that not only were the Chinese friends and neighbors but also that "we together shed our blood for three years."[46] To repair the damage, a Soviet delegation headed by Aleksei Kosygin, which included CPSU secretary Iurii Andropov, visited Pyongyang on May 5. Because Khrushchev was unable to come to Pyongyang, as Kim had wanted, Kosygin invited Kim to visit Moscow to conclude the Treaty of Alliance. Kim accepted this invitation to visit Moscow and Kiev, scheduled from June 29 through July 12, 1961. He concluded the Treaty of Alliance with Moscow on July 6, eight years after the United States and South Korea concluded their defense treaty.

It is important to point out that Kim suddenly decided to go to Beijing directly from Kiev, one day before his scheduled departure, and succeeded in concluding an alliance treaty with China on July 11, only five days after the conclusion of the alliance treaty with the USSR. The almost simultaneous conclusion of the alliance treaties with China and with the USSR may appear to merely have been a demonstration of socialist solidarity. The truth is, however, that it signified the DPRK's deteriorating relations with the Soviet Union.

It turned out that Kim had clandestinely negotiated the alliance treaty with Beijing and had already come to a general agreement on June 28, a day before his planned departure for Moscow. Chinese diplomatic sources reveal that Chinese ambassador Qiao Shaoguan had met with the DPRK's foreign minister, Pak Son-ch'ol, on June 27, and had handed over the Chinese draft of the treaty. Kim had met with Ambassador Qiao the next day and had agreed to sign the treaty with China, though Soviet ambassador Puzanov was totally uninformed of these negotiations.

Not knowing that Kim was secretly negotiating with Beijing, Khrushchev bluntly told Kim that once U.S.-USSR relations improved, the Soviet-DPRK alliance treaty might be annulled. Ambassador Puzanov accompanied Kim to Moscow and Kiev, but his diary in the Russian foreign archives lacks an account of the most important period from June 29 through July 12. Kim revealed to the Soviet ambassador only on July 10 in Kiev that he planned to go directly from the Soviet Union to Beijing, without saying overtly that he had planned to sign a Treaty of Alliance with China.[47]

The Sino-DPRK Treaty of Friendship, Cooperation, and Mutual Assistance was signed in Beijing on July 11. Kim is likely to never have mentioned anything about his planned visit to China to Khrushchev. Ambassador Puzanov's diary shows that Kim and others in the North Korean leadership had successfully concealed these secret negotiations with Beijing from him. Puzanov was personally far more positively disposed toward Kim than his predecessor Ivanov had been, and was instrumental in bringing Pyongyang around to Moscow's side. Still, Puzanov did not know about Kim's secret negotiations with Beijing in advance.

After coming back from Moscow to Beijing, Puzanov was asked by the Polish ambassador, Yuzef Dryglyas, whether he had known in advance of Kim's visit to Beijing. Puzanov answered:

> It became known from the Korean delegation on the forthcoming visit to Beijing when we were staying in Kiev after we signed the treaty. In our talks with Kim Il Sung, he told me that two or three days before our departure for the Soviet Union, the Chinese ambassador had visited Pak Son-ch'ol, the DPRK foreign minister, and

> had presented a proposal for the Treaty of Friendship, Cooperation, and Mutual Assistance. Kim also mentioned that Pak had received an invitation for a DPRK party and governmental delegation to come to Beijing and that the Central Committee of the KWP had accepted the invitation.[48]

On July 15, Puzanov met Kim at the Pyongyang airport. Puzanov writes that at this meeting, Kim told him how hot the weather was in Beijing and that he "signed the treaty with Mao Zedong at the Airport." After this Pyongyang airport meeting with Puzanov, Kim suddenly canceled his entire planned schedule to ratify the treaty with the Soviet Union and took the whole summer to rest. On July 17, Puzanov met Pak Yŏng-guk, head of the International Department of the KWP, but Pak also refused to pass on any concrete information about the alliance treaty with China to the Soviet ambassador.[49] It was not until August 8 that Kim finally met with Ambassador Puzanov to explain about the treaty with China.

The treaty with the Soviet Union was weaker in its guarantee of security compared with the treaty with China. The treaty with the Soviet Union was effective for only ten years, whereas the treaty with China was effective for an indefinite period. The treaty with the Soviet Union also stipulated that the alliance was to go into effect only when either country was actually attacked, whereas the treaty with China defined the bilateral relations as an alliance. Kim quietly played the two Big Brothers off against each other, and he managed to make a better deal with Beijing than with Moscow.[50]

The tense relationship between Beijing and Moscow came to a head in the fall of 1961. At the Twenty-second Congress of the CPSU in October 1961, Chinese premier Zhou Enlai openly attacked the Soviets on de-Stalinization. The issue of Albania also became a measure of Moscow-Pyongyang relations in this case, when the Albanian Communist Party chief, Enver Hoxha, challenged Khrushchev's doctrine of peaceful coexistence with his remarks at a November 7, 1961, address in Moscow.[51] Hoxha's open defiance of Khrushchev's authority appealed to the North Koreans. In a closed meeting, the DPRK Foreign Ministry declared that the Koreans regarded Stalin's cult as a "domestic issue of the CPSU," and suggested that the Soviet comrades were taking "incorrect attitudes toward Albania," according to information received by the Czechoslovakian Embassy.[52] The North Koreans, however, did not attack the Soviet Union as openly as had the Albanians and the Chinese. Kim Il Sung himself seemed less vocal when the Soviet ambassador met him on April 13, 1962, and only underlined Communist unity.[53]

North Korea's Policy toward the Developing World, and Moscow's Role

There is a good reason why North Korea did not openly attack the Soviet Union and did not completely sever its ties with Moscow. Because the DPRK recognized the emerging role of the developing world in the 1960s, its diplomacy began to target developing Asian countries, as well as neutral African nations like Mali, Egypt, and Nigeria, especially from 1962 to 1963. And even as Pyongyang's policies began to clash with Moscow's, Pyongyang pursued them without consulting Moscow. This, of course, was also intended as an attempt to mobilize support against the ROK, where Park Chung Hee had come to power after a coup in May 1961 and established a military dictatorship. Pyongyang calculated that Park Chung Hee's authoritarian government was unlikely to garner support from other countries.

Nevertheless, if Pyongyang wanted to pursue its policy toward the developing world, it could not afford to alienate Moscow irreparably. The DPRK had always suggested that because the United Nations had been its enemy during the Korean War, the United Nations could not be a neutral and fair arbitrator of the unification issue. This issue, it insisted, should be resolved peacefully by the Korean people. As peace in Asia became an agenda item for the UN, however, the DPRK could no longer remain indifferent when the Korean issue came before the UN General Assembly in September of every year. As the United States vigorously pushed its policy to have the ROK become a member of the United Nations, Pyongyang had to rely on the USSR to veto this policy. The UN issue tied Pyongyang to Moscow, though relations between the two capitals remained strained. North Korea had no way to coordinate its policy with the leaders of the developing world without calling on Moscow's influence inside the UN. In this respect, China was no help.

Kim Il Sung's health problems also somewhat helped to improve Soviet-DPRK relations. When Kim became ill in 1962, Puzanov and his embassy tried to cultivate an improved relationship by sending doctors to look after Kim. A successful operation was performed under Soviet supervision.[54] Although the Soviets saved his life, this did not prevent the ungrateful Kim from quietly negotiating with Beijing.

Puzanov's departure from Pyongyang in June 1962 marked the end of the generally benign relationship between the USSR and DPRK that lasted from 1957 to 1962. After Puzanov left the North Korean capital, the DPRK foreign minister, Pak Son-ch'ol, remarked that "no other ambassadors were invited to his [Kim's] apartment or dacha. . . . Kim Il Sung considers you [Puzanov] the representative of the CPSU, not merely an ambassador."[55]

Lips and Teeth: Again with Mao

The underlying reason for Kim's sharp turn toward Beijing was revealed in October 1962, when the PRC and the DPRK renegotiated their border issues, which resulted in the PRC-DPRK Border Treaty signed by Zhou Enlai and Kim Il Sung on October 12. Remarkably, these negotiations went unnoticed by the Soviet and Eastern European embassies in Pyongyang.[56]

Moscow's newly appointed ambassador, V. P. Moskovskii, came to Pyongyang and first met with DPRK foreign minister Pak Son Chol on August 10, 1962, and then with Kim Il Sung on August 14.[57] It is noteworthy that Pak was a Chinese-Korean and a Kim loyalist.[58] The experienced Bulgarian ambassador, Georgi Kostov-Bodanov, suggested to Moskovskii that although Kim was paying lip service to the "cult of personality" issue raised by Khrushchev at the Twenty-second Congress of the CPSU 1961, "the essence [of the situation] is not changed." This implied that Eastern European diplomats saw growing anti-Soviet trends in Pyongyang's politics.

The crucial negotiations over border demarcation with regard to Pektusan were at that very time being kept secret from Ambassador Moskovskii. The ambassador tried to meet with the former foreign minister, Nam Il, a Soviet-Korean loyal to Kim, and eventually succeeded in arranging a meeting for September 15. He discovered, however, that Nam was totally isolated and was not even free to talk openly with the Soviet ambassador.[59] This was followed by the resignation of Bulgarian ambassador Kostov-Bogdanov, who left Pyongyang in protest after four Korean students were abducted from Sofia by North Korean agents in September 1962.

Tension again developed between the North Korean authorities and the embassies of their Eastern European allies. At the beginning of October 1962, the Polish ambassador characterized this relationship as "gloomy."[60] The East German ambassador, Kurt Schneidewind, who perceptively grasped the political climate in Pyongyang at that time, suggested to Moskovskii on October 11, before Zhou Enlai's visit to Pyongyang, that the North Korean leadership was leaning toward China, although he was not likely to have known of Zhou's arrival.[61] Opinions on North Korea's leanings toward China were divided among the ambassadors of the allied socialist countries. The Czechoslovakian ambassador, for example, tended to believe that Kim was sincere about his denunciation of Stalin's "cult of personality" at the Twenty-second CPSU Congress. But it became clear that the relationship between the DPRK and the Soviet Union and its Eastern European allies sharply deteriorated toward the end of 1962. As a keen observer of DPRK politics, Schneidewind informed the Soviet ambassador on November 24: "In the summer of 1962, when China and the DPRK negotiated on the contested Pektusan border issue, they managed to reach a compromise. The Chinese made concessions on the issue of the border, while the Koreans' concessions were political rather than territorial."[62] Though it is difficult to gauge this bargain, China is likely to have lured the DPRK to its side with the concession on the territory.[63]

After these negotiations, North Korea truly became a legitimate Chinese ally. The East German ambassador sympathized with the thankless job of the Soviet ambassador at that time, for Deputy Premier Minister Kim Il had kept Moskovskii from seeing Kim Il Sung for at least half a year. On June 11, 1963, Moskovskii was informed that "Kim Il Sung was ill and had to remain under special medical observation for two or three years." As it turned out, however, the ambassador finally got to see Kim on September 8, although at this meeting Kim did not speak a word to him, while having a friendly chat with the Chinese ambassador.[64] This was followed by curious provocations toward the Soviet Embassy in Pyongyang, where self-proclaimed "political" émigrés ensconced themselves.[65]

The economic issue mattered a great deal in Kim's maneuvers, as reflected in the mutual distrust between Moscow and Pyongyang over arms sales. The Soviets wanted to sell arms to North Korea on credit, but Kim wanted the Soviets to provide him with weapons free of charge. By the end of 1962, the relationship was very nearly severed. DPRK defense minister Kim Ch'ang-bong came to Moscow to negotiate a way out of this dispute, but no concession came from the Soviets and he simply returned home empty-handed. The DPRK leaders immediately called a party plenum, where some delegates even advocated breaking diplomatic relations with the USSR.[66] Some of the anger behind these demands also stemmed from friction over the nuclear cooperation issue, though the details of this were not known.

The issue of the arms sale broke the camel's back, and Pyongyang now aligned itself with Beijing in the Sino-Soviet conflict. In the years 1963–64, the DPRK press was busy criticizing "revisionism" and denouncing those who wanted to negotiate with the United States.

Pyongyang's Uneasy Partnership with Moscow, October 1964 to 1968

Khrushchev's sudden departure from the political scene in October 1964 marked the end of the adversarial relationship between Moscow and Pyongyang. At the very least, such was the illusion that overshadowed bilateral relations for a while. Until the beginning of the 1970s, the Soviet Union was under a collective leadership headed by Leonid Brezhnev as the CPSU's first secretary (and later general secretary) and Aleksei Kosygin as premier. Kosygin played a major role in the international arena, especially in Asian affairs.

Despite Beijing's recent first successful nuclear test, which dealt another blow to the Soviets as leaders of the socialist camp, it was the Chinese themselves who proposed normalizing relations with the USSR through a mutual China-DPRK visit to Moscow in November 1964. Beijing's attempt at rapprochement with Moscow failed, however, because Zhou Enlai found a thoroughly anti-Mao climate in Moscow and had to return to China.[67]

Moscow-Pyongyang relations proved somewhat more resilient than Beijing-Moscow relations. Pyongyang stopped its anti-Soviet campaign soon after Khrushchev's ouster. Vice Foreign Minister Kim Yŏn-nam met his counterpart, Vladimir Kuznetsov, in February 1965, when Soviet premier Kosygin visited Pyongyang, and the two found some common ground for discussion, though they still did not completely see eye to eye. In fact, Kuznetsov and Kim had difficulty finding words for the Joint Communiqué. Kuznetsov underlined the importance of "peaceful coexistence," while Kim emphasized the "revolutionary force against aggression and war of the imperialists."[68] Even so, in May 1965, Moscow and Pyongyang agreed to strengthen their military and economic cooperation.

The Chinese "Great Cultural Revolution," which began in 1966, added another dimension to Asia's Cold War political landscape. Beijing's radicalization seriously alienated the PRC from those Asian socialist elements that had formerly supported it. Specific aggravations, like the Chinese Red Guards' criticism of Kim's regime, for example, negatively affected DPRK-PRC relations. Pyongyang was unhappy with the general atmosphere of constant iconoclastic upheavals in China.

This drove Kim back into Moscow's embrace, or more accurately, Kim publicly portrayed himself as more pro-Moscow. Brezhnev reportedly commented that "the departure of the Korean comrades from the Chinese course is an actual fact."[69] In addition to keeping his distance from Mao's violent revolution, Kim had other reasons to lean toward Moscow. First, the ROK had normalized relations with Japan in 1965 and had begun to industrialize. North Korea's image as an industrialized country was discredited as Seoul rapidly modernized its economy following the Japanese model. Furthermore, the "United States–Japan–ROK triangle" seemed to pose a serious security threat, though such an "alliance" did not, in fact, exist. It seems that the North Koreans overestimated the level of cooperation between the three countries.

Another reason for the DPRK to lean further toward Moscow was the increasing competition with the ROK over membership in the United Nations. Of course, the DPRK had always been the enemy of the United States, and its leaders had always stressed the importance of an independent path toward Korean unification. Kim and his spokesmen had claimed that unification was the cause of the whole Korean people, and all foreign armies—that is, U.S. troops—should be withdrawn from the Korean Peninsula. Meanwhile, such neutral states as India and Pakistan had wanted to extend UN membership to both Koreas simultaneously, and this idea began to seem an increasingly attractive solution by the 1960s, especially in developing countries.

The USSR was a UN Security Council member and had the power to veto any unfavorable proposals. Moscow was instrumental in contacting and organizing supporters, especially in neutral Asian and African countries, to counter the U.S.-ROK bloc. All the while, DPRK foreign delegations inevitably had to depend on Moscow, even for such basic help as travel to developing countries like Iran and Afghanistan, and the increasing number of independent African countries drove this point home for Pyongyang. Close contact with Moscow was thus highly desirable for Kim, and another visit to Moscow was the first step on this road.

Nevertheless, the USSR seemed less than fully supportive of Kim's initiatives on this front. The neutral countries were mostly passive, because, as a Soviet official explained to the DPRK ambassador in Moscow in March 1963, they could not understand how North Korea could view the UN as the enemy and yet demand a UN resolution for the withdrawal of the U.S.-UN army from the South.[70]

The changing international situation in 1965, however, influenced DPRK-USSR relations. In 1965 the Indonesian Communist Party was destroyed after the events of September 30, 1965. This indicated the danger of aligning too closely with China. The U.S. commitment in Vietnam was a serious challenge to Moscow's legitimacy as the Big Brother of socialist Vietnam. Kosygin's role was instrumental in countering U.S. moves to escalate the Vietnam War. In this context, Moscow was prepared to restore relations with Pyongyang. Ambassador Kim Pŏn-jik informed his Soviet counterpart that Kim Il Sung wanted to meet with Brezhnev as soon as possible in person at the end of 1965.[71]

Kosygin wanted a concerted effort of Asian socialist allies against the United States. The Soviet premier attempted to address the Korean unification issue during his visit to Pyongyang, when he suggested to Kim that perhaps Charles de Gaulle might be able to use his good offices to help mediate between Kim and the South.[72] In fact, a visit by de Gaulle to Pyongyang was contemplated at that time, though it never materialized. Thus, Moscow achieved at least temporary, though superficial, détente with Kim. A high-level delegation, headed by Ch'oe Yong-gŏn, was invited to the Twenty-third CPSU Congress in March 1966. Kim Il Sung seemed not to be hostile to such a move.

Further developments came in December 1966, when Brezhnev met with Kim Il Sung, first in Vladivostok and then in Moscow, in a series of high-level talks. Though few documents are available on these meetings, it appears that both sides agreed that the U.S. conflict with North Vietnam had entered a critical stage. China was almost in a state of civil war following Chairman Mao's instigation of the Cultural Revolution. Japan had normalized relations with South Korea in 1965, which threatened Kim's regime. Thus, from Kim Il Sung's point of view, a higher level of contact and some kind of working relationship with Moscow had to be reestablished. The newly appointed ambassador, Kim Ch'un-bin, later said to Gromyko that Kim Il Sung was satisfied with his meeting with Brezhnev.[73] Nikolai Podgorny, chairman of the Supreme Soviet, talked with the new DPRK ambassador, Kim Ch'un-bin, and told him that the Chinese "Cultural Revolution would only benefit the U.S."[74]

However, this cooperation was based on a misperception of who their common enemies were. Pyongyang initiated the "Japanese threat" campaign to enlist Soviet help in countering "Sato [Eisaku]'s right-wing conservative government."[75] However, the Soviet Embassy in Pyongyang, specifically Ambassador Aleksandr Gorchakov, had already informed Moscow in June 1966 that "the North may emphasize the threat of Japanese militarism. . . . Therefore, it is desirable that we should inform Pak Son-ch'ol [the foreign minister] of the real aim of Gromyko's visit to Tokyo."[76] The Soviets aimed at achieving rapprochement with Japan, which was at variance with Kim's anti-Japanese campaign.

Moscow also wanted Pyongyang to keep a low profile in the broader world community, especially with nonaligned Asian and African states and in international organizations. In return, Moscow offered to secure a place for the DPRK in the International Federation of Standardization in The Hague. Gromyko also helped the DPRK join the World Health Organization in 1972.[77] With these measures, Moscow wanted Pyongyang to have broader contact with international organizations, and eventually to be integrated into the broader world community.

However, Kim's détente with Moscow remained illusory, as Pyongyang again radicalized its stance on the unification issue and adopted aggressive political tactics. From 1966, Pyongyang began to build up its military forces, apparently gearing up to unify the peninsula by Kim's sixtieth birthday in 1972. A domestic purge was also conducted in May 1967, when Kim loyalists finally monopolized all real power, as the Sixth Congress of the KWP demonstrated.[78] In this purge, even Kim loyalists and the old guards of the "Partisan" faction, like Pak Kim-chŏl or Yi Hyo-sun, could not escape disgrace.

A great deal of Soviet aid was funneled into this military buildup. Vice Foreign Minister Ho Sŏk-t'ae remarked that "a new war in the Korean Peninsula is inevitable," that "the Japanese militarist spirit is well known," and that is why "our party is strengthening the nation's defensive capability even at the cost of economic growth." However, this had little effect on Soviet diplomats, like Vice Foreign Minister Vladimir Kuznetsov, who remained unconvinced, dismissing Ho's views and simply remarking: "We have no such information." Kuznetsov dismissed any alleged rise of Japanese militarism.[79]

Thus, Soviet-DPRK relations once again deteriorated as their mutual expectations never meshed. When Gromyko met with Korean foreign minister Pak Son-ch'ol in April 1966, Pak tried to convince him to devote substantial economic resources to the military buildup against U.S. and Japanese militarism. Hearing this, Gromyko replied: "We will fight against them by diplomatic means."[80] The North Koreans saw war as inevitable, while the Soviets categorically denied the plausibility of such an event. The DPRK's ambassador to Moscow, Kim Ch'un-bin, bitterly complained about the Soviet media's neglecting to print "some materials that express the love of our leader, by Kim Il Sung." Vice Foreign Minister Sergei Vinogradov simply informed Kim that editorial decisions were made by the editors of the publications involved.[81] Ambassador Kim's stay in Moscow may have been cut short by this affair, his failed attempt to print a DPRK condemnation of Japan in the paper *Sovetskaia Rossia*.[82]

The *Pueblo* Incident

It was in this context that the North Koreans escalated the aggressiveness of their tactics against the United Sates. They attacked and captured the U.S. "spy" ship *Pueblo* on January 23, 1968, following the unsuccessful attempt by a guerrilla unit to kill ROK president Park Chung Hee at the Blue House in the same month. Newly revealed documents on Soviet-DPRK relations in 1968 brought to light by Sergei Radchenko show just how far bilateral relations had deteriorated by 1968.[83] The North Korean government began to evacuate some urban residents and urged foreign diplomats to seek shelter. Moscow was not informed of these events in advance, and it never endorsed Kim's maneuvers. Foreign Minister Gromyko met a DPRK diplomat, Kan Ch'un-gŭm, on January 29, 1968, to inform him of Soviet mediation efforts at the UN.[84] He hinted that the UN secretary-general, U Thant, was also involved in the mediation. Even Canadian ambassador Robert Ford asked Moscow to intervene in the *Pueblo* affair.[85]

In turn, Kim Il Sung was in a combative mood and asked for Soviet military aid in accordance with the alliance treaty on January 30.[86] Moscow invited Defense Minister Kim Ch'ang-bong to Moscow. The CPSU secretary, Boris Ponomarev, also visited Pyongyang to persuade Kim to negotiate, though the details of this visit are not known.[87] The U.S. ambassador to Moscow, Llewellyn E. Thompson, met with Gromyko on February 27 to urge the Soviets to rein in Pyongyang.[88]

Kim, however, rejected these requests and kept the *Pueblo* crew until December 1968. Moscow had known how difficult it was to handle its junior partner, and now it had an opportunity to reconfirm this fact. In short, just as with U.S.-DPRK relations, 1968 was also a critical year for Soviet-DPRK relations. The USSR was the DPRK's top trading partner, and the volume of trade increased 20 percent from its 1967 level, but the Soviet side admitted that both could not fulfill the target for 1968.[89]

Kim Il Sung, Sino-Soviet Military Conflict, and U.S.-Chinese Rapprochement

The Russian Foreign Ministry's archival documents contain very few substantial materials on bilateral relations during the period when N. G. Sudalikov served as the ambassador to Pyongyang from 1967 until 1974. Moscow's lukewarm attitude toward Pyongyang was also partly due to intensifying USSR-China relations, as was shown in the Damanskii/Zhenbao Island incident in March 1969.[90] When the Sino-Soviet conflict was elevated to military confrontation, both Moscow and Beijing became more eager to recruit Pyongyang to their side. The visit of the Supreme Soviet chair, Nikolai Podgorny, to Pyongyang might have been related to this political move. On October 1, 1969, Mao Zedong stated that China wanted a special relationship with the DPRK.[91] Zhou Enlai's ostentatious visit to Pyongyang in April 1970 was well calculated on both sides.

Soviet-DPRK relations had not improved by December 1969, when, at his meeting with Brezhnev, Foreign Minister Pak Son-ch'ol still stuck to fiery rhetoric and preached a revolutionary war with the United States.[92] Both men had different agendas and differing expectations, which the other partner was unlikely to meet. Thus, Soviet-DPRK relations simply remained on a plateau, and few Soviet leaders visited Pyongyang throughout the 1970s. It is true that the KWP held its Fifth Congress in November 1970 and had to sum up the results of the Seven-Year Plan. Kim Kŭn-lŏn, chairman of the Foreign Economic Commission, talked with Ambassador Nikolai Sudarikov to ask for more aid with construction and other projects, while the ambassador complained of the poor utilization of the aid.[93] Symbolic ritual meetings took place between the two countries, like that of the chairman of the Supreme People's Assembly, Ch'oe Yong-gŏn, and the chairman of the Presidium of the Supreme Soviet, Nikolai Podgornyi, in April 1971. In addition, on the tenth anniversary of the

Treaty of Alliance, a delegation headed by Politburo member K. T. Mazurov was dispatched to Pyongyang.[94] But relations remained at a stalemate.

Kim's Proposal for Confederation

Meanwhile, tacit contact between Pyongyang and Seoul began during 1971. On August 6, Kim Il Sung hinted in his article in the *Rodong Sinbun* that he might meet a South Korean delegation of all strata, though without President Park Chung Hee. Paek Nam-un, chair of the Supreme People's Assembly, also sent a letter to Seoul to the effect that Park's "marionette" regime was dangerous and was preventing peaceful unification.[95] Still, Pek's appeal on January 1, 1972, for peaceful and autonomous unification seemed ritualistic. However, when a Supreme Soviet official, Aleksei Shtikov, met with Chŏng Tu-kwan on January 24, 1972, in Moscow, Ten underlined that the conditions for peaceful unification were "favorable." The newly appointed ambassador, Kwŏn Ku-gŭn, also underlined Kim's willingness to come to Moscow. Kim's move confused Moscow. Contrary to Kim's seemingly conciliatory gesture, his article on August 6, 1971, had underlined the importance of the leadership of "Lenin and Stalin" and seemed to defy Moscow.[96]

Meanwhile, a Politburo candidate, S. Rashidov, visited Pyongyang in January 1972. This was remembered as an occasion when Kim bemoaned his country's recent economic difficulties and asked Rashidov for economic aid. Moscow reluctantly had to pay.[97] Rashidov's visit to the DPRK seemed to indicate a Soviet reaction to the changing political landscape in the Asia-Pacific region triggered by U.S.-PRC rapprochement.

Meanwhile, Kim made an unexpected political move when he declared on July 4, 1972, that he was willing to form a "Confederation of Korea" with the ROK. The idea of such a confederation had been floated at the Geneva Conference in 1954 and again in 1960, but since 1960 Kim had categorically opposed this move.

China's strategic turn to accommodate itself with the United States following the announcement on July 15, 1971, of President Richard Nixon's visit to Beijing in 1972 definitely played a crucial role in this shift. Kim Il Sung's address of August 1971 also hinted at a new kind of settlement, but few had expected such a move or could explain why Kim and his South Korean counterpart were behaving this way. One plausible explanation may be attributed to the long-indoctrinated "unification" campaign on the occasion of Kim's sixtieth birthday, April 15, 1972. Because an armed effort for unification had failed in 1968, Kim and his entourage were forced to try a new approach by 1972. This was a nationalistic campaign for Kim's regime at a time when both

Moscow and Beijing were seeking détente with the United States. According to the account of a Soviet diplomat, M.S. Kapitsa, some DPRK diplomats even hinted at the possibility of canceling the alliance treaties with the USSR and China.[98] Vice Foreign Minister Li Chong-ok visited Moscow to gauge the Soviet leadership's reaction to this move.

However, this turned out to be another propaganda maneuver. In fact, Kim commemorated the drafting of a new Constitution on December 28, 1972, and was elevated to the position of the first president of the DPRK. Thus, Kim's confederation plan was another item in his self-glorification process as the father of Korean unification. This had an ambivalent impact on the DPRK-USSR relationship. On the one hand, it was in line with Moscow's wishes, but on the other it was a move inspired by Korean nationalism. The CPSU secretary, K. F. Katyshev, visited Pyongyang on September 3 after the July declaration of confederation, though the contents of his talks with Kim are not known.[99] In any case, this turned out to be an empty gesture. Neither the ROK nor the DPRK had committed to the cause of détente firmly enough to construct any kind of fundamentally different relationship, and things soon turned to confusion. False promises were left unrealized. Moscow's archival documents tell very little of why the effort eventually failed. Kim's regime soon started accusing President Park Chung Hee and the Korean Central Intelligence Agency of failure. Moscow also had foreseen this and had few illusions of North-South rapprochement.

Conclusion

In December 1973, the Soviet Foreign Ministry submitted a document titled "Some Problems in USSR-Korean Relations," which mentioned these four points: (1) illegal fishing by DPRK fishermen, (2) 15,000 North Koreans residing in the Soviet Far East, (3) the distribution of Chinese publications inside the Soviet Union that described the USSR as a socialist-imperialist power, and (4) ill will resulting from unrealized oral invitations to upper-level Soviet officials to visit North Korea. Of course, this list does not touch on the fundamental problems of USSR-DPRK relations. But by merely mentioning these trivial items without addressing fundamental issues, Moscow was demonstrating its eagerness to avoid more trouble with Pyongyang.

Kim Il Sung's regime was installed in power by the Soviet Red Army in 1945. Despite Kim's later claims that he had risen to his current position by virtue of his independent revolutionary activities before 1940, Moscow was the key element upon which he had to rely. However, it cannot be denied that by the 1960s, he had turned himself into an autonomous and independent politician through his bitter opposition to the Big Brothers' intervention in 1956. He successfully maneuvered between Moscow and Beijing and maintained his independence, taking advantage of the Sino-Soviet conflict without completely committing himself to either side. His alliance strategy was always based on a consideration of his domestic position as well as the international milieu—above all, the USSR and China.

A particularly serious gap between Moscow and Pyongyang emerged over the issue of "peaceful unification" following the Geneva Conference of 1954. For Kim, this was not simply a foreign policy issue but also one involving the domestic power struggle. Kim was committed to building a united socialist Korea by any means, not excluding violent ones, whereas Moscow had no vested interest in this cause. Moscow's calculation was based on its own geopolitical interests and ideological and military confrontation with Mao's China, particularly in the 1960s and 1970s.

Kim's foreign gestures and moves were sometimes symbolic, were not substantial, and were lacking in any real commitment. Such was the case with the alliance treaty with the USSR in 1961 and the Declaration on the Confederation with the ROK in 1972. Still, as long as the United States and Japan were regarded as hostile forces, and while the Big Brothers were turning out to be unreliable partners, Kim had to pursue "peaceful coexistence" with the ROK for cosmetic, and perhaps domestic, consumption.

Notes

1. *Cold War International History Project Bulletin,* no. 16 (2008): 447–63 (see James Person's introduction); A. Lankov, *From Stalin to Kim Il Sung: The Formation of North Korea 1945–1960* (New Brunswick, N.J.: Rutgers University Press, 2002); A. Lankov, *Crisis in North Korea: The Failure of De-Stalinization* (Honolulu: University of Hawaii Press, 2005); Balázs Szalontai, *Kim Il Sung in the Khrushchev Era: Soviet-DPRK Relations and the Roots of North Korean Despotism, 1953–1964* (Washington, D.C., and Stanford, Calif.: Woodrow Wilson Center Press and Stanford University Press, 2005).

2. A. M. Aleksandrov-Agentov, *Ot Kollontai do Gorbacheva* [From Kollontai to Gorbachev] (Moscow: Mezhdunarodnye otnosheniia, 1994), 93.

3. Arkhiv Vneshnei Politiki Rossiiskoi Federatsii (hereafter AVP RF), fond (f.) 102, opis' (op.) 10, papka (p.) 52, delo (d.) 8, listy (ll.) 66–67.

4. For Kim's purge of his rivals, see AVP RF, f. 102, op. 9. p. 44, d. 9, ll. 42, 75, 95, 110, 125, 178; Rossiiskii gosudarstvennyi arkhiv sotsial'no-politicheskoi istorii (hereafter RGASPI), f. 5, op. 28. d. 314, l. 97; Nobuo Shimotomai, *Mosukuwa to Kin Nissei* [Moscow and Kim Il Sung] (Tokyo: Iwanami shoten, 2006), 146–48.

5. AVP RF, f. 102, op. 11, p. 60, d. 15, l. 3.

6. Russiiskii Gosudarstvennyi Arkhiv Noveishei Istorii (hereafter RGANI), f. 5, op. 28, d. 314, ll. 67–99. According to this draft, the DPRK, as the basis for the unification,

entered the socialist stage. However, Moscow simply thought it premature, because Korea was not united, and advised emphasis on the activities of the united front organization with the South instead (l. 262).

7. RGANI, f. 5, op. 28, d. 314, l. 262.

8. AVP RF, f. 102, op. 11, p. 60, d. 7, l. 35.

9. Ibid., l. 185.

10. The term "*chuche*" might have originated in the Japanese Marxist philosophical debates at the end of 1940s. *Shutai-sei ronso,* or the issue of subjectivity in history and the role of humanity, was hotly debated, though in a different context. However, the official version of the December 1955 Kim Il Sung speech is questionable, because it might have been revised later. Kim Il Sung, *Chosakushu* [Works] (Japanese edition) [Chosakushu], vol. 9, 426–35.

11. Shimotomai, *Mosukuwa to Kin Nissei,* 229.

12. AVP RF, f. 102, op. 9, p. 44, d. 9, l. 125; Shimotomai, *Mosukuwa to Kin Nissei,* 147.

13. See note 1 above.

14. Shimotomai, *Mosukuwa to Kin Nissei,* 183.

15. AVP RF, f. 102, op. 13, p. 72, d. 5, l. 42.

16. Ibid., l. 252, Puzanov's diary for November 13.

17. AVP RF, f. 102, op. 13, p. 72, d. 6, l. 37.

18. Incidentally, the Soviets wanted the Chinese volunteer army to stay in North Korea, as was shown in the statement of Foreign Minister D. Shepilov on January 4, 1957 (Shen zhiha document, or SD10187, in North East Normal University).

19. According to one academician, Li Si En, who had access to the Soviet Embassy, Kim Tu-bong wanted to introduce either Cyrillicization or alphabetization of the Korean language. This was also regarded as another reason for the accusation; AVP RF, f. 102, op. 14, p. 75, d. 5, l. 109.

20. RGANI, f. 1, op. 3, d. 3, l. 75; information provided by S. Radchenko.

21. AVP RF, f. 102, op. 14, p. 75, d. 6, l. 64.

22. AVP RF, f. 102, op. 14, p. 75, d. 7, l. 469. Former deputy premier Pak Chang-ok and Pak Yi ban were Soviet-Koreans, whereas Ko Bongi, the Pyongyang city party boss, was pro-Chinese. They were charged with conspiracy against the party and the government. Pak Yi ban's family was sent to the USSR.

23. Szalontai, *Kim Il Sung in the Khrushchev Era,* 129.

24. Author's interview with one of the students who never returned to the DPRK, Moscow, October 6, 2008.

25. AVP RF, f. 102, op. 15, p. 81, d. 7, l. 329.

26. AVP RF, f. 102, op. 14, p. 75, d. 4, l. 76.

27. AVP RF, f. 102, op. 14, p. 75, d. 4, ll. 3–5.

28. Vadim P. Tkachenko, *Koreiskii poluostrov i interesy Rossii* [The Korean Peninsula and the interests of Russia] (Moscow: Vostochnaia Literatura, 2000), 16–18.

29. AVP RF, f. 102, op. 15, p. 81, d. 7, l. 30.

30. Shimotomai, *Mosukuwa to Kin Nissei,* 278; AVP RF, f. 102, op. 15. p. 81, d. 7, l. 86. Foreign Minister Nam Il was also not well informed of the reason. In fact, he was soon replaced by Pak Son Chol.

31. This incident shows that Kim's regime was not immune to protests by other socialist countries. Trouble occurred again in September 1962, this time with Bulgaria,

when four Korean students were forced to return home. The Bulgarian government was furious and recalled Ambassador Kostov-Bogdanov, a longtime veteran in Pyongyang diplomatic circles, to Sofia as a protest. However, the DPRK's ambassador justified the action by saying that "we should not mechanically apply bourgeois law to this case." AVP RF, f. 102, op. 18, p. 93, d. 5, l. 47.

32. Ibid., l. 385.

33. 33 AVP RF, f. 102, op. 16, p. 85, d. 6, l. 169.

34. AVP RF, f. 102, op. 108. p. 93, d. 13, l. 128.

35. AVP RF, f. 102, op. 18, p. 93, d. 5, l. 63. Ambassador Moskovskii's meeting with Nam Il on September 15, 1963. He was apparently heavily guarded, and the meeting was reported by two workers from the KWP and Foreign Ministry.

36. AVP RF, f. 102, op. 20, p. 35, d. 5, l. 476.

37. Shimotomai, *Mosukuwa to Kin Nissei,* 183; AVP RF, f. 102, op. 15, p. 83, d. 32, l. 2.

38. AVP RF, f. 102, op. 16. p. 85, d. 6, ll. 36–37.

39. AVP RF, f. 102, op. 16, p. 85, d. 7, l. 5. The Soviet side had already decided to leak the November 1956 document to Kim just after Khrushchev's return from Beijing. *Prezidium TsK KPSS 1954–64, chernovye protokolnye zapisi zasedanii, stenogrammy, postanovlenia v 3 tomakh* [The Presidum of the CPSU Central Committee 1954–64, Draft notes of the minutes of meetings, stenographs, and resolutions in 3 vols.] (Moscow, 2003), vol. 1, 443. According to A. Puzanov, who attended this meeting, Kim was apparently shocked by Mao's statement and remained silent for a while. He then said to the Soviet ambassador that "Chinese leadership is defective." Kim had a five-hour conversation with Khrushchev, but no record was kept in the AVP RF archives. Incidentally, Vadim Tkachenko, a CPSU official in charge of the DPRK, kept a record of this meeting. According to this record, Kim was skeptical about disarming unilaterally and asked to sign the alliance agreement. Khrushchev was positively disposed toward his visit to Pyongyang next year, but this visit never materialized.

40. AVP RF, f. 102, op. 16, p. 85, d. 7, l. 19.

41. Ibid.

42. Diary of Shesterikov, Talk with Vice Foreign Minister Pak Gil En on July 7, AVP RF, f. 102, op. 14, p. 35, d. 8, l. 201.

43. AVP RF, f. 102, op. 20, p. 26, d. 11, l. 3.

44. AVP RF, f. 102, op. 16, p. 85, d. 7, l. 135.

45. Ibid., l. 167.

46. AVP RF, f. 102, op. 17, p. 89, d. 5, l. 11.

47. Telegram from the Chinese Foreign Ministry to the DPRK Embassy on June 29, 1961, no. 595, Archives of the Chinese Foreign Ministry, 201-00765-03, 13.

48. AVP RF, f. 102, op. 17, p. 89, d. 5, l. 26.

49. Ibid., l. 23.

50. Shimotomai, *Mosukuwa to Kin Nissei,* 293.

51. *Prezidium TsK KPSS 1954–64,* vol. 3, 269.

52. AVP RF, f. 102, op. 18, p. 93, d. 4, ll. 88–89.

53. Ibid., ll. 92–93.

54. Ibid., l. 183. Kim seems to have suffered from kidney stones; an operation was performed on May 15, 1962, and the CPSU made available special medical treatment by dispatching two doctors to care for Kim.

55. Ibid., l. 242.
56. AVP RF, f. 102, op. 18, p. 93, d. 5, l. 186.
57. Ibid., ll. 2, 4.
58. Pak's Chinese origin was hinted at by Romanian ambassador Bodnepash to V. Moskovskii; ibid., l. 116.
59. Ibid., l. 63. Ambassador Moskovskii wanted to talk with Nam freely, but he found that two workers from the party and Foreign Ministry were writing down every statement, thus preventing a free discussion.
60. Ibid., l. 91. Kim was fully informed of Eastern European divisions and was to utilize these differences. Romania was ambivalent on the Stalin issue and also critical of Russian chauvinistic tendency. Thus Kim could tell Polish ambassador Driglyas in the summer of 1963 that he regretted having shot several "Soviet-Korean" leaders in 1958. He even hinted that he might be willing to reexamine events from the different point of view; AVP RF, f. 102, op. 19, p. 97, d. 5, l. 84.
61. AVP RF, f. 102, op. 18, p. 93, d. 5, l. 99.
62. Ibid., l. 186.
63. Of course, a territorial issue is always accompanied by nationalism, and South Koreans were critical of Kim for not obtaining all of Pektusan.
64. AVP RF, f. 102, op. 19, p. 97, d. 5, l. 74.
65. Ibid., l. 155.
66. Tkachenko, *Koreiskii poluostrov,* 29.
67. Aleksandrov-Agentov, *Ot Kollontai do Gorbacheva,* 169.
68. AVP RF, f. 102, op. 21, p. 105, d. 2, ll. 2–5.
69. S. S. Radchenko, *The Soviet Union and the North Korean Seizure of the USS* Pueblo*: Evidence from the Russian Archives,* Cold War International History Project Working Paper 47 (Washington, D.C.: Cold War International History Project, Woodrow Wilson International Center for Scholars, 2005), 11.
70. AVP RF, f. 102, op. 19, p. 97, d. 2, l. 1.
71. RGANI, f. 5, op. 30, d. 475, l. 38.
72. AVP RF, f.102, op. 27, p. 53, d. 2, l. 2.
73. AVP RF, f. 102, op. 23, p. 110, d. 3, l. 7.
74. Ibid., l. 10.
75. AVP RF, f. 102, op. 26, p. 52, d. 2, l. 1.
76. AVP RF, f .102, op.22. p. 108, d. 13, l. 1.
77. AVP RF, f. 102, op. 33, p. 67, d. 2, l. 12.
78. AVP RF, f. 102, op. 23, p. 111, d. 12, l. 25.
79. AVP RF, f. 102, op. 23, p. 110, d. 3, l. 38.
80. AVP RF, f. 102, op. 23, p. 111, d. 12, l. 25.
81. AVP RF, f. 102, op. 22, p. 107, d. 4, ll. 1–5.
82. Ibid., l. 86.
83. Radchenko, *Soviet Union and the North Korean Seizure of the USS Pueblo.*
84. AVP RF, f. 102, op. 28, p. 55, d. 2, l. 5.
85. Ibid., ll. 7–11.
86. RGANI, f. 2, op. 3, d. 95, ll. 50–58. The original was obtained and translated for the Cold War International History Project by Sergey Radchenko; see note 69 above.
87. Tkachenko, *Koreiskii poluostrov,* 37.

88. AVP RF, f. 102, op. 28, p. 55, d. 2, l. 22.

89. AVP RF, f. 102, op. 29, p. 57, d. 9, l. 1.

90. Unfortunately, Ambassador Sudalikov's diary for April 1969 is missing from the archives. AVP RF, f. 102, op. 29, p. 57, d. 6, ll. 16–28.

91. Chen Jian and Wilson, "New Evidence on Sino-Soviet Rapprochement: 'All under Heaven Is Great Chaos,'" *Cold War International History Project Bulletin,* no. 11 (1998): 172.

92. Tkachenko, *Koreiskii poluostrov,* 31.

93. AVP RF, f. 102, op. 30, p. 59, d. 4, ll. 16–21.

94. AVP RF, f. 102, op. 31, p. 63, d. 7, l. 120.

95. AVP RF, f. 102, op. 32, p. 66, d. 10, ll. 2–13.

96. Ibid., l. 36.

97. AVP RF, f. 102, op. 32, p. 66, d. 11, l. 4.

98. M. S. Kapitsa, *Na raznyikh paralleliakh: Zapiski diplomata* [On various parallels: Notes of a diplomat] (Moscow: Kniga i biziness, 1996), 240.

99. AVP RF, f. 102, op. 32, p. 65, d. 1, l. 17.

6. Chinese Foreign Policy, 1960–1979

Lorenz Lüthi

China's place in the world after the foundation of the People's Republic of China (PRC) in 1949 was an anomaly in international affairs. As a member of the socialist camp, it challenged much of the existing liberal world order. Yet, despite being the de facto representative of most of the Chinese people, it was forced to remain outside the one international organization with which even the socialist world was willing to engage: the United Nations system. Throughout the first half of the Cold War, China remained one of the very few countries unfettered by the existing international system; it even went to war with the United Nations during the Korean War. However, this prevented the PRC neither from aspiring to become a member of the UN system nor from attempting to break out from its international isolation, which had been both imposed from the outside and self-chosen.

The year 1960 rattled China's policy of ideological and institutional absence from the larger world. The sudden withdrawal of the Soviet advisers from the PRC symbolized the ongoing collapse of the country's economic relations with most of the socialist world. Furthermore, the Great Leap Forward (1958–60) had failed to bring the economic windfall Chairman Mao Zedong had envisioned; instead, it caused famines, an economic contraction, and a decrease in China's foreign trade. The year 1960 thus was not only disastrous but also a chance to rethink the country's place in the world.

The dominance of theoretical concepts and of U.S.-centered approaches in the literature on Chinese foreign policy obscures the analysis of the reasons for

---

The author is grateful to Chen Jian for a document from the Fujian Provincial Archives, to Joyce Ng for research assistance, and to Tsuyoshi Hasegawa and Odd Arne Westad for comments.

China's trajectory from pariah nation to a respected world power from 1960 to 1979. Instead of focusing on changes within the so-called Chinese-Soviet-American triangle, the prism of ideology and modernization helps to elucidate the domestic sources of China's foreign policy changes. In the first of four sections, this chapter explores the conflict between revolutionary and modernizing impulses that led the country to international political isolation *and* global economic integration by the first years of the Cultural Revolution (1966–76). The second section covers China's rapid emergence in international relations from 1968 to 1972, triggered by internal and external causes. Finally, the last two sections address the success of the moderate policy line of modernization. The Chinese evidence on foreign policy decisionmaking during these years is still very fragmentary. Swiss, East German, British, and American archival materials, mostly from the embassies in Beijing or from talks with Chinese leaders, are important supplements to Chinese-language sources.

The "Line Struggles" in China's Foreign Relations, 1960–68

The official history of the Chinese Communist Party (CCP) is full of "line struggles"—conflicts among various party factions about the correct policy line. The tug of war over the direction of China's foreign policy in the 1960s epitomized such internal tensions. It primarily was about China's relationship with the whole outside world—the Soviet system, the imperialist world, the developing world, and international institutions. In a nutshell, the radical line still saw China as a Communist challenger of the international system, as an opponent of both the Soviet and imperialist worlds, and as the leading representative of the oppressed developing world struggling against an unjust world order. The moderate line envisioned economic integration with the outside world for the sake of economic reconstruction and modernization in the long term.

The Radical Line

The radical line emerged in the early 1960s as the result of the deterioration of Sino-Soviet ideological relations and Mao's rejection of economic reconstruction policies at home. The ideological fallout stemmed from his disagreement with Nikita Khrushchev's pragmatic, but ultimately failed, policy of peaceful coexistence with the United States under President Dwight Eisenhower.[1] Mao's aversion to economic reconstruction arose over his belief that the reintroduction of private plots and small-scale rural markets, which were designed to overcome the food and goods shortages in China that had occurred as a result of Mao's failed Great Leap Forward, amounted to the reintroduction of capitalism. This argument served him in attacking Liu Shaoqi, Deng Xiaoping, and their supporters, who not only formulated and implemented these policies but also had managed to limit Mao's influence in daily policymaking after the collapse of the Great Leap Forward.[2]

The CCP work conference in Beidaihe in the summer of 1962 marked not only the turning point in this domestic conflict but also a return of Chairman Mao's influence in foreign policy. By accusing those who promoted the recovery policies of overtaking the Khrushchevite revisionists in the Soviet Union in abolishing socialism, Mao was able to recoup control in daily policymaking.[3] His new, domestic radicalism had an immediate influence on international affairs, because he saw both as closely connected: "International and domestic [affairs] share the same set of problems, that is, whether the Revolution is led by the proletariat or the bourgeoisie."[4]

After the Beidaihe conference, Mao refined his views on international affairs. In the late 1940s, he had argued that the world was divided into two camps—one headed by the Soviet Union, and the other by United States—that were struggling over the vast intermediate zone. Starting in 1962, he argued that there were in fact two intermediate zones: developed Europe plus Japan and Australia, and the underdeveloped Asian–African–Latin American world. China, leading the large zone of underdeveloped countries, opposed both superpowers.[5] At the Sixth All-Country Foreign Affairs Conference that gathered CCP and government leaders working on foreign affairs in the fall of 1962, he made anti-Soviet struggle; the propagation of Mao Zedong Thought abroad; the focus on national liberation movements in Asia, Africa, and Latin America; and limited cooperation with nonsocialist states exclusively in the spheres of the economy and science into the guiding principles of China's foreign policy.[6] The Soviet missile withdrawal at the end of the Cuban Missile Crisis, which occurred only weeks after these fundamental changes in China's foreign policy, served Mao as proof of both a Soviet betrayal of world revolution and, hence, his own correct ideological positions.[7]

Yet it took time for this radicalism to have an impact on China's foreign relations. After the collapse in the summer of 1963 of Sino-Soviet party talks, which were designed to produce ideological reconciliation, Chairman Mao sent Prime Minister Zhou Enlai on a tour throughout the Middle East and Africa at the turn of the year to mobilize support for China in the Asian–African–Latin American intermediate zone. If one believes the contemporaneous Egyptian evidence, this Chinese visit was more a political stunt than evidence of true interest in or understanding of the region.[8]

More important was China's support for North Vietnam in the escalating

Second Indochina War. Beijing was alarmed by the political instability in South Vietnam after the assassination of its president, Ngo Dinh Diem, in late 1963 and by the possibility of increased American engagement. Thus Beijing decided by mid-1964—before the Gulf of Tonkin incident that triggered Washington's escalation—to commit military aid to Hanoi and to relocate strategic industries and cities to the country's interior.[9] Although Chinese policy toward the emerging conflict remained moderate for some months, the prospect of massive Soviet military aid to North Vietnam and the landing of U.S. ground troops in South Vietnam in early 1965 stiffened China's attitude.[10] Beijing obstructed the flow of Moscow's military aid with the goal of restricting Soviet influence and demanded that Hanoi fight a protracted guerrilla conflict within a larger anti-American united front in Southeast Asia.[11] Soviet military aid provided North Vietnam with modern weapons; Chinese aid aimed at strengthening the guerrilla forces in South Vietnam.[12] Hanoi's decision to seek a speedy victory during the Tet Offensive in early 1968, and, after that offensive's military failure, its determination to seek an end to the conflict through negotiations with Washington contradicted Beijing's demands for guerrilla war and its rejection of any diplomatic solution. With aid continuing to flow to the southern guerrillas into the 1970s, the PRC's assistance to North Vietnam nevertheless decreased for some years.[13]

A similar ideological dedication to national liberation governed China's commitment to the Palestinian cause. Because the PRC had defined the Palestinian struggle against Israel as the "Vietnam War" against U.S. imperialism in the Middle East, China was among the first countries to recognize the Palestine Liberation Organization (PLO), in May 1965, as the legitimate representative of the Palestinian people.[14] Although the precise form of Chinese aid is still a matter of dispute, Beijing's support came at a politically important point for the PLO. After the Arab defeat in the Six-Day War in mid-1967, however, the PLO increasingly turned to China's ideological archenemy—the Soviet Union—for support.[15] The lack of unity within the PLO, among other factors (see also below), convinced China to disengage from the Palestinian cause in the early 1970s.[16]

One of the primary factors in the radicalization of Chinese foreign policy in the mid-1960s was the increased militancy of domestic politics. After Mao had made resistance to revisionism a goal in foreign and domestic affairs, he hoped for Khrushchev's removal from power to help him claim supreme leadership in the socialist world and at home. However, after Khrushchev's fall in mid-October 1964, the new Soviet leadership continued Khrushchev's policy almost unchanged—except with regard to agriculture and Vietnam. Mao realized that his strategy of seeking to attain political supremacy at home by winning ideological preeminence in the socialist world had failed. Thus, at the turn of 1964–65, he decided to turn against his internal rivals in what would develop into the Cultural Revolution by mid-1966.[17]

The need to create an atmosphere of China's hostile encirclement—with the circle supposedly consisting of the revisionist Soviet Union, militarist Japan, bourgeois India, and the imperialist United States—for the purpose of mobilizing the Chinese citizenry to engage in the purge of allegedly unreliable CCP and government officials required the further radicalization of foreign policy.[18] However, this also led to China's political self-isolation in the world. In the winter of 1965–66, many of the diplomatic gains that China had made in Africa since the early 1960s evaporated when Beijing started to preach revolution against the postcolonial governments of countries that had only recently gained independence.[19] Soon thereafter, Mao broke the CCP's relations with the Communist Party of the Soviet Union by refusing to send the customary delegation to its Twenty-third Congress.[20] After the start of the Cultural Revolution in the late summer of 1966, Beijing demolished its foreign policy apparatus by withdrawing personnel from its embassies around the world (including all ambassadors except the one to Egypt), by ordering the skeleton staff to engage as "red diplomatic warriors of Chairman Mao" in revolutionary actions against their host countries, and by permitting physical violence against foreign embassy personnel in China.[21] This purposeful disrespect of diplomatic customs through the introduction of "proletarian" diplomacy, whatever it was supposed to mean, amounted to a clear challenge to the international order.[22]

The Moderate Line

Although Prime Minister Zhou Enlai often sided with Mao's radical policies toward the Soviet Union and national liberation movements, he nevertheless tried to pursue a moderate foreign policy that included the economic opening toward the outside world for the purpose of modernization.[23] Economic needs thereby often trumped both ideological blinders and the One-China Principle (the doctrine that no third country could recognize both the PRC and the Republic of China on Taiwan at the same time). In fact, his policy aimed at moving equitably toward both intermediate zones; while following Mao's policy of engaging with the Asian–African–Latin American world, he advocated an opening toward the whole outside world, but particularly the developed intermediate zone.

In this context, the PRC did not make the One-China Principle an obstacle to the rapid development of trade with nonsocialist countries. The largest among the new trading partners—Japan, Canada, Australia, and West Germany, for example—continued to recognize Taiwan as the legal representative of China until the early 1970s.[24] As early as August 1960, Beijing had in fact offered Tokyo an improvement of trade relations while permitting Tokyo to keep diplomatic relations with Taipei.[25] Already by 1965, Japan, with more than 10 percent of China's total trade, had become the PRC's largest foreign trading partner. Conversely, in the years after the sudden withdrawal of Soviet advisers in mid-1960, China's economic relations with the Soviet Union and Eastern Europe rapidly diminished. This was partly due to the continued contraction of the Chinese economy even after the end of the Great Leap Forward by late 1960,[26] and partly to the decision to refocus the country's foreign economic relations toward the nonsocialist world.[27]

In the years 1960–65, China's foreign trade was primarily driven by the needs of famine relief.[28] The country spent much of its scarce foreign currency resources to buy grain on the world market.[29] In 1961 and 1962, Beijing even turned to Moscow for famine relief.[30] From 1962 to 1965, once the worst of the food crisis had been overcome, the country also bought sixty-five industrial plants in the fields of metallurgy, oil, chemical engineering, machinery, electronics, light industry, and textiles from the United Kingdom, West Germany, Sweden, Switzerland, the Netherlands, Belgium, Austria, Japan, Italy, and France.[31]

It was against this background that Zhou supported the *sanhe yishao,* a policy proposal that had been formulated by the CCP Central Committee secretary, Wang Jiaxiang, in early 1962 and sought Three Reconciliations with the Soviet Union, the United States, and India, and One Reduction in foreign aid to other countries for ideological reasons.[32] At the same time, the prime minister, together with Foreign Minister Chen Yi, ordered the establishment of the Second Beijing Foreign Language University with the aim of training future Foreign Ministry and Foreign Trade Ministry cadres in English, French, Arabic, Spanish, and Russian. The last two languages were replaced with Japanese and German when the new university opened in September 1964,[33] which clearly reflected the change in contemporaneous trade patterns.[34] Yet Mao's reassertion of political influence at the Beidaihe work conference in the late summer of 1962, as described above, quickly terminated the *sanhe yishao.*[35]

In view of the impending final debt repayment to the Soviet Union in early 1965,[36] Zhou outlined his economic visions for the PRC in a speech to the Third National People's Congress on December 21, 1964. For the Third Five-Year Plan (1966–70), he called for *sihua* (*si xiandaihua*)—the Four Modernizations of agriculture, industry, defense, and science and technology (in that order). To achieve this goal, foreign trade around the globe was crucial as long as China would not again become heavily dependent on only one partner, as it had during the 1950s in its trade relations with the Soviet Union.[37]

This had not been the first time that Zhou had called for *sihua.* As early as September 23, 1954, he had announced the modernizations of industry, agriculture, defense, and transportation (in that order); and in February 1960, he had called for the modernizations of industry, agriculture, science, and defense (in that order). In both cases, however, developments beyond his control had undermined his plans.[38] With the Socialist High Tide in 1955 and the Great Leap Forward in 1958, Mao endorsed a radical and utopian economic development model, and in 1960 the collapse of the Great Leap Forward and the need for famine relief once more postponed the implementation of any systematic modernization policy.[39] The resulting famines explain why Zhou stressed the modernization of agriculture in late 1964.

Yet Zhou's renewed announcement of *sihua* on December 21, 1964, again came at an inopportune moment. Only a week later, Mao clashed with Liu Shaoqi and Deng Xiaoping about CCP rectification; subsequently, Mao decided to move against them outside party channels in what would become the Cultural Revolution.[40] And in the spring of 1965, under the weight of the U.S. escalation of the Vietnam War, the Chinese leadership shifted the strategic relocation of industries and cities into high gear.[41] Fearing interruptions of production, Zhou called for the maintenance of high-yield production in agriculture and for the prioritization of certain industrial projects to limit the negative economic impact of the strategic relocation program.[42] On May 5, Zhou announced the *sibao* (*si baocang;* the Four Preservations), which were designed to protect the Chinese economy from political interference.[43] The Five-Year Plan adopted in the fall of 1965 primarily called for investments in defense, military industry, strategic relocation, and the progressive transformation of China's industrial geography.[44]

With *sihua* shelved again and political radicalism increasing, foreign trade, however, did not suffer immediately. This paradox was obvious in the clash between the radical and the pragmatic lines in May 1965. Although the PRC recognized the PLO, thereby supporting its struggle against Israel,[45] West Germany coincidentally recognized Israel for unrelated reasons and provided military support against its Arab neighbors.[46] This put the dilemma before the PRC of either supporting the PLO against Israel or continuing trade relations with pro-Israeli West Germany.[47] In the end, Beijing's goods exchange with Bonn increased by a record 87 percent in 1965 and continued to grow in the following years.[48] By 1967, West Germany was China's third-largest trading partner after Japan and the United Kingdom; economic pragmatism had trumped political radicalism.

Although the radicalism of the Cultural Revolution virtually paralyzed the institutional and human resources of China's diplomatic apparatus, the Foreign Trade Ministry seemed to have escaped much of the political unrest. And though the Foreign Ministry was the scene of a seizure by radicalized junior cadres,[49] most of the other ministries experienced only "Chinese opera–style" takeovers.[50] Furthermore, Zhou Enlai sent the People's Liberation Army to check any radical influence in most of the ministries in May 1967.[51] Similarly, the pre–Cultural Revolution trends in trade developments continued. Japan, the United Kingdom, and West Germany accounted for 25 to 30 percent of China's foreign trade during the late 1960s.[52]

Foreign trade started to suffer in the 1967–69 period due to its susceptibility to changes in domestic economic developments.[53] China had experienced four years of economic growth starting in 1963, only to dive into a contraction in 1967. As early as June 1966, the CCP Central Committee had reactivated one of the disastrous Great Leap Forward slogans: "Bigger, Faster, Better."[54] Once Mao had called on the Red Guards to mobilize workers and peasants, in late 1966,[55] political radicalism swept into China's economic sphere.[56] Workers and peasants embraced passive resistance (absenteeism, strikes, sabotage, and waste) or instrumentalized the radical rhetoric of the Cultural Revolution to advance their own economic interests (higher bonuses, shorter working hours, etc.). Both, however, damaged economic production and led to repeated calls by the government for the strikers to return to their work sites.[57]

By August 1967, Zhou Enlai publicly condemned the interference by the Red Guards in China's economy.[58] A Swiss Embassy report late that year called his efforts to shield the economy from radicalism only partially successful, especially because many experienced economic cadres had been purged. Yet, though the report maintained that the *overall* damages to the economy were minor, it asserted that *most* of the damage occurred in industry, which made up only 10 percent of China's economic output. The Swiss Embassy's assessment concluded that the contraction of 1967, although minor in view of the overall economy, was responsible for the exponentially negative trends in foreign trade, which in turn would cause a long-term "setback" for China's modernization.[59] Indeed, the policy of importing technology was officially suspended in 1968.[60] Thus overall trade and imports decreased by 12.6 and 18.7 percent, respectively, during the 1967–69 period, but imports of machinery and whole sets of factories—the backbone of modernization—declined by 44.9 and 93.3 percent, respectively.[61]

Imports of technology also shouldered the brunt of the decline in trade because China was unable to alter recurring import costs in other areas. Given the endemic problems in food supplies, the PRC was dependent on imports of both foodstuffs and chemicals for fertilizer production. Throughout the second half of the 1960s, these two categories remained at 39.4 to 45.7 percent, respectively, of the overall import budget each year.[62] No wonder that Zhou repeatedly called for the maintenance of high levels of food production during the chaos of the early Cultural Revolution.[63] Thus, while the strategic relocation triggered by the Vietnam War had delayed *sihua,* the Cultural Revolution threatened to postpone the Four Modernizations even further.

By 1967–68, the line of revolutionary radicalism seemed to have pushed the pragmatic economic line out of the limelight. While Mao worked on the completion of his project for an isolated model revolutionary society, Zhou was left to protect the economic fundamentals for the sake of future modernization. In politics, however, nothing stays the same for long.

Toward Reintegration with the World, 1968–72

China escaped its institutional absence and self-chosen political isolation from the world in a short period from 1968 to 1972. Several factors contributed to the country's stunning reintegration after its two decades of being the odd man out in international affairs. First, Mao realized that he had led China into a dead end. Second, economic needs forced the country to open up even more. And finally, the world had come around to accepting the PRC into its fold.

Diplomatic Resurgence

The burning of a building of the British legation in Beijing on August 22, 1967, which was executed by Red Guards but organized by radicalized Foreign Ministry officials,[64] revealed to Mao both the negative effects of the Cultural Revolution on China's ability to implement a meaningful foreign policy and the degree to which he had lost control over political developments. Although it took years to reestablish order in the Foreign Ministry in particular and in China at large, Chairman Mao, together with Prime Minister Zhou, did not lose time in purging the Foreign Ministry of its radicals and prohibiting any further attacks on embassies.[65] Later that year, Mao also apologized to the prime minister of Congo (Brazzaville) for the "breach of diplomatic etiquette" by the Chinese Embassy in that African country. At that time, preparations for the redispatching of ambassadors abroad reportedly were under way as well.[66]

In a series of decrees in the first half of 1968, the chairman rescinded his 1962 instruction to use Mao Zedong Thought in the conduct of foreign relations.[67]

The Soviet intervention in Czechoslovakia on August 21, 1968, drove the danger of the country's self-isolation in the world home to the Chinese leadership. Moscow's actions testified to its willingness to intervene in other socialist states if it saw its interests threatened; Bucharest and Beijing feared being next.[68] For many foreign observers in China, this event was the decisive moment that triggered "China's reappearance on the world stage."[69] Yet changes in China's diplomacy necessitated the reconstruction of central CCP and government organs capable of implementing new polices. For a long time, Mao had postponed calling for the convention of the Ninth Party Congress necessary for that task because he had feared that the lack of provincial organs would lead to a top-heavy central bureaucracy.[70] The last provincial revolutionary committees, which were designed to function as new midlevel administrative institutions, however, happened to be established in Tibet and Xinjiang the following month.[71] Thus the chairman called for the first CCP Central Committee plenum since August 1966 to be convened in October 1968. That meeting was supposed to prepare for the April 1969 Party Congress,[72] which Mao wanted to be the final curtain call for the Cultural Revolution.[73]

Most important, China seemed to be again engaged in diplomacy. On November 25, it signaled to the United States the resumption of the unofficial ambassadorial talks, which had started in 1955 but had ended with the beginning of the Cultural Revolution, in late February in Warsaw.[74] This decision occurred against the background earlier that month of the election to the U.S. presidency of Richard Nixon, who had advocated rapprochement with China for a year,[75] and the related hope of solving the thorny Taiwan issue.[76] Furthermore, the Chinese signal occurred eight days after Mao, in a conversation with Vietnamese prime minister Pham Van Dong, had finally endorsed the North Vietnamese strategy of negotiating with the Americans in Paris while continuing to fight on the ground in Indochina.[77] These two events represented a marked change in Chinese foreign policy, which had until recently rejected negotiations under any circumstances.[78] Before, Foreign Minister Chen Yi had still equated the Soviet intervention in Czechoslovakia with the American aggression in Vietnam.[79]

Yet, in a last bout of self-isolationism, Mao canceled the ambassadorial talks after a Chinese consular officer in the Netherlands defected to the United States on February 19, 1969.[80] Two weeks later, on March 2, in an attempt to reassert its claims over Damanskii/Zhenbao Island—a small island in an isolated stretch of the Ussuri River—China provoked a massive, though unsuccessful, Soviet counterattack on March 15, followed by the Soviet threat of a nuclear strike.[81] In its wake, Mao decided to make the impending CCP convention into a "congress of unity," which would seek to bring together the different factions of the party, including some of those who had recently been purged.[82]

Although the reconstitution of the CCP's central organs moved factional infighting into the newly established Politburo and the Central Committee,[83] Mao and Zhou immediately proceeded with the reconstruction of China's foreign policy apparatus. On May 1, the chairman invited the ambassadors of eight countries to attend the Labor Day festivities on the top of Tiananmen Gate—a rare honor—to announce the redispatching of Chinese ambassadors abroad, to apologize for the Cultural Revolution violence against embassies, and to blame "ultraleftists" for the damage done to China's foreign relations.[84] From May 15 to August 17, the PRC stationed ambassadors in seventeen countries, thereby vastly increasing China's ambassadorial representation abroad beyond the lonely Chinese representative in Egypt.[85] Yet Beijing made no overtures to the United States. Zhou only instructed Lei Yang, who left for Warsaw in June to become chargé d'affaires, "to pay close attention to developments in U.S. policy."[86]

With that, China's reintegration with the world had started. Its new foreign policy line found support in a report from four marshals, whom Mao and Zhou had asked to analyze the international situation. Although the report oozed ideological concepts, it concluded that China's best global strategy consisted of increasing diplomatic efforts around the globe in order to "expand the international united front of anti-imperialism and anti-revisionism."[87]

Economic Needs

The second important reason for China's reintegration was the drab economic situation at home. The decrease in foreign trade, in general, and of the importing of technology for the sake of modernization, in particular, have already been addressed above. Yet at a meeting of the Chinese leadership in May 1968, radicals and moderates could not agree on the future of the Cultural Revolution, although the withdrawal of politics from the economic sphere was a point of discussion.[88] Similar to the diplomatic resurgence after the Soviet intervention in Czechoslovakia, economics moved to center stage in the fall, when Zhou called several times for a "Great Leap Forward" (*sic!*) in production.[89] In fact, the year 1969, in the words of a British observer, was a "year of undramatic consolidation," with 11.1 percent growth in the nation's gross domestic product.[90]

In 1970, Zhou stressed the continuation of a policy of establishing small and medium-sized factories that only required the import of machinery but not of complete sets of factories. However, grain and chemical fertilizer imports, as a British report noted, continued "at a high level." Yet, as newspaper articles published in China that year testify, the country's leadership was discussing the resumption of constructing large and integrated factories.[91] But this required the production of a steady supply of high-quality commodities for export in exchange for the purchase of such technology. According to another British report, the PRC experienced problems throughout 1970 in delivering such commodities of the quality and quantity contractually agreed to with foreign business partners.[92]

It was only after the demise of Lin Biao, Mao's appointed successor—who died in mid-September 1971 in a plane crash in Outer Mongolia during an attempt to escape to the Soviet Union—that Zhou regained complete control over the decisionmaking process in economic affairs. With the promotion of foreign trade as the key to modernization, imports of Japanese technology, in particular, helped make the period from 1971 to 1973 a time of renewed economic growth. However, by 1974, the "Gang of Four"—Mao's wife, Jiang Qing, and three of her collaborators during the Cultural Revolution—launched the "Criticize Lin Biao and Confucius" campaign, which was spearheaded against Zhou, derided foreign expertise, and promoted the idea of modernization on the basis of China's own domestic efforts.[93] As a result, the growth in gross domestic product in the first half of the 1970s was erratic, though not negative, and imports reached a new peak for the PRC in 1973–74 before falling again for some years.[94]

The World's Acceptance of a Communist China

The final reason for China's reintegration was the world's growing acceptance of the PRC as a fact in international life. Despite the fact that China had a falling out with most of the socialist camp in the early 1960s, no socialist country ever disputed that the PRC was the legitimate and only representative of the Chinese people. On the other side of the Cold War divide, however, the story was different.

Great Britain had recognized China as early as January 6, 1950, because it followed the doctrine of recognizing de facto governments.[95] Charles de Gaulle's France, dropping its recognition of Taiwan, established relations with the PRC on January 27, 1964, mainly for the purpose of reasserting its own independent role in world affairs after having given up its colonial possessions.[96] Japan, because of its booming trade with China, tried to copy France's diplomatic success in 1965, but the concurrent political radicalization in China stalled this endeavor.[97] Despite increased Canadian wheat deliveries to China since 1961, it was only in the summer of 1968 that the Sinophile Pierre Trudeau reviewed Canada's foreign policy, shortly after becoming prime minister. Given that the PRC had refused to sign the Nuclear Non-Proliferation Treaty, Trudeau hoped to stabilize the international order by embracing it diplomatically. By 1969, Beijing and Ottawa were negotiating recognition.[98]

The United States, the leading power of the Western world and a staunch supporter of Taiwan, refused to recognize the PRC diplomatically until January 1, 1979. As early as John F. Kennedy's presidency, however, Washington had pondered rapprochement with Beijing.[99] But the unofficial Sino-American ambassadorial talks since 1955 did not further this goal, especially once Chinese domestic politics progressed toward the Cultural Revolution.[100] It was only after the fall 1969 war scare in China, which stemmed from Soviet psychological warfare starting in mid-August, that Beijing and Washington revived the ambassadorial talks.[101] By early 1970, the PRC even communicated with the United States via Pakistan that it had abandoned its assessment of the Soviet-American great power collusion in international affairs.[102]

However, no Sino-American rapprochement followed. The U.S. involvement in the right-wing military coup in Cambodia against King Sihanouk, China's ally, in the early spring of 1970 triggered Beijing's attempts to seek rapprochement with Moscow.[103] On May 1, Mao received the vice head of the Soviet border negotiation team on top of Tiananmen Gate, stating his wish for "good-neighborly relations."[104] The same year, China redispatched fourteen ambassadors, among them those to the Soviet Union, Hungary, North Korea, Poland, and East Germany.[105] Apparently, in the first half of 1970, Mao was trying to hedge his bets between U.S. imperialism and Soviet revisionism. And then, on October 13, the PRC established diplomatic relations with Canada—the first country in five years, apart from the People's Republic of Yemen in 1968—with nineteen more countries to follow by the end of 1971.[106] In all cases, these countries had to abide by the One-China Principle and cut official relations with Taiwan.

Against this background, Sino-American rapprochement resumed in the second half of 1970. Once the Cambodian issue had receded into the background,[107] the PRC invited Edgar Snow, an American journalist who had been sympathetic to the Communist cause since the 1930s, to make an extended visit to the PRC in the late summer of 1970. Mao even received him on October 1 on top of Tiananmen Gate and on December 18 for a long interview, but these two signals were lost on the Americans.[108] In early 1971, the PRC asked Romania to pass an invitation to the U.S. president to visit China, but, again, the recipient did not reply.[109] Yet the PRC was not discouraged; in early March,

Vice Foreign Minister Qiao Guanhua hinted to the Swiss ambassador that major changes in China's foreign policy were impending.[110] Once ping-pong diplomacy had occurred, Zhou sent a letter on April 21 through Pakistan to Nixon, inviting a representative of the president to secret talks in China.[111] After the seminal secret visit of Henry Kissinger, then the president's national security adviser, to Beijing on July 9–10, 1971, both sides announced Nixon's visit for February 1972.[112]

Rapprochement with the enemy of twenty years was not uncontested at home, even if it seemed to bring the solution of the Taiwan issue closer. According to what Mao told French foreign minister Maurice Schumann in 1972, Lin Biao had been an opponent of Sino-American rapprochement.[113] Although Mao courted more moderate Chinese leaders who had suffered during the Cultural Revolution for promoting less radical foreign policy ideas after Lin's death, it was still difficult to make rapprochement with the United States palatable to many CCP members.[114] In a report to the party in December 1971, Zhou once more reconfirmed the theory of the two camps and the two intermediate zones while portraying the impending visit by the U.S. president as a "victory" for China and as a magnanimous gesture of consent to "Nixon's *request*" to come.[115] However, the visit was more symbolic than substantive, and it served Washington as an instrument for achieving détente with Moscow.[116]

Finally, the United Nations moved toward recognition of the PRC. Throughout most of the 1960s, the advocacy of PRC membership had been a minority position among the member states; support for Communist China had never been even close to the two-thirds majority of votes in the General Assembly necessary for obtaining UN membership and thus replacing Taiwan. The increasing number of votes in 1969 and 1970, however, suggested that the tide was turning.[117] It was only a matter of a few years at most until the PRC would replace Taiwan. In fact, on October 26, 1971, the General Assembly voted to seat the PRC and expel Taiwan, with seventy-six yes votes (68.5 percent of those cast) to thirty-five no votes.[118] Kissinger's secret visit to Beijing only four months earlier had been a sign that American resistance to the inevitable was fading.

The PRC was not prepared for UN membership in institutional and political terms, however. The initial talks between the Chinese UN ambassador, Huang Hua, and American representatives reveal the level of Chinese ignorance about the functioning of the UN system, even about such basic matters as procedures in the Security Council and the General Assembly.[119] The PRC also refused to recognize all past UN resolutions, particularly those dating back to the Korean War.[120]

Yet, through the act of entering the UN, the PRC embraced the very institution it had denounced as "an instrument of great power politics" as late as

February 1969.[121] The greatest change in China's foreign policy, however, revolved around its decreasing support for national liberation movements that aimed to overthrow legal governments around the globe. Most of its support for these movements—except the National Liberation Front in South Vietnam—ended in the early 1970s. To garner African votes at the UN, the PRC had renounced its support for revolutions against postcolonial governments.[122] Anti-Soviet policy guided the realignment of the PRC with the shah's regime in Iran and terminated support for pro-Chinese Iranian opposition parties.[123] And despite Qiao Guanhua's denouncement of the "aggression against the Palestinian . . . peoples by Israeli Zionism" in his inaugural speech at the UN in November 1971,[124] Sino-PLO relations were cooling down, largely because of Soviet-Palestinian rapprochement and the rise of international Palestinian terrorism.[125] In the long term, however, the PRC not only abandoned its challenge to the international order but also became one of its staunchest defenders against any change. Communist China was, and still is, particularly concerned about developments in international law—especially with regard to human rights—that undermine the dogma of noninterference in domestic affairs.[126]

Wooing the Intermediate Zones, 1972–76

The available Chinese evidence does not reveal precisely what Beijing had hoped to obtain from rapprochement with Washington beyond some progress on the Taiwan issue and some sort of strategic realignment.[127] It must have been more, because the PRC was frustrated by the lack of further developments in Sino-American relations afterward and by the subsequent Soviet-American détente. On December 2, 1975, Mao told visiting President Gerald Ford: "It seems to me at present there is nothing very much between our two countries, your country and mine. Probably this year, next year, the year after there will not be anything great happening between our countries. Perhaps afterward the situation might become a bit better."[128] At the same time, however, rapprochement with the former Soviet ally did not work out either.

In the final years of Mao's life, the foreign policy of the PRC focused on the two intermediate zones. The new CCP Constitution of August 1973 asserted that China's foreign policy strategy was to "firmly unite" with "the proletariat, the oppressed people and nations of the *whole* world" in order "to oppose the hegemonism of the two superpowers."[129] Half a year later, Mao and his lieutenants started to propagate the three-world theory, according to which the imperialist exploiters, the United States and the Soviet Union, formed the first world; the simultaneously exploited and exploiting developed countries, one of the former intermediate zones, made up the second world; and the large remainder of nations composed the exploited third world. Although the PRC continued to claim a leadership position in the so-called third world (the former Asian–African–Latin American intermediate zone), it now emphasized economic development and cooperation within that world *over* Communist revolution and confrontation, as Deng Xiaoping told the UN General Assembly in early 1974.[130]

It was in this context that the PRC showed continued interest in developing closer relations with the so-called second world, particularly with Japan and the European Economic Community (EEC; or the Common Market). Trade with China's most important trading partner, Japan, made up between 16.5 and 25.7 percent of overall trade in 1971–76, and with the United Kingdom and West Germany another 10 percent each. During the same period, goods exchanges with the two superpowers were negligent.[131]

Although Japan was playing in a league of its own as a source of foreign technology for the PRC, China's interest in Western Europe was more than just economic. At the time of Nixon's visit, the PRC showed an increased interest in the EEC because the Common Market "improved [the] economic and political strength of smaller countries and therefore their ability to resist [the] imperialist pressure of [the] superpowers," as the Chinese ambassador in Moscow told his British counterpart.[132] The accession of the United Kingdom to the EEC, which became final on January 22, 1972, particularly pleased the PRC, because, according to Zhou Enlai, it symbolized the fall of the United States and the Soviet Union from positions of world power.[133] As a British report concluded in late 1974, Chinese interests in the EEC were primarily twofold: establishing a "counterweight to the Soviet Union (and to a lesser extent the United States)" and finding "a trading partner and source of advanced technology."[134]

By the mid-1970s, China's economic growth had become erratic but positive. The country's grain production had doubled since the Great Leap Forward, but its net grain imports in 1973–74 were as high as in 1961–64. With regard to foreign trade, China returned to where it had been in 1963–67.[135] Against the background of this unsettled but rebounding economy, Zhou returned to *sihua* on January 13, 1975. At the Fourth National People's Congress, in what would be his last public appearance, he called for the "overall modernization of agriculture, industry, national defense, and science and technology before the end of the century."[136] Throughout 1975, Deng enacted many of Zhou's ideas, which resulted in overall increases in agricultural and even more in industrial production. However, late that year, the radicals around Jiang Qing once more moved against these new policies.[137]

The End of Revolution, 1976–79

After Zhou's and Mao's deaths in 1976, it took the PRC two years to implement new foreign and domestic policies. Although foreign trade remained roughly at the same level throughout the 1974–78 period, the import of whole sets of factories and machinery decreased sharply after 1976.[138] In mid-1978, the PRC and the United States started to negotiate about the full establishment of diplomatic relations. In late 1978, a Joint Communiqué announced the establishment of diplomatic relations on January 1, 1979.

China's economic modernization, as envisioned by Zhou since the 1950s, required an increased transfer of technology from the West. The deepening of China's relations with the capitalist world, however, was only possible through the normalization of relations with its economic powerhouses—Japan and, particularly, the United States, its most important member and technological leader.[139] Most of 1977 was spent sorting out problems in the PRC's communication and transportation system.[140] As early as the beginning of that year, however, China and Japan both were eager to initiate negotiations on a peace treaty, which they eventually signed in mid-August 1978. This agreement not only officially ended World War II in East Asia but also elevated the two nations' existing close trade links to the level of government relations.[141] Yet this was only a harbinger of greater changes to come in the remainder of the year.

On May 7, 1978, in a conversation with a delegation from Madagascar, Deng asserted that the September 1976 purge of the "Gang of Four" had not only ended a dark chapter in China's recent history but also reopened the path to *sihua.*[142] On June 6, *Renmin Ribao* (*People's Daily*) publicly mentioned the policy of the Four Modernizations. The following month, the Central Committee adopted decisions to accelerate industrial development; in September, the State Council discussed *sihua,* after twenty years of systemic modernization had been lost, as the economic specialist Li Xiannian asserted. The Third Plenum of the Eleventh Central Committee in December eventually approved *sihua,* thereby marking the decisive turn to Zhou's longtime call for China's modernization and the start of economic policies that led to astonishing changes in the PRC that continue to this very day.[143]

Equally important in China's strategic turn to the United States was the Soviet threat. By mid-1978, border incidents between Vietnam, a Soviet ally except in name, and Pol Pot's Cambodia, China's ally since 1975, occurred at more frequent intervals.[144] Simultaneously, the Soviet Union stationed SS-20 intermediate-range ballistic missiles in Siberia.[145] Washington had good reasons to reciprocate China's entreaties. President Jimmy Carter had focused on Soviet-American détente in his first year in office,[146] but Moscow dragged its feet on the second round of the Strategic Arms Limitation Talks (SALT II) negotiations.[147] By early 1978, Soviet-American relations had worsened over Soviet and Cuban assistance to Ethiopia in its conflict with Somalia.[148] This formed the impetus for the United States to play the China card in order to apply pressure on the Soviet Union.[149] On January 1, 1979, after almost thirty years of official alienation, the two greatest Cold War antagonists in East Asia established not only official relations but also a quasi-alliance against the Soviet Union. Thus, the United States' Cold War containment of the revolutionary Sino-Soviet alliance was transformed into Sino-American strategic containment of a perceived Soviet global expansionism. The last step in ending Sino-American antagonism was the reaffirmation of the status quo on the question of Chinese national unity: the de facto existence of Taiwan.[150]

The containment of Vietnam and the related Chinese commitment to status quo politics in Southeast Asia followed the same logic. During the Sino-American talks in 1978, the PRC repeatedly raised Vietnamese expansionism and Soviet support behind it.[151] On November 3, Moscow and Hanoi concluded a Treaty of Friendship and Cooperation that allowed the Soviet Union to station its navy at the former U.S. base on Cam Ranh Bay.[152] A week later, Deng publicly railed against the treaty, calling Vietnam a "small hegemonist," a pawn in Soviet global strategy, and the "Cuba of the Orient."[153] Hanoi, in turn, accused Beijing, its former revolutionary ally, of having sold out world revolution.[154]

Given Vietnam's visible preparations by late 1978 to intervene in Cambodia, the PRC faced the puzzle of dissecting its neighbor's overall aims in the region. Vietnamese peace diplomacy—in the form of Pham Van Dong's visits to the Association of Southeast Asian Nations (ASEAN) member states from September 6 to October 17—was supposed to disguise what was in fact (as Hanoi communicated to East Berlin) a policy of "internationalist duty," the spread of revolution, throughout Southeast Asia.[155] Although virtually no direct Chinese evidence has surfaced on how Beijing perceived this prospect, the PRC certainly was concerned. In the first half of January 1979, after Vietnam's occupation of Cambodia, Deng secretly visited Thailand for the purpose of setting up a Sino-ASEAN quasi-alliance against its neighbor.[156] According to what CCP Chairman Hua Guofeng told West German Chancellor Helmut Schmidt almost a year later, Chinese thinking in late 1978 followed both political and strategic lines. The PRC could hardly prevent the impending second Vietnamese step to alter the status quo in Southeast Asia after the reunification in 1975 of that country itself, but it had to ponder how to turn this into Vietnam's last challenge to the regional order: "China's struggle against any kind of hegemony was intended to be genuine. . . . If China had not acted, then Thailand and Malaysia would have been the next victims; the ASEAN countries would not [have been able to] resist in that case. With that, the Soviet Union would have gained access to the Strait of Malacca and thereby control over a crucial maritime link between the Pacific and Indian oceans. That would have had an impact on the Persian Gulf, on the Red Sea, and definitely on the world's oil supply."[157] With Moscow's support, Hanoi had assumed the role of exporter of world revolution to which Beijing had aspired in the 1960s but which Mao's successors had given up.

It was in this context that Deng arrived in Washington on January 28, 1979, reciprocating Nixon's trip to Beijing with a visit to President Carter. Although most of the original documents have not yet been declassified, the available evidence paints a clear picture of Deng's talks with the U.S. president. In the first meeting on January 29, the Chinese leader was gloomy about the possibility of war[158]—he even went so far as to assert that the Soviet Union wanted to start one[159]—and called for cooperation between the United States, China, Japan, and Western Europe against the Soviet Union.[160] If the United States took the leading role, Deng asserted, China would cooperate.[161] Turning to East Asia, Deng suggested maintaining the status quo on the Korean Peninsula.[162] Finally, Deng accused the Soviet Union of using Cuba for its expansionist policies in Africa and exploiting Vietnam for the same purpose in Southeast Asia.[163]

When Deng left the United States, the world was bracing for another war in Southeast Asia. On February 15, 1979, the Chinese ambassador informed the Carter administration that Beijing had fully considered U.S. concerns about international repercussions but had decided to take self-defensive measures.[164] Carter was sympathetic to the Chinese aims.[165] The following day, Deng ordered military action for February 17.[166] The Sino-Vietnamese war marked the definitive end of revolutionary unity among the Asian Communist parties that had been held together by China's support for national liberation from the Korean War through the Vietnam War. In Beijing, sheer balance-of-power thinking had replaced revolutionary expansionism. China had entered its post-revolutionary age.

Conclusion

The 1960–79 period witnessed the transformation of an isolated, revolutionary People's Republic into a globally integrated, status quo–oriented China. The sources of this remarkable transformation were manifold. First, the PRC gave up its ideological radicalism, partly because Mao had achieved his domestic goals of purging real and invented enemies at home, but also because he realized that he had led the country into a global dead end. Thus, in the late 1970s, the Vietnamese accused the Chinese of just what the PRC had accused the Soviet Union of in the early 1960s: selling out world revolution for the sake of great power collusion. Second, Mao's ideological radicalism of the 1960s concealed an economic pragmatism that gradually led to the country's integration with the world economy—even before its diplomatic opening. Although Mao's policies continued to be detrimental to the country's economic health, he at least refrained from intervening too overtly in economic policy. Even during the Cultural Revolution, the PRC continued to trade globally for the sake of economic modernization. Finally, by the late 1960s, both China and the wider world recognized the necessity of normalizing relations. Parts of the Western world had pushed for this development since the early 1960s, while the 1968–69 period was crucial for China's turn toward the outside world.

The attempt to understand the changes in China's policies on the twin levels of domestic politics and international affairs, and not with theoretical concepts like a triangular Sino-Soviet-American relationship, relegates the superpowers to a less dominant role in China's reintegration with the world. This is not to say that they did not play important roles in this process, because their actions clearly helped to push and pull China into global politics. But as recent Cold War historiography has revealed, smaller states often played roles that were greater than previously assumed in the monumental changes of the Cold War because they had greater independence in formulating and implementing their own policies.

Notes

1. Lorenz Lüthi, *The Sino-Soviet Split: Cold War in the Communist World* (Princeton, N.J.: Princeton University Press, 2008), 151–52.
2. Ibid., chaps. 6, 7, and 9.
3. Ibid., 221.
4. Zhonggong zhongyang wenxian yanjiushi bian [Chinese Communist Party, Central Committee, Research Office of Government Documents], ed., *Mao Zedong zhuan (1949–1976)* [Biography of Mao Zedong (1949–1976); hereafter *MZDZ*] (Beijing: Zhongyang wenxian chubanshe, 2003), 1235.
5. "Two Intermediate Zones (1963/9, 1964/1, 7)," in *Mao Zedong wenji* [A collection of Mao Zedong's papers], by Mao Zedong, vol. 8 (Beijing: Renmin chubanshe, 1999), 343–44.
6. "Communication of the Main Points of the 6th All-Country Foreign Affairs Conference," n.d., Jiangsu Sheng Dang'anguan (Jiangsu Provincial Archives; hereafter JSSDAG), 3124, zhang 145, 2–13.
7. Lüthi, *Sino-Soviet Split,* 224–28.
8. "Information," n.d., Stiftung Archiv der Parteien und Massenorganisationen der DDR im Bundesarchiv (Foundation Archive of Parties and Mass Organizations of the GDR in the Federal Archive, Berlin; hereafter SAPMO-Barch), DY 30/IV A 2/20/890,

1–13. See also Ji Chaozhu, who claims that the trip was about getting Middle Eastern and African support for Chinese membership in the United Nations; Ji Chaozhu, *The Man on Mao's Right: From Harvard Yard to Tiananmen Square—My Life Inside China's Foreign Ministry* (New York: Random House, 2008), 210.

9. Lorenz Lüthi, "The Early 2nd Vietnam War and China's 3rd-Line Defense Planning before the Cultural Revolution, 1964–1966," *Journal of Cold War Studies* 10, no. 1 (2008): 31.

10. Lüthi, *Sino-Soviet Split,* 305–24.

11. Han Suyin, *Eldest Son: Zhou Enlai and the Making of Modern China, 1898–1976* (London: Pimlico, 1994), 304; "Winzer to Ulbricht, Stoph, Honecker," December 21, 1965, SAPMO-BArch, NY 4182/1222, 95–96.

12. "Reception for Michałowski," January 15, 1966, Arkhiv Vneshnei Politiki Rossiiskoi Federatsii, Moscow (Archive of Foreign Policy of the Russian Federation; hereafter AVP RF), fond (f.) 100, opis' (op.) 59, papka (p.) 525, delo (d.) 5, list (l.) 2.

13. Zhai Qiang, *China and the Vietnam Wars, 1950–1975* (Chapel Hill: University of North Carolina Press, 2000), 179.

14. Xiao Sike, "Xu Yixin: Zhonggongdangshi shang de 'bangge renwu'" [Xu Yixin: The "semi-person" in CCP history], *Wenshi Bolan,* no. 10, 2007, 26.

15. "Note," June 25, 1966, Politisches Archiv des Auswärtigen Amtes, Bestand: Ministerium für Auswärtige Angelegenheiten (Files of the Ministry for Foreign Affairs in the Political Archive of the Office for Foreign Affairs, Berlin; hereafter PAAA-MfAA), Abteilung Arabische Staaten Gesamtarabische Fragen, A 13343, 81–82.

16. "Political Report no. 17," June 26, 1972, Bundesarchiv Bern (Federal Archive Berne; hereafter BA Bern), E 2300-01, Akzession 1977/29, 17, "1972 p.a. 21.31 Moskau Politische Berichte," 1–13. Shi Yanchun, "Zhou Enlai yu Zhongdong: Jinian Zhou Enlai zongli shishi 30 zhounian" [Zhou Enlai and the Middle East: The 30th anniversary of Zhou Enlai's passing], *Dangshi Zongheng,* no. 1, 2006, 8.

17. Lüthi, *Sino-Soviet Split,* 285–92.

18. "Information No. 51/65," 10/2/1965, SAPMO-BArch, DY 30/IV A 2/20/220, 2.

19. Alaba Ogunsanwo, *China's Policy in Africa, 1958–1971* (Cambridge: Cambridge University Press, 1974), 194; Alan Hutchison, *China's African Revolution* (London: Hutchinson, 1975), 103–32; G. P. Deshpande and H. K. Gupta, *United Front against Imperialism: China's Foreign Policy in Africa* (Bombay: Somaiya, 1986), 130–50.

20. Wu Lengxi, *Yi Mao zhuxi: Wo qinshen jingli de ruogan zhongda lishi shijian pianduan* [Remembering Chairman Mao: A part of a series of important historical events I personally experienced] (Beijing: Xinhua, 1995), 151–52; Wu Lengxi, *Shinian lunzhan, 1956–1966: ZhongSu guanxi huiyulu* [Ten years of debate, 1956–1966: Recollections of Sino-Soviet relations] (Beijing: Zhongyang wenxian, 1999), 937–39.

21. Ma Jisen, *The Cultural Revolution in the Foreign Ministry of China* (Hong Kong: Chinese University Press, 2004), 73–77; "Political Report no. 11," July 17, 1967, BA Bern, E 2300-01, Akzession 1973/156, 18, "1967 p.a. 21.31 Peking Politische Berichte," 1–2 (quotation).

22. "Tel no. 180," 2/10/1967, National Archives of the United Kingdom, Kew (hereafter NA UK), FCO 21/8, "Political Affairs (Internal), General Situation and Policy," 1.

23. "Political Letter," January 16, 1962, BA Bern, E 2300, Akzession 1000/716, 360, "Politische Briefe, 1962," 1–2.

24. For the development of trade relations, see Dangdai Zhongguo congshi [Contemporary China collection], *Dangdai Zhongguo duiwai maoyi* [Contemporary China trade], vol. 2 (Beijing: Dangdai Zhongguo chubanshe, 1992), 371–88. For the recognition of China instead of Taiwan, see Xinhua News Agency, *China's Foreign Relations: A Chronology of Events (1949–1988)* (Beijing: Foreign Languages Press, 1989), 225, 407, 415, 452, 489, 518, 534, 559.

25. Xiao Donglian, *Qiusuo Zhongguo: Wenge qian shinian shi* [In search of China: The history of the decade before the Cultural Revolution], vol. 2 (Beijing: Hongqi, 1999), 919. *Dangdai Zhongguo duiwai maoyi,* vol. 1, 30, including note 1.

26. For data on the developments related to gross domestic product, see Penn World Tables, http://pwt.econ.upenn.edu/php_site/pwt62/pwt62_form.php. For trade developments, see *Dangdai Zhongguo duiwai maoyi,* vol. 2, 371–88.

27. "Record of Conversation with Chen Yi," October 26, 1960, AVP RF, f. 100, op. 53, d. 9, p. 454, l. 62.

28. Feng Lu, *China's Grain Trade Policy and Its Domestic Grain Economy,* CFER Working Paper E1997002 (Beijing: Center for Economic Research, Peking University, 1997), 22.

29. Xiao, *Qiusuo Zhongguo,* vol. 2, 759–61.

30. Lüthi, *Sino-Soviet Split,* 198–201.

31. Xiao, *Qiusuo Zhongguo,* vol. 2, 919. Also see *Dangdai Zhongguo duiwai maoyi,* vol. 1, 31.

32. Xu Zehao, *Wang Jiaxiang zhuan* [Biography of Wang Jiaxiang] (Beijing: Dangdai Zhongguo, 1996), 555–63.

33. Zhonggong zhongyang wenxian yanjiushi bian [CCP, Central Documents Research Office], ed., *Zhou Enlai nianpu, 1949–1976* [A chronicle of Zhou Enlai's life: 1949–1976], vol. 2 [hereafter *ZELNP*2] (Beijing: Zhongyang wenxian, 1997), 465; Jin Changru, "Qunce qunli yingyun ersheng: Beijing dier waiguoyu xueyuan choujian jingguo" [Teamwork in favorable conditions: The establishment of the Second Foreign Language School in Beijing], *Beijing dier waiguoyu xueyuan xuebao* 5 (1994): 1–6.

34. *Dangdai Zhongguo duiwai maoyi,* vol. 2, 371–88.

35. Roderick MacFarquhar, *The Origins of the Cultural Revolution,* vol. 3 (New York: Columbia University Press, 1997), 290.

36. "Record of Conversation with the Vice-Minister of Trade of the PRC Li Qiang," April 5, 1965, AVP RF, f. 100, op. 58, d. 5, p. 516, ll. 68–69.

37. Zhou Enlai, "Major Tasks for Developing the National Economy," December 21, 1964, in *Selected Works,* by Zhou Enlai, vol. 2 (Beijing: Foreign Languages Press, 1989), 458–61.

38. Zhonggong zhongyang wenxian yanjiu shibian, ed., *Zhou Enlai zhuan* [A biography of Zhou Enlai], vol. 2 [hereafter *ZELZ*2] (Beijing: Zhonggong zhongyang wenxian chubanshe, 1998), 1534–36.

39. Lüthi, *Sino-Soviet Split,* 43, 85.

40. Ibid., 292–93.

41. Lüthi, "Early 2nd Vietnam War," 35–37.

42. *ZELNP*2, 716–17; Sun Dongsheng, "Woguo jingji jianshe zhanlüe buju de da zhuanbian: San xian jianshe juece xingcheng shu lüe" [The big changes in the capital construction strategy of our country: A brief account of how the policy decision on the three line construction took place], *Dangde wenxian,* no. 3, 1995, 46; "Speeches of Liu,

Zhou, and Deng in the Politburo," April 12, 1965," Fujian Sheng Dang'anguan (Fujian Provincial Archives), 101-4-384, 71–77; "Comrade Wang Wei Communicates the Speeches of Some Responsible Comrades Discussing the 'War Preparedness Instructions' in the Politburo," JSSDAG, 3011, zhang 1162, 45–47.

43. *ZELZ2*, 1803.

44. Dong Baoxun, "Yingxiang sanxian jianshe juece xiangguan yinsu de lishi touxi" [An analysis of the factor correlated with the 3rd-front construction policymaking], *Shandong Daxue Xuebao,* no. 1, 2001, 91; Li Yin, "Sanxian yuanqi" [Origins of the third-line defense], *Dangde Zongheng,* no. 4, 2005, 55.

45. Xiao, "Xu Yixin," 26.

46. *New York Times,* May 14, 1965.

47. Ibid.

48. *Dangdai Zhongguo duiwai maoyi,* vol. 2, 371–88.

49. "Tel no. 180," February 10, 1967, NA UK, FCO 21/8, "Political Affairs (Internal), General Situation and Policy," 1.

50. "Dear David," May 24, 1967, NA UK, FCO 21/11, "Political Affairs (Internal): General Situation and Policy," 4.

51. Roderick MacFarquhar and Michael Schoenhals, *Mao's Last Revolution* (Cambridge, Mass.: Belknap Press of Harvard University, 2008), 159–61.

52. *Dangdai Zhongguo duiwai maoyi,* vol. 2, 371–88.

53. Ibid.

54. "Political Report no. 4," February 21, 1967, BA Bern, E 2300-01, Akzession 1973/156, 18, "1967 p.a. 21.31 Peking Politische Berichte," addendum 2, 1.

55. "Political Report no. 1," 1/16/1967, BA Bern, E 2300-01, Akzession 1973/156, 18, "1967 p.a. 21.31 Peking Politische Berichte," 3; MacFarquhar, *Mao's Last Revolution,* 140–44.

56. "Tel no. 92," January 23, 1967, NA UK, FCO 21/8, "Political Affairs (Internal), General Situation and Policy," 1–3.

57. "Political Report no. 4," February 21, 1967, BA Bern, E 2300-01, Akzession 1973/156, 18, "1967 p.a. 21.31 Peking Politische Berichte," addendum 2, 1–2; "Political Report no. 3," 2/6/1967, BA Bern, E 2300-01, Akzession 1973/156, 18, "1967 p.a. 21.31 Peking Politische Berichte," 7.

58. "Tel no. 917," September 13, 1967, NA UK, FCO 21/12, "Political Affairs (Internal): General Situation and Policy," 1.

59. "Political Report no. 12," October 30, 1967, BA Bern, E 2300-01, Akzession 1973/156, 18, "1967 p.a. 21.31 Peking Politische Berichte," 2–3, 8–9.

60. *Dangdai Zhongguo duiwai maoyi,* vol. 1, 34.

61. Ibid., vol. 2, 370, 392–93.

62. Ibid.

63. "Political Report no. 12," October 30, 1967, BA Bern, E 2300-01, Akzession 1973/156, 18, "1967 p.a. 21.31 Peking Politische Berichte," 1–10.

64. MacFarquhar, *Mao's Last Revolution,* 222–27; Ji Chaozhu, *Man on Mao's Right,* 232.

65. Gong Li, "Chinese Decision Making and the Thawing of U.S.-China Relations," in *Re-examining the Cold War: U.S.-China Diplomacy, 1954–1973,* ed. Robert S. Ross and Jiang Changbin (Cambridge, Mass.: Harvard University Press, 2001), 322–23. Also see Li Jie, "Changes in China's Domestic Situation in the 1960s and Sino-U.S.

Relations," in *Re-examining the Cold War,* ed. Ross and Jiang, 308; "Dear David," September 4, 1967, NA UK, FCO 21/12, "Political Affairs (Internal): General Situation and Policy," 1–3.

66. "Dear John," January 23, 1968, NA UK, FCO 21/13, "Internal Political Situation and Policy: In China," 1–2.

67. "Memo about Mao Zedong on Foreign Propaganda," July 12, 1968, JSSDAG, 3072 Provincial People's Committee General Office, 3124, zhang 305, 1–3.

68. Author's interview with Ioan Romulus Budura, Bucharest, July 10, 2004.

69. "Telegram no. 51," August 24, 1968, BA Bern, E 2200.174 Peking, Akzession 1985/195, 11, "China-Tschechoslowakei 1968," 1.

70. "The Ninth Party Congress," June 28, 1968, NA UK, FCO 21/14, "Internal Political Situation and Policy: In China."

71. "Political Report No. 3: New Administrative System—Start of the Final Phase of the Cultural Revolution," October 11, 1968, BA Bern, E 2300-01, Akzession 1973/156, 28, "1968 p.a. 21.31 Peking Politische Berichte," 1–2.

72. *MZDZ,* 1530–37.

73. Yang Kuisong. "The Sino-Soviet Border Clash of 1969: From Zhenbao Island to Sino-American Rapprochement," *Cold War History* 1, no. 1 (2000): 22.

74. Zhang Baijia, "The Changing International Scene and Chinese Policy toward the United States, 1954–1970," in *Re-examining the Cold War,* ed. Ross and Jiang, 68.

75. Richard Nixon, "Asia after Viet Nam," *Foreign Affairs* 46, no. 1 (October 1967): 111–25.

76. That Taiwan was on the minds of the Chinese leaders is clear from the telegram sent agreeing to the resumption of the Warsaw talks; see "Telegram from American Embassy in Warsaw to Secretary of State," November 25, 1968, National Archives and Records Administration (hereafter NARA), State Department, RG 59, Central Files, 1967–69, Box 1972, Political Aff. & Rel. Chicom-Us 1968.

77. "Conversation between Mao Zedong and Pham Van Dong; Beijing, 17 November 1968," in *77 Conversations between Chinese and Foreign Leaders on the Wars in Indochina, 1964–1977,* CWIHP Working Paper 22, ed. O. Arne Westad, Chen Jian, Stein Tonnesson, Nguyen Yu Tung, and James G. Hershberg (Washington, D.C.: Cold War International History Project, Woodrow Wilson International Center for Scholars, 1998), 146.

78. *ZELNP*3, 256. Li Jiasong, ed., *Zhonghua renmin gongheguo waijiao dashiji* [Chronicle of foreign affairs of the People's Republic of China], vol. 3 (Beijing: Shijie zhishi chubanshe, 2002), 201.

79. "Speech by Vice Prime Minister Chen Yi at the Reception in Honor of the National Holiday of Mali," September 22, 1968, BA Bern, E 2200.174 Peking, Akzession 1985/195, 11, "China-Tschecheslowakei 1968," 2.

80. Xiong Xianghui, "Dakai ZhongMei guanxi de qianzhou: 1969nian siwei laoshi dui guoji xingshi yanjiu he jianyi de qianqianhouhou" [Prelude to the Opening of Sino-American Relations: The whole story of the study and recommendations on the world situation of the four teachers in 1969], *Zhonggong dangshi ziliao* 42 (1992): 56–57.

81. Lüthi, *Sino-Soviet Split,* 340–41.

82. *ZELNP*3, 285. *MZDZ,* 1541–43.

83. Gong, "Chinese Decision Making," 324.

84. *Current Background* [hereafter *CB*] 886 (August 8, 1969): 15; Zhang Baojun,

"1969nian qianhou dang dui waijiao zhanlüe de zhongda tiaozheng" [The significant readjustment of the party's foreign policy strategy in 1969], *Zhonggong dangshi yanjiu,* no. 1 (1996): 63; Gong, "Chinese Decision Making," 323–24; Liu Zhinan, "1969nian, Zhongguozhanbei yu dui MeiSu guanxi de yanjiu he diaozheng" [China's war preparation and study and balance toward Soviet-American relations in 1969], *Dangdai Zhongguo shi yanjiu,* no. 3 (1999): 54.

85. "New Ambassadors of the PR China," August 8, 1969, PAAA-MfAA, Abteilung Ferner Osten–Sektor China, Microfiche C 186/74, 68–69. Also see "Telegram from American Consulate in Hong Kong to the Department of State," August 8, 1969, NARA, State Department, RG 59, Central Files, 1967–1969, box 1968, Pol 17-5 Chicom 1/1/67. *New York Times,* June 9, 1969.

86. Gong, "Chinese Decision Making," 336.

87. "Document No. 9: Report by Four Chinese Marshals—Chen Yi, Ye Jianying, Xu Xiangqian, and Nie Rongzhen—to the Central Committee, 'A Preliminary Evaluation of the War Situation' (excerpt)," July 11, 1969, *Cold War International History Project Bulletin* 11 (1998): 168.

88. "Excerpts from a Letter of the Extraordinary and Plenipotentiary Ambassador of the GDR to the PR China, Comrade Bierbach, to State Secretary Hegen on 6/22/1968," July 9, 1968, SAPMO-BArch, DY 30/IV A 2/2.028/144, 44–48.

89. "Political Report No. 3: New Administrative System—Start of the Final Phase of the Cultural Revolution," October 11, 1968, BA Bern, E 2300-01, Akzession 1973/156, 28, "1968 p.a. 21.31 Peking Politische Berichte," 6.

90. "China: Annual Review for 1969," February 6, 1970, NA UK, FCO 21/643, "Annual Review of China for 1969," 1.

91. "Walking on Two Legs in Industry," September 2, 1970, NA UK, FCO 21/672, "Economic Situation in China," 1.

92. "Far Eastern Department," June 8, 1970, NA UK, FCO 21/672, "Economic Situation in China," 1.

93. *Dangdai Zhongguo duiwai maoyi,* vol. 1, 34–35. This source misdates Lin Biao's demise by providing his year of death as 1970. See also Dangdai Zhongguo congshi [Contemporary China collection], *Dangdai Zhongguo de jingji tizhi gaige* [The reform of the economic system of contemporary China] (Beijing: Dangdai Zhongguo chubanshe, 1984), 147–48.

94. *Dangdai Zhongguo duiwai maoyi,* vol. 2, 371–88.

95. *New York Times,* January 6, 1950.

96. *New York Times,* January 28, 1964.

97. "Political Report No. 34," September 6, 1965, BA Bern, E 2300, Akzession 1000/716, 361, "Politische Berichte, 1965," 1–3.

98. F. Q. Quo, and Akira Ichikawa, "Sino-Canadian Relations: A New Chapter," *Asian Survey* 12, no. 5 (May 1972): 386–98.

99. Gordon H. Chang, *Friends and Enemies: The United States, China, and the Soviet Union, 1948–1972* (Stanford, Calif.: Stanford University Press, 1990), 217–24; Warren Cohen, *Dean Rusk* (Totowa, N.J.: Cooper Square, 1980), 163–70.

100. Steven M. Goldstein, "Dialogue of the Deaf? The Sino-American Ambassadorial-Level Talks, 1955–1970," in *Re-examining the Cold War,* ed. Ross and Jiang, 200–237.

101. Lüthi, *Sino-Soviet Split,* 343–44.

102. "Memorandum for the President," February 23, 1970, NARA, Nixon, NSC, box 1032, Cookies II, 1–2.

103. "Substantial Summary of the Talks on the Occasion of My Farewell Visits to Leading Romanian Comrades," August 25, 1970, SAPMO-BArch, DY 30/IV A 2/20/363, 5.

104. Zhang Baojun, "1969nian," 63.

105. Ma, *Cultural Revolution,* 320.

106. Xinhua, *China's Foreign Relations,* 518; Ma, *Cultural Revolution,* 321.

107. Xiong Xianghui, "Dakai," 93.

108. Chen Jian, *Mao's China and the Cold War* (Chapel Hill: University of North Carolina Press, 2001), 255–56.

109. Jeffrey Kimball, *Nixon's Vietnam War* (Lawrence: University Press of Kansas, 1998), 262.

110. "Political Report No. 2," March 4, 1971, in BA Bern, E 2300-01, Akzession 1977/29, 7, 1971, "p.a. 21.31 Peking Politische Berichte," 1–7.

111. "Message from Premier Chou En-lai," April 21, 1971, NARA, Nixon Presidential Materials Project at the National Archives, box 1031, Exchanges Leading Up to HAK Trip to China—December 1969–July 1971 (1), no page numbers.

112. F. S. Aijazuddin, *From a Head, through a Head, to a Head: The Secret Channel between the US and China through Pakistan* (Karachi: Oxford University Press, 2000), 116.

113. "FM Peking 190430Z," July 19, 1972, in NA UK, FCO 21/963, "Political Situation in China," 1–2.

114. MacFarquhar, *Mao's Last Revolution,* 339.

115. Zhou Enlai, "Why Did Our Country Accede to Nixon's Request for a Visit?" Zhou Enlai's Internal Report to the Party on the International Situation, December 1971, in *China and the Three Worlds: A Foreign Policy Reader,* ed. King C. Chen (White Plains, N.Y.: M. E. Sharpe, 1979), 137–40; emphasis added.

116. Wang Zhongchun, "The Soviet Factor in Sino-American Normalization, 1969–1979," in *Normalization of U.S.-China Relations: An International History,* ed. William C. Kirby, Robert S. Ross, and Gong Li (Cambridge, Mass.: Harvard University Press, 2005), 158; Warren I. Cohen, *America's Response to China: A History of Sino-American Relations,* 4th ed. (New York: Columbia University Press, 2000), 199.

117. *New York Times,* November 12, 1969, and November 21, 1970.

118. *New York Times,* October 26, 1971.

119. "Top Secret, Memorandum of Conversation," November 23, 1971, Digital National Security Archive (hereafter DNSA), KT00393, 10–11. See also *New York Times,* November 9, 1971.

120. "Political Report No. 16," November 24, 1971, BA Bern, E 2300-01, Akzession 1977/29, 7, "1971 p.a. 21.31 Peking Politische Berichte," 4; "Political Report No. 15," November 3, 1971, BA Bern, E 2300-01, Akzession 1977/29, 7, "1971 p.a. 21.31 Peking Politische Berichte," 3.

121. Li Jiasong, *Zhonghua,* vol. 3, 210.

122. Hutchison, *China's African Revolution,* 165–66.

123. Hashim S. H. Behbehani, *China's Foreign Policy in the Arab World, 1955–1975*

(London: KPI, 1981), 219–21; Mohamed Bin Huwaidin, *China's Relations with Arabia and the Gulf, 1949–1999* (London: RoutledgeCurzon, 2002), 153–59.

124. *New York Times,* November 16, 1971; Yezid Sayigh, *Armed Struggle and the Search for a State: The Palestinian National Movement, 1949–1993* (Oxford: Oxford University Press, 1999), 182.

125. Lillian Craig Harris, *China Considers the Middle East* (London: I. B. Tauris, 1993), 131.

126. Andrew J. Nathan, "Human Rights in Chinese Foreign Policy," *China Quarterly* 139 (1994): 622.

127. Xia Yafeng, *Negotiating with the Enemy: U.S.-China Talks during the Cold War, 1949–1972* (Bloomington: Indiana University Press, 2006), 210–12.

128. "Secret, Memorandum of Conversation," December 2, 1975, DNSA, KT01839, 5.

129. Quoted by Chen, *China and the Three Worlds,* 39; emphasis added.

130. Mao Zedong, "On the Question of the Differentiation of the Three Worlds" (February 22, 1974), in *On Diplomacy,* by Mao Zedong (Beijing: Foreign Languages Press, 1998), 454; *New York Times,* April 12, 1974.

131. *Dangdai Zhongguo duiwai maoyi,* vol. 2, 371–88.

132. "FM Moscow 302 Feb 14/72," 2/14/1972, NA UK, FCO 21/974, "Foreign Policy of China," 3.

133. "FM Peking 140940Z," April 14, 1972, NA UK, FCO 21/974, "Foreign Policy of China," 1–2. See also "Chinese Foreign Policy," September 18, 1972, NA UK, FCO 21/975, "Foreign Policy of China, 1972," 11.

134. "Chinese Foreign Policy during the 1970's," December 16, 1974, NA UK, FCO 21/1230, "Foreign Policy of China," 11.

135. *Dangdai Zhongguo duiwai maoyi,* vol. 2, 371–88.

136. "Marching towards the Splendid Goal of the Four Modernizations" (January 13, 1975), in *Selected Works,* by Zhou Enlai, vol. 2, 504.

137. *Dangdai Zhongguo de jingji tizhi gaige,* 151, 156; MacFarquhar, *Mao's Last Revolution,* 379–412.

138. *Dangdai Zhongguo duiwai maoyi,* vol. 2, 370, 392–93.

139. Zhonggong zhongyang wenxian yanjiushi [Chinese Communist Party, Central Committee, Research Office of Government Documents], ed., *Deng Xiaoping nian pu (1975–1997)* [Chronicle of the life of Deng Xiaoping (1975–1979)], vol. 1 (hereafter *DXPNP*1) (Beijing: Zhongyang wenxian chubanshe, 2004), 43–44; Li, "Changes in China's Domestic Situation," 80.

140. *Dangdai Zhongguo de jingji tizhi gaige,* 159.

141. For a good discussion of this issue, see chapter 8 in this volume, by Tsuyoshi Hasegawa.

142. *DXPNP*1, 307.

143. *Dangdai Zhongguo de jingji tizhi gaige,* 160, 162, 164, 166; Richard Evans, *Deng Xiaoping and the Making of Modern China* (London: Hamish Hamilton, 1993), 230.

144. Raymond L. Garthoff, *Détente and Confrontation: American-Soviet Relations from Nixon to Reagan* (Washington, D.C.: Brookings Institution Press, 1994), 661 n. 22.

145. Wang Zhongchun, "Soviet Factor," 166.

146. Li, "Changes in China's Domestic Situation," 83.

147. Garthoff, *Détente,* 632–36.

148. Ibid., 653–54.

149. Zbigniew Brzezinski, *Power and Principle: Memoirs of the National Security Adviser, 1977–1981* (New York: Farrar, Straus & Giroux, 1983), 207–9; Garthoff, *Détente,* 660–62.

150. In the fall of 1978, Deng said that China would wait "1,000 years" to settle the Taiwan conflict peacefully; see [No title], n.d., Jimmy Carter Library, National Security Affairs, 26 Staff Material Far East, box 1, "Armacost Chron File 9-10/78," 1.

151. Garthoff, *Détente,* 773.

152. King C. Chen, *China's War with Vietnam, 1979: Issues, Decisions, and Implications* (Stanford, Calif.: Hoover Institution Press, 1987), 27, 169–72; John H. Holdridge, *Crossing the Divide: An Insider's Account of Normalization of U.S.-China Relations* (Lanham, Md.: Rowman & Littlefield, 1997), 180.

153. *New York Times,* November 9, 1978.

154. "Note," September 12, 1978, PAAA-MfAA, Abteilung Ferner Osten, C 5450, 51–52.

155. "Statements of the SRV Ambassador," November 6, 1978, PAAA-MfAA, Abteilung Ferner Osten, C 5487, 19–20.

156. Christopher Goscha, "Vietnam and the Meltdown of Asian Internationalism," in *The Third Indochina War: Conflict between China, Vietnam, and Cambodia, 1972–1979,* ed. O. Arne Westad and Sophie Quinn-Judge (London: Routledge, 2006), 179.

157. Helmut Schmidt, *Menschen und Mächte* [Humans and World Powers] (Berlin: Siedler, 1987), 378.

158. *DXPNP*1, 476; Patrick Tyler, *A Great Wall: Six Presidents and China—An Investigative History* (New York: PublicAffairs, 1999), 275.

159. Gong Li, *Deng Xiaoping yu Meiguo* [Deng Xiaoping and America] (Beijing: Zhonggong dangshi chubanshe, 2004), 258.

160. Tyler, *Great Wall,* 275.

161. Ibid.

162. *DXPNP*1, 476; Gong, *Deng Xiaoping yu Meiguo,* 258; Jimmy Carter, *Keeping Faith: Memoirs of a President* (Toronto: Bantam Books, 1982), 206.

163. Gong, *Deng Xiaoping yu Meiguo,* 257–58. Carter only remembered that Deng called Vietnam the Cuba of the East; see Carter, *Keeping Faith,* 204–5.

164. Brzezinski, *Power and Principle,* 411–12.

165. Tyler, *Great Wall,* 279.

166. *DXPNP*1, 489.

7. Japan's Foreign Policy under Détente: Relations with China and the Soviet Union, 1971–1973

Kazuhiko Togo

This chapter focuses on Japan's foreign policy initiatives from 1971 to 1973, which took shape in response to the diplomacy of détente conducted by the United States, the People's Republic of China (PRC), and the Soviet Union. Before this period, for about a quarter century after the end of World War II, Japanese foreign policy was more or less preoccupied with resolving major issues originating from the end of World War II, and there was no room for Japan to consider playing an active role in structuring the framework of Cold War international relations. By the early 1970s, Japan had resolved most of these major issues, but two outstanding issues remained unsettled: the resumption of diplomatic relations with mainland China, and the conclusion of a peace treaty with the Soviet Union. The détente politics that began to dominate the international diplomatic scene in the initial years of the 1970s gave Japan a new opportunity to become a substantial player in the international power structure of East Asia through a substantial improvement of its relations with the PRC and the Soviet Union.

Sino-Japanese Relations before the Nixon Shock

Japan established diplomatic relations with the Republic of China (ROC, Taiwan) in 1952, and from then on, normalization of relations with the PRC became one of its major foreign policy objectives. Although bilateral ties gradually developed, under Prime Minister Sato Eisaku from 1965 until 1971, political ties experienced a chill, partly because of the overall ossification of Chinese foreign policy during the Cultural Revolution from 1966 onward. Matters were not helped by Sato's attention to the return of Okinawa, which the PRC viewed as Japan's greater association with the anti-Chinese policy of the United States.

In February 1965, Sato refused to allow Japan's Export-Import Bank to extend loans for exporting plant equipment to China. *People's Daily* carried a sharp article criticizing Sato, saying the "Chinese people hold no illusions about Sato."[1] In November 1969, Sato and Nixon agreed in a communiqué to revert control of Okinawa to Japan. In that communiqué, Sato assured the president that "the maintenance of peace and security in the Taiwan area was also a most important factor for the security of Japan."[2] China's criticism of Sato reached its peak after this communiqué.[3]

But the standard analysis that Sato was too preoccupied with the United States and was not interested in exerting any initiative for improving relations with China is not entirely correct. On January 22, 1971, Sato used the name "People's Republic of China" for the first time in his New Year policy speech, as opposed to "Communist China"; in May, Miyazawa Kiichi, minister of finance, publicly stated that the Japanese government would reevaluate its decision to disallow Japan's Export-Import Bank to extend loans to China. Scholars of the highest stature formed a group to give advice on a new China policy and met for the first time on August 26, 1971.[4]

On the critical issue on Taiwan, however, Sato, though willing to improve ties with China, was not prepared to jeopardize relations with Taiwan. Hashimoto Hiroshi, who served as the director of the China Division of the Ministry of Foreign Affairs from 1968 until 1973, later confirmed this by saying that "including Sato, the Liberal Democratic Party [LDP] and the Ministry of Foreign Affairs [MOFA] were eager to open diplomatic relations with China, but did not want to cut ties with Taiwan."[5] China, therefore, did not react to Sato's initiative. Rather, the first important message from the PRC on the conditions for normalizing relations emerged with their meeting with representatives of the Komei Party (Komeito). At a time when official contact was restrained because formal diplomatic relations had not been established, the Komeito had become an effective channel of communications between the leaders of the two countries.[6] The first delegation, led by Takeiri Yoshikatsu, chairman of the Komeito, visited Beijing from June 16 to July 4, 1971, just before the confidential talks between Mao Zedong, Zhou Enlai, and U.S. national security adviser Henry Kissinger to prepare for U.S. president Richard Nixon's visit to China. A joint declaration between the Komeito and the China-Japan Friendship Association was signed by Takeiri and Wang Guoquan, the association's chairman, on July 2. In this declaration, the Komeito enunciated five principles for the normalization of Sino-Japanese relations, and the Chinese side "applauded and supported them" and "recognized that should the Japanese government accept these principles, it would be possible to establish China-Japan state-to-state relations." The Komeito's five principles were as follows:[7]

1. China is one entity. The People's Republic of China is the sole legitimate government that represents the Chinese people.
2. Taiwan is a part of China. It is an inalienable part of the territory of China. The Taiwan issue is a domestic issue for China.
3. The Treaty between Japan and Taiwan of 1952 is unlawful and invalid.
4. The United States should withdraw its troops from Taiwan.
5. The PRC becomes a permanent member of the UN Security Council and Chiang Kai-shek's (Jiang Jieshi's) representatives must be ousted from the UN.

Point 5 was satisfied by a UN decision in the fall of that year, and the first three conditions became known as China's three conditions for normalization. Point 4 was not an issue where Japan could take a decision, but the question of Taiwan's security in the context of the Japan-U.S. Security Treaty became an important hidden agenda in the normalization talks between Japan and China.

The Nixon Shock and Sato's Painful Policy Choices

Immediately after the Komeito-PRC joint declaration, the Sino-Japanese normalization process was overtaken by the so-called Nixon shock. Japan's participation in the great game of détente was greatly affected by this shock, and it took on a typically reactive character. When, on July 15, 1971, President Nixon announced his intention to visit China, he did not share the news with Prime Minister Sato until three minutes before its public announcement.[8] The former Japanese ambassador to the United States, Asakai Koichiro, had previously said that he had nightmares that "when I would wake up, relations between China and the U.S. will have been established."[9] This nightmare scenario actually did unfold.[10]

Why did the American leadership keep this crucial information from Japan until the last moment without any previous consultation with the Japanese government whatsoever? Kissinger later explained the motive by borrowing three points from Ambassador Armin Meyer's memoir:[11] that the Japanese might leak the information; that it would be necessary to inform other allies, if Japan were informed; and that Japanese policy was not really undercut but preempted. But as Nancy Bernkopf Tucker argues, none of these points is convincing.[12] Wakaizumi Kei, Sato's secret representative for the Okinawa reversion negotiations, suggested an entirely different reason: Nixon's disregard of Japan was his "revenge" for Japan's breach of trust in relation to the handling of textile negotiations during the Okinawa reversion negotiations.[13] A British journalist, Henry Brandon, concurs with Wakaizumi's observation.[14] Whatever the reason for Nixon's secret diplomacy, it prompted Japan to adopt a more autonomous policy from the United States, as would be demonstrated in its future relations with the PRC, Mongolia, and North Vietnam.[15] Kissinger later wrote that "I believe in retrospect that we could have chosen a more sensitive method of informing the Japanese. It would have surely been more courteous and thoughtful, for example, to send one of my associates from the Peking trip to Tokyo to brief Sato a few hours before the official announcement."[16]

After Nixon's China shock, Sato had to go through a painful period of policy adjustment. The historian Sadako Ogata vividly described the state of shock among the top Japanese policymakers. Upon hearing this news, Sato was "numbed"; the party secretary, Hori Shigeru, was "shaken"; officials of the MOFA in charge "were taken aback"; and "there was thus a widely shared sense of betrayal on the part of government leaders."[17] A tearful Sato told the visiting Australian Labor leader Gough Whitlam: "I have done everything they [the Americans] have asked, but they have let me down."[18] On September 9, 1971, U.S. secretary of state William Rogers reported to the president: "Although the blow was severe, responsible Japanese opinion is prepared to consider the fact that we did not consult with them before your July 15 announcement of your visit to Peking as a matter of past history."[19]

After the initial wound of the Nixon shock healed, the UN vote on China's seat in the UN Security Council became the central issue between the two governments. The United States decided to support a dual representation formula, that is, to advocate Beijing's entry but oppose Taiwan's expulsion in the form of a reverse Important Question Resolution, requiring a two-thirds majority for the expulsion of Taiwan. After announcing this policy on August 2, the State Department pressed the Japanese government to cosponsor this resolution through its UN delegation in New York. In Tokyo, both the MOFA and LDP generally favored dual representation, but as for the actual decision on how to handle the United States–sponsored resolution, it was left to Sato. Sato announced his decision to cosponsor the resolution on September 22. Strong urging by the United States and obligations to Taiwan were two fundamental reasons for his cosponsorship.[20] However, Sato is also said to have supported the U.S. position because he feared that otherwise the ratification of the Okinawa Reversion Treaty by the U.S. Senate, where the issue was being debated from September to October 1971, could be jeopardized.[21]

Sato's government made further efforts to help Taiwan save face. Former prime minister Kishi Nobusuke, Sato's brother, visited Taipei and Washington to try to manage the situation. In Taipei, Kishi frankly told Chiang Kai-shek to let the PRC occupy the Chinese UN seat and for his regime to remain represented in the UN as Taiwan. Chiang Kai-shek flatly refused Kishi's advice.[22] Had Chiang agreed to Kishi's proposal, could Taiwan have remained in the UN? This counterfactual question is very difficult to answer in a clear manner. On the second day of his meeting with Kissinger, on July 10, 1971, Zhou had told him that "we do not consider the matter of regaining our seat in the UN an urgent matter. . . . We do not attach any importance to the UN question." Zhou had further stated that "to people who ask for our attitude [on the reverse Important Question Resolution], we will of course say that all China's legitimate rights in the UN must be restored." Kissinger agreed to disagree, and Zhou nodded.[23] This is the reason why the State Department advanced the dual representation formula.[24] Chiang's refusal probably deprived Taiwan of its last opportunity to remain in the United Nations. Thus, when Kishi visited Nixon in Washington on October 22, he could just express his wish "that both countries continue to push as hard as they could" the UN-cosponsored resolution, and convey his impression, based on his meeting with Chiang, that Chiang "would voluntarily walk out of the UN if the reverse-IQ Resolution failed."[25]

The failure of the UN vote became a crucial motivating factor in Japan's recognition of the PRC. The Japanese government was not yet clear as to how to deal with Taiwan. But delaying the recognition of the PRC was no longer an option. Togo Fumihiko, who became deputy minister for political affairs in August 1972, recounted that "as far as I can see, the turning point was the UN resolution of 1971."[26] Whereas in the United States, the defeat of the dual representative form was viewed with bitterness and fostered a negative attitude toward the UN, in Japan this decision was taken as the push toward accepting the PRC as a full member of the international community.[27]

With this changing tide as the backdrop, after the defeat of his cosponsored bill by the UN Security Council, Sato eagerly launched an initiative to resume ties with the PRC. On November 10, 1971, LDP secretary-general Hori Shigeru passed a confidential letter to Zhou Enlai through Tokyo governor Minobe Ryokichi. However, the letter was unclear about whether the government of Japan recognized the PRC as the "only" government representing China, and whether it recognized Taiwan as an inalienable part of the PRC. The expression that "Taiwan is a part of the territory of the peoples of China" fell short of specifying it as "a part of the territory of the PRC." Zhou Enlai disclosed the content of the letter and criticized that it did not meet China's requirements.[28]

Notwithstanding this rigid position expressed by Zhou, at the San Clemente meeting between Sato and Nixon on January 6, 1972, just before Nixon's visit to China, Sato expressed bluntly that "if Japan's normalization policy succeeds, it will have its principal political and economic relations with Peking, and only economic relations with Taiwan."[29] Sato explained to Nixon the state of shock of the Japanese people induced by the Nixon shock on July 15.[30] Nixon's position at San Clemente appeared to be more on the defensive. He stated that what would come out from his China visit "is not normalization; . . . what would come out, he hoped, is a channel of communication and progress in other areas."[31] In fact, Kissinger had told Zhou in his July 9 and 10, 1971, meetings that "there is no possibility for us to recognize in the next one and a half years the PRC as the sole government of China in a formal way" but that "we would not support the Taiwan Independence Movement, [nor] one China, one Taiwan, [nor] two Chinas."[32] But when President Nixon visited China in February 1972, U.S. support of the one-China policy was formulated in a nuanced expression of acknowledging the fact that "all Chinese on either side of the Taiwan Strait maintain there is but one China."[33]

On the issue of security across the Taiwan Strait, President Nixon first assured Sato that "his forthcoming visit to Peking [will] in no way be at the expense of the commitments the United States has to its friends and allies in the Pacific, Japan, the ROK, and Taiwan." Sato did not seem to be impressed, and just told the president that "the position of Taiwan has not changed in terms of the mutual Security Treaty between Japan and the United States."[34] This position confirmed by Sato converged with the U.S. interest. In fact, in Kissinger's talks with Zhou in July, Japan's position on Taiwan's security was one of the most serious issues discussed. Zhou raised concern about Japan's expansion to Taiwan: "The new China will not practice expansionism; it's not the same for Japan." Kissinger immediately responded that the United States–Japan security relationship would act as a cap on Japan's expansion to Taiwan: "Our defense relationship with Japan keeps Japan from pursuing aggressive policies."[35]

After the Sato-Nixon meeting at San Clemente, on January 6, 1972, President Nixon and Prime Minster Zhou met in Beijing on February 24, 1972. Zhou expressed strong concern about the possible reintroduction of Japanese forces to Taiwan, and Nixon reassured him that the U.S.-Japan Security Treaty did not provide for this, and the United States would not let it happen. The following conversation ensued:

> Zhou: "You will discourage the Japanese from coming in while they are there?"
> [Note by the author: coming to Taiwan while U.S. troops are in Taiwan.]
>
> Nixon: "I will go further. We will try to keep Japanese forces from coming into Taiwan after our forces leave."

Zhou: "That is to say, while you still have forces in Japan?"
Nixon: "Precisely that. Unless we have forces in Japan, they won't pay any attention to us."[36]

In Japan on March 6, 1972, as a result of tense parliamentary debate on Taiwan, the Sato government formulated a three-point position:[37]

1. Japan considers that since it has renounced all right and title to Taiwan by the San Francisco Peace Treaty, it is unable to pronounce whether or not Taiwan is a part of China.
2. Japan fully understands the stand of the government of the People's Republic of China that Taiwan is an inalienable part of the territory of the PRC in view of what has taken place in the past, and also of the fact that the PRC has come to represent China in the United Nations.
3. Based on the above understanding, the government will make all efforts to achieve normalization of relations with China.

It is interesting to note that the basic logic by which Tanaka Kakuei and his team negotiated with Zhou later in September had already been clearly outlined under Sato. However, the Chinese government issued no response. Sato's political record most likely led the Chinese to conclude that they would wait for a change of government in Japan to normalize relations.

Therefore, this was as far as Sato's Cabinet could go. Sadako Ogata stated: "Once Sato was crowned with the formal reversion of Okinawa on May 15, all contenders to his succession began to agitate openly. The agreed feeling was that . . . the China issue should be handled by his successor."[38] Sato's leaving office signified the necessity of restoring diplomatic relations with the PRC, but serious concerns remained. As Gene Hsiao stated, "In what form the existing friendly and goodwill relations with the Nationalist government will be maintained is another question."[39]

Tanaka Kakuei and the Normalization of Relations with the PRC

By this time, Japanese business groups, LDP members, and bureaucracies had all come to see the importance of the enormous Chinese market.[40] If the United States relaxed its own policy toward the PRC, there was no reason for Japan not to revise its own policy toward China. In addition, if this change could be used to Japan's advantage on the East Asian regional political scene, no ambitious politician was to pass up the opportunity.

In the early 1990s, Akira Iriye analyzed the Sino-Japanese relations of this period by using a three-layer approach, viewing events from the perspectives of *security, economic relations,* and *cultural ties.* On *security,* he outlined the process by which both Japan and China were incorporated as indispensable players on opposing sides of the Cold War divide but had no specific reasons to target at each other.[41] Given the fundamental changes occurring in the Cold War structure, prompted by the United States' revision of its policy toward China, Japan had few security concerns that would have prevented it from opening relations with the PRC. On the contrary, this would provide an opportunity for Japan to assert its greater role in the emerging regional power politics. On *economic relations,* Iriye focused on the trend toward "expanding ties and growing interdependence."[42] Sometimes, politics affected economics. Japanese exports to China became constrained by the restrictions imposed by the Coordinating Committee for Export Controls and China Committee. Trade figures shrank from 1958 to 1962. Iriye analyzed how this sharp drop was caused by the drastic cooling of the political climate due to the Chinese government's concern about Prime Minister Kishi's pro-American security policy. But trade figures saw a clear rise after Kishi's departure and continued to expand in the 1960s.[43] Iriye used *cultural ties* in a nondeterministic and nonreductionist manner, defining them as "those aspects of national or international affairs that are not usually put in categories of security and economics." He pointed out that "in the wake of the brutal war in which [the Japanese] had caused the suffering of millions in China, Japanese intellectuals and other leaders wanted to repent and to turn to China for some spiritual guidance."[44] Thus, from all these three perspectives—that is, the changing Cold War structure of détente, the accumulating wishes of mainstream Japanese businesses to establish fully open economic ties, and longtime uneasiness on the part of many Japanese of having wronged China—conditions were ripe for normalizing the relations between the PRC and Japan.

But the central issue at stake was Taiwan. From all three considerations of security, economic relations, and cultural ties, Japan was not in a position to neglect Taiwan. Taiwan was still a U.S. ally under the U.S.-ROC Mutual Security Treaty. It was an important geostrategic area where maintaining peace and security was a common concern of both the United States and Japan, as a part of the "Far East" as defined by the Japan-U.S. Security Treaty of 1960. Taiwan-Japanese economic relations were expanding, as Taiwan was about to take off on a period of rapid economic growth. It was imperative, therefore, for many business enterprises in both countries to keep up friendly relations. Furthermore, Chiang Kai-shek's magnanimity in forgoing wartime reparations from Japan was remembered with a sense of gratitude by many Japanese.

The tasks of how to balance this dual importance of continental China and Taiwan, and how to normalize relations with Beijing by taking into account the Taiwan factor, fell on Sato's successor, Tanaka Kakuei, and a select group of individuals who wielded real influence over his policy decisions.[45] In the post-Sato succession scramble of 1972, Tanaka showed his masterful ability of power politics, in which the Sino-Japanese normalization issue played a key role. To outvote Fukuda, Sato's chosen heir, Tanaka successfully aligned himself with two other candidates, Ohira Masayoshi and Miki Takeo, both known to be strong supporters of normalizing relations with China.[46] After Tanaka staged a political coup on May 9 by forming his own group within the Sato faction to which he had belonged, the second Komeito delegation, led by Ninomiya Fumizo, visited China in May 1972 and received a clear message from Zhou Enlai that China would welcome an official visit by Tanaka Kakuei as Japan's new prime minister. "Thus, China became the rallying point around which political alignments were formed."[47] Tanaka later explained that three factors led him to establish relations with the PRC: the need to resolve Japan's domestic problems; the scale and potential of the Chinese market, with its nearly 1 billion people; and the desire to form a stable triangular Japan–United States–China relationship that would keep peace in the Far East.[48]

Tanaka announced immediately after he formed his Cabinet on July 7 that his Cabinet would expedite the process for normalizing relations with China.[49] Given the general domestic expectations for Tanaka to tackle the China issue, this was a shrewd and anticipated approach, provided that he would follow it up with measures to reassure the United States. As mentioned below, he accomplished this in Honolulu within two months. But apparently it was the Komeito's third delegation, again headed by Takeiri, which visited China and had a breakthrough meeting with Zhou Enlai on July 27–29, that made Tanaka's final decision to visit China possible. Zhou sent an eight-point proposal with three other confidential undisclosed proposals for agreement.[50] The key issue of Taiwan was dealt with as follows:

> Point 1. The state of war between the PRC and Japan is terminated on the day this statement becomes public.
>
> Point 2. The Japanese government fully understands the three principles set by the PRC for normalization of relations and recognizes the Government of the PRC as the sole legal Government of China. Based on this, both governments will establish diplomatic relations and exchange ambassadors.
>
> (Undisclosed agreement 1): Taiwan is a territory of the PRC. The liberation of Taiwan is China's internal matter.

Point 7 stated that China would abandon the reparation rights, and outside the eight-point proposal Zhou stated that it would not object to the Japan-U.S.

Security Treaty.[51] Takeiri later narrated to the editors of the book edited by Ishii and colleagues that when he met Tanaka on July 23, the prime minister was indecisive about visiting China. At his meeting with Zhou, Takeiri later explained to the editors, he had appreciated most China's renunciation of claims to reparations and acceptance of the Japan-U.S. Security Treaty. On the Taiwan issue, Takeiri had guarded his position, knowing that it would become the most controversial issue for the Japanese. Zhou had reassured Takeiri that "he is not going to put Tanaka in an awkward position, so [Tanaka should] come to China reassured." On August 4, Takeiri transmitted to Tanaka the full record of his talks with Zhou. Tanaka told Takeiri on August 5 that he had decided to visit China.[52]

Hashimoto Hiroshi, the director of the China Division of MOFA from 1968 to 1973, recounted that in his numerous personal meetings with Tanaka and Ohira before the Tanaka Cabinet was formed, Hashimoto succeeded in convincing the two politicians that the only way to normalize relations with the PRC was to acknowledge the PRC's one-China policy and to break relations with the ROC. According to Hashimoto, Tanaka and Ohira's decision to break diplomatic relations with Taiwan, while carefully exercising maximum courtesy to ensure that Taiwan's sensitivities would not be hurt, led to the PRC's decision not to ask for reparations, as well as its acknowledgment of the Japan-U.S. Security Treaty, and made the normalization of relations possible.[53]

How did Tanaka handle the United States in his China policy? Throughout Tanaka's career as a leading Japanese politician, there is nothing to indicate that he had ever pursued any anti-American initiatives. There is a consensus that, as the minister of international trade and industry in the Sato Cabinet, he had handled a tough round of negotiations on textiles with his American counterpart in Washington in September 1971, but then had exerted powerful domestic leadership to introduce voluntary export restraints while ensuring subsidies for Japanese textile manufacturers that totaled ¥200 billion. It is also warmly recorded in all Japanese biographies of Tanaka that at the San Clemente Sato-Nixon summit in January 1972, Nixon had specifically invited Tanaka to sit with him in order to express his gratitude for successfully concluding the textile negotiations.[54]

In embarking on his Beijing visit, Tanaka met with Nixon in Honolulu on August 31 and September 1, 1972. Now that U.S. policy toward its normalization of relations with China had been firmly established, the United States had only one fundamental concern. Kissinger emphasized in his memorandum to the president as of August 29 that "Japan's normalization of relations with the PRC is a process upon which the Japanese are irrevocably embarked [but] we have a definite interest that Japan not agree to possible PRC requirements which would further restrict our access to bases in Japan and inhibit our ability to fulfill our defense commitments, particularly with respect to Taiwan and Korea."[55] Nixon and Kissinger had already implanted in the mind of Chinese leaders the fundamental importance of the Japan-U.S. Security Treaty for China's own interest. But this memorandum shows the concern on the part of the United States that Tanaka might go too fast, damaging the proper functioning of the security treaty and risking the U.S. cross-strait security interest. Tanaka, acknowledging that "the domestic situation within Japan has now developed to the point, where it is almost impossible for Japan not to normalize relations with the PRC," repeatedly stated in an abstract form that "Japan would not consider any restoration of diplomatic relations with the PRC that would be disadvantageous to Japan–United States relations." Nixon just mildly spoke that "this [Japan's opening of relations with the PRC] should not be done at the expense of Japan's friends,"[56] leaving the outcome of Tanaka's visit in September in Tanaka's hands.[57] It is possible to conclude that Tanaka reached a tacit agreement with the United States on his China policy without sacrificing Japan's independence.

Breaking Diplomatic Relations with Taiwan

To show maximum respect for Taiwan, the Tanaka Cabinet sent Shiina Etsusaburo, vice president of the LDP, to meet with Chiang Ching-kuo [Jians Jingguo] on July 19. Although Japan's general decision to open diplomatic relations with the PRC at the expense of diplomatic relations with the ROC had already been made, Shiina used maximum circumlocution so as not to aggravate the ill will it could engender. He referred to the resolution adopted by the Council for Normalization of Japan-China Relations, saying that "in view of the close relationship between Japan and the ROC, negotiations should be conducted giving sufficient consideration to the continuation of that relationship." Shiina explained that "that relationship encompasses a diplomatic relationship," and that "the negotiations with the PRC should take this point into account." He did not promise anything but tried to convey a general feeling of goodwill. Chiang Ching-kuo responded that he could not but take Foreign Minister Ohira's statement to Taiwan's ambassador in Tokyo that "in the eventuality of normalization of relations with China, the Japan-ROC Treaty will cease to exist," which was essentially a statement that his government would sever diplomatic relations in case relations were normalized with the PRC. Shiina insisted that Chiang was misinterpreting the statement.[58] Ogura Kazuo, the deputy director of the China Division of MOFA, also recounted that the Japanese side deleted all references from Tanaka's letter that Shiina brought to

Chiang Kai-shek regarding the severance of diplomatic relations with the ROC after Japan established relations with the PRC.[59]

The way the Japanese government projected its position was obscure and vague. This vagueness was probably due to a combination of three factors: trying to avoid definitive statements while the outcome of the Beijing negotiations was not entirely clear; presenting harsh reality with soft diplomatic language; and reverting to the traditional practice of expressing official positions with intentionally ambiguous words, letting the intended audience read between the lines. At the same time, it is now known that Ohira let it be known through a Taiwanese private-sector channel that even if diplomatic relations with the ROC were severed, economic and other practical relations with the ROC would continue. This second-track message was very important for the Taiwanese to keep in mind in preparing for the eventuality of severed diplomatic relations.[60]

Tanaka telegraphed the formal message severing diplomatic relations with the ROC from Beijing, addressed to Chiang Kai-shek, on September 29, 1972, after an agreement on all points was reached between Japan and the PRC.[61] It was meant to be the final message, intended to bring this painful process to a close.

During Tanaka's visit to China on September 25–30, 1972, the first issue that divided the two sides over Taiwan was the validity of the Japan-ROC Peace Treaty concluded in 1952. Closely connected to this issue was the question of the termination of the state of war, which had already been addressed in that treaty. The PRC declared that the 1952 Japan-ROC Treaty was "unlawful and invalid," which was the third condition of the July 1971 proposal, and therefore the state of war between Japan and China should end with the 1972 Joint Communiqué. This would have required Japan to disavow the whole history of Japan-ROC relations from 1952 to 1972, and this was something that Japan could not accept. Japan therefore proposed in the draft a joint declaration that "the government of Japan and the PRC *confirm* that the state of war between Japan and China herewith ends."[62] On September 26, at the morning session of the foreign ministerial meeting, Takashima Masuo, director-general of MOFA's Treaties Bureau, explained the Japanese position in detail.[63] At the afternoon session between Tanaka and Zhou Enlai, Zhou lambasted Takashima over the Japan-ROC Treaty. That evening, Tanaka, Ohira, Takashima, and Hashimoto had an in-depth informal discussion over dinner. Upon Hashimoto's proposal, the phrase "the abnormal state of affairs" was substituted for "state of war." Zhou accepted this at subsequent sessions.[64] Paragraph 1 of the 1972 Joint Communiqué now read: "The abnormal state of affairs that has hitherto existed between Japan and the ROC is terminated on the date on which this Joint Communiqué is issued." Once this issue was resolved, Ohira simply announced the termination of the Japan-ROC Treaty in his concluding press conference on September 29.

On the issue of the status of Taiwan, recognizing China as one entity (the first condition of the July 1971 proposal) did not cause any problems, and so paragraph 2 of the 1972 Joint Communiqué read: "The Government of Japan recognizes the Government of the People's Republic of China as the sole legal government of China."

But just how to treat Taiwan (the second condition of the July 1971 proposal) proved a more difficult and sensitive issue. The language for the communiqué that was finally agreed upon was as follows:

> 3. The Government of the People's Republic of China reiterates that Taiwan is an inalienable part of the territory of the People's Republic of China. The Government of Japan fully understands and respects this stand of the Government of the People's Republic of China, and it firmly maintains its stand under Article 8 of the Potsdam Declaration.

The Japanese position was based on the government view formulated under Prime Minister Sato on March 6, 1972. The original proposed draft communiqué read: "The Government of the PRC reiterates that Taiwan is an inalienable part of the territory of the PRC. The government of Japan fully understands and respects this stand of the Government of the PRC."[65] The words "and respects" were not included in the March 6 position paper formulated by the Sato government and added anew in this proposal. However, Takashima, in his explanatory statement during the morning session between the two foreign ministers on September 26, had already stated that "Japan is not in a position to make any original judgment on the legal status of present Taiwan since it has relinquished all rights concerning Taiwan in the San Francisco Peace Treaty. However, it is the consistent view of the Government of Japan that, in light of the Cairo and Potsdam declarations, Taiwan *should* be returned to China as these declarations intended."[66] According to Kuriyama Takakazu, the head of the Treaties Division assisting Takashima, faced with China's refusal to accept a communiqué that contained the phrase "understands and respects," it was the Japanese side that proposed what eventually became the last words of paragraph 3: "firmly maintains its stand under Article 8 of the Potsdam Declaration."[67] Kuriyama's explanation is convincing because, as stated above, that line of thinking had already been expressed by Takashima during the meeting on September 26, although some analysts maintain that the reference to the Potsdam Declaration was included at China's insistence.[68]

Paragraph 3, legalistic as it may seem, probably represented the most important part of the agreement reached between Japan and China, because its implications still persist to the present. Undeniably, three political consequences stemmed from this clause. The first is that whatever the legal argument, China's position and Japan's position differed in not using identical language. Understanding and interpreting this disparity is left up to the two governments and their experts. The second is that from 1972 to this day, there has not been any definitive official interpretation of the paragraph issued by the two governments. The third consequence is that, because this question has remained unexplored, the language has lost none of its ambiguity or saliency. In fact, in all the talking points I was able to use in parliamentary debates during my own tenure as director-general of the Treaties Bureau from 1998 to 1999, phrases like "maintaining Article 3 of the 1972 Joint Communiqué," and "wishing for a peaceful resolution,"[69] were all the statements on Taiwan policy that could be used. Suffice it to mention that in the communiqué adopted on the occasion of Wen Jinbao's visit in February 2007 and Hu Jintao's visit in May 2008, the references to Taiwan were identical: "Regarding the Taiwan issue, the Japanese side again expresses its adherence to the position enunciated in the Joint Communiqué of the Government of Japan and the Government of the People's Republic of China."[70]

From the 1980s on, after the democratization and Taiwanization movements in Taiwan, cross-strait relations became a politically sensitive issue for all parties concerned: China, Taiwan, the United States, and Japan. Each party thought a little differently, but all agreed on the maintenance of the status quo. Using the thirty-year-old language without bothering with elaborate interpretations is politically the wisest approach, if one's aim is not to rock the boat and to maintain the delicate status quo.

Interpretation of the Japan-U.S. Security Treaty

Another issue that had fundamental importance for Japan's position on Taiwan was the Japan-U.S. Security Treaty. In a meeting with Takeiri on July 27, 1972, Zhou Enlai made a decisive comment that apparently facilitated a breakthrough on this issue. He stated the following as conditions for normalization: "I want to reassure Prime Minister Tanaka and Foreign Minister Ohira. The Japan-U.S. Security Treaty would not be a problem. If China-Japan relations were restored, the Security Treaty would lose its effectiveness toward China. The Sato-Nixon Joint Statement of 1969 would not be touched upon either."[71] None of the Japanese leaders then knew that behind Zhou's statement was Kissinger's message to view the Japan-U.S. Security Treaty as a cap to possible Japanese aggression, as analyzed above.

The official minutes of the meeting between Tanaka and Zhou, in principle, confirm that Tanaka did not have to depart from the position that he had promised to Nixon in Hawaii. At the first Tanaka-Zhou meeting, on September 25, Zhou stated: "We will not touch on Japan-U.S. relations. This is Japan's problem. The cross-strait situation is changing, therefore the implications of the treaty are also changing. . . . The Chinese side will not touch upon the issue of the Japan-U.S. Security Treaty, nor on the issue of the U.S.-ROC Defense Treaty. I leave the handling of Japan-U.S. relations to you."[72] At their second meeting, on September 26, Zhou further stated: "As far as the Japan-U.S. Security Treaty is concerned, I don't think that we are going to liberate Taiwan by force. You will not be held responsible for the 1969 Sato-Nixon Communiqué. . . . Now that Sato has retired, we are not going to take issue with this communiqué. . . . We are not happy with the Security Treaty but understand that it should be maintained as it is. We need not touch upon the Security Treaty while normalizing relations."[73]

Japanese political leaders and MOFA officials were aware that in 1960, at the time when the revised security treaty was being intensely debated in Japan, the Japanese government had defined as part of the "Far East" any area where the U.S. troops stationed in Japan might be deployed to contribute to the maintenance of international peace and security as specified under Article VI, specifically, "North of the Philippines and Japan and its surrounding areas, including areas under the control of Korea and the Republic of China (Taiwan)." The Taiwan clause of the Sato-Nixon 1969 Communiqué reinforced the political importance of Taiwan to Japan's security, but we can see that even without this clause, the legally defined jurisdiction of the term "Far East" in the Security Treaty, as read by Japanese officials, already included Taiwan.

In fact, when Foreign Minister Ohira called on President Nixon at the Oval Office on October 18, 1972, the first question the president asked was "whether the PRC leaders gave the Japanese any difficulties on the Security Treaty." Ohira replied "not at all" and observed that "the Chinese indicated the Security Treaty is a matter between Japan and the United States."[74] But reading carefully statements made by Zhou to Takeiri on July 27 and to Tanaka on September 25, one notices that Zhou qualified his nonobjection to the Security Treaty. He stated that "he would not object to the Japan-U.S. security treaty (July 27)," but also that "the cross-strait situation is changing, therefore the implications of the treaty are also changing (September 25)." The September 25 statement might indicate that Zhou was not objecting to the Japan-U.S. Security Treaty because of the changing interpretation of the treaty in relation to Taiwan. In fact it is reported that Foreign Minister Chi Peng-fei [Shi Pengfei] told a representative of the Democratic Socialist Party in the fall of 1973 that "because the 1972 China-Japan joint statement had nullified the Taiwan clause of the U.S.-Japan defense treaty, Beijing no longer objected to it."[75]

This seed of possible future disagreements did not come to surface in the 1970s or the 1980s, when China saw the usefulness of the Japan-U.S. security agreement because it acted as a brake on any revival of Japanese militarism. After the Sino-Soviet split, it may well have been that China considered the security treaty a useful counterweight against the Soviet threat.

But from the middle of the 1990s, this situation showed signs of change. When Japan and the United States reaffirmed the alliance in 1996 and introduced a new guideline in 1997 based on "situational," as opposed to "geographic," cooperation, China expressed strong concern over whether this new understanding could possibly be applied to the subject of cross-strait relations. Then the February 2005 Japan-U.S. joint statement of Two plus Two—that is, the meeting of the Japanese ministers of foreign affairs and defense with the U.S. secretaries of state and defense—identified peaceful resolution of the Taiwan Strait issue as an area where Japan and the United States share a strategic interest, a point that criticism from Beijing highlighted. The wording of the security treaty was never brought to the forefront of debate, but it was clear that China was objecting to the possibility that Japan-U.S. security cooperation could extend to Taiwan.

The Chinese position directly contradicted Japan's interpretation of the treaty, unchanged from 1960, still believing that Taiwan fell under the specified definition of "Far East," an area that was clearly defined as one where Japan and the United States share common security concerns.[76] Thus, the language and positions taken by both governments in 1972 are at the root of the present-day delicate but important difference in security concerns between Japan and China.

Summarizing China's Position toward Japan

As I have demonstrated above, the key factor of détente was the restructuring of the geopolitical balance of power. For China, the first immediate imperative was that it needed the United States to counterbalance the USSR. However, once this task was complete, the second objective on China's agenda was to prevent the revival of Japanese militarism. The Japan-U.S. Security Treaty became an important issue for China, and it decided to recognize its usefulness as a cap on any possible revival of Japanese militarism. Nixon and Kissinger exploited in full the Chinese fear of the revival of Japanese militarism and convinced them of the usefulness of the Japan-U.S. Security Treaty as a cap. Japanese leaders were delighted to learn of China's general acceptance of the

Japan-U.S. Security Treaty, but few noticed that Zhou's smile belied his deep distrust of Japan.

Furthermore, for China, normalization of its relations with the United States and Japan meant above all the recognition of its full territorial rights over Taiwan, and the denial of that island's claim to sovereignty. Therefore, both the United States and Japan had to cross a rather narrow bridge to overcome the Taiwan situation. Japan did this in the 1972 Joint Communiqué. The United States started the process with the 1972 Shanghai Communiqué and concluded it with the 1978–79 Communiqué and Taiwan Relations Act. Nothing indicates that China considered Japan strong enough to utilize as an ally in its geopolitical contest with the United States or the USSR. Politically, Japan became an important player in countering the Soviet Union, but this happened only later, centering on the issue of the conclusion of the Peace and Friendship Treaty and the inclusion of the anti-hegemony clause therein.

Establishing Diplomatic Relations with the Soviet Union in 1956

The Soviet Union did not sign the San Francisco Peace Treaty, and in 1955–56 the two countries negotiated a peace treaty and agreed to a Joint Declaration in October 1956. The only remaining question was the territorial issue. The Japanese side requested the return of the four Kuril Islands: Habomai, Shikotan, Kunashiri, and Etorofu. The Soviet side agreed to return Habomai and Shikotan, as it was written in the 1956 Joint Declaration, but not to the return of Kunashiri and Etorofu.

The U.S. position was ambivalent. It had agreed to "hand over" the Kuril Islands to the USSR at the Yalta Conference in February 1945, in order to secure Soviet participation in the war against Japan. John Foster Dulles later rejected the two-islands formula of Foreign Minister Shigemitsu Mamoru in August 1956, with the threat never to return Okinawa.[77] U.S. support of the Japanese government's four islands formula in September 1956 and May 1957 exacerbated the continuing tension between Japan and the Soviet Union in Cold War power politics.

China's position was no different. In 1951, the Chinese Foreign Ministry compiled a document stating that although the commitments made at Yalta should be honored, Habomai and Shikotan did not belong to the Soviet Union. This view might actually reflect the Soviet government's position of that period.[78] In the 1970s, many leading Chinese public figures did not hesitate to support Japan's position on the Northern Territories as an extension of the Sino-Soviet rivalry.[79] Recently, this discourse has not been employed by Chinese public figures due to the normalization of its relations with the Soviet Union / Russia.

Détente and Its Impact upon Soviet-Japanese Relations

Sino-American rapprochement in the latter half of 1971 and Japan's enthusiasm to open diplomatic relations with the PRC caused Soviet anxiety over becoming encircled. The best policy to counter these moves was to woo Japan and bring it to the Soviet side, thereby detaching it from China.[80]

Soviet foreign minister Andrei Gromyko visited Japan in January 1972. The conservative Japanese press wrote that "the rapprochement of China and Japan played an important role, for this was something the Soviet Union had wanted to pre-empt."[81] Gromyko met Prime Minister Sato on January 27, 1972, and according to the Russian Foreign Ministry's minutes of that meeting, later reported by a Japanese journalist, the Soviet foreign minister stated that "the Soviet side is prepared to resolve the issue on the basis of the [1956] Joint Declaration." Sato's response was passive, if not entirely negative: "The positions of the two sides differ, and we cannot agree immediately to the Russian proposal. At this point, I would like to reserve my comments."[82] But the Soviets kept paying close attention to Japan. When Tanaka became prime minister in July 1972, the Soviet leader, Leonid Brezhnev, sent a personal letter expressing his desire for a closer relationship with Japan.[83]

Retrospectively, 1972 was probably the time of greatest opportunity to find a breakthrough in Japanese-Soviet relations. But the task of establishing diplomatic relations with China, as described above, was overwhelmingly more important for Japan, particularly after the Nixon shock, than repairing relations with the Soviet Union. Tanaka's diplomatic activities focused on China in the second half of 1972, and it was only after relations were normalized with the PRC that Tanaka shifted his attention toward the Soviet Union. After he accomplished normalization with China, Tanaka spoke out loudly in private that "now the next task is the Soviet Union!"[84]

Tanaka was soon to be disappointed, however. Niiseki Kinya, then Japanese ambassador to the USSR, noticed that until August 1972 the Soviets were keen on concluding a peace treaty as soon as possible, but from October on, they became markedly cooler in their enthusiasm. Foreign Minister Ohira's visit to Moscow in October was very different from Gromyko's trip in January. The Soviets no longer mentioned anything about the possibility of going back to 1956.[85] Mikhail Kapitsa, the deputy foreign minister, left a detailed account in his memoir on the Gromyko-Ohira meeting. Gromyko pointedly asked Ohira a question on the Sino-Japanese Communiqué's anti-hegemony clause,[86] and he was not satisfied with Ohira's response that this clause was a mere repetition from the Shanghai Communiqué. Gromyko further stated: "We do not consider the hegemony clause as being neutral. . . . We are against two or more governments creating a scheme or coalition directed against the Soviet Union or other countries." Kapitsa wrote that the Soviet side became satisfied with Ohira's response: "The Sino-Japanese normalization must not be a coalition. Japanese-Soviet relations must be independent and free from any hints from a third country."[87]

It is not clear whether Ohira's discourse had a real impact on the Soviet side, but Brezhnev sent a signal of his willingness to improve Soviet-Japanese relations. He made a speech on December 21, stating that "the purpose of the Soviet-Japanese negotiations, which are to take place next year, is to resolve *remaining issues* from the time of WWII." In March 1973, Brezhnev reintroduced his multilateral collective security proposal that he had first proposed in 1969. On January 20, 1973, in Tokyo, Arai Hirokazu assumed the post of director of the First East Asian Division of the European and Oceania Department of MOFA, which was directly responsible for the Soviet Union. He became the chief architect of Japan's policy toward the Soviet Union to implement Tanaka's wish to improve relations with the Soviet Union for the next few years.

Arai had detected the Soviets' intention to arrest Sino-Japanese rapprochement in Gromyko's visit in January 1972. Arai also saw that the Soviets were eager to achieve greater economic cooperation with Japan, which had become the number two economic power in the Free World. Encouraged by Brezhnev's speech on December 21, Arai proposed that Tanaka send a letter to Brezhnev. He drafted the letter, making two modifications to Brezhnev's December speech. First, he used the singular term, *issue,* not the plural, *issues,* making it clear that the issue pertained only to the territorial dispute. Second, he added the expression of Japan's "readiness" on Siberian development based "on the principle of mutual benefit" in order to respond to Brezhnev's interest on the Siberian development.[88] Tanaka and Ohira strongly agreed with this approach, the letter was sent on March 6, and Brezhnev responded positively on March 28.[89]

The two sides began hard negotiations on how to structure Tanaka's visit to Moscow. By July 1973, it was agreed that Tanaka's visit to Moscow would take place from October 7 to 10, 1973. Arai summarized the basic policy toward the visit in these four points: (1) The major objective is to improve Brezhnev's understanding of Japan to ensure the solid development of bilateral relations. (2) Maximum efforts would be made to make the visit a real starting point for the resolution of the territorial problem, but it cannot be expected that a single visit would resolve such a truly difficult issue; a two-islands solution or the

Peace and Friendship Treaty without any territorial resolution shall be rejected. (3) The Soviet side would request Japan's cooperation in exploiting Siberian resources, and, subject to the overall situation of the negotiations, this could be considered. (4) The Asian collective security proposal cannot be accepted because it envisages the reorganization of the postwar frontier and the United States' withdrawal from Asia.[90]

The Tanaka-Brezhnev Summit, 1973

The Tanaka-Brezhnev summit began on the morning of October 8, 1973. Oleg Troianovskii, then Soviet ambassador in Tokyo, who attended this meeting, described in his memoir the unfortunate way it started. The war in the Middle East and frequent memos submitted to the Soviet leaders and their whispering with each other at the table "naturally irritated the Japanese."[91] At the second meeting, in the afternoon of October 8, Brezhnev made a long presentation about future cooperation in Siberia. Tanaka responded bluntly, asking both sides to take notes, and said that the "obligation and destiny of politicians on both sides are to resolve the territorial issue."[92] Brezhnev proposed to end the meeting right then, and while standing up from his seat, said rather loudly: "We shall give them nothing."[93] The third meeting, on October 9, became more constructive, but no convergence on the territorial issue was in sight. It was the overnight contacts that took place that evening, when both sides came up with the same approach of using Brezhnev's speech from December 1972 as the basis for a mutually acceptable draft "to conclude a peace treaty by resolving the unresolved issue(s) since World War II." The Japanese side urged putting the word "issues" in the singular, but the Soviet side did not agree and insisted that the word should be plural.[94]

At the final meeting between the two leaders, at noon on October 10, Brezhnev requested that *unresolved issues* should be in the plural. Tanaka asked Brezhnev whether he could confirm that the "four islands" were included in these *issues.* Brezhnev first said "I know." Tanaka asked again, and Brezhnev said "Yes." Both sides accepted an agreement—albeit an oral one—for the first time in the history of Japan-Soviet negotiations that Kunashiri and Etorofu were *unresolved issues* from World War II.[95]

The communiqué was signed on the evening of October 10. This became the high point of Soviet-Japanese negotiations in the period of détente. The oil shock that befell the world economy began with the war in the Middle East, while Tanaka was in Moscow, and had diplomatic repercussions that seemed to have weakened Japan's economic position while strengthening the USSR's position, due to its large oil reserves. Tanaka's domestic political status declined because of a scandal involving Lockheed. President Nixon became implicated in the Watergate incident, which resulted in his resignation in August 1974. The USSR soon overcame its fear of encirclement and began to utilize the prevailing mood of détente to expand its influence in Indochina and Africa. As the détente process was experiencing crisis, Soviet-Japanese bilateral relations also began to deteriorate.

Why Did Japan's Attempt at Rapprochement with the Soviet Union Fail?

How should we evaluate Japan's limited achievements in this short period of one year, from 1972 to 1973? Did Japan miss a great historic opportunity because of the failure of its strategy, or did it achieve more or less what was realistically possible in the given conditions?

We begin by ascertaining the historical facts about the meaning of the Joint Communiqué of October 1973 with regard to the territorial question. It is well known that already from the middle of the 1970s, the Soviet side began to undermine the Japanese interpretation of the 1973 Brezhnev-Tanaka meeting. Gromyko began to use the term "unfounded territorial claim" in 1975, and Brezhnev stated in 1977 in his response to *Asahi Shinbun* "the interpretation that there exists an unresolved issue between Japan and the Soviet Union is one-sided and inaccurate."[96] Troianovskii revealed an account with more nuances that Kosygin was concerned that the wording of the communiqué might imply Soviet acknowledgment of the territorial issue, and therefore he warned Ambassador Niizeki after the meeting "not to publicly interpret the final document in your own favor because it might invite a negative reaction on the Soviet side."[97] The Soviet account closest to the Japanese one was made by Kapitsa. He revealed in 1995 to Hasegawa Tsuyoshi orally that the Japanese interpretation on the Tanaka-Brezhnev Joint Communiqué was basically correct.[98] But he wrote in his memoir published in 1996 that "our representatives confirmed that Brezhnev said 'Yes, I know' but the Japanese insisted on their own [version]."[99] The difference is subtle, because the Japanese version was "I know" and "yes." Ultimately, because there is no written, agreed-on version, it is difficult to determine which is correct. But because the Japanese version is based on statements by those who were actually present, there does not seem to be a plausible reason that the Japanese side embarked on a campaign of lies immediately after the meeting, and Kapitsa's version indicates a close enough hint at what really happened, I consider the Japanese version to be correct.

This ambiguity leads us to consider whether it was not possible for Tanaka to achieve more, for instance to secure in writing what Brezhnev stated during his last meeting with Tanaka. Hirano wrote that MOFA had difficulty in convincing foreign diplomats in Tokyo that some progress was made on the territorial issue, when even the names of contentious islands failed to appear in the agreement.[100] As some of the Japanese diplomats would have preferred, it certainly would have been better to fix the position taken in 1973 by the Soviets in writing.[101] Why did Tanaka not request Brezhnev to put in writing that the "unresolved issues" included "the issue of the four islands"? The obvious risk of insisting on this point was Brezhnev's refusal of his oral acknowledgment of the four islands issue. An indication of Brezhnev's rigidity on the territorial issue is his statement that "we shall give nothing," made at the end of the second meeting on October 8, 1973, as stated above. If that is the case, did not Japan have the option to not sign the Joint Communiqué? The Tanaka team must have considered that it was better to have an agreement based on an oral exchange, however weak it may have been, than not have any agreement at all, because for the first time the Soviet side acknowledged the existence of the "four islands issue."

This issue in turn leads us to raise a question: What led the Soviets to change their mind from 1972 to 1973? If it was not possible to have the Soviets acknowledge the validity of the 1956 Joint Declaration in 1973, did Japan miss the chance to accept Gromyko's proposal to Sato in 1972, when Gromyko proposed the solution of the territorial question on the basis of the 1956 Joint Declaration? Why did Prime Minister Sato ignore Gromyko's proposal in January 1972? Even if China was the overwhelming priority after the Nixon shock, if the Japanese side had greater interest in the content of the proposal, could not the result of the negotiations have been different? Wada Haruki argues that Sato was probably preoccupied with Okinawa and had no particular interest in taking up the Soviet issue before his retirement, with the result that Japan therefore lost its opportunity to regain Habomai and Shikotan.[102] Kimura Hiroshi asserts that because the Japanese government could not have accepted such a proposal based on the 1956 Joint Declaration, the result would have been the same anyway.[103] Hasegawa asks several valuable questions about the implications of Okinawa, China, and domestic politics in relation to Sato's attitude, and he concludes that, had Japan been serious toward the Soviets, a lot more might have developed from Gromyko's proposal.[104] After the Nixon shock, pushing the normalization agenda with China first became an imperative for Sato, and then for Tanaka. Reaching rapprochement with the Soviet Union became a second priority. The most interesting criticism against Japan, however, comes from the Soviet side. Aleksandr Panov, ambassador to Japan in the late 1990s, wrote in his memoirs that Troianovskii later wrote in *Yomiuri Shinbun* that "it is understandable that Japan could not be satisfied with two islands, but was there not a possibility to begin negotiations on that basis and lead the negotiations to another direction?"[105] It may well be that from the Russian point of view, proceeding "based on 1956" could have indicated a start, but for the Japanese leaders at this time, it would have looked as if they were abandoning the bid for Kunashiri and Etorofu. If that was the case, the psychological mismatch between the two sides is regrettable.

If Sino-Japanese rapprochement in 1972 was the major reason for the Soviet government's hardening of its position, what exactly prompted the Soviet Union to change its previous conciliatory attitude toward Japan? Did the inclusion of the anti-hegemony clause in the September 1972 Japan-China Joint Communiqué antagonize the USSR, or did Sino-Japanese rapprochement in general displease the Soviet Union? It appears that at least public pronouncements by the Soviet officials indicate that the inclusion of the anti-hegemony clause could have made the acceptance of Sino-Japanese rapprochement difficult for the Soviet leaders. Gromyko raised this issue seriously in his October 1972 meeting with Ohira, warning against the inclusion of the anti-hegemony clause. Georgii Kunadze, a scholar at the Institute of World Economy and International Relations (known as IMEMO), later underlined this concern by quoting Ishikawa Tadao, who argued that for the Chinese leaders, "hegemony" clearly meant the Soviet Union.[106] For the Japanese negotiators in Beijing in September 1972, although they preferred not to include this clause in the communiqué, it was a concession that they thought acceptable, particularly after the Sino-American Shanghai Communiqué had included the same anti-hegemony clause.[107] The Japanese negotiators probably could not comprehend that in the negotiations with the United States, the anti-hegemony clause had only minor significance. Whereas with Japan, which was still considered a politically weak appendage of the United States, the anti-hegemony clause was more of an influence in hardening Soviet policy toward Japan. Still, in 1972, the fundamental change in Sino-Japanese relations was probably a more dominant factor, which made the "Japan card" less valuable for the Soviets. But during the 1978 negotiations on the Peace and Friendship Treaty, this issue became central to Japan-USSR-China relations.

Another important issue that contributed to the failure of Soviet-Japanese rapprochement was Japan's rejection of the Soviet proposal for Asian collective security. To what extent did the Japanese government's rigid approach to collective security affect the Soviet position on the Northern Territories? It can be argued that the impact was limited because the collective security proposal did not get anywhere, in either 1969 or 1973. Several interpretations have been put forward since then on the subject of this proposal. Given the fact that it was launched just after the Sino-Soviet military collision at Damanskii/Zhenbao

Island in March 1969, many interpreted this as a proposal aimed at encircling China with countries friendly to the USSR.[108] But others considered that the proposal "genuinely contained elements for a new collective security framework."[109] The Japanese Foreign Ministry, however, understood it more as an attempt to weaken the U.S. military presence in East Asia and therefore took a strong position against it. Arai later explained that he reacted very negatively to this proposal because "it was evident that this proposal was aimed at U.S. withdrawal and fixation of the border."[110]

Another issue to be examined is whether or not Japan could have utilized the Siberian cooperation card more effectively to extract Soviet concessions on the territorial question. Kimura seems to be the strongest critic of Tanaka's handling of economic leverage, arguing that Tanaka completely wasted this card. He argues that Tanaka intentionally decoupled economics from politics and stated that Japan would cooperate with the Siberian development with the USSR.[111] Hasegawa also agrees that Tanaka revealed his greatest trump card before the negotiations started.[112]

The Japanese side was not unaware of the role of the "economic card" in shaping the Soviet position toward Japan. Arai later wrote that during the preparatory stage of Tanaka's visit in August and September 1973, the government reached a consensus that the "Economic Cooperation Agreement shall not be concluded before the resolution of the territorial problems."[113] In that sense, the principle of *seikei fukabun* (the inseparability of politics and economics) was a pro forma policy direction. But in reality, the Japanese approach was more flexible, and in the preparatory stage it was decided "to leave a little room for Japan's participation in the Siberian resource development, subject to the conditions" to be agreed on with the Soviets.[114] The business community was vitally interested in Siberian energy to diversify Japan's energy sources. Tanaka's statement before the visit, expressing a willingness for Siberian cooperation, was probably a reflection of these Japanese interests as well as his effort to raise Soviet interest in Japan's participation. At the third meeting, on October 9, Tanaka secured Brezhnev's agreement to the three conditions on Siberian development: technical feasibility, government assurance for smooth implementation, and inclusiveness of third-country (implying U.S.) companies.[115]

The Tanaka-Arai policy actually meant maintaining a basic willingness for Siberian development, but at the same time making it clear that a resolution of the four islands problem would be critically important. This is precisely the spirit if not the wording of *kakudai kinko* (balanced expansion).[116] It was not an unwise policy. Fixating the government's position in the rigid policy of *seikei fukabun* (the inseparability of politics and economics) has never produced results in Japan-Russia relations from the 1980s on. Even if the gains were limited, Tanaka and Arai clearly took a step forward both on the territorial issue and in the realm of economic relations.

Thus, from the end of the 1960s until the beginning of the 1980s, altogether nine Siberian resource projects were implemented with Japanese cooperation.[117] On the Tyumen (Tiumen) oil project, however, the Soviet side proposed increasingly harder conditions from 1972 to 1973, which eventually became the primary cause of Japan's withdrawal from it. It is interesting to note that the hardening of the Russian attitude coincided with Chinese concern, "voiced privately to Japanese groups, over the strategic implications of an improved supply of oil to the Soviet Far East."[118]

Finally, we must consider the clash of personalities between Brezhnev and Tanaka for the failure of Soviet-Japanese rapprochement.[119] Many commentators have concluded that the way Tanaka conducted his talks with Brezhnev antagonized the proud Soviet leader. Arai left an account that Tanaka did not like the long and high-handed speech on economic cooperation made by Brezhnev at the second meeting on October 8, 1973.[120] Troianovskii also left an account about Tanaka asking to take notes, and that in turn irritated Brezhnev.[121] Panov went on to state that it was because of Tanaka's unworthy behavior of asking the participants to take notes at the second meeting on October 8 that Brezhnev decided to withdraw his position to go back to the 1956 Joint Declaration.[122]

Like Hasegawa, I do not consider this a mismatch purely on the basis of a personality clash. The way Brezhnev and Tanaka behaved at their second meeting, on the afternoon of October 8, was a reflection of their perception of the world, and their perception of their own country and the other in this world. Brezhnev represented the USSR, a superpower eager to receive all the honor due a victor in World War II, and was the leader of the socialist camp. Its fortunes were on the rise, and economic cooperation with Japan, an economic power rapidly rising in the international society, seemed very logical. Tanaka represented Japan, a rising regional power by virtue of its miraculous economic growth during the 1960s, and a diplomatic power that had just normalized its relations with China. For Tanaka, the next diplomatic question was the Soviet Union, and the territorial issue was at the center of their relationship, not economic cooperation. There was a fundamental gap in understanding and perception.[123]

Conclusion

During the period of détente in the early 1970s, the Japanese government envisaged undertaking an active and autonomous policy to overcome two of the major outstanding unresolved issues from World War II: reestablishing relations with the PRC, and concluding a peace treaty with the Soviet Union. The realization of these two goals would have considerably strengthened Japan's diplomatic stature and make it a more serious political player in the international Cold War structure of East Asia.

With regard to China, the Japanese government more or less achieved its objective. It has long been considered that the Nixon shock pushed Japan's policymakers to take a much more autonomous position than they otherwise would have adopted, and this resulted in the drastic decision to sever political relations with Taiwan in September 1972. In fact, Japan established diplomatic relations with China seven years earlier than the United States. But with the diligence of diplomats and the strong wills of politicians, the Japanese negotiators ensured that Japan's security treaty with the United States would be left intact, that its interpretation would remain unchanged, and that the slightly divergent views on the status of Taiwan between Beijing and Tokyo could be left alone.

With regard to the Soviet Union, what little was achieved in 1972 and 1973 did not last. The Soviet government bluntly began to negate its oral acknowledgment that "four islands" were the object of negotiations, and a postdétente exacerbation of international relations sharply affected Soviet-Japanese relations starting in the later 1970s. A serious reconsideration of the relationship began only in the later 1980s, during perestroika.

Why did Japan succeed in its rapprochement with China but fail in its relations with the Soviet Union? For Japan, détente opened a possibility to tackle concerns with both China and the Soviet Union. Theoretically, Japan had three options: Tackle China first, and then the Soviet Union; tackle the Soviet Union first, and then China; or tackle both simultaneously. Was the second way really feasible? In reality, as has been discussed, there was no great Japanese domestic frustration with the failure to achieve rapprochement with the Soviet Union, as there was with China. Tanaka had no choice but to act on China. But, then, was it possible to move on two fronts simultaneously? After all, didn't Nixon and Kissinger do exactly that? Yes, they did, because they were U.S. leaders and their goal was to achieve geopolitical superiority over the Soviet Union by achieving rapprochement with China. In the American case, the two operations had to go side by side. But Japan's main objective was different, and more limited: to bring to a close unresolved issues from World War II. There was no real reason to move simultaneously with respect to both the Soviet Union and China. Furthermore, there was not enough diplomatic capability to implement the two operations simultaneously. Neither among political leaders nor in MOFA was there enough initiative to implement this kind of synthetic foreign policy. So Japan's options were reduced to one at a time, and when Tanaka intended to move on the Soviet Union, it was too late to achieve a lasting breakthrough.

Notes

1. Tanaka Akihiko, *Nicchukankei 1945–1990* [Japan-China Relations 1945–1990] (Tokyo: Tokyo daigaku shuppankai, 1991), 59.

2. Joint Communiqué between President Richard M. Nixon and Prime Minister Eisaku Sato, November 21 1969, paragraph 4, http://www.ioc.u-tokyo.ac.jp/~world jpn/documents/texts/docs/19691121.D1E.html.

3. Tanaka Akihito, *Nicchukankei,* 60.

4. The group included Ishikawa Tadao, Imahori Seiji, Ichiko Chuizo, Umesao Tadao, Eto Shinkichi, Eto Jun, Kamiya Fuji, Kosaka Masataka, Nakajima Mineo, Miyashita Tadao, Nagai Yonosuke, and Yamazaki Masakazu. Tanaka Akihito, *Nicchukankei,* 69; Chalmers Johnson, "The Patterns of Japanese Relations with China, 1952–1982," *Pacific Affairs* 59, no. 3 (Autumn 1986): 412.

5. Ishii Akira, Shu Kenei, Soeya Yoshihide, and Lin Xioa Guang, eds., *Nicchu kokko seijoka: Nicchu heiwa yuko joyaku kosho* [Normalization of Japan-China relations: Negotiations to conclude a Peace and Friendship Treaty between Japan and China] (Tokyo: Iwanami, 2003), 212.

6. Go Ito, *Alliance in Anxiety: Détente and the Sino-American-Japanese Triangle* (London: Routledge, 2003), 95–97, 108.

7. Nicchukokkokaifuku Giinrenmei, *Nicchukokkokaifuku Kankeishiryoshu* [Collection of materials concerning the restoration of diplomatic relations between Japan and China] (Tokyo: Nicchukokkoshiryoiinnkai 1972), 139–41.

8. In Tokyo three minutes before Nixon's speech, Kusuda Minoru, Sato's secretary, encountered the prime minister emerging from a Cabinet meeting and conveyed the news. Kusuda recounted these events in a presentation at the Wilson Center March 11, 1996. Michael Schaller, *The Nixon "Shocks" and U.S.-Japan Strategic Relations–74,* Working Paper 2, U.S.-Japan Project Working Papers Series, National Security Archives, http://www.gwu.edu/~nsarchiv/japan/schaller.htm, 11.

9. Nakanishi Hiroshi, "Chapter 4, Jiritsuteki Kyochono Mosaku" [Search for Autonomous Cooperation], in *Sengo Nihon Gaikoshi* [Postwar Japanese Diplomatic History], ed. Iokibe Makoto (Tokyo: Yuhikaku, 1999), 151.

10. In Washington, when Alex Johnson made telephone contact with the Japanese ambassador, Ushiba Nobuhiko, minutes before Nixon's address, Ushiba cried out: "Alex, the Asakai nightmare has happened." Schaller, *Nixon "Shocks."*

11. Armin Meyer was U.S. ambassador to Japan from 1969 to 1972.

12. Nancy Bernkopf Tucker introduces Meyer's three points and questions: (1) What is the evidence for Japan's leak record? (2) Was there any other country among U.S. allies for which China policy mattered so much, other than Taiwan? (3) How does one explain Japan's rush to establish diplomatic relations with China ahead of the United States if one does not take into consideration the gravity of this shock? Nancy Bernkopf Tucker, *U.S.-Japan Relations and the Opening to China,* Working Paper 4, U.S.-Japan Project Working Papers Series, National Security Archives, http://www.gwu.edu/~nsarchiv/

japan/tucker.htm, 6–7. It was only on June 29, 1998, that President Bill Clinton publicly stated in his Shanghai community leaders' meeting that "we don't support independence for Taiwan or two Chinas or one Taiwan, one China." Clinton then added America's position on international organizations, but this aspect is outside the framework of this chapter's analysis; Robert Suettlinger, *Beyond Tiananmen: The Politics of U.S.-China Relations 1989–2000* (Washington, D.C.: Brookings Institution Press, 2003), 348.

13. Wakaizumi Kei, *Tasaku nakarishi o shinzemuto hossu* [Wanting to believe that there were no other measures] (Tokyo: Bungeishunju, 1994), 608.

14. As cited by Schaller, *Nixon "Shocks."*

15. Ito, *Alliance in Anxiety,* 79–80.

16. Henry Kissinger, *White House Years* (Boston, Little, Brown, 1979), 762.

17. Sadako Ogata, *Normalization with China: A Contemporary Study of U.S. and Japanese Processes* (Berkeley: University of California Press, 1988), 37.

18. Quoted by Schaller, *Nixon "Shocks."*

19. Memorandum for the president dated September 9 concerning his meeting with Foreign Minister Fukuda on September 10, 1971, Digital National Security Archive, no. 01434, 2.

20. Ogata described in detail the process of decisionmaking in Tokyo to cosponsor the Important Question Resolution. Ogata, *Normalization with China,* 40–43.

21. Ito, *Alliance in Anxiety,* 82.

22. Fukada Yusuke and Kim Mirei, *Tekiwa Chugokuniari* [The Enemy Is China] (Tokyo: Kobunsha, 2000), 223–25.

23. Memorandum of conversation between Henry Kissinger and Zhou Enlai, July 10, 1971, Great Hall of the People, Digital National Security Archive, no. 00304, 17–19.

24. As a note, a Taiwanese senior diplomat who participated in the process flatly rejected the possibility that the PRC would have allowed Taiwan to stay in the UN in whatever capacity. This observation is based on my interview on October 13, 2006, with a former Taiwanese diplomat who worked on the UN representation issue in this period.

25. Memorandum of conversation, the president, Alexander Haig, and Nobusuke Kishi, White House Office, October 22, 1971, Digital National Security Archive, no. 01451, 5.

26. Togo Fumihiko, *Nichibeigaiko 30nen* [30 Years of Japan-U.S. Diplomacy] (Tokyo: Sekaino Ugokisha, 1982), 204.

27. Ogata, *Normalization with China,* 43.

28. Ibid., 39–40; Ito, *Alliance in Anxiety,* 84–85. Hori's letter reads as follows: "I understand and recognize that there has been one China, which is now represented by the PRC, and that Taiwan has been a part of the territory of the peoples of China." Quoted by Ito, *Alliance in Anxiety,* 85.

29. Meeting with Eisaku Sato, Japanese prime minister, on Thursday, January 6, 1972, at San Clemente, Digital National Security Archive, no. 01499, 13.

30. Sato reiterated directly to Nixon in their meeting at San Clemente on January 7, 1972, that "the announcement of the President's visit to Peking had come as a great shock. He himself understood that this had been arranged behind Japan's back (over its head) but the Japanese people did not share his understanding." Digital National Security Archive, no. 01500, 3.

31. Meeting with Sato on January 6, 1972, Digital National Security Archive, no. 01499, 9. Also see Ito, *Alliance in Anxiety,* 87–89.

32. Conversation with Zhou Enlai, July 9, 1971, Digital National Security Archive, no. 00303, 16; Conversation with Zhou Enlai, July 10, 1971, Digital National Security Archive, no. 00304, 16.

33. The relevant part of the Shanghai Communiqué dated February 27, 1972, reads as follows: "The US side declared: The United States acknowledges that all Chinese on either side of the Taiwan Strait maintain there is but one China and that Taiwan is a part of China. The United States Government does not challenge that position." http://www.ioc.u-tokyo.ac.jp/~worldjpn/documents/texts/docs/19720227.D1E.html.

34. Meeting with Eisaku Sato on January 6, 1972, at San Clemente, Digital National Security Archive, no. 01499, 6, 13.

35. Two quotations from a conversation with Zhou Enlai, July 9, 1971, Digital National Security Archive, no. 00303, 42.

36. Nixon's trip to China, document 3, memorandum of conversation, February 24, 1972, 5:15 p.m.–8:05 p.m., http://www.gwu.edu/~nsarchiv/NSAEBB/NSAEBB106/NZ-3.pdf, 13.

37. Ogata, *Normalization with China,* 45.

38. Ibid., 46.

39. Gene T. Hsiao, "The Sino-Japanese Rapprochement: A Relationship of Ambivalence," *China Quarterly,* no. 57, (January–March 1974): 108.

40. Ito, *Alliance in Anxiety,* 80.

41. Akira Iriye, "Chinese-Japanese Relations, 1945–90," *China Quarterly,* no. 124 (Special Issue on China and Japan: History, Trends, and Prospects, December 1990): 624–29.

42. Ibid., 629.

43. Ibid., 631–33.

44. Ibid, 634–35.

45. Tanaka Kakuei, born in 1918 the son of poor farmer in Niigata, only had a primary school education. He served in the army in Manchuria, opened a construction firm in Niigata during World War II, was elected as a member of the House of Representatives in 1947, and had since rapidly expanded his power and influence in the conservative party. He had already held such important posts as minister of finance and LDP general secretary and was minister of international trade and industry in the Sato Cabinet. Later nicknamed "the bulldozer with a computer," he was known to be the master of party power politics and spearheaded the Japanese drive for economic development known as the "Period of High Growth" during the 1960s, although he was not particularly known for his views on foreign policy, including China.

46. Lee W. Farnsworth, "Japan 1972: New Faces and New Friends," *Asian Survey* 13, no. 1 (January 1973): 113–15; Ogata, *Normalization with China,* 45–46.

47. Ogata, *Normalization with China,* 47; Farnsworth, "Japan 1972," 114.

48. Quoted by Tanaka Akihiko, *Nicchukankei,* 75–76.

49. Quoted by Ogata, *Normalization with China,* 47.

50. Ishii et al., *Nicchu kokko seijoka,* 29–34 (documents); Ogata, *Normalization with China,* 49; Tanaka Akihiko, *Nicchukankei,* 79–79.

51. Ishii et al., *Nicchu kokko seijoka,* 11, 14, 32 (documents).

52. Ibid., 197–207.

53. Ishii et al, *Nicchu kokko seijoka,* 213–16 (testimonies).

54. Tsumoto Yo, *Igyono Shogun II* [Unusual Shogun II] (Tokyo: Gentosha Bunko,

2004), 126–32, 137–39; Mizuki Yo, *Tanaka Kakuei: Sono kyozen to kyoaku* [Tanaka Kakuei, Mighty Good and Mighty Evil] (Tokyo: Bungeishunju, 2001), 221–25, 230; Sugita Nozomu, *Tensai daiakuto* [Genius and Tyrant] (Tokyo: Daiwashobo, 2006), 123–31, 142–43.

55. "Your Meeting with Japanese Prime Minister Tanaka in Honolulu on August 31 and September 1, 1972," memorandum from Henry Kissinger to Richard Nixon, Digital National Security Archive, no. 01624, 4.

56. Prime Minister Tanaka's call on President Nixon, August 31, 1972, Hawaii, National Security Archive, 01635, 9, 10, 12.

57. A joint statement was issued on September 1, 1972, in which Tanaka and Nixon "shared the hope that the forthcoming visit of the Prime Minister to the PRC would also serve to further the trend for the relaxation of tension"; http://www.ioc.u-tokyo.ac.jp/~worldjpn/documents/texts/JPUS/19720901.D1E.html. Hirano Minoru, an informed Japanese journalist, later wrote that in the original draft prepared by the U.S. side, "shared the view" was toned down to "shared the hope" and "this change was interpreted as reflecting the fact that the U.S. side did not wholeheartedly agree to the normalization of the Japan-China relationship." Hirano Minoru, *Gaiko Kisha nikki: Ohira Gaiko no ninen* [Diary of a foreign policy correspondent: Two years of Ohira diplomacy], vol. 1 (Tokyo: Gyosei tsushinsha, 1978), 52.

58. Ishii et al., *Nicchu kokko seijoka,* 135–38 (documents).

59. Ibid., 229–33.

60. This is based on my interview on October 13, 2006, in Taipei with a senior Taiwanese opinion leader who was directly engaged in transmitting the message from Ohira to the Taiwanese leadership.

61. This is based on Ogura's testimony. Ishii et al., *Nicchu kokko seijoka,* 232 (testimonies).

62. Ishii et al., *Nicchu kokko seijoka,* 117 (documents).

63. Ibid., 111.

64. This is based on Hashimoto's testimony. Ishii et al., *Nicchu kokko seijoka,* 218–22 (testimonies).

65. Ishii et al., *Nicchu kokko seijoka,* 117 (documents).

66. Ishii et al., *Nicchu kokko seijoka,* 113 (records). The standard interpretation of this clause is that Article 8 of the Potsdam Declaration stated that the terms of the Cairo Declaration of 1943 shall be carried out and the Cairo Declaration stated that all territories Japan has stolen from the Chinese such as Manchuria, Formosa and the Pescadores shall be restored to the Republic of China. The ROC was at the time understood to be the sole representative of China, a role that was now taken over by the PRC. Kazuhiko Togo, *Japan's Foreign Policy 1945–2003* (Leiden: Brill, 2005), 130.

67. Kuriyama Takakazu, *Kakankai Kaiho* [Report by Kakankai], October 2007, 13.

68. Hsiao, "Sino-Chinese Rapprochement," 116.

69. Takashima, in his statement made at the September 26 morning session, had already clearly mentioned that "since it is the wish of all Japanese people that war between China and the U.S. should be averted, the Government of Japan considers that the Taiwan issue has to be resolved peacefully." Ishii et al., *Nicchu kokko seijoka,* 113 (documents).

70. See http://www.mofa.go.jp/region/asia-paci/china/joint0805.html.

71. Ishii et al., *Nicchu kokko seijoka,* 11 (documents); Article 4 of the 1969 Sato-

Nixon Communiqué includes the following: "The President referred to the treaty obligations of his country to the Republic of China which the United States would uphold. The Prime Minister said that the maintenance of peace and security in the Taiwan area was also a most important factor for the security of Japan"; http://www.ioc.u-tokyo.ac.jp/~worldjpn/documents/texts/docs/19691121.D1E.html.

72. Ishii et al., *Nicchu kokko seijoka,* 57 (documents).

73. Ibid.

74. "Foreign Minister Ohira's call on the President on October 18, 1972, at the Oval Office," National Security Archive, 01660, 2.

75. Sheldon Simon, "The Japan-China-USSR Triangle," *Pacific Affairs* 47, no. 2 (Summer 1974): 135.

76. Through my personal experience as the director-general of the Treaties Bureau from August 1998 until August 1999, during which period I had access to all MOFA documents concerning interpretation of international treaties that Japan was party to, including the U.S. Security Treaty, I have not come across any documents that indicated the change of its interpretation.

77. Tanaka Takahiko, *Nissokokkokaifukuno Shitekikenkyu* [Historical research on the restoration of Japanese-Soviet relations] (Tokyo; Yuhikaku, 1993), 254–57.

78. See http://www5f.biglobe.ne.jp/~kokumin-shinbun/H16/1607/1607044north.html.

79. Joachim Glaubitz, *Between Tokyo and Moscow: The History of an Uneasy Relationship, 1972 to the 1990s* (London: Hurst & Company, 1995), 136–43.

80. Wada Haruki, *Hopporyodo Mondai* [Northern Territories Problem] (Tokyo: Asahi, 1999), 278; Kimura Hiroshi, *Nichiro kokkyo koshoshi* [History of the Russo-Japanese border negotiations] (Tokyo: Chukoshinsho, 1993), 148.

81. Glaubitz, *Between Tokyo and Moscow,* 50.

82. Nagoshi Kenro, a Sankei correspondent in Moscow, consulted the Russian Foreign Ministry archive and published the quoted passage; see Nagoshi Kenro, *Kuremurin himitsu bunsho wa kataru* [What secret Kremlin documents tell] (Tokyo: Chukoshinsho, 1994), 233. Mikhail Kapitsa, who attended that meeting, wrote in his memoir practically the same proposal and concluded that "the Japanese Prime Minister did not react to this sounding"; Mikhail Kapitsa, *Na raznykh paralleliakh: Zapiski diplomata* [On several parallels: Notes of a diplomat] (Moscow: Kniga i Biznes, 1996). Wada Haruki checked *Sato Eisaku's Diary,* vol. 5, published in 1997, on this meeting: "We talked just two of us at my office. There is still a gap on the Kuril issue but that gap is diminishing"; Wada, *Hopporyodo Mondai,* 279–80. Hasegawa made further detailed analysis on other sources; see Tsuyoshi Hasegawa, *The Northern Territories Dispute and Russo-Japanese Relations,* vol. 1, *Between War and Peace, 1697–1985* (Berkeley: International and Area Studies, University of California, 1998), 149–50, and in particular 213 n. 19.

83. Hasegawa, *Northern Territories Dispute,* 151.

84. Tanaka Akihiko, *Nicchu kankei,* 76.

85. Hasegawa, *Northern Territories Dispute,* 152.

86. Sino-Japanese Communiqué of September 29, 1972, clause 7: "The normalization of relations between Japan and China is not directed against any third Country. Neither of the two countries should seek hegemony in the Asia-Pacific region and

each is opposed to efforts by any other country or group of countries to establish such hegemony."

87. Kapitsa, *Na raznykh paralleliakh,* 160. Hirano also left an account very similar to Kapitsa's; Hirano, *Gaiko kisha nikki,* vol. 1 (Tokyo: Gyosei tsushinsha, 1978), 109.

88. Arai Hirokazu, "Taiso gaiko hiwa" [Secret story of foreign policy toward the Soviet Union], *Shokun,* January 2000, 79–80.

89. Ministry of Foreign Affairs, *Warerano Hopporyodo: Shiryohen* [Our Northern Territories: Documents] (Tokyo: Ministry of Foreign Affairs, 2001), 58; Hasegawa, *Northern Territories Dispute,* 152.

90. Arai, "Taiso gaiko hiwa," 83–85.

91. Oleg Troianovskii, *Cherez gody i rasstoianie: Istoriia odnoi semii* [Through the years and distance: Story of a family] (Moscow: Vagrius, 1997), 288.

92. Arai, "Taiso gaiko hiwa," 92.

93. Troianovskii, *Cherez gody i rasstoianie,* 288.

94. Arai, "Taiso gaiko hiwa," 93–96.

95. Ibid., 97. Hasegawa, *Northern Territories Dispute,* 156; Kimura, *Nichiro kokkyo koshoshi,* 153.

96. Kimura, *Nichiro kokkyo koshoshi,* 155.

97. Troianovskii, *Cherez gody i rasstoyanie,* 289. Arai also noticed at the third meeting that Kosygin's response was much tougher on the territorial issue than Brezhnev's; Arai, "Taiso gaiko hiwa," 94.

98. Interview by Hasegawa with Kapitsa, May 19 1995. Hasegawa, *Northern Territories Dispute,* 214.

99. Kapitsa, *Na raznykh paralleliakh,* 162.

100. Hirano, *Gaiko kisha nikki,* vol. 2, 148–51.

101. Hasegawa, *Northern Territories Dispute,* 214 n. 34.

102. Wada, *Hopporyodo mondai,* 280.

103. Kimura, *Nichiro kokkyo koshoshi,* 148–50.

104. Hasegawa, *Northern Territories Dispute,* 150.

105. Alexander Panov, *Kaminari nochi hare* [After the thundering, blue sky] (Tokyo: NHK Shuppan, 2004), 240–41.

106. Georgii Kunadze, *Iapono-Kitaiskie otnosheniia na sovremennom etape 1972–1982* [Japan-China relations in the contemporary period 1972–1982], (Moscow: Nauka, 1983), 42–43.

107. Ito, *Alliance in Anxiety,* 100.

108. Kimura, *Nichiro kokkyo koshoshi,* 145.

109. Hasegawa, *Northern Territories Dispute,* 148.

110. Arai, "Taiso gaiko hiwa, " 83.

111. Kimura, *Nichiro kokkyo koshoshi,* 151.

112. Hasegawa, *Northern Territories Dispute,* 154.

113. Arai, "Taiso gaiko hiwa," 86.

114. Ibid., 85.

115. Ibid., 93.

116. The Japanese government formally adopted this concept in 1989 in dealing with Gorbachev's Soviet Union.

117. Togo, *Japan's Foreign Policy,* 242.

118. Allen Whiting, *Siberian Development and East Asia: Threat or Promise?* (Stanford, Calif.: Stanford University Press, 1981), 138–39.

119. Arai, "Taiso Gaiko Hiwa," 92; Hasegawa, *Northern Territories Dispute,* 155–56.

120. At the dinner with Japanese officials on October 8, Tanaka grumbled that "Brezhnev behaved like an assistant professor teaching a deputy-director of a government agency." Arai, "Taiso Gaiko Hiwa," 92.

121. Troianovskii, *Cherez gody i rasstoyanie,* 289.

122. Alexander Panov, *Fushin kara Shinraie* [Beyond distrust to trust] (Tokyo: Simul Shuppan, 1992), 68.

123. Hasegawa, *Northern Territories Dispute,* 155–57.

8. A Strategic Quadrangle: The Superpowers and the Sino-Japanese Treaty of Peace and Friendship, 1977–1978

Tsuyoshi Hasegawa

The Cold War in Asia evolved along a different path from that taken in Europe. In Asia, dynamic and changing relations among four major powers—the United States, Japan, the Soviet Union, and China—created a more complicated picture for the structure of the Cold War than in Europe, where the East/West fault line was clearly drawn.[1] This was especially true during the 1970s. Three factors that emerged during the 1970s made the structure of the Cold War in Asia fundamentally different from that in Europe. First and foremost, the Sino-Soviet split that had begun as an ideological conflict in the 1960s developed into a military conflict in 1969. Mao Zedong began to view the Soviet Union as a more dangerous hegemonic power threatening China's security than the United States. Second, the U.S. defeat in the Vietnam War seriously eroded the prestige and power of the United States, and revealed the limit of the United States' commitment to defend its Asian allies. The strategic triangle that in the 1970s replaced the bipolarity of the first stage of the Cold War resulted from the combination of these two factors. China, which had once been a junior partner of the Soviet Union in the Communist camp, became an independent strategic player to be courted by the United States in seeking to counter the Soviet threat; and this in turn gave China an opportunity to enter the international arena as a great power. Third, during this decade Japan attained the status of an economic great power, which gave it confidence as an independent player in its foreign policy. Although the U.S.-Japanese security alliance continued to be the basis for Japan's foreign policy, the United States was no longer in a position to dictate its hegemonic will to Japan, as it had done during the earlier Cold War period.

This chapter reassesses the power reconfiguration in the second half of the 1970s, using Japan as the analytical pivot from which to see how the other three powers—the United States, China, and the Soviet Union—responded to the changing circumstances. The goal is to view the reconfiguration of power relations in the 1970s not in the triangular relationship but in the quadrangular relations by including Japan, and thus offer a corrective to triangular analyses of the power reconfiguration in Asia during the 1970s.[2]

Japan and the Strategic Triangle, 1968–77

According to Henry Kissinger, détente is an extension of containment by a different means. From the perspective of the former U.S. secretary of state, détente was not meant to be a relaxation of superpower conflict but a means to contain the Soviet expansionism at a time when the United States was losing its prestige and power after its defeat in the Vietnam War.[3] One way to achieve this goal was to reach rapprochement with the People's Republic of China (PRC).

Realizing the limit of U.S. power, President Richard Nixon enunciated the Nixon Doctrine, indicating the United States' retrenchment from its commitment in Asia. The American withdrawal of troops from Vietnam in 1973, and the eventual victory of North Vietnam in the Vietnam War in 1975, gave rise to the Chinese leaders' concern. The Soviet invasion of Czechoslovakia in 1969, the military confrontation with the Soviet forces on Damanskii/Zhenbao Island, and the subsequent Soviet military buildup along the Soviet-Chinese border, on the one hand, and the emergence of united Vietnam, assisted by the Soviet Union as a hegemonic power in Southeast Asia, on the other, heightened the Chinese sense of the Soviet threat. The Sino-American rapprochement was a major diplomatic revolution that served the interests of China and the United States—each sought in the other a counterweight to Soviet expansionism.

Where does Japan fit in the reconfiguration of powers in the 1970s? During the 1970s, Japan gradually began to shed its U.S. tutelage and attempted to assert its own independent foreign policy.[4] Nixon's rapprochement with the PRC without consultation with Japan was a profound shock to the Japanese. In the wake of the Nixon shock, Prime Minister Tanaka Kakuei immediately normalized Japan's relations with the PRC in 1972, going a step further than the United States. In the following year, he had a summit meeting with Leonid Brezhnev in Moscow. Although he could not achieve the resolution of the Northern Territories question, the summit initiated Japan's active involvement in large-scale Siberian projects that were to last until the beginning of the 1980s.

Tanaka's foreign policy represented Japan's attempt to stake out an independent space in the new reality of the strategic triangle.[5] It also reflected Japan's new assertiveness commensurate with its economic great power status. The operative principle that guided its foreign policy in the first half of the 1970s was "equidistance." Equidistance, of course, did not mean neutrality. Japan's relations with the United States, with its security relations and growing economic interdependence, continued to constitute the core of its foreign policy, and set the parameters of its equidistance, which meant, more than anything else, that Japan attempted to keep an equal distance from the PRC and the Soviet Union. This policy was also a reaction to the retrenchment of the United States' commitment to Asia. It was prudent to seek equidistance from China and the Soviet Union so that Japan would not be entangled in a Sino-Soviet military conflict. Furthermore, to conclude a peace treaty with the Soviet Union and with the PRC, thereby putting an end to the past war, was a precondition for Japan to enter the international arena, free from the legacies of the war.

Under the Miki Takeo government that was formed in December 1974 after Tanaka's resignation, the Sino-Japanese negotiations for the Peace and Friendship Treaty (PFT) became stalled, because the Chinese insisted on the inclusion of an anti-hegemony clause. Japan had originally accepted the anti-hegemony clause in the 1972 Joint Communiqué, because it was a complete replica of the Shanghai Communiqué between the United States and China, and also because this clause was tempered by the qualification that it was not directed at any third party. Foreign Minister Miyazawa Kiichi enunciated Japan's four principles with regard to the anti-hegemony clause: (1) Japan would oppose any hegemonism, not only the Asia-Pacific region but also elsewhere in the world; (2) Japan's opposition to hegemonism was not directed against any specific third country; (3) Japan's opposition to hegemonism would not mean Sino-Japanese joint actions; and (4) Japan would not accept anything that would contradict the spirit of the United Nations Charter. The Chinese side vehemently rejected Miyawaza's four principles.[6] The Sino-Japanese negotiations became deadlocked in the spring of 1975, and they did not see any tangible progress until the fall of 1977.

In July 1976, Miyazawa publicly cautioned that hasty U.S. abrogation of diplomatic relations and the defense treaty with Taiwan would destabilize the East Asian region as a whole. This argument was admittedly one-sided, because Japan itself had normalized its diplomatic relations with the PRC ahead of the United States, while maintaining de facto relations with Taiwan, and because it was asking the United States not to follow its own example. But in a geostrategic sense, Japan was not in the same league as the United States. Taiwan's security was guaranteed by the United States, not by Japan, and U.S. normalization with the PRC, if it were accompanied by an abandonment of the U.S. security guarantee for Taiwan, would threaten Japan's economic and security interests. Miyazawa's comments provoked sharp Chinese criticism. Thereafter, the Japanese government refrained from public comments on this subject, but the Japanese continued to be concerned with U.S. normalization with the PRC, especially when their memory of Nixon's China shock was still vivid.[7]

The hiatus in Sino-Japanese negotiations for a peace treaty coincided with the stagnation of Sino-American relations after 1973. Three factors contributed to this stalemate. First, they differed over strategy toward the Soviet Union. Kissinger wanted to use the China card to establish détente with the Soviet Union. While China feared that it would be sacrificed by the United States for the U.S.-Soviet condominium, the United States was concerned that if it leaned too heavily toward the Chinese side, it might be drawn into a Sino-Soviet conflict.[8] Second, both differed over the Taiwan issue. Kissinger hoped that the United States could normalize relations with Beijing while maintaining its formal relations with Taiwan, but this position was strenuously opposed by the Chinese, who set three preconditions for normalization: (1) to break off diplomatic relations with Taiwan, (2) to abrogate the U.S.-Taiwan Security Treaty, and (3) to withdraw all American troops from Taiwan. And third, domestic politics in China and the United Stated worked against the normalization of relations between the two countries. The Sino-American rapprochement advocated by Zhou Enlai was criticized by the radicals led by the Gang of Four (Mao Zedong's wife, Jiang Qing, and three of her collaborators during the Cultural Revolution). Zhou Enlai died at the beginning of 1976, and Deng Xiaoping, who emerged as the leader, had only shaky control. The United States was hampered by the Watergate scandal and growing isolationist sentiment in Congress.[9]

The suspension of Sino-Japanese negotiations, however, did not facilitate an improvement in Soviet-Japanese relations. Moscow's new ambassador to Tokyo, Dmitrii Polianskii, who was demoted from Politburo membership to this position, replacing Oleg Troianovskii, managed to alienate the Japanese with his high-handed manner.[10] The Belenko affair—in which a Soviet air force pilot, Lieutenant Viktor Belenko, flew to Hakodate and defected to Japan with his MiG 25, and the Japanese government shipped the aircraft and Belenko to the United States—further exacerbated Soviet-Japanese relations.[11] In the midst of the Belenko affair, Miyazawa visited Cape Nosappu, thus becoming the first Japanese foreign minister to inspect the Northern Territories from the cape. The acrimonious fishing negotiations that coincided with the Belenko affair further contributed to the deterioration of bilateral relations. Despite avowed "equidistance," Japan's relations with both China and the Soviet Union considerably worsened.

Thus, from 1973 to 1976, all four powers found themselves in a stalemate. Yet the Soviet Union, while gloating over the correlation of forces in international relations inexorably moving in its favor, was unable to translate this favorable condition into the creation of a stable international system in Asia. Brezhnev's 1969 proposal for Asian collective security was perceived as patently anti-Chinese, and it was rejected by the United States and Japan. If the Soviets displayed intransigence against the Chinese, they treated the Japanese with arrogance by offering no concessions on the crucial territorial issue in order to prevent this increasingly powerful economic giant from seeking a peace treaty with the Chinese.

The last half of 1976 was the time for change in governments. In September, Mao Zedong died, One month after his death, the Gang of Four was arrested, which eventually led to the return of Deng Xiaoping. In November 1976, Jimmy Carter was elected the thirty-ninth president of the United States. In December 1976, Fukuda Takeo replaced Miki as prime minister of Japan. As these new players and new environment fully emerged, they reconfigured the strategic quadrangle.

Fukuda's Omnidirectional Foreign Policy and Carter's Initial Asian Policy

Fukuda's assumption of the premiership meant that Japan had entered a period of stability, after the turbulence in the wake of the Lockheed scandal and the power struggle between Miki and Fukuda. As soon as he became prime minister, Fukuda declared that he would pursue an "omnidirectional" foreign policy. This policy was in a sense the Japanese reaction to America's disengagement from Asia. Because the domestic constraints precluded the possibility of Japan's developing its own independent military force, armed with nuclear weapons, its best option was to balance the Soviet Union and China while maintaining the framework of the U.S.-Japanese Security Treaty.[12] Fukuda's task was therefore to persuade the United States to maintain its commitment to Asia, while improving Japan's relations with China and the Soviet Union.

Unlike President Gerald Ford, who banished the term "détente," Carter had fully embraced the U.S. pursuit of détente during the presidential campaign. And once Carter was elected, reaching an agreement on arms control with the Soviet Union was his top foreign policy priority. His plan to withdraw ground forces from South Korea, which he announced less than a week after his inauguration, was an important part of his overall policy for the relaxation of tensions in the framework of détente.[13]

The new U.S. administration was also interested in normalizing relations with China, but this issue was a low priority.[14] There was a division within the Carter administration with regard to U.S. policy toward China. Shortly after taking office, Carter began an internal assessment of policy toward China, which resulted in a document, Presidential Review Memorandum 24, known as PRM-24, which was an attempt to reconcile two opposing views on U.S. policy toward China. The first view advocated a quick normalization of relations with China by accepting the three conditions about Taiwan that the Chinese had presented as the precondition for normalization. This group, headed by National Security Adviser Zbigniew Brzezinski and Secretary of Defense Harold Brown, called for more extensive security relations with China, including sharing intelligence and exporting American weapons. The second group, represented by the State Department and Secretary of State Cyrus Vance, cautioned against hasty normalization with the PRC and development of close security ties that would jeopardize détente with the Soviet Union. The president initially sided with the second view.[15] Carter's policy to withdraw ground troops from South Korea greatly disturbed the Japanese. In the wake of the fall of Saigon and the U.S. economic difficulties that contributed to the domestic backlash against defense spending, they took Carter's policy as leading to the United States' overall retrenchment from its Asian commitment.[16]

The Carter administration was quick to allay Japan's fears. The president dispatched Vice President Walter Mondale to Tokyo in February 1977. The vice president attempted to stress the United States' continuing commitment to stability of Asia, explaining that the withdrawal of troops from South Korea would be limited only to ground force units without involving air force units. The reduction of ground troops would be done in a way that would keep the defense structure on the Korean Peninsula intact. Furthermore, Mondale assured the Japanese that whatever decisions to be made would be implemented with full consultation with the Japanese government.[17]

As for Taiwan, Fukuda expressed the concern that the United States' eventual normalization of relations with the PRC should be done in such a way as to avoid military conflict between the PRC and Taiwan. Mondale stated that U.S. policy was to "proceed toward normalization along the lines set forth in the Shanghai Communiqué."[18] Mondale was faithfully presenting Vance's stance on the China policy, endorsed at that time by the president. Although Mondale's visit was successful in allaying Japan's fear of a lack of consultation, Japan's skepticism about Carter's Asian policy was not fully removed even by the first Carter-Fukuda summit in March 1977 in Washington.[19]

In May 1977, Vance visited China, and he made it clear to the Chinese that the United States was not prepared to sacrifice Taiwan for the sake of normalizing relations. Deng Xiaoping's reaction was stern and confrontational: He flatly stated that Vance's position was a "retreat from proposals advanced by former President Gerald R. Ford and former Secretary of State Henry Kissinger." According to Deng, Ford had promised that, if reelected, "he would resolve the Taiwan problem in the same way as the Japanese had done."[20] Deng was pitting the United States against Japan in the race for normalization.

The Soviet Reaction to Fukuda's Omnidirectional Foreign Policy

As soon as Fukuda announced his "omnidirectional" foreign policy, the Soviet Union and China each attempted to entice Japan into its own camp against the other. Fukuda's statement initially received favorable treatment from the Soviet Union, but it was denounced by the Chinese as bowing to Soviet hegemonic interests.[21] It should be noted that Fukuda's assumption of power coincided with the time when Sino-Soviet relations took a turn toward the worse. The Soviets, who had restrained criticism of China since Mao's death, resumed their strident denunciations of China, while the border negotiations that had been conducted since November 1976 were suddenly broken off.[22] A contest between the Soviet Union and China to court Japan had begun.

It turned out that China had the upper hand in this competition. But this was not because the Soviets completely lacked flexibility. In May, the Soviet Union and Japan concluded a trade agreement for 1976–80.[23] Brezhnev proposed in his reply to *Asahi Shinbun* the conclusion of a treaty of good-neighborliness and cooperation, as a step toward an eventual peace treaty, but Brezhnev rejected the Japanese assertion that the "unresolved questions" in the 1973 Joint Communiqué included the territorial question as "one-sided and inaccurate."[24] The Japanese Ministry of Foreign Affairs rejected Brezhnev's proposal for a treaty of good-neighborliness out of hand, stating that the Japanese government firmly stood for the return of all four contested Kuril Islands, which the Japanese called the "Northern Territories" (see chapter 7).[25] Fukuda sent the Liberal Democratic Party's (LDP's) pro-Soviet Diet member, Ishida Hakuei, to Moscow in June to explore the possibility of making progress toward the conclusion of a peace treaty. Ishida requested the release of twenty-three Japanese fishermen who had been captured by the Soviets. As a goodwill gesture, Soviet premier Aleksei Kosygin agreed to release all these fishermen, but there was no progress on the territorial question.[26]

The Soviet approach to Japan in other areas was not necessarily conducive to elicit Japan's positive response. During the highly confrontational fishing negotiations that lasted from February through May 1977, the Soviet representatives demonstrated high-handed intransigence, notifying the Japanese of the abolition of the existing fishing agreement, and demanding that Japan recognize Soviet sovereignty over the disputed Northern Territories, which they claimed to be within their 200-mile territorial waters.[27] The Soviet tactics of bullying Japan on this issue succeeded, but at the cost of angering and frustrating the Japanese.[28]

In June, Ambassador Polianskii held his first press conference since taking the position in April 1976. He was eager to ameliorate ill feelings resulting from the MiG 25 incident and the fishing negotiations. And yet, when he was asked about the territorial question, the ambassador repeated the Soviet official position that "on the so-called northern territorial issue, . . . there is no such theme as an 'unsettled territorial problem.'"[29]

Polianskii's rare press conference indicated Moscow's strategy. The Soviets recognized the necessity of improving Soviet-Japanese relations, but not at the cost of placing the territorial issue on the agenda. They thus opted to explore the possibility of concluding a treaty of good-neighborliness rather than aiming to conclude a peace treaty. But this strategy was from the beginning doomed to fail. Without meaningful concessions on the territorial dispute, there was little chance that Japan would be forthcoming in improving its relations with the Soviet Union.

China's Reaction to Japan's Omnidirectional Policy

In contrast to the Soviet Union, China conducted more skillful diplomacy. Though they were greatly disappointed by Carter's reluctance to resume normalization negotiations, the Chinese leaders hoped that the Peace and Friendship Treaty with Japan would prompt the United States to achieve normalization. Otherwise, the United States would leave the lucrative Chinese market for Japan to dominate.

For Fukuda, the conclusion of the PFT was one of the most important foreign policy goals. But there were many obstacles. Initially, Fukuda maintained a cautious attitude toward China. His government was a product of factional compromise, and his faction included many hard-line pro-Taiwan supporters.[30] But he quietly sent a signal to China about his intention to resume negotiations for a peace treaty.

Fukuda's chief Cabinet secretary was Sonoda Sunao, who exerted a more powerful influence on Fukuda's foreign policy than Foreign Minister Hatoyama Iichiro. The chief Cabinet secretary occupies a unique position in the Japanese government and political structure. Next to the prime minister, he is one of the few very important men in the Cabinet, serving as the chief of staff to the prime minister, senior government spokesman, and chief coordinator for the prime minister between the ruling LDP and government ministries. Unlike the majority of his Cabinet ministers, who graduated from elite universities, Sonoda was a self-made man with a middle-school education who served in the Imperial Army during the war and rose from local politics in Kumamoto to the position of chief of the LDP elite in the Diet. Although his strength was domestic affairs, he served as the parliamentary vice minister of foreign affairs, and was known as an early proponent of improved ties with the PRC.[31]

In January 1977, shortly after he became prime minister, Fukuda asked Takeiri Yoshikazu of the Komei Party (Komeito) to send his personal message, during the latter's trip to Beijing, to Liao Chengzhi, the head of the Sino-Japanese Friendship Association, expressing his interest in resuming negotiations with the Chinese. In his first policy statement in the Diet at the end of January, the prime minister spoke of the importance of establishing good-neighborly relations with China and emphasized that both governments were united in seeing the need to conclude a peace treaty in a form beneficial to the interests of both. In February, Fukuda sent another message through Ambassador Ogawa Heishiro to the Chinese, expressing his interest in resuming negotiations on the PFT. Nevertheless, the Chinese remained skeptical about Fukuda's determination. They pointedly emphasized the importance of the anti-hegemony clause and their opposition to Miyazawa's four principles.[32]

Two factors contributed to the change in the Chinese attitude. The first was Fukuda's tour of Southeast Asia in August 1977. At the end of this tour, he issued the Fukuda Doctrine to establish Japan's relations with its Asian neighbors on the principles (1) that Japan would never become a military hegemonic power, (2) that Japan would establish mutually beneficial economic and political relations with the Southeast Asian countries, and (3) that Japan would strive for the establishment of peace and prosperity in the region. These principles were equally applicable to Japan's relationship with China. The Chinese press reported favorably on the Fukuda Doctrine, in contrast to the Soviet press, which characterized it as expressing Japan's imperialist intentions.[33]

The second factor was the Chinese domestic situation. In July 1977, Deng Xiaoping made his second comeback. In August, the Chinese Communist Party held its Eleventh Congress, which made two crucial decisions. The first was the resolution that declared the party's resolute struggle against "hegemonism of two superpowers, the Soviet Union and the United States," singling out the Soviet Union as its first enemy. The second was the decision to adopt "four modernizations." These two decisions had profound implications for Sino-Japanese relations.[34] Having recalled all ambassadors from major countries after the arrest of the Gang of Four, the Chinese government chose Japan as the first country to appoint a new ambassador, the veteran diplomat Fu Hao, who arrived in Tokyo on August 2.[35] The new Japanese ambassador, Sato Shoji, was sent to Beijing on August 10. The framework for negotiations was established.[36] On September 10, Deng told the Japanese parliamentary delegation that all the problems with regard to a peace treaty would be resolved "in one second" once Fukuda decided to conclude it.[37] At the end of September, a Sino-Japanese foreign ministerial conference was held in New York for the first time since the formation of the Fukuda government. Both foreign ministers agreed on the need for the early conclusion of the PFT.[38]

The "anti-hegemony" clause, however, continued to be a stumbling block for the conclusion of the PFT. In September 1977, Nikaido Susumu, a powerful politician in the LDP's Tanaka faction, visited China and presented a compromise proposal to resolve the difference on the anti-hegemonic clause by adding another clause: "The development of friendship between China and Japan envisaged in this peace treaty is not directed against any third country." Presumably, Deng was receptive to this idea.[39] Under strong pressure from pro-PRC conservatives, Fukuda finally instructed the Ministry of Foreign Affairs to make preparations for negotiations with China for the PFT, irrespective of Japan's relations with the Soviet Union.[40]

In November 1977, Fukuda appointed Sonoda Susumu as the new foreign minister in his second-term Cabinet. Simultaneously, the prime minister summoned Ambassador Sato Shoji from Beijing for consultation. Before his return to Japan, Sato sounded out China's reaction to the negotiations on the PFT, and he felt China's softening position on the anti-hegemony clause. He duly reported his findings to Sonoda and Fukuda, and recommended that the time was ripe for Japan to open negotiations.[41] By the end of December, the Japanese government had composed a draft peace proposal, which included a provision opposing the anti-hegemony clause.[42]

In March 1978, the general secretary of Komeito, Yano Junya, who was visiting Beijing, brought back China's proposal on Miyazawa's four principles, which indicated China's softening position.[43] On March 22, Prime Minister Fukuda, Foreign Minister Sonoda, Chief Cabinet Minister Abe Shintaro, and key Ministry of Foreign Affairs officials had a crucial meeting in which the Japanese government began the process of redrafting a Japanese proposal for the treaty. At this meeting, whether or not Japan should accept the anti-hegemony clause was no longer an issue; the question was to have China accept the clause indicating that the anti-hegemonic provision would not be directed against any third party.[44]

Soviet Reactions to Japan's Negotiations with China

Sino-Japanese relations under the Fukuda government were deeply influenced by the Soviet factor. Throughout the process of negotiations with China, the Japanese side carefully attempted to avoid provoking hostile reactions from the Soviet Union. In September 1977, Fukuda made it clear that seeking the PFT with China would not hinder Japan's relationship with the Soviet Union.[45]

The Soviet reaction to Japan's move to seek rapprochement with China was predictable. Alarmed by the impending Sino-Japanese rapprochement, the Soviets tried to intervene to block the Sino-Japanese negotiations. But the manner in which the Soviets intervened was clumsy and counterproductive. In the fall of 1977, Foreign Minister Hatoyama Iichiro requested Soviet agreement for his Moscow visit designed to allay Moscow's fears about Sino-Japanese rapprochement. This request was repeatedly rejected, presumably to make the point that Moscow was displeased with Japan's approach to China.[46] A flurry of comments warning Japan about the consequences of concluding the PFT with the anti-hegemonic clause appeared in the Soviet press.[47] *Pravda* warned: "Of course, it is up to Japan to decide whom to establish diplomatic relations with. However, Japan should bear in mind that by concluding the treaty with China, which has an anti-hegemony clause, it will impair its diplomatic credence and negatively affect Soviet-Japanese relations as a whole."[48] Only in January 1978 did Ambassador Polianskii belatedly invite the new foreign minister, Sonoda, and propose a foreign ministerial conference in 1978 to explore the possibility of concluding a peace treaty.[49]

Sonoda visited Moscow in January 1978 to resume the foreign ministerial conference that had been suspended since Miyazawa's visit to Moscow in January 1975. Sonoda's purpose was to restore the state of the territorial dispute to the condition that had existed when Tanaka and Brezhnev issued the Joint Communiqué in 1973, which acknowledged that there were "unresolved questions" left from World War II (see chapter 7). The Japanese had interpreted these questions to include the territorial question. Since then, the Soviets had taken the position that there was no territorial dispute between the two countries, rejecting Japan's interpretation. The Soviet government immediately rebuffed Sonoda's demand for negotiations for a peace treaty by resolving the "unresolved question." Although the Soviet leaders did not take their usual inflexible stand that the territorial question had already been resolved, they still did not offer any concessions on this problem. Instead, they offered a treaty of good-neighborliness and cooperation. When Andrei Gromyko gave Sonoda a document that contained the Soviet draft for this treaty, the Japanese foreign minister refused to read the proposal, let alone discuss it, stating that before anything else, it would be necessary to resolve the territorial question. The Moscow foreign ministerial conference only demonstrated how widely the two sides differed. They even failed to issue the customary joint declaration after the meeting. Sonoda left Moscow a day earlier than planned.[50]

What Moscow intended to achieve at this foreign ministerial conference is not clear. It may well be that, given Japan's eagerness to shelve the Senkaku Islands issue with the PRC, Moscow may have believed that Tokyo might be willing to shelve the Northern Territories problem with evenhandedness. Perhaps the leaders in Moscow believed that the big Siberian projects were sufficient bait to entice Japan to conclude this treaty. They must have known that without any concessions on the territorial dispute, they stood no chance of gaining Japan's consent to resume peace negotiations. During the conference, however, the Soviets did not raise as strong objections to Japan's peace overtures to China as the Japanese had expected. Gromyko expressed "apprehension over Japan's relations with 'the third country' from the point of view of Soviet-Japanese good-neighborliness."[51] But this objection was so mild that the Foreign Ministry officials concluded (1) that the Soviets had reluctantly accepted Sino-Japanese rapprochement as a fait accompli, and (2) that the Soviets were already positioning themselves for the eventuality of the Sino-Japanese PFT.[52] The debacle of the Moscow foreign ministerial conference did not fail to please the Chinese. Vice Prime Minister Ji Dengkui praised Japan for courageously sticking to its justifiable demand for the return of the Northern Territories, suggesting that "the only way for Japan to resolve the territorial problem . . . is to struggle against the Soviet Union."[53]

If the Moscow foreign ministerial conference did not yield any tangible benefits for Moscow, what followed further angered the Japanese. In February 1978, Polianskii visited Fukuda and handed him Brezhnev's letter expressing the general secretary's grave concern over the prospect of Sino-Japanese peace at the expense of the Soviet Union, and proposed that Japan and the Soviet Union conclude a treaty of good-neighborliness.[54] When Fukuda refused to consider such a treaty before the resolution of the territorial question, the Soviet government unilaterally announced the contents of the draft treaty of good-neighborliness that Gromyko had handed to Sonoda in Moscow. The draft proposal stated: "Neither the Soviet Union nor Japan demand any privilege or prerogatives over any problems in the world, including the demand for the right of control in the Asia-Pacific region, nor recognize such demands." This clause was obviously directed against Chinese efforts to seek Japan's support for the anti-hegemony clause. Moreover, this proposal stipulated that both sides had the obligation not to have a third country use its territory for actions that would damage the security of the other. This clause was tantamount to demanding that Japan abrogate the existing U.S.-Japanese security arrangement.[55] This attitude infuriated the Japanese all the more, because Tokyo took this proposal as an attempt not only to derail the process of Sino-Japanese rapprochement but also to undermine the U.S.-Japanese alliance. Even worse, the Soviets were trying to achieve these impossible goals without making any concessions on the territorial question. The Soviet attitude deeply wounded Japan's sense of pride and greatly damaged the willingness of the Japanese government to maintain equidistance with the Soviet Union, irrevocably pushing Japan to move closer to the Chinese position.[56]

The Senkaku Islands Incident

For Japan to take the final step in the negotiations with the Chinese for the PFT, it needed the tacit approval of the United States. Although Fukuda decided to enter negotiations with China for the PFT in March 1978, it took two months to convince the anti-PRC faction within the LDP to accept his position. In the meantime, a crisis struck in April. Chinese fishermen armed with machine guns sailed close to the disputed Senkaku (or Diaoyutai) Islands, whose contested nationality had remained unresolved in 1972, when the two countries normalized relations. Some of them even ventured into what the Japanese considered their territorial waters. The incident hardened the anti-PRC conservative opposition in Japan to negotiations, and forced Fukuda to take a strong stand on this issue. Exploiting this incident, the Soviets pointed out that the Chinese incursions around the Senkaku Islands represented Chinese encroachment on Japan's sovereign rights.[57] Met with Japan's protest, the Chinese backed off, characterizing the incident as a mere accident, and sending the fishing boats out of the troubled waters. Fukuda, however, found it necessary to pursue the issue further, instructing Ambassador Sato to conduct high-level negotiations. On May 10, Vice Minister Han Nianlong gave Sato an assurance that the Senkaku Islands issue would be dealt with "from the viewpoint of the overall importance of Sino-Japanese relations." He further stated that China was prepared to conclude the PFT "in accordance with the Joint Communiqué of 1972," thus indicating that China would be prepared to conclude a peace treaty by shelving the territorial dispute.[58]

Without access to Chinese archives, it is difficult to interpret the real meaning of the Senkaku incident. It is possible, as the Japanese government assumed, to interpret it as an attempt by the Chinese government to concoct the incident to put pressure on Japan. But it is also possible to speculate that a genuine popular nationalist outburst against the Japanese led to the incident. If so, both the Japanese government and the public at large misread the Chinese nationalistic sentiment that was hidden behind the negotiations. The Chinese Communist leadership was strong enough to silence this sentiment for what it perceived to be China's national interest.[59]

Interestingly, Soviet commentators viewed the Senkaku incident not as a territorial dispute that the Soviet Union and the PRC shared in common with the Japanese but as a quintessential example of China's hegemonism, provoking popular protest to put pressure on Japan to conclude the PFT.[60] The Senkaku formula that the PRC and Japan were to later adopt to resolve their territorial dispute could have served as an example for solving the Soviet-Japanese territorial dispute. But the Soviets, preoccupied with China's threat, could not see it that way, which demonstrated the shortsightedness of Soviet thinking.

The Change in U.S. Policy toward China and Brzezinski's Pressure on Japan

How did the Carter administration change its policy vis-à-vis Japan's omnidirectional policy at the end of 1977? Richard Holbrooke's memo to Vance in preparation for Vance's Tokyo trip on August 26–27, 1977, succinctly summarized the U.S. position in mid-1977. As for Japan's attitude toward U.S.-PRC normalization, Holbrooke stated that, having normalized relations with the PRC, Japan was not in a position to oppose the process. But since then, Japan had cultivated productive relations with both the PRC and Taiwan, and therefore it was "extremely sensitive to the security and economic implications of any change in the U.S. relationship with either capital." Japan would, therefore, prefer the status quo, and there was a general sense that Japan should stay ahead of, or at least remain even with, the United States in improving relations with the PRC. In addition, Holbrooke continued, the Japanese considered the consultation process about normalization a test of U.S. sincerity as an ally. The scars of the "Nixon China shock" had largely been healed, but its trauma had not been forgotten. Holbrooke therefore recommended that Vance make two arguments: (1) Any move by the United States toward the PRC should not result in the sudden destabilization of Taiwan, which would have adverse effects on the region as a whole; and (2) Japan should be given advance warning of any U.S. actions about normalization. Japan, like the United States, continued to strive for a stable balance between Beijing and Moscow. It was unlikely that the Japanese would "steer too far from their cautious central course between Peking and Moscow."[61]

But that was in mid-1977. By the end of 1977, U.S. policy toward China had undergone a drastic change. By 1978, the Carter administration had reevaluated its policy to seek détente with the Soviet Union, for this policy had encountered difficulties on two fundamental fronts: the developing world (then known as the Third World) and arms control. Soviet support for revolutionary regimes in Ethiopia, Angola, South Yemen, and Afghanistan alarmed the United States, while the Soviet rejection of Carter's proposal for deep cuts in the second round of negotiations for the Strategic Arms Limitation Talks (SALT II) and the deployment of SS-20 missiles and Backfire bombers raised serious doubts as to Soviet intentions about the future of arms control.

In these new circumstances, Carter now espoused a harder line toward the Soviet Union. He adopted a new China policy in favor of normalization by accepting the three conditions that China had demanded and extending military aid to China. This signified a repudiation of Vance's policy and the adoption of Brzezinski's policy. Over Vance's objections, the president sent Brzezinski to Beijing in May 1978 to resume normalization talks and to convey the message that the United States had made up its mind.[62] Unlike Kissinger and Nixon, who used the China card as bait to force the Soviets to make concessions, Carter and Brzezinski now sought to mobilize China in an attempt to form an alliance against the Soviet Union.[63]

Fukuda must have realized the fundamental shift in U.S. policy toward China when he met with Carter in Washington in May 1978. After returning from this summit, Fukuda began to take the initiative to seek an early settlement for a peace treaty with China. The declassified record of the Carter-Fukuda summit indicates that Carter made it clear that Japan's acceptance of the anti-hegemony clause would give the United States no concern. Although this was not necessarily Carter's pressure on Fukuda to seek negotiations for the PFT, it certainly served as a go-ahead signal that nudged Japan toward the acceptance of the anti-hegemony clause.[64] Carter's go-ahead signal was a major turning point for Fukuda to resume negotiations. Receiving Carter's imprimatur also served as the major factor in silencing the anti-PRC faction within Fukuda's own party.

The Chinese had been frustrated by the lack of progress in Sino-Japanese negotiations, and they decided to exploit the United States to put pressure on the Japanese. At a meeting with Brzezinski in Beijing, Hua Guofeng and Deng Xiaoping directly appealed to Brzezinski to intervene on their behalf to put pressure on Japan. After his visit to China, Brzezinski stopped in Tokyo and offered "more than subtle encouragement" to Fukuda and Sonoda to conclude the PFT by accepting the anti-hegemony clause.[65] On May 23, Brzezinski met Fukuda. Brzezinski related that "there was complete agreement with the Chinese that U.S.-Japan relations were a major factor for peace and stability in the Far East," and he noted that "the Chinese viewed U.S.-Japan relations positively." He further stated: "The Chinese had explained at length their view that the anti-hegemony clause was for everyone's benefit. The Chinese expressed a real sense of hope and even impatience in concluding the PFT."[66] This description of the memorandum of this conversation strongly implies that the Chinese were counting on Brzezinski's help to put pressure on Japan to move forward to conclude the PFT with an anti-hegemony clause.

Before the meeting, Brzezinski's National Security Council aide, Michael Armacost, recommended to Brzezinski: "With respect to Sino-Japanese relations, you should emphasize that you and the Chinese agreed on the importance of good Sino-Japanese relations and that the Chinese acknowledged their familiar position that they attach great importance to the preservation of close U.S.-Japanese links." Armacost further suggested that when Brzezinski had a tête-à-tête meeting with Fukuda, he should read the following remarks that the Chinese had made during his meeting with the Chinese leaders:

> We think it is in the interest of the Japanese to conclude the Treaty of Peace and Friendship in China, to incorporate the anti-hegemony clause in toto into the operative phases of the Treaty. It will be a restraint on China. Under the Treaty, China will be committed never to seek hegemony and actually it is our consistent policy not to seek it. Through the conclusion of the Treaty, China will undertake the legal commitment. It would also be beneficial to the image of Japan. During the Second World War, Japan invaded many Asian countries which still have vivid memories of the Japanese atrocities during that time. The conclusion of the Treaty will change their views on Japan and improve the image of Japan among those countries. It is also beneficial to Japanese resistance against Soviet pressure. So we think the conclusion of the Treaty is in the interests of the Japanese side.[67]

This document underscores three important points. First, Brzezinski was to urge the Japanese to accept the anti-hegemony clause. Second, the Chinese were interested in mobilizing Japan in the common front against the Soviet Union. Third, and more interestingly, the Chinese were using historical memories as leverage to pressure Japan.[68]

Brzezinski's intervention finally broke the resistance of the Japanese government.[69] It was reported that during his meeting with Sonoda, Brzezinski's strident anti-Sovietism and use of the term "anti-hegemonism" shocked the Japanese foreign minister.[70] The Chinese, for their part, accepted the Japanese soft version to ameliorate the impact of the anti-hegemony clause as a provision.[71] The Soviets suspected, correctly, that there was strong U.S. pressure behind Japan's decision to conclude the PFT with the anti-hegemony clause.[72]

The Soviet government warned that it "cannot remain a spectator in a question which could involve its own interests." Should the Japanese government agree to conclude a peace treaty that would include the anti-hegemonic clause, the Soviet government would "draw the necessary conclusions and make alterations necessary in its own politics with reference to relations with Japan."[73]

Signing the Sino-Japanese Peace and Friendship Treaty

The Sino-Japanese negotiations for the PFT resumed on July 21, 1978.[74] The focus of the negotiations was no longer the inclusion of the anti-hegemony clause, but rather the inclusion of the third-party clause to indicate that the peace treaty was not directed at any third party. Now confident of U.S. support on this issue, the Chinese opposed the Japanese draft to include a clause that would nullify the anti-hegemony clause. As far as the Chinese were concerned, the value of the anti-hegemony clause consisted in committing Japan to a coalition against the Soviet Union, a purpose Japan wanted to avoid by proposing the additional clause. The Chinese rejected Japan's earlier version intended to strip the anti-hegemony clause of anti-Soviet intention by inserting the third-country clause before the anti-hegemony clause. The negotiations were deadlocked. But when Sonoda went to Beijing to iron out the differences on this matter, the Chinese accepted the inclusion of Japan's softened version: "This treaty shall not affect either party in its relations to other third parties," but this article was pushed to Article 4, two articles after the article on anti-hegemony article. With this amendment, the Sino-Japanese Treaty of Peace and Friendship was finally signed in August 12, 1978.[75] Ambassador Sato told the Chinese that after the PFT was signed, Japan expected China to break the Sino-Soviet Defense Treaty when it came up for renewal the following February. The Chinese did not respond to this demand, but Fukuda had instructed Sonoda to pursue this matter, partly for domestic reasons.[76] Deng Xiaoping made a historic, triumphant visit to Japan in October to exchange the ratified peace treaty.

As soon as the peace treaty was made public, the Soviet representative protested to the Foreign Ministry, and stated that by accepting the PFT including the anti-hegemony clause, the Japanese government had lent its support to Beijing's expansionist policy, taking the side of China against the Soviet Union. He also warned that as long as the Sino-Japanese treaty had gone beyond bilateral relations, the Soviet Union could not be indifferent and would have to take appropriate measures.[77] According to Glaubitz, however, the Soviet reaction was by and large characterized by a "wait-and-see" attitude without immediately resorting to countermeasures.[78] The State Department's classified assessment also supported Glaubitz's conclusion: "Despite Soviet complaints about Japan's signing of the PFT, the Soviets have not taken any significant steps to demonstrate their displeasure. The Soviets continue to have a strong interest in strengthening economic ties with Japan, and given other developments in Asia such as the normalization of relations between the U.S. and the PRC, the Soviets would be unlikely to take actions which would contribute to the deterioration of relations with Japan. The Japanese, on the other hand, will continue to make every attempt to avoid becoming involved in Sino-Soviet rivalry and will be receptive to opportunities to improve relations with the USSR."[79]

Although the Japanese were careful not to provoke the Soviets, the Chinese went out of their way to emphasize that the Soviet occupation of the Northern Territories was a good example of Soviet hegemonism: "While stubbornly refusing to return these four Japanese islands, the Soviet revisionists have also established naval and air bases there, frequently intruded upon the territorial airspace and waters of Japan, and conducted ruthless activities against the Japanese fishermen."[80] During his trip to Japan, Deng went so far as to suggest that Japan strengthen its own Self-Defense Force, and he made it clear that China supported the U.S.-Japanese security alliance.[81]

Economic Factors: The Long-Term Trade Agreement

Economic considerations provided a powerful motivation behind Japan's seeking rapprochement with China. With Deng Xiaoping's rehabilitation, China embarked on a program of modernization. A major turning point for Japan's economic relations with China came when the Keidanren (Japan Business Federation) and representatives of the Ministry of International Trade and Industry visited Beijing to conclude the Long-Term Trade Agreement in February 1978. The agreement was to be in force for eight years, from 1978 to 1985, and during this period Japan was expected to export technology, plants, construction materials, and machinery worth $10 billion in return for China's crude oil and coal.

The Long-Term Trade Agreement was immensely beneficial for both countries. For Japan, the new market in China would brunt the criticism of industrial nations that Japan's aggressive export policy was causing trade deficits in these nations, especially in the United States. Trade with China helped Japan to diversify its energy sources. For China, Japan was a logical economic partner from which to seek the economic assistance needed for modernization.[82] The Chinese National People's Congress passed a number of new laws to accommodate joint ventures, and the government undertook other reforms in banking, insurance, and finance to facilitate foreign investment. The Chinese were way ahead of the Soviet Union in economic modernization, laying the foundations for future economic interactions with foreign countries. The Japanese business community also supported Japan's economic relations with the Soviet Union, but the Soviet economy showed stagnation in the second half of the 1970s, and all the big Siberian projects were to be completed in the first half of the 1980s. As far as the Japanese business community was concerned, the China market provided greater possibilities for expansion than the stagnating Soviet market.

Sino-American Normalization

Brzezinski's visit to Beijing in May 1978 was a major breakthrough for the process of U.S.-Chinese normalization. The United States accepted China's three conditions on Taiwan, and it abandoned the insistence on Chinese acceptance of peaceful unification. Nonetheless, Carter's insistence that the United States would continue to sell defensive weapons to Taiwan became a sticking point that prevented the immediate conclusion of the normalization negotiations. To induce China's concession, the United States invited Deng Xiaoping to the United States before the expected U.S.-Soviet summit to conclude the SALT II Treaty. In the meantime, the Soviet Union concluded a Treaty of Friendship and Cooperation with Vietnam in November 1978, heightening a sense of crisis among the Chinese. Finally, Deng broke the deadlock by making concessions to the United States. On December 15, four months after Japan and China concluded a treaty to normalize relations, Washington and Beijing announced that both countries would establish diplomatic relations in January 1979.[83]

The Japanese remained apprehensive about the pace with which the United States was attempting to forge a military alliance with China against the Soviet Union. When the U.S. secretary of defense, Harold Brown, met the Japanese director of the Defense Agency, Kanemaru Shin, in Tokyo in November 1978, Kanemaru expressed his deep concern that the United States was abandoning its mutual security treaty with Taiwan. Brown equivocated by explaining that the "PRC government was prepared to be very patient about the eventual union of Taiwan with the rest of China." Kanemaru asked Brown whether the PRC had the capability to attack Taiwan, to which Brown responded that at that point, it would not have that capability for another five or even more years. Kanemaru reiterated that the Taiwan issue should be resolved "in a manner wherein the United States could exercise some form of influence and control over Taiwan." Brown responded that "the U.S. wished to move in a way that would insure our commercial and cultural relations with the island of Taiwan and would continue as was the case in Japan's normalization." To this, Kanemaru replied that the difference was that the United States had a Mutual Security Treaty with Taiwan, unilateral termination of which would be injurious to the region and to Japan.[84] A briefing memo for Brown, prepared before his meeting with Fukuda on November 9, recommended that "if pressed on our policy on arms sales to the PRC," Brown would respond that the United States would not sell arms to the PRC.[85] Though Japan concluded the PFT with China, it was more skeptical about China's behavior, expressing apprehension about the United States' penchant to plunge head-on into military cooperation with the PRC.

The close security cooperation between the United States and China did not immediately follow from the normalization treaty. During his tour of the United States, Deng spoke in favor of a military alliance with the United States and informed his American hosts of China's intention to invade Vietnam. But Congress passed the Taiwan Relations Act to ensure the continuing sale of defense weapons to Taiwan and prevent the use of force to unify Taiwan with the mainland. Yet throughout 1979, security cooperation remained restrained, and the United States did not support China's plan for invading Vietnam.[86]

Aftermaths and Assessments

Who won and who lost in the reconfigurations of East Asian power relations in 1977 and 1978? The clear winner was China, which ended its diplomatic isolation and forged an anti-Soviet entente by concluding the PFT with Japan and normalizing its relations with the United States. By tilting decidedly toward China, the United States also gained a counterweight against Soviet expansionism. But this was accomplished at the cost of détente. Given the Soviet Union's aggressive policy in the developing world, further erosion of U.S. prestige in Iran, and the domestic backlash against the Soviet Union, however, it is doubtful that the Carter administration had the option to pursue the continuation of détente.

Japan managed to conclude the PFT with China, thus formally ending the state of war with the PRC and establishing the foundations for a further expansion of economic relations. Nevertheless, by accepting the anti-hegemony clause, it failed to maintain its omnidirectional foreign policy, tilting decidedly toward entente with China but against the Soviet Union. Contrary to Japan's expectations that signing the peace treaty with China would contribute to the stability of Asian international relations, it exacerbated the conflict, triggering the Soviets' signing of the Treaty of Friendship and Cooperation with Vietnam, and Soviet troops occupying Danang and Cam Ranh Bay, controlling the important strategic point for the Strait of Malacca, a crucial Middle Eastern route for transporting oil to Japan. Arguably, Japan's strategic position had worsened.

The clear loser was the Soviet Union, which pushed Japan and the United State into an anti-Soviet entente with the PRC. The problem for Moscow was the lack of leverage sufficient to sway Japan's policy. Some within the leadership may have contemplated the possibility of striking a deal on the Northern Territories issue on the basis of the 1956 Joint Declaration, but all the tentative signals of Moscow's flexibility were nipped in the bud by the Japanese Ministry of Foreign Affairs, which stubbornly clung to the demand for the return of *all* four islands. No one in the Kremlin advocated the return of all four islands, and as long as the Soviet leaders were not prepared to go that far, there was little they could do to win Japan's support in competition with China. The treaty of good-neighborliness reflected this ambiguity. It represented Moscow's determination to make a point, but without a conviction that it would carry weight in influencing Japanese decisionmaking.

If the Soviet Union was seriously concerned about the threat from China, why could it not exploit the Japan card more effectively to lure Japan, if not into an alliance against China then at least into a position to maintain equidistance? After all, the Japanese were genuinely concerned about the deterioration of their relations with the Soviet Union, and they would have preferred, had the chance been given, to improve their relations with it.[87] This question goes to the heart of Soviet policy toward Japan in the postwar period. Four factors must be considered.

The first was psychological. The Soviet leadership belonged to the war generation. To these men, the legitimacy of the Communist Party was integrally connected with the Soviet victory in World War II. The possession of the contested Northern Territories represented the symbol of this victory in the Pacific. Second, the Soviet acquisition of strategic parity with the United States during the 1970s also affected their psychological approach to Japan. For the Soviet leaders, the USSR's superpower status was measured above all by its military power. Thus, Japan's attaining a global economic status meant little to them. In fact, Japan's increasingly aggressive territorial demands appeared insolent. Thus, the Soviet leaders—long accustomed to looking at Japan merely as an appendage of the United States, and at their policy toward Japan as nothing but a function of U.S.-Soviet relations—found it difficult to craft a policy fine-tuned to Japan's situation.[88]

A question might be raised here about the difference between the Soviet Union's approach to Japan and its approach to West Germany. How can one explain the subtle and flexible approach the Soviets took toward West Germany, although West German security was also closely tied to the United

States' extended deterrence, and Germany and Japan were the defeated nations during World War II? The difference partly lay in the Eurocentric perception of the world held by the Soviet leaders, and partly in West Germany's flexibility in dealing with the Soviet Union, as exemplified by Willy Brandt's *Ostpolitik.* It was also connected with the specific circumstances that characterized the arms race in Asia. The only bargaining leverage that the Soviet Union could have used to fundamentally change Japan's policy toward it would have been a major concession on the territorial question. But the Soviet global strategy required the possession of the Northern Territories. Contrary to the widely held view that the Soviet Union's deployment of troops in these territories was its retaliation for Japan's conclusion of the peace treaty with China, this move was largely prompted by the Soviet strategic demand in the context of the U.S.-Soviet strategic balance.[89] As long as the Soviets' top priority in the Pacific was the need to counter the U.S. strategic threat, it was impossible for the Soviet Union to craft an independent Japan policy.

Did Japan have alternatives? Could Japan have played the Soviet card to induce China to abandon the anti-hegemonic clause? In view of China's subsequent equidistant foreign policy, was Japan's conclusion of the PFT premature? Should Japan have maintained its omnidirectional foreign policy even at the risk of not concluding the PFT with China? The conclusion of the PFT was not the result of a national consensus; in fact, the popularity of China among the Japanese steadily declined from 1973 to 1978, when Japan concluded the PFT. Nevertheless, the factors favoring Japan's seeking the PFT were overwhelming. Among others, they included the Japanese sense of guilt about the war against China; the long history of cultural ties with China; the existence of a powerful, pro-PRC lobby that cut across political parties; the support of the business community; and above all, the blessing of the United States. In contrast, the Soviets lacked leverage, had to work against the backdrop of overwhelming anti-Soviet feelings nurtured by the memory of the Soviet-Japanese war from August to September 1945, and had no Soviet lobby in Japan comparable to the China lobby.[90] Rapprochement with the Soviet Union was not an option, as long as the Soviet Union did not come up with a far-reaching compromise on the territorial dispute. Even if Soviet diplomacy had displayed more subtlety, it would have been an uphill struggle to keep Japan's equidistance, certainly because any compromise proposal short of the return of all four disputed islands would have been rejected by Japan. In fact, it appears that in the heightened Cold War atmosphere in the late 1970s, it would have been difficult for Japan to maintain an omnidirectional foreign policy.

In November 1978, Fukuda Takeo was defeated by Ohira Masayoshi in the Liberal Democratic Party presidential primaries and resigned as prime minister. Thus, 1979 began with Ohira's premiership. The Chinese invaded Vietnam in February, which the Japanese took as a blatant display of hegemonism. And in December 1979, the Soviet Union invaded Afghanistan. Détente had ended. In the new situation, Japan became closely aligned with the United States, seeking to actively cooperate with the U.S. global strategy in an unprecedented fashion. Ironically, as the United States and Japan stepped up their security collaboration, China began to pursue its own omnidirectional foreign policy, criticizing the hegemony of both the Soviet Union and the United States. In response to Leonid Brezhnev's Tashkent speech in 1982, which extended an olive branch to the Chinese to end the hostility, China gingerly began the process of negotiations with the Soviet Union. The new era that began in 1979 was to lead to another reconfiguration of the strategic quadrangle.

Notes

1. See Chen Jian, *Mao's China and the Cold War* (Chapel Hill: University of North Carolina Press, 2001); Ilya V. Gaiduk, *Confronting Vietnam: Soviet Policy toward the Indochina Conflict, 1954–1963* (Washington, D.C., and Stanford, Calif.: Woodrow Wilson Center Press and Stanford University Press, 2003); Zhu Jianrong (Shu Kenei), *Mo Takuto no chosen senso* [Mao Zedong's Korean War] (Tokyo: Iwanami shoten, 1991); Zhu Jianrong (Shu Kenei), *Mo Takuto no Betonamu senso* [Mao Zedong's Vietnam War] (Tokyo: Tokyo daigaku shuppankai, 2001); and Shimotomai Nobuo, *Ajia reisenshi* [History of the Cold War in Asia] (Tokyo: Chuko shinsho, 2004).

2. Seeing the power reconfiguration in Asia in the second half of the 1970s, using Japan as the analytical pivot, has not been widely attempted, with the notable exception of Robert E. Bedeski, *The Fragile Entente: The 1978 Japan-China Peace Treaty in a Global Context* (Boulder, Colo.: Westview Press, 1983). Roger Buckley does not say anything about the role played by the Soviet Union in U.S.-Japanese relations during this period; see Roger Buckley, *US-Japan Alliance Diplomacy, 1945–1990* (Cambridge: Cambridge University Press, 1992), 138–74. Raymond Garthoff's massive volume on U.S.-Soviet relations, *Détente and Confrontation: American and Soviet Relations from Nixon to Reagan* (Washington, D.C.: Brookings Institution Press, 1985), has nothing to say about Japan in the strategic triangle. Generally, Soviet-Japanese relations during the Brezhnev period have been little studied. The only exceptions are Allen S. Whiting, *Siberian Development and East Asia* (Stanford, Calif.: Stanford University Press, 1981); Kimura Hiroshi, *Hoppôryôdo: Kiseki to henkan eno josô* [The Northern Territories: Background and steps for their return] (Tokyo: Jiji shuppansha, 1989); Joachim Glaubitz, *Between Tokyo and Moscow: The History of an Uneasy Relationship, 1972 to the 1990s* (Honolulu: University of Hawaii Press, 1995); Myles L. C. Robertson, *Soviet Policy toward Japan: An Analysis of Trends in the 1970's and 1980's* (Cambridge: Cambridge University Press, 1988); and Hiroshi Kimura, *Islands or Security? Japanese-Soviet Relations under Brezhnev and Andropov* (Kyoto: International Research Center for Japanese Studies, 1998). For a Soviet view on this issue, see L. N. Kutakov, *Moskva-Tokio: Ocherki diplomaticheskikh otnoshenii, 1956–1986* [Moscow-Tokyo: Study of diplomatic relations, 1956–1986] (Moscow: Mezhdunarodnye

otnosheniia, 1988), 146–49. The most detailed study of Sino-Japanese relations in the 1970s is by G. F. Kunadze, *Iapono-Kitaiskie otnosheniia na sovremennom etape, 1972–1982* [Japanese-Chinese relations at the contemporary stage, 1972–1982] (Moscow: Nauka, 1983), but Kunadze, most likely for obvious political sensitivity, avoids expanding his analysis beyond Sino-Japanese relations, especially, their implications for Sino-Soviet and Soviet-Japanese relations.

3. For Kissinger's definition of détente, see Henry Kissinger, *Years of Upheaval* (Boston: Little, Brown, 1982), 235–46.

4. See chapter 7 in this volume, by Kazuhiko Togo.

5. Ogata notes that "there was intense pressure in Japan for Japan to achieve normalization ahead of the United States." Sadako Ogata, *Normalization with China: A Comparative Study of U.S. and Japanese Processes* (Berkeley: Institute of East Asian Studies, University of California, 1988), 50.

6. Furusawa Kenichi, *Showa hishi: Nicchu heiwa yuko joyaku* [A secret history of Showa: The Sino-Japanese Treaty of Peace and Friendship] (Tokyo: Kodansha, 1988), 22.

7. Department of State, Briefing Paper, "Japanese Attitudes toward US-PRC Normalization," United States–Japan Relations, 1977–1992, Digital Document Collection (hereafter USJRD), JA00269, August 25, 1977, National Security Archive (hereafter NSA).

8. Harry Harding, *A Fragile Relationship: The United States and China since 1972* (Washington, D.C.: Brookings Institution Press, 1992), 48–49.

9. Ibid., 50–54; Robert S. Ross, "U.S. Relations with China," in *The Golden Age of the U.S.-China-Japan Triangle, 1972–1989,* ed. Ezra F. Vogel, Yuan Ming, and Tanaka Akihiko (Cambridge, Mass.: Harvard University Asia Center, 2002), 84–86.

10. For Troianovskii's service as ambassador in Tokyo, see Oleg Troianovskii, *Cherez godyi i rasstoianiia: istoriia odnoi sem'i* [Through the years and distances: A history of one family] (Moscow: Vagrius, 1997), 275–306.

11. *Yomiuri Shinbun,* May 16, 1977. For Belenko's escape, see *John Barron, MiG Pilot: The Final Escape of Lieutenant Belenko* (New York: McGraw-Hill, 1982).

12. Bedeski, *Fragile Entente,* 3–7.

13. For Carter's plan to withdraw ground troops from Korea, see Fred Hoffman, "The Role of Intelligence in President Jimmy Carter's Troop Withdrawal Decisions," *Military Intelligence Professional Bulletin,* December 12, 2008, http://findarticles.com/p/articles/mi_m01BS/is_1_28/ai_82351485.

14. Harding, *Fragile Relationship,* 69–70; Ross, "U.S. Relations with China," 89.

15. Harding, *Fragile Relationship,* 70–75; Ross, "U.S. Relations with China," 89–90. The State Department Briefing Paper prepared for Vice President Walter Mondale's visit to Japan states that "Japan's efforts to maintain a balanced pattern of relationships with China and the Soviet Union generally parallel our own," indicating the State Department represented Vance's line. "Department of State Briefing Paper: Vice President Mondale's Visit to Japan," 12, USJRD, JA00163, January 23, 1977, NSA. In contrast, Mike Armacost's briefing memo to Brzezinski for the latter's meeting with Mondale states: "Note our intent to continue playing a central role in preserving the Asian balance of power" and "Affirm our interest in pursuing full normalization of relations with China." Armacost to Brzezinski, USJRD, JA00164, January 26, 1977, NSA.

16. Department of State, Briefing Paper, "Japanese Views on Korean Troop Withdrawal," USJRD, JA00269, August 25, 1977, NSA; Secret memo, American Embassy to Secretary of State, USJRD. JA 00165, January 28, 1977, 5, NSA.

17. Department of State, Memorandum of Conversation, "Vice President Mondale–Prime Minister Fukuda Conversation II," USJRD, JA00167, February 1, 1977, 3, NSA.

18. Ibid., 2, 4.

19. Thomas Shoesmith to Richard Holbrooke, USJRD, JA00168, February 2, 1977, 1, NSA; Secretary of State to All East Asian and Pacific Diplomatic Posts Priority, USJRD, JA00189, March 25, 1977, NSA. Also see Harold Brown's briefing to the Japanese on the troop withdrawal plan: Department of State, incoming telegram, "Consultations on Korea: Brown/Habib Meeting with Prime Minister Fukuda," USJRD, JA 00207, May 17, 1977, 1–3, NSA.

20. Ogata, *Normalization with China,* 63.

21. *Yomiuri Shinbun,* February 4, 1977; *Krasnaia zvezda,* February 1, 1977, quoted by Foreign Broadcast Information Service: The Soviet Union (hereafter FBIS-Sov), February 4, 1977.

22. *Yomiuri Shinbun,* February 11, February 26, and May 8, 1977. FBIS-Sov, March 21, March 28, March 30, April 5, April 6, and April 21, 1977.

23. FBIS-Sov, May 31, 1977.

24. "Burejinefu shokicho no *Asahi Shinbun* eno kaito" [General Secretary Brezhnev's reply to *Asahi Shinbun*], June 7, 1977, quoted by Shigeta Shigeru and Suezawa Shoji, eds., *Nisso kihon bunsho shiryoshu* [Collection of basic documents on Japanese-Soviet relations] (Tokyo: Sekaino ugokisha, 1988), 216–17.

25. *Yomiuri Shinbun,* June 13, 1977.

26. FBIS-Sov, June 15, 1977.

27. Tsuyoshi Hasegawa, *The Northern Territories Dispute and Russo-Japanese Relations,* vol. 1, *Between War and Peace, 1697–1985* (Berkeley: International and Area Studies, University of California, 1998), 159–60; State Department Confidential Memorandum on Soviet-Japanese Fishing Negotiations Stalemate, undated and prepared by S. Goldberg, NSA.

28. *Yomiuri Shinbun,* April 19, June 7, and June 14, 1977.

29. FBIS-Sov, June 17, 1977.

30. Furusawa, *Showa hishi,* 30–35. For Fukuda's initial policy toward China, see Kunadze, *Iapono-Kitaiskie otnosheniia,* 72–75.

31. "Confidential Memorandum from U.S. Embassy to the Secretary of State on Sunao Sonoda," USJRD, JA00159, January 19, 1977, NSA.

32. Furusawa, *Showa hishi,* 35–41, 44–45, 47–49. For the critical view on Fukuda's China policy from the Soviet viewpoint, see Kunadze, *Iapono-kitaiskie otnosheniia,* 72–75.

33. Furusawa, *Showa hishi,* 64–69. As for Soviet reactions to the Fukuda doctrine, see *Izvestiia,* August 9, 1977, as reported in FBIS-Sov, August 12, 1977, and also TASS, August 19, FBIS-Sov, August 22, 1977; V. Kondrashov, in *Izvestiia,* August 21, 1977, cited in FBIS-Sov, August 24, 1977.

34. Kunadze, *Iapono-kitaiskie otnosheniia,* 75–76.

35. *Yomiuri Shinbun,* May 8, 1977.

36. Furusawa, *Showa hishi,* 70–71.

37. *Yomiuri Shinbun,* September 11, 1977; Furusawa, *Showa hishi,* 71; Tanaka

Akihito, *Nicchukankei, 1945–1990* [Japanese-Chinese relations, 1945–1990] (Tokyo: Tokyodaigaku shuppankai, 1991), 96.

38. Furusawa, *Showa hishi,* 74.

39. Tanaka Akihito, *Nicchukankei,* 96–97.

40. *Yomiuri Shinbun,* October 30, 1977; Furusawa, *Showa hishi,* 75–79.

41. Ogata, *Normalization with China,* 86–87; Furusawa, *Showa hishi,* 90–95.

42. *Yomiuri Shinbun,* January 1, 1998.

43. According to Kunadze, Liao Chengzhi and Deng Xiaoping made two concessions: (1) that the anti-hegemony clause was not directed at a specific third party; and (2) that the anti-hegemony clause would not mean that China and Japan would take a joint action. Kunadze, *Iapono-kitaiskie otnosheniia,* 80–81.

44. Tanaka Akihito, *Nicchukankei,* 97–98; Ogata, *Normalization with China,* 88.

45. *Yomiuri Shinbun,* September 17, 1997. Furusawa, *Showa hishi,* 75–79.

46. *Yomiuri Shinbun,* September 26, 1977.

47. FBIS-Sov, December 2, 1977.

48. Quoted in the commentary by Nikolaev, "Japan, PRC Treaty Criticized: Friendship with USSR Urged," FBIS-Sov, January 4, 1978. Also see Iu Bandura's comments in *Izvestiia,* December 1, 1977, quoted in FBIS-Sov, December 7, 1977; *Pravda,* November 26, 1977, quoted in FBIS-Sov, December 8, 1977; G. Krasin, *Novoe vremia,* no. 49, December 2, 1977, quoted in FBIS-Sov, December 13, 1977, Nikolaev's commentary rejecting Japan's territorial demand and proposing the conclusion of a treaty of good-neighborliness, FBIS-Sov, December 29, 1977.

49. *Yomiuri Shinbun,* December 1 and 2, 1978.

50. *Yomiuri Shinbun,* January 10 (evening), 11, 11 (evening), and 12, 1978; Glaubitz, *Between Tokyo and Moscow,* 148–49. For the Soviet view, see Kunadze, *Iapono-kitaiskie otnosheniia,* 78.

51. *Yomiuri Shinbun,* January 10, 1978.

52. *Yomiuri Shinbun,* January 11, 1978.

53. *Yomiuri Shinbun,* January 14, 1978; *Izvestiia,* February 1, 1978, FBIS-Sov, February 8, 1978.

54. *Yomiuri Shinbun,* February 22, 1978; Glaubitz, *Between Tokyo and Moscow,* 149.

55. "Nisso zenrin kyoryoku joyaku soren seifu soan" [The Soviet draft proposal for the Japanese-Soviet Good Neighbor Cooperation Treaty], in *Nisso kihon bunsho shiryôshû,* ed. Shigeta and Suezawa, 219–20.

56. *Yomiuri Shinbun,* February 24 and 24 (evening), 1978; Kimura, *Hopporyodo,* 70–71; Glaubitz, *Between Tokyo and Moscow,* 150. For the entire text of the draft proposal, see Shigeta and Suezawa, *Nisso kihon bunsho shiryoshu,* 219–20; and Glaubitz, *Between Tokyo and Moscow,* 269–71. For a Soviet view on this issue, see Kutakov, *Moskva-Tokio,* 146–49.

57. Bedeski, *Fragile entente,* 121; Kunadze, *Iaponsko-kitaikie otnosheniia,* 82, 86.

58. Ogata, *Normalization with China,* 88–89; Bedeskki, *Fragile Entente,* 35–37; Kunadze, *Iapono-kitaiskie otnosheniia,* 86–87.

59. See Tsuyoshi Hasegawa and Kazuhiko Togo, *East Asia's Haunted Present: Historical Memories and the Resurgence of Nationalism* (Westport, Conn.: Praeger Security International, 2008).

60. See Arlov's commentary, FBIS-Sov, May 3, 1978; TASS, FBIS-Sov, May 5, 1978; *Pravda,* May 7, 1978, in FBIS-Sov, May 10, 1978.

61. Department of State, Briefing Memorandum, Richard Holbrooke to the Secretary of State through Habib, USJRD, JA 00296, August 25, 1977, NSA.

62. Zbigniew Brzezinski, *Power and Principle: Memoir of the National Security Advisor* (New York; Farrar, Straus & Giroux, 1983), 208; Ogata, *Normalization with China,* 64–65; Ross, "U.S. Relations with China," 91–92; Harding, *Fragile Relationship,* 75–81.

63. For Carter's instructions to Brzezinski before the latter's trip to Beijing, see Brzezinski, *Power and Principle,* appendix I, 551.

64. Vance to Carter, "Your Meeting with Takeo Fukuda, Prime Minister of Japan, May 3, 1978," USJRD, JA00380, April 30, 1978, NSA; White House, Memorandum of Conversation, "Summary of the President's Meeting with Prime Minister Takeo Fukuda," USFRD, JA00384, May 3, 1978, NSA; Vance to Brzezinski, USJRD, JA00388, 1978/05/16, NSA.

65. Brzezinski, *Power and Principle,* 218.

66. White House, Memorandum of Conversation [Brzezinski/Fukuda meeting, May 23, 1978], USJRD, JA00392, May 23, 1978, NSA. The memo has two copies, the original and the other with the excised portion of the text blocked out. Comparing the two texts, it is clear that any reference to Korea was excised. The Chinese advocated a U.S. withdrawal of troops from South Korea, and expressed hope for the peaceful unification of the two Koreas. When asked by Fukuda whether the Chinese had mentioned the Japan-Korea Continental Shelf Agreement, Brzezinski answered in the negative. The latter may imply that the Chinese objection to the Japan-Korea Continental Shelf agreement was merely an excuse to put pressure on Japan.

67. National Security Council Memorandum, Armacost to Brzezinski, May 23, 1978, USJRD, JA00391, NSA.

68. Ibid.

69. Brzezinski, *Power and Principle,* 218; Tanaka Akihito, *Nicchukankei,* 102, 104–5. Ogata challenges this view as an exaggeration. She believes that "there is no indication from the policy debate in Tokyo that the U.S. attitude toward 'anti-hegemonism' was an issue of much concern." Ogata, *Normalization with China,* 95.

70. *Yomiuri Shinbun,* May 24, 1978.

71. Ogata, *Normalization with China,* 95.

72. *Yomiuri Shinbun,* May 27, 1978; *Sovetskaia Rossiia,* November 19, 1978, quoted in FBIS-Sov, November 24, 1978.

73. "Moscow Gives Tokyo Statement on Treaty with PRC," FBIS-Sov, June 19, 1978; Glaubitz, *Between Tokyo and Moscow,* 151–52; *Yomiuri Shinbun,* June 19 (evening), 1978.

74. For the domestic political reasons for Fukuda's anxiousness to conclude the PFT, see Kunadze, *Iapono-kitaiskie otnosheniia,* 82–86, 88–89.

75. See Glaubitz, *Between Tokyo and Moscow,* 100–105; and Kunadze, *Iapono-kitaiskie otnosheniia,* 89–93. Also see http://www.mofa.gov.jp/mofaj/area/china/nc_heiwa.html.

76. National Security Council Memorandum, Oksenberg to Brzezinski, "Sino-Japanese Treaty of Peace and Friendship," USJRD, JA00423, August 8, 1978, NSA. Michael Oksenberg's memo indicates that Sino-Japanese negotiations in Beijing were closely relayed to the U.S. government through Ambassador Mike Mansfield.

77. Tanaka Akihito, *Nicchukankei,* 103–4; *Nisso kihon bunsho,* 222–23, 464.

78. Glaubitz, *Between Tokyo and Moscow,* 153; M. S. Kapitsa, *Na raznykh paral-*

leliakh: Zapiski diplomata [On various parallels: Notes of a diplomat] (Moscow: Kniga i bizines,1991), 166.

79. Department of State, "Japanese Background Papers," n.d., declassified Department of State Secret document (790087 593), NSA.

80. Quoted by Bedeski, *Fragile Entente,* 62.

81. Ibid., 62–63; for other Chinese statements supporting the U.S-Japanese security alliance, see ibid., 100–101.

82. Bedeski, *Fragile Entente,* 85–88; Kunadze, *Iapono-kitaiskie otnosheniia,* 93–94.

83. Harding, *Fragile Relationship,* 78–81; Ross, "U.S. Relations with China," 92–93; Kunadze, *Iapono-kitaiskie otnosheniia,* 97.

84. "Memorandum of Conversation between Harold Brown and Shin Kanemaru," November 8, 1978, NSA, in *Power and Prosperity: Linkage between Security and Economies in U.S.-Japanese Relations since 1960* (Washington, D.C.: National Security Archive, n.d.), ed. Robert Wampler, II, 405.

85. Department of Defense, Briefing Memorandum, "Your Meeting with Prime Minister Fukuda," USJRD, JA00460, November 9, 1978, NSA.

86. Harding, *Fragile Relationship,* 82–94.

87. Interview with Ambassador Tajima Takashi, then the China Desk section chief and deeply involved in negotiations with China.

88. G. F. Kunadze, "V poiskakh novogo myshleniia: Politika SSSR v otnosheniia Iaponii" [In search of new thinking: Soviet policy in its relations with Japan], in *SSSR v mirovom soobshchestve: Ot starogo myshleniia k novomu* [USSR in the world community: From the old thinking to the new] (Moscow: Progress, 1990), 294; Semen I. Verbitskii, "Soviet Misperceptions of Japan in the USSR during the Cold War and Perestroika," *Carl Beck Papers,* no. 1503 (October 2000): 5–41.

89. For the view that the deployment of troops in the Northern Territories was Soviet retaliation for Japan's conclusion of the peace treaty, see Bedeski, *Fragile Entente,* 50.

90. See Tsuyoshi Hasegawa, "Japanese Perceptions of the Soviet Union, 1960–1985," *Acta Slavica Iaponica* 5 (1987); and Tsuyoshi Hasegawa, "Japanese Perceptions of the Soviet Union and Russia in the Postwar Period," in *Japan and Russia: The Tortuous Path to Normalization, 1949–1999,* ed. Gilbert Rozman (New York: St. Martin's Press, 2000).

9. Korea's Great Divergence: North and South Korea between 1972 and 1987

Gregg Brazinsky

Observers traveling through North Korea and South Korea in 1972 would have had difficulty making a very compelling case for the superiority of capitalism and allegiance to the Free World based on what they saw. Roughly two and a half decades earlier, these two Korean states had taken on very different shapes under the guidance and supervision of their great power patrons. But by the early 1970s, the two countries were fairly similar when it came to their standards of living and per capita income. South Korea's authoritarian state, led by Park Chung Hee, was not as rigid as the totalitarian regime of Kim Il Sung that governed North Korea. But political liberty, fair elections, and freedom of expression did not prevail in either of the two Koreas. The governments in both Seoul and Pyongyang seemed to command the loyalty of some but not all of those they ruled. The two Koreas had very different systems, but both were considered reasonably successful examples of nation building by their allies.

In only another fifteen years, however, it was readily apparent to almost the entire world that South Korea, or the Republic of Korea (ROK), was leaving North Korea, or the Democratic People's Republic of Korea (DPRK), behind in the dust. Between 1972 and 1987, the ROK's economy expanded rapidly while that of the DPRK stagnated and began to decline. Seoul had become an increasingly significant player in international organizations and was moving to improve relations with members of the rapidly disintegrating Eastern Bloc. Pyongyang, conversely, was moving toward greater isolation from both the Free World and its Communist allies. By 1987, few would question that the Korean version of capitalism had been far more successful at creating a prosperous, forward-looking society than had the Korean version of communism.

What accounted for this great divergence of fortunes between North Korea and South Korea during these years? What allowed South Korea to become a paragon of the virtues of capitalism while its northern rival withered away into irrelevance? The answer to these questions lies, to a great extent, in the ways that the two Korean states adapted to changing global political and economic circumstances during the 1970s and 1980s. Politically, the easing of Cold War frictions and the advent of détente posed challenges to the political rulers in Seoul and Pyongyang. Both regimes had to struggle with the question of how to adjust their relationships with friends and foes alike during a time of shifting allegiances and strategic uncertainty. Economically, the period was marked by the emergence of what Walter LaFeber has called "the new global capitalism," which was fueled by information age technology that promoted greater economic integration and made it easier for well-positioned corporations to sell their products in every corner of the globe.[1] In many ways, North Korea and South Korea had very similar instincts in how they adapted to these challenges. Both tried to find ways to balance the loss of firm support from their superpower patrons, and both tried to take advantage of the changing global economy. But the South Korean system proved much more capable of adapting to the changing political and economic climate of the 1970s than did the North Korean system. By the mid-1980s, the ROK was gaining in both global influence and economic wealth while the DPRK was moving toward the seclusion and poverty that would eventually turn it into an international outcast.

Dealing with Détente

The 1970s brought a dramatic shift in the structure of the Cold War. Upon assuming power in 1968, the new administration of Richard Nixon sought to move American foreign policy away from the constraints of ideological competition and seek common interests with the United States' Cold War adversaries. The goal of this strategy was for Washington to have better relations with Moscow and Beijing than the two Communist giants had with each other. The Nixon administration sought to negotiate arms control agreements with the Soviet Union and engage in summitry with its leaders. More significantly for the two Koreas, Nixon pulled off some dramatic victories when it came to thawing relations between the United States and the People's Republic of China (PRC). Relations between Washington and Beijing improved significantly after Nixon's dramatic visit to China in 1972, and suddenly the two countries seemed capable of working together on a wide variety of issues.[2]

The repercussions of Nixon's dramatic visit to Beijing in 1972 could be felt throughout the world, but they were felt with particular intensity on the Korean

Peninsula. For the two Korean states, whose very creation was a product of the Cold War, the relaxation of tensions that occurred during the 1970s was bound to have a strong influence. Cold War frictions had a more real and more horrifying impact on Korea than on virtually any other place in the world. But they had also brought opportunities that Korean political leaders deftly exploited for all they were worth. Korea was perched right atop one of the key geostrategic fault lines in the battle between the Free and Communist worlds. Moreover, during the Korean War, the United States and the PRC had invested their own credibility and resources in the survival of their respective Korean allies. After the war ended, they could never tolerate Korea's reunification on the terms of the other side. In the two decades after the war, the United States and its Communist adversaries lavished vast sums of aid on Seoul and Pyongyang in efforts to assure that these regimes survived and prospered.[3] The North and South Korean governments had in turn done everything they could to maximize assistance from the wealthier powers.

But the 1970s marked the beginning of the end of superpower indulgence toward the two Koreas. Even before he traveled to Beijing, Nixon had actively sought to reduce America's investments in its Asian allies, including the ROK. Several months after taking office, he issued the Nixon Doctrine, which declared that the United States would help "the defense and development of allies and friends" but would not "undertake all the defense of the free nations of the world."[4] This doctrine provided the impetus for National Security Decision Memorandum 48, which withdrew one full division of American combat forces (approximately 20,000 troops) from the Korean Peninsula.[5] This scaling back of the U.S. military presence was accompanied by reductions in economic aid. The Lyndon Johnson administration had begun tapering U.S. economic assistance to the ROK during the mid-1960s as it started to experience more rapid development, but Nixon had virtually eliminated all nonmilitary forms of aid by 1971.[6]

In the extensive Sino-American dialogue that blossomed in the wake of Nixon's China visit, both sides hoped to find ways to reduce the high costs of their involvement in the two Koreas. American and Chinese officials recognized that greater stability on the peninsula would be the key to this objective. If the risks of war in Korea could be reduced, then the United States and the PRC would have a logical excuse for scaling back military and economic assistance. By the end of 1972, Sino-American diplomacy had produced a tacit accord on how the two powers could mange their sometimes-prickly Korean allies. The United States and the PRC agreed to restrain Pyongyang and Seoul from the types of provocative behavior that might lead to a destabilizing military conflict. The Chinese came to expect that the United States would exert a moderating influence on South Korea, while Americans came to expect that the Chinese would exert a similar influence on North Korea.[7] Of course, agreement on these basic issues did not allow Beijing and Washington to extricate themselves completely from their commitments to the two Korean states. But they no longer felt it necessary to offer the levels of economic, military, and diplomatic support that they had given their Korean allies in earlier decades.

During the mid-1970s, both the United States and the PRC continued to try to reassure their Korean allies that they would not abandon them; but at the same time, they clearly demonstrated an unwillingness to support risk taking on the part of Seoul or Pyongyang. When Gerald Ford assumed the presidency in 1974, he made a two-day visit to Seoul on his way to Vladivostok and reassured the Park Chung Hee government of America's determination to "render prompt and effective assistance to repel armed attack against the Republic of Korea in accordance with the Mutual Security Treaty."[8] But the Ford administration disappointed the ROK in its response to an incident that occurred in the Demilitarized Zone (DMZ) between the two Korean states in 1976. In August of that year, DPRK guards using axes killed two American officials who had entered the DMZ to prune a tree that was obstructing their view. Some, including the Park government, called for some form of military retaliation against the DPRK, but the Ford administration accepted a statement of regret from Kim Il Sung and excluded the ROK from a negotiated settlement of the crisis.[9] These divergent reactions of Seoul and Washington to the crisis demonstrated that, though the two remained allies, Washington was more concerned with stability and preventing a new crisis than with backing Seoul's desire to take the toughest possible stance in dealing with Pyongyang.

Along similar lines, Beijing's diplomacy toward the DPRK continued to attach importance to good relations with its long-standing ally, but it also reflected a growing interest in stability and a greater willingness to restrain the North Koreans under certain circumstances. Chinese propaganda generally continued to offer strong support for Pyongyang on international issues and offered praise for its policy of *chuche* (self-reliance) as a creative application of socialism. Moreover, during the early 1970s, the economic and cultural ties between the PRC and the DPRK deepened, and growing numbers of trade and cultural delegations traversed the Sino-DPRK border.[10] But even while Beijing's propaganda remained strongly supportive of North Korea, its actual policies were at odds with those of the Kim Il Sung regime on many critical issues. By the early 1970s, Soviet observers could clearly discern that the PRC had a very different stance from the DPRK on the question of Korean reunification. Though Kim Il Sung had remained insistent that the Korean Peninsula should be unified under Communist rule, Soviet observers in China were reporting that

Beijing thought a divided Korea would better serve its interests. The Soviets were, in fact, "firmly convinced that the Chinese" were "not interested in reunification." They claimed that the PRC was afraid that "a unified Korea with a population of more than 50 million would become an important political factor and stress its independence even more strongly." The North Koreans were also disappointed that Chairman Mao Zedong did not push harder for the withdrawal of American forces from the peninsula during Nixon's visit to China. The Soviets reported to their East German comrades that "the DPRK expected more from the Chinese talks with Kissinger. The Chinese were said not to have insisted enough on the withdrawal of U.S. troops from South Korea."[11] Much as American policies had become a disappointment to Seoul during the early 1970s, some Chinese policies had become a disappointment to Pyongyang despite the facade of Chinese-DPRK solidarity.

Pyongyang's growing disappointment with China's lukewarm support was exacerbated by reductions in Soviet assistance. Although frictions between Beijing and Moscow persisted, the Soviets generally shared the PRC's apprehensions about any sort of instability on the Korean Peninsula. Both the 1976 axe murder incident in the DMZ and the downing of an American EC-121 fighter plane by the North Korean air force in 1968 had caused consternation among Soviet officials that Kim Il Sung would ignite a new military conflagration. Although Leonid Brezhnev's regime continued to furnish North Korea with conventional arms, during the years between 1972 and 1979 it generally avoided supplying the DPRK with the newest and most sophisticated Soviet weapons.[12]

Faced with declining support from their great power patrons, both Koreas strove for greater political and economic autonomy, although they did so in very different ways. The political authorities in both Pyongyang and Seoul took measures to strengthen their grasp on power and limit the influence of foreign powers on their internal affairs. They viewed such measures as necessary to preserve their legitimacy at a time when they seemed to be losing the endorsement of their great power patrons. Both the ROK and the DPRK also shifted their foreign policies during the 1970s. They struggled to find ways to compensate for the fact that their allies could no longer offer them the same kind of firm guarantees of support that they once had. The different approaches that the two Koreas took to resolving the problems created by détente would define the politics of the Korean Peninsula and exert an enormous influence on the politics of the Asian region for the next two decades.

There were interesting similarities in the ways that the regimes in Seoul and Pyongyang strove to strengthen themselves as superpower support declined. Both Korean governments increasingly sought to centralize political power and strove to eliminate potential dissent. Neither the ROK nor the DPRK had been democratic before détente began, but during the 1970s a trend toward increased state suppression was visible on both sides of the 38th Parallel. Reconciliation between the superpowers provided an exogenous shock that made Korean leaders anxious about losing power. Cold War hostilities were a significant part of the raison d'être for both Korean states, and reductions in tensions had the potential to stir domestic dissent, especially in South Korea, where there was some semblance of civil society. Moreover, the regimes in Pyongyang and Seoul had always relied on assistance from their wealthier allies to build their bases of support. With less American and Communist Bloc aid, they lost one of their key tools for keeping resistance under control. Thus détente created an atmosphere of crisis in both North and South Korea that the authorities tried to solve by deepening their own political dominance.

In South Korea, a move toward greater authoritarianism had been under way since the late 1960s but accelerated as a result of changing American policies in the early 1970s. The government that ruled South Korea during the mid-1960s can best be described as quasi-democratic. It had a freely elected president and legislature, and some measure of dissent was generally allowed, but the executive branch was extremely strong and usually got its way on critical issues. In 1969, the ROK's president, Park Chung Hee, had forced an amendment to the South Korean Constitution through the National Assembly that allowed him to seek a third term despite protests from both his political opposition and the United States. Though American officials did not greet Park's power grab with much enthusiasm, they did little to oppose it. They not only remained reluctant to act in way that might jeopardize the country's stability but also found that as U.S. aid to South Korea had dwindled, their capacity to influence events there had also declined.

Although Park won election to a third term as president in 1971, the election results troubled him. He had run against Kim Dae Jung, who was then a young and energetic crusader against the continuing military domination of Korean politics (and who would one day become South Korea's president). But despite the fact that Park had mobilized both vast financial resources and a powerful nationwide network of progovernment political organizations during the campaign, he had won by a much narrower margin than he had anticipated, receiving 53 percent of the vote to Kim's 45 percent.[13] Kim's success in capturing the popular imagination and nearly pulling off an upset victory had heightened Park's fears that if he did not take drastic measures, his political dominance would slip away.

In October 1972, Park declared martial law, banned political parties, dissolved the National Assembly, and closed the country's universities. On December 13, Park ended martial law but announced the new Yusin (meaning literally "revitalization") Constitution. The new system gave Park the authority to appoint one-third of the National Assembly; to appoint and dismiss all members of the Cabinet, including the prime minister; and to issue emergency decrees that became law immediately. Presidential elections were removed from the public sphere and assigned instead to an electoral college. Finally, Park would be allowed to serve an unlimited number of six-year terms.[14]

Although the unexpectedly close election results were the most immediate cause for Park's sudden turn toward outright authoritarianism, the ROK president's bold move cannot be understood without reference to Nixon's surprise visit to Beijing, which had occurred just eight months before the promulgation of the Yusin Constitution. When Park formally announced the inauguration of Yusin, he specifically cited the "uncertain political environment in East Asia" as a justification for the move. American intelligence officers had little doubt that Sino-American détente was at the heart of the matter. One National Intelligence Estimate on South Korea had noted that Park had perceived the development "from a viewpoint more like that of Taipei than Washington." It noted that as the leader of a small state, he could "not view with equanimity great-power dealings in which the interests of small states like South Korea might be subordinated to the pursuit—however laudable—of a generalized reduction in regional tensions."[15]

Understanding the rationale behind domestic political developments in North Korea during the 1970s remains far more difficult than probing those that occurred in Seoul. Since its creation in 1948, the DPRK regime had maintained a remarkably firm grip on power while allowing little dissent. The stark realities of North Korea's politics make speaking of a shift toward greater authoritarianism or centralization there somewhat complicated. But as Cold War frictions eased during the 1970s, North Korea's leadership made some interesting moves to shelter itself from potential international criticism. Increasingly, North Korean propaganda touted the nation's path to socialism as "the only correct and exemplary one for other countries." In March 1972, the East German Embassy in Pyongyang reported that Korean propaganda "is currently leading a broad campaign that defines all parties as supporters of revisionism which do not agree with positions of Kim Il Sung on questions like personality cult, dictatorship of the proletariat, class struggle, and so on."[16] This sort of propaganda effort made it easier for the North Koreans to simply label any criticism of their system coming from elsewhere in the Communist world as "revisionist" and head off any dissent that might arise as a result of criticism by the PRC or the Soviet Union.

Moreover, in 1973, Kim Il Sung launched the "Three Revolutions" movement, whose ostensible purpose was to carry out ideological, technical, and cultural revolutions in the DPRK. In reality, the "Three Revolutions" campaign focused on promoting proper thinking among key sectors of society. The regime organized teams of twenty-five to fifty college students, intellectuals, and technocrats who had demonstrated unswerving loyalty to the Korean Workers' Party. These teams descended on schools and factories, where they attempted to eliminate opposition to Kim Il Sung and his successor, his son Kim Jong Il.[17] It is difficult to tell how this campaign was related to the changing security environment in East Asia, given the paucity of materials about the DPRK during these years. Nevertheless, the North Korean regime's effort to clamp down on dissent in the wake of Nixon's visit to China presents a striking parallel to the sudden increase in political repression that occurred in South Korea at the same time.

Perhaps most significantly, during the 1970s Kim Il Sung began to build up Kim Jong Il as his successor. Kim Jong Il was elected secretary in charge of organization propaganda and agitation in the Central Committee of the Korean Workers' Party in 1973. By 1980, he had assumed new positions in the Secretariat, the Politburo, and the Military Commission and had emerged as the second most important political leader in North Korea. Over the course of the 1980s, DPRK propaganda did much to portray Kim Jong Il as brilliant, charismatic, and capable of becoming another "Great Leader." All these moves helped to pave the way for a smooth power transition from father to son.[18] Thus, although they did so in very different ways, the political rulers of both North and South Korea tried to respond to increasingly uncertain international circumstances by reducing political uncertainty at home.

Similarities were also apparent in the way that the two Koreas modified their foreign policies—at least initially—in the aftermath of superpower détente. In particular, the two Koreas showed a sudden interest in pursuing limited dialogue and negotiation. During the months after Nixon's historic trip to China, both Koreas sent high-level officials to each other's capitals. These visits resulted in the creation of the Joint Communiqué on July 4, 1972, which announced that the two Koreas would seek peaceful reunification by transcending the differences in their systems and ideologies. Both sides agreed as well that Korean reunification should be achieved without the interference of foreign powers.[19] With the support of their great power patrons looking increasingly uncertain, it was natural for both Seoul and Pyongyang to seek a measure of stability in their relationship.

Both North and South Korea also launched initiatives to improve their relationships with the neutral nations of Asia, Africa, and Latin America during the 1970s. They viewed this as a way to boost their international prestige and to show a measure of autonomy from their great power patrons. One report, written by the East German ambassador to Pyongyang in 1975, explained that the DPRK's leaders were "moving toward seeking new friends, especially among the nonaligned countries of the 'Third World.'" The North Koreans, he reported, believed that "these countries have to play a pivotal role in strengthening the DPRK's international positions and creating favorable conditions for Korean unification."[20]

Although with assistance from China, the DPRK did succeed in extending its relations with neutral countries to some degree, Seoul was more successful at this venture than Pyongyang. The Park Chung Hee government focused much of its effort to forge new diplomatic relationships on South America and Africa. By the end of 1978, the ROK had established relations with twenty-six Latin American countries and twenty-seven countries in Africa. Although these efforts were never central to South Korean foreign policy, they did become more extensive as the ROK economy continued to grow and Seoul was increasingly able to devote resources to such endeavors. During the 1980s, South Korean president Chun Doo Hwan stepped up these kinds of activities by traveling to many countries in the developing world that none of his predecessors had visited. In August 1982, Chun traveled to four African countries, including Kenya and Nigeria. In October 1983, he followed up on this trip with a tour of several Southeast Asian nations. This, of course, included his trip to Burma, where the infamous Rangoon bombing—an attack by North Korean terrorists that killed several members of Chun's entourage—occurred.[21] Although neither North nor South Korea really became a major player in the developing world, their growing involvement in it helped them to slightly step out of the shadow of their superpower patrons.

However, though both Koreas sought to improve relations with neutral nations and the developing world, their leaders were well aware that they could not rely on these new allies to compensate for the economic and military backing they had received from their great power patrons. Interestingly, both Seoul and Pyongyang looked to strengthen relationships with other significant powers in their respective "camps." Both succeeded to some degree in replacing the support they had once received from their superpower patrons. Though the DPRK attempted to do this in a manner that would enable it to preserve its independence in the name of *chuche,* the ROK simply pursued economic development and integration with the capitalist world. Ironically, South Korea's approach ultimately enabled it to gain greater autonomy and self-reliance, whereas North Korea's left it perpetually dependent on foreign sources of support.

Yet North Korea had one option open to it that South Korea lacked. In previous decades, both the Soviet Union and the PRC had given North Korea significant amounts of aid. Both Communist giants looked at the DPRK as an extremely valuable ally, not only in the global struggle against capitalism and imperialism but also in the struggle for influence within the Communist world. From the late 1950s onward, as friction developed between the PRC and the Soviet Union, both Moscow and Beijing had vied for Pyongyang's loyalty in the conflict. Although aid from both the PRC and the Soviet Union had declined, the two continued their efforts to capture the loyalties of Pyongyang. One East German report from 1972 noted that "delegation traffic" between North Korea and China had "increased significantly, and that during Chinese visits anti-Soviet literature was regularly distributed."[22] The Soviets and their allies sought to counter these Chinese efforts. The Soviet ambassador in Pyongyang explained in one lecture to his fellow ambassadors from fraternal socialist countries that "we will also continue to look out for opportunities to improve and develop Soviet-Korean relations in several areas with the simultaneous focus to weaken political and other effects by the Chinese leadership on the DPRK."[23]

The friction between the two Communist giants created an opportunity for North Korea. The DPRK always had the option of playing its two allies off against each other, using a strategy that sought to secure aid from both sides of the Sino-Soviet split while enabling it to maintain an independent posture. Although the Soviets were deeply concerned about increasing ties between China and North Korea during the 1970s, they also reported that the situation was not completely hopeless for the DPRK's relations with Moscow and its allies. The Soviet ambassador also noted that, unlike the PRC, "the DPRK agrees to support actions of European socialist countries to achieve and maintain security in that geographical area." He further reported that "the DPRK does not condone the Chinese cooperation with the imperialist and reactionary forces on global policy issues in an antisocialist and anti-Soviet fashion."[24] Throughout the 1970s and 1980s, Pyongyang would continue to attempt to balance its relations with Moscow and Beijing in this manner. It sought to repair the damage that was done to Sino-DPRK relations during the Cultural Revolution while being careful not to take any positions that would alienate it from other potential supporters in the Communist camp. Thus, by carefully orchestrating its diplomacy toward the PRC and the Soviet Union, the DPRK managed to remain virtually the only country to successfully maintain its neutrality in the conflict.

Although South Korea did not have the luxury of playing two superpowers against each other, it did increasingly seek to balance American influence with Japanese influence. The legacy of Japanese colonialism had left the two countries as bitter rivals at the end of World War II, and normalization of relations between the two nations had been achieved only after constant pressure from the United States on both the South Korean and Japanese governments. For the United States, this represented a way of transferring some of the enormous costs of containing Communism in the Pacific to its allies. The story of the tortuous road to this normalization agreement, which was signed in 1965, has been told elsewhere and will not be repeated here.[25] The most significant and disputed component of the treaty was the payments that Japan made to the ROK as reparations for Japanese colonialism. Under the terms of the normalization treaty, the Japanese government agreed to grant the ROK $300 million in unconditional grants, $200 million in low-interest loans, and $100 million in commercial credit as reparations for Japanese colonialism. This money would play a pivotal role in enabling the ROK government to avoid being subject to American guidance.

Although the United States itself had been a major driving force behind the conclusion of this agreement, the influx of Japanese capital complicated the efforts of American officials to steer the South Korean government toward what they considered good decisions. Moreover, Japanese views of what was in the best interests of the ROK's economy did not necessarily correspond with American views. Within a few months of having reached the normalization agreement, the Japanese government was already proposing investment projects in South Korea, such as the construction of new cement and fertilizer plants, that the U.S. Operations Mission to Korea believed conflicted with the ROK's best interest. The United States even briefly considered a diplomatic initiative to "forestall [the] development of U.S.-GOJ [Government of Japan] conflict over [the] direction of respective aid and export assistance programs and over trends in ROK economic development."[26] Americans also feared that the Park government would use funds acquired from Japan to pursue development projects that they deemed impractical. The State Department, concerned about the attraction that the ROK government had exhibited for "showy" projects in the past, began seeking to coordinate aid efforts with Japan "to minimize friction, to dissuade [the ROK government] from expensive show-case projects and to avoid loss to U.S. of opportunities in appropriate sectors of [the ROK] economy."[27]

During the 1970s, cooperation between South Korea and Japan continued to intensify. As American aid to and interest in South Korea declined during the Nixon, Ford, and Carter administrations, Seoul increasingly turned to Tokyo as an alternate source of support. Domestically, the deepening ties between the ROK and its erstwhile colonizer were extremely unpopular and bolstered political dissent against Park Chung Hee's government. But the economic and, to a lesser extent, political benefits of increasing cooperation with

Japan were enormous for South Korea's economy. Japan relocated many declining industries to South Korea and took advantage of its relatively cheap but highly trained workforce.

Collaboration with Japan proved particularly crucial to incubating South Korea's electronics industry. The Park Chung Hee government provided special incentives to lure Japanese companies interested in subcontracting parts of their operations. By the late 1970s, South Korea had already become the first choice of many Japanese electronics firms for filling subcontracting orders. Eventually, large domestic manufacturing firms took the place of Japanese ones, and South Korea surprised much of the world with the rapid growth of its electronics industry.[28] The development of this industry benefited South Korea in myriad ways. Many electronics components had clear military applications, and South Korea's ability to manufacture them swiftly and efficiently enhanced its autonomous defense capacities. Moreover, the emergence of homegrown electronics companies primed South Korea to become a cutting-edge member of the globalized economy within two decades.

In some instances, Japan's support for South Korea was not only economic but also political and diplomatic. Nixon's efforts to reduce America's commitments to the Asian region had stirred anxieties in Japan along with South Korea, and Tokyo often joined Seoul in protesting U.S. efforts to reduce its presence in the region. The withdrawal of American forces from the Korean Peninsula was particularly worrisome to Japan. In 1978, when the Jimmy Carter administration considered drawing down U.S. forces in the ROK beyond the one division that Nixon had already redeployed, Japanese prime minister Fukuda Takeo strongly protested. In one meeting with the U.S. ambassador to Japan, Mike Mansfield, Fukuda even criticized the Carter administration for depreciating the value of the entire Pacific region.[29] Eventually, Carter shelved his plan to withdraw another 6,000 American soldiers from the peninsula in the face of opposition from U.S. allies around the world.[30]

Japan also supported the South Korean government in the face of the Carter administration's criticisms of its human rights policies. Frictions had flared between the ROK and Japan over the issue in 1973, after agents of the Korean Central Intelligence Agency had abducted the dissident politician Kim Dae Jung from a hotel room in Tokyo. In the aftermath of the incident, Japan had temporarily cut off economic aid to the ROK and demanded an apology. In November 1973, however, Park Chung Hee dispatched ROK premier Kim Chong-p'il to meet with his Japanese counterpart and offer an apology. The two managed a face-saving compromise that papered over differences and led to the restoration of Japanese aid.[31] By the mid-1970s, Japan was increasingly shying away from joining in international criticisms of South Korea on human rights questions. Although the Park government was reviled in the eyes of the Japanese public, Japan's government was reluctant to join the Carter administration's efforts to pressure Seoul on the issue. Before a visit to the United States in March 1977, Prime Minister Fukuda openly acknowledged that differences existed between the United States and Japan on human rights policies toward other countries in Asia. After Carter visited South Korea and pressed Park on the issue of human rights, Fukuda stated that while he supported human rights, "the situation where Japan is located is different from that of the [United] States, and I believe that Japan should work out its own implementation."[32] Although Japan avoided strong endorsements of the Park government, its willingness to overlook South Korea's human rights record in exchange for increased trade made Tokyo an ideal ally for Seoul in its efforts to compensate for the decline in the strength of American support.

A final way that both North and South Korea strove to cope with weakening support from their patron states was by seeking improved relations with major powers in rival camps. Thus, during the 1970s, Seoul initiated efforts to reach out to Moscow and Beijing that would enable it to normalize relations with both within two decades. At the same time, Pyongyang made several abortive efforts to reach out to a generally unresponsive Washington. Once again, the relative success of the ROK's efforts in this area enabled it to make further gains in the fierce competition for international prestige and recognition that it was waging with the DPRK.

Seoul's efforts to pursue improved relations with Moscow began soon after Sino-American rapprochement. By 1974, officials in the Park government were noting subtle shifts in the Soviet Union's position toward the ROK, which one Foreign Ministry report characterized as "avoiding hostile behavior as much as possible." The report went on to call for Seoul to gradually seek reconciliation with the Communist superpower in a way that would not put the Kremlin's leadership in an awkward position. In particular, it put forward the idea that allowing private, nonofficial organizations to build some mutually beneficial linkages with the Soviets in the short term might lead to more formal relations between Seoul and Moscow in the more distant future.[33] By 1978, this policy seemed to be bearing some fruit. South Korean delegations found it easier to acquire visas for international conferences and events held in the USSR, while sports teams from the ROK visited Leningrad and other Soviet cities to compete in tournaments and play exhibition games. Moreover, Soviet diplomats had begun seeking limited contacts with South Korean diplomats abroad, although the Park government suspected that KGB operatives were involved in this process.[34]

By the 1980s, observers in the Kremlin were increasingly impressed with

South Korea's economic prowess, and many were beginning to advocate more substantial contacts with Seoul. For instance, during a closed session of the Central Committee of the Communist Party in 1984, Georgii Kim, the Korean-born deputy director of Institute for Oriental Studies, commented that the ROK was a successful country that was interested in friendship with the Soviet Union. He encouraged those in attendance to make a more positive effort to respond to South Korean overtures. Two years later, a Politburo document recognized that Seoul had become an increasingly significant force in international affairs and that trade and other forms of economic exchange with the ROK should be encouraged.[35] When Mikhail Gorbachev assumed power in 1985, he doubtless recognized that South Korea's growing economic strength would make it difficult to shut out if Moscow genuinely sought better relations with the West.

Although South Korea succeeded in gradually increasing its contacts with the Soviet Union, North Korea faced far greater difficulties in trying to improve relations with the United States during the same period. The DPRK government attempted to reach out to the United States through third countries, such as Romania, during the early 1970s. In a 1974 meeting with U.S. secretary of state Henry Kissinger, one Romanian official broached the subject with him. At the time, Kissinger expressed his willingness to open contacts with Kim Il Sung, if he "were to act in a restrained manner toward South Korea and in the UN on the issues before it."[36] North Korean officials also met with the banker David Rockefeller, who was fairly close to Kissinger, several times during the early 1970s to discuss the possibility of broader contacts between the two countries. In his private conversations with Rockefeller, Kissinger continued to express some interest in having such contacts, but he insisted that they be kept secret and be accompanied by a DPRK nonaggression pledge.[37]

The ultimate reason that these limited contacts between the United States and the DPRK did not develop into a more significant informal relationship like that between the ROK and the Soviet Union is unclear. But there are several likely possibilities. Because it was obsessed with secrecy, the Nixon administration insisted that DPRK officials keep any efforts to initiate contacts secret. But unlike their Communist neighbors in Beijing, the North Koreans seemed to have little grasp of the subtleties of Nixon-Kissinger diplomacy. In one instance, the DPRK even attempted to make an overture to the United States through Congress. Naturally, the secretive Nixon administration refused to respond.[38] It is also possible that Washington did not want to run the risk of causing further consternation in Seoul, where Nixon's policy was already leading many to question the depth of America's commitment.[39] Finally, the combination of the DMZ axe murder incident in 1976 and the 1977 shooting down of an American C-47 helicopter that had strayed into DPRK airspace probably raised frictions to the point where both sides lost interest in such contacts. The end result was that the DPRK was far less successful in building relations with the leaders of its rival camp than was South Korea.

Although the North and South Korean governments showed some very similar instincts in how they responded to superpower détente, these responses had very different ramifications. Both Koreas sought new allies or ways to counterbalance the perceived loss of support from their patron states. The DPRK's efforts to play the Soviets and the Chinese against each other brought it greater independence in the short run and enabled it to claim that its policy of *chuche* was a success. This policy enabled the DPRK to shelter itself from world economic trends, but at the same time would ultimately make it more difficult for the DPRK to participate in the new global economy. The ROK, conversely, by edging closer to Japan, sacrificed some measure of its economic independence but moved firmly in the direction of greater economic integration. Much more than the path chosen by the DPRK, the route that the ROK followed would put it in an ideal position to benefit from the new global capitalism.

North Korea, South Korea, and the New Global Capitalism

Recently, historians have begun to point to the 1970s as a time of highly significant change in the world economy. In particular, it marked an era when both capital and new transnational corporations, abetted by the development of new information technologies, began to move swiftly around the globe. The South Koreans proved far more adept at taking advantage of these trends than their North Korean brethren. Part of the reason for this was, of course, historical. During the Cold War, the United States had already begun the process of inducing the ROK's participation in the global capitalist system. At the same time, however, it is also necessary to look at some of the specific choices made by the two Koreas during the era. Both the ROK government and leading South Korean companies aggressively sought to take advantage of the new global capitalism by developing industries that could thrive in the changing world trade environment and seeking new economic partnerships abroad. The DPRK, conversely, attempted to shelter itself from these changes. The end result was a rapid expansion of the ROK's influence in international affairs and the dramatic decline of the DPRK's.

One important dimension of the world economy during the 1970s was the growing availability of loans to developing countries. The sudden rise in petroleum prices during the decade led oil-producing countries to deposit large sums of capital in commercial banks located in Europe and the United States.

At the same time, high oil prices had helped to bring on a recession in many industrial countries, in turn leading to a decline in the demand for loans in these regions. As a result, the World Bank, the International Monetary Fund, and commercial banks in wealthier countries began offering loans at extremely low interest rates to countries in the developing world. Many governments in Asia, Africa, and Latin America were eager to seize the opportunity presented by the sudden largesse of these banks in hopes of spurring industrialization in their countries.[40] Capital flowed from commercial banks and global financial institutions into developing countries at unprecedented rates. In much of the world, this sudden increase in borrowing ultimately had disastrous consequences. Many political rulers in the developing world simply used the debt to strengthen their regimes or for corrupt, personal gain. Within a decade, this excessive borrowing had created a major debt crisis that spanned much of the global South.[41]

South Korea, however, proved to be one of the few developing countries to use the sudden increase in the availability of credit to make significant, long-term improvements in its economy. In the early 1970s, the nation started to take advantage of the new, easy availability of credit, and within five years it had become the world's third-largest developing debtor nation. The South Korean state generally used these loans as subsidies for a few select entrepreneurs and firms that had already started to achieve impressive records either as exporters or by entering into the heavy and chemical industries. Unlike many other governments in the developing world, the Park Chung Hee regime managed to develop a fairly efficient system that allocated loans at cheap interest rates to those firms that seemed most capable of performing. This kind of financing ultimately proved invaluable for South Korea's "big push" into industries such as iron and steel, automobiles, and machine tools during the 1970s. South Korean business conglomerates, or *chaebol,* such as Hyundai and Samsung grew into major international companies during this period, thanks to the Park Chung Hee government's largesse and its determination to make the ROK more autonomous politically and economically through rapid economic growth. Of course, the results of these policies were not all good. The *chaebol* became a dominating and at times destabilizing influence in South Korea's economy and society. But still, the strategic use of debt by the ROK government enabled the nation's economy to soar at a time when most others in the developing world were floundering.[42]

The South Korean government's skillful use of the new availability of credit to build a powerful industrial economy during the 1970s stood in contrast to the DPRK's greatly misguided use of international credit during the same period. Of course, commercial banks in the United States and Europe were far less willing to loan to the DPRK than to the ROK. Nevertheless, Pyongyang did find lenders during this era of very easy credit. Ultimately, it borrowed hundreds of millions of dollars to buy new factories from Japan and Western Europe. It hoped that these new technologies would generate export income that could ultimately be used to repay the debt. This policy failed miserably, however, due to both the slow growth of the global economy during these years and the country's lack of experience in efficiently using the technologies that it imported.[43] By the 1980s, North Korea still vowed to its allies that it would repay these loans. In a meeting with East German chancellor Erich Honecker in 1984, for instance, Kim Il Sung mentioned the $700 million that the DPRK had borrowed from Western European nations. With little sense of realism, Kim brushed aside these loans as insignificant and explained that "we are not very deeply in debt." He claimed that North Korea would be able to repay these loans within two years.[44] Of course, it did not. And by the mid-1980s, much of the international community had come to see North Korea as a sort of a deadbeat, making it difficult for Pyongyang to find new sources of foreign credit.[45]

The contrast in how the two Koreas utilized the rapid expansion of global credit during the early 1970s could not have been greater. South Korea had developed industries that made it a much bigger player in the global economy and integrated it more thoroughly with the world's more prosperous nations. Thus, it was much more independent economically at the end of the decade than in 1970. North Korea, conversely, had failed to benefit much from its own borrowing binge. In fact, its failure closely resembled that of numerous other developing countries during the era. It had accrued massive debts that it could not pay off, and this in turn served to further isolate it from the new system of global finance.

Perhaps more significantly, by the late 1970s South Korea had something that North Korea did not and seemed highly unlikely to develop: multinational companies with the capacity to take advantage of the new global capitalism. Many of these companies had taken off during the late 1960s as a result of some of the special opportunities the United States had given South Korea in exchange for its participation in the Vietnam War. In return for Park Chung Hee's decision to dispatch two South Korean combat divisions to South Vietnam, the United States had provided opportunities for South Korean contractors to participate in construction projects undertaken by the U.S. government and American contractors in Southeast Asia. Thus, several South Korean firms that would later become large business conglomerates gained a valuable chance to participate in new kinds of international ventures.[46]

The Park regime continued to nurture these companies through the use of preferential loans in subsequent years and helped to turn them into significant players in the global economy. Over the course of the 1970s and 1980s, this difference would prove important not only economically but also politically. As South Korea's new conglomerates looked abroad both for markets and places to invest, they also helped to knit the ROK into webs of interdependence with some of the other countries of Asia. Closer economic ties necessitated greater political interaction, and greater political interaction resulted in improved relations between South Korea and nations that had been some of its most fervent adversaries during the Cold War. This was particularly true of the ROK's relationship with the People's Republic of China, which had almost helped to obliterate South Korea during the Korean War. But the eagerness of both these countries to participate in the new world economic order would eventually transform these erstwhile adversaries into partners.

Improved economic ties between the two countries first took the form of informal trade, which began to increase steadily after Deng Xiaoping began making more dramatic efforts to open the PRC's economy in 1978. The two sides at first carried out most of their trade relations through intermediaries such as Singapore, Japan, and Hong Kong, but by 1981 they had already started shipping goods directly to each other in vessels with third-party registries. China generally exported raw materials, especially coal, to South Korea, while South Koreans began exporting electronics and other manufactured goods to the PRC. This informal trade grew from a negligible amount at the time Deng first gained power to $300 million in 1980 and more than $500 million in 1981.[47] These numbers continued to grow throughout the decade as both nations recognized the benefits of increased trade ties. By 1991, the year before the PRC and ROK established formal relations, Chinese exports to South Korea had reached $3.4 billion and South Korean exports to China had reached $1 billion.[48]

As informal trade between the countries started to increase, South Korean firms clamored to take advantage of investment opportunities in China. Conglomerates such as Samsung found innovative ways of creating "front" companies in Hong Kong that constructed factories in Shenzhen, Weihai, and Yantai.[49] South Korean business leaders viewed operations in the latter two cities, both of which are situated in China's northeastern Shandong Province and in very close proximity to the Korean Peninsula, as logical steps toward making further inroads into the Chinese economy. By 1988, South Korean activity in Shandong had grown to such a high level that the PRC and ROK governments decided to quietly allow direct trade in the province. Chinese officials hoped that by quietly opening trade in the region they could safely build economic ties with the ROK while not drawing too much attention from the international community.[50] The penetration of the Chinese market by South Korean capital naturally continued to expand after this agreement, reaching a total of 255 investment projects by May 1992. Shandong continued to grow as a major hub of ROK investment in China. These projects of course much more reflected the initiative of South Korean firms than of the Chinese government. But they certainly added incentives for Beijing to rethink its policies toward South Korea.

Growing trade contacts between the PRC and the ROK led each to recognize the need for new mechanisms to coordinate and facilitate economic interactions. By the late 1980s, the two countries were already thinking about the possibility of establishing unofficial trade offices in each other's territory to assist with these tasks. By October 1990, the China International Chamber of Commerce and the Korea Trade and Investment Promotion Agency had reached an agreement to establish such offices in Seoul and Beijing. The use of these semiofficial organizations to strengthen trade ties was an important step toward normalizing relations between the two countries. Pyongyang, which at this point could clearly see the direction of the tides, viewed this move with great suspicion.[51] As the ROK and PRC continued to move toward normalizing relations, these trade offices helped to forge economic ties between the two countries that were far more dynamic than those between Beijing and Pyongyang. Although Beijing maintained amicable relations with Pyongyang, Seoul's economic diplomacy had pulled Beijing away from its firm support for Pyongyang on many international issues.

Although South Korean investment in China marked perhaps the most dramatic shift in the ROK's economic orientation from earlier decades, this new China trade was only part of a much broader pattern of growth in Korean investment abroad during the 1970s and 1980s. South Korean firms also began to invest in more developed Western countries during the 1980s to assure continued access to American and European export markets. Much of this new foreign investment was led by Samsung, Lucky-Goldstar, and Daewoo, South Korea's three largest business conglomerates. By the late 1980s, South Korean firms had either completed or planned to complete six factories in Europe that produced electronics. The *chaebol* were also planning to build new factories in Central and Eastern Europe in the hope of gaining new, low-cost production bases that could be used to further boost South Korean exports to Western Europe. Along similar lines, LG set up a plant in Mexico to produce color television chassis that were ultimately shipped to a final production plant in Huntsville, Alabama. Finally, during the 1980s South Korean foreign investment flowed into Southeast Asia, where the *chaebol* hoped to both find new sources of cheap labor and lay the groundwork for acquiring market share in the future. By the late 1980s, South Korean firms had, in a short period of time, managed to learn how to invest in a broad range of foreign countries with great deftness and celerity.[52]

By utilizing foreign direct investment, South Korean firms managed to continue to increase their exports to the United States and Western Europe during the 1980s, despite the fact that some of these countries were erecting new barriers to foreign goods, especially in sectors such as automobiles and electronics. South Korean electronics exports in particular exploded during the 1980s, reaching $15 billion by 1988 after experiencing annual growth rates of up to 40 percent.[53] Moreover, the ROK also seized growing shares of world export markets in industries where the country did not rely as heavily on foreign direct investment. For instance, despite the fact that economists in industrial countries had been widely skeptical in the 1970s when South Korea announced its plan to launch a shipbuilding industry, it had managed to capture 20 percent of new orders for ships by the late 1980s.[54]

The end result of this rapid adaptation to the changing global economy was, for the most part, rapid economic growth in South Korea, which persisted despite growing conflict between the authoritarian state and prodemocratic forces. South Korea achieved an average annual economic growth rate of 9.2 percent between 1982 and 1987. By the late 1980s, Seoul was also achieving significant surpluses in its balance of payments for the first time in its modern history.[55] By 1987, South Korea already had a significant middle class that was growing in size and political influence.

Although South Korea's economic growth did not necessarily translate directly into political power, the model that its government used to achieve this growth did give the country a form of "soft power" that shaped the overall outcome of the Cold War. Joseph Nye has defined soft power as the ability to make others "want what you want." Generally this occurs when nations come to admire the values, emulate the example, and aspire to the level of prosperity of a particular country or society.[56] Nye has most often used this term in conjunction with discussions of American globalism, but he has also pointed out that smaller states like the Vatican can also have significant measures of soft power. For a variety of reasons, South Korea's stunning successes in the economic sphere made it a country that others in the developing world sought to emulate. The attractiveness of its model enabled it to make its influence felt in ways that it could not before the late 1970s.

Part of what made South Korea's industrialization so important to international politics was the fact that it produced some of its most remarkable results at precisely the historical juncture when most left-wing revolutionary states were suffering abysmal failures. Odd Arne Westad has noted that the early 1980s proved to be a "time of disappointments and severe setbacks" for many leftist regimes in Asia, Africa, and Latin America, as it became clear that their policies could not offer a viable alternative to capitalism.[57] The failure of non-capitalist modes of development and the relative success of once-impoverished capitalist countries such as South Korea were important factors in ending the Cold War in the developing world. As China and other parts of the Communist world attempted to diversify their economies and pursue market reforms, they quickly realized that South Korea was a country from which they had much to learn.

It is difficult to determine whether China and other Asian nations deliberately imitated the South Korean development strategy. Nevertheless, the ROK's rise to prosperity had made it abundantly clear to political leaders around the globe that state planning, autocratic modes of government, and markets could coexist. This was especially crucial to the leaders of the Chinese Communist Party because it offered them the possibility of maintaining political control and improving their country's economic performance at the same time. The similarity of the policies adopted by China as it reformed its economy during the 1970s and 1980s and those that had been pioneered in South Korea further invalidated Communist models of development and underscored the importance of the Korean one. Bruce Cumings has even written that "the 'Korean model' generalized to Southeast Asia and then to China broke the back of Stalinism as a model of development not just in North Korea but all over the world."[58] In this sense, South Korea contributed greatly to the economic downfall of Communism in Asia and the developing world.

The prestige that South Korea gained from its economic triumphs was reflected in the International Olympic Committee's decision to hold the 1988 summer games in Seoul. The ROK's selection as the host country for the games was meant to highlight the country's economic achievements and illustrate the virtues of capitalist development. Ultimately, the Seoul Olympics not only demonstrated South Korea's soft power but also strengthened it. As people all over the world got a glimpse of Seoul's modern landscape and high living standard, they were stunned that such prosperity could be found in a country that had been struggling to survive just thirty years earlier. More than ever, they came to see South Korea's society and economy as attractive.

Conclusion

By 1987, the contrast between North Korea and South Korea in both economic prosperity and international prestige could not have been clearer. South Korea had a thriving economy and was gaining the admiration of even its erstwhile adversaries in the Communist world. North Korea, conversely, was economically stagnant and was losing the respect of its most reliable allies. Although there were similarities in the ways that the ROK and the DPRK responded to the political and economic upheavals that occurred during the 1970s, the specific choices that they made played a critical role in shaping their subsequent very divergent fortunes. In South Korea, both the public and private sectors had found ways to weather the challenges presented by the global upheavals of the 1970s while taking full advantage of the opportunities they provided. The North Korean regime had managed to survive and, to some degree, preserve its independence. But it had not learned to thrive in this changing global environment. In short, the 1970s marked the end of an era of unlimited superpower indulgence for client states and the use of large-scale aid to build capitalism and Communism in the developing world. The South Koreans proved far more capable of adapting to these changes than their North Korean brethren, and as a result they were in a much better position to become significant players in world affairs by 1987.

Notes

1. See Walter LaFeber, *Michael Jordan and the New Global Capitalism* (New York: W. W. Norton, 1999).

2. For a good basic summary of détente, see Jussi Hanhimaki, "Détente," in *Encyclopedia of the Cold War,* vol. 1, ed. Ruud Van Dijk (New York: Routledge, 2008), 250–54.

3. On U.S. assistance to the ROK, see Gregg Brazinsky, *Nation Building in South Korea: Koreans, Americans, and the Making of a Democracy* (Chapel Hill: University of North Carolina Press, 2007). On Communist assistance to the DPRK, see Charles Armstrong, "Fraternal Socialism: The International Reconstruction of North Korea, 1953–1962," *Cold War History* 5, no. 2 (May 2005): 161–87.

4. LaFeber, *American Age,* 638–39.

5. Kim Ch'angsu, "Hanmi kwan'gye, chongsok kwa kaltung" [Korean-American relations: Subordination and conflict], in *Pak chonghui rul nomoso* [Beyond Park Chung Hee], ed. Han'guk chongch'i yon'guhoe (Seoul, 1998), 333–34.

6. "United States Economic Assistance to Korea, 1954–1973: Fact Book," U.S. Agency for International Development Library, Washington.

7. I elaborated on this in "Controlling the Two Koreas: Détente and Sino-American Diplomacy toward the Korean Peninsula, 1971–1992," paper prepared for the conference "Transforming the Cold War," East China Normal University, Shanghai, December 20–21, 2006.

8. Cited by Chae-jin Lee, *A Troubled Peace: U.S. Policy and the Two Koreas* (Baltimore: Johns Hopkins University Press, 2006), 75–76.

9. Ibid., 80.

10. Note on a conversation with USSR Embassy counselor Comrade Denisov, January 22, 1973, GDR Embassy to DPRK, PolA AA, MfAA, C 295/78, North Korea International Documentation Project, Woodrow Wilson International Center for Scholars (hereafter NKIDP).

11. Note on a Conversation with Comrade Kurbatov, First Secretary of the USSR

Embassy, March 26, 1973, in the USSR Embassy, GDR Embassy to DPRK 28 March 1973, PolA AA, MfAA, C 295/78, NKIDP.

12. Sông-im Chông, "Puk-rô kwan'gye" [Soviet-DPRK relations], in *Pukhan ûi taeoe kwan'gye* [North Korea's foreign relations], ed. Sejong Yôn'guso (Seoul: Hanul, 2007), 335.

13. John Kie-Chang Oh, *Korean Politics: The Quest for Democratization and Economic Development* (Ithaca, N.Y.: Cornell University Press, 1999), 58–59.

14. Brazinsky, *Nation Building in South Korea,* 160.

15. "Special National Intelligence Estimate: The Political Outlook in South Korea, October 26, 1972," Korea Declassification Projects, National Security Archive.

16. Note on a Conversation with the First Secretary of the USSR Embassy, Comrade Kurbatov, March 10, 1972, in the GDR Embassy, PolA AA, MfAA, C 1080/78, NKIDP.

17. Bradley K. Martin, *Under the Loving Care of the Fatherly Leader: North Korea and the Kim Dynasty* (New York: St. Martin's Press, 2006), 173–75.

18. Charles Armstrong, *The Koreas* (New York: Routledge, 2007), 75–79.

19. Lee, *Troubled Peace,* 73–74.

20. GDR Embassy to DPRK to Ministry for Foreign Affairs, January 14, 1975, NKIDP.

21. Kim Chôngwôn, *Han'guk oegyo balchôllon* (Seoul: Chimmundang, 1996), 210–11, 238–39.

22. GDR Embassy to DPRK, Pyongyang, February 1, 1973, NKIDP.

23. GDR Embassy to DPRK, Pyongyang, January 14, 1975, NKIDP.

24. Ibid.

25. See Victor Cha, *Alignment Despite Antagonism: The United States–Korea–Japan Security Triangle* (Stanford, Calif.: Stanford University Press, 1999).

26. "U.S.-GOJ Coordination on Projects in Korea," March 9, 1966, NA/RG 59 General Records of the Department of State, Central Foreign Policy File, 1964-1966, box 567.

27. Ibid.

28. Jung-En Woo, *Race to the Swift: State and Finance in Korean Industrialization* (New York: Columbia University Press, 1991), 144–47.

29. Summary of a meeting on Japanese matters, February 7, 1978, Declassified Documents Reference Service (hereafter DDRS).

30. Brazinsky, *Nation Building in South Korea,* 230; William H. Gleysteen, *Massive Entanglement, Marginal Influence: Carter and Korea in Crisis* (Washington, D.C.: Brookings Institution Press, 1999), 20–30.

31. *New York Times,* November 3, 1973.

32. *New York Times,* March 11, 1977.

33. Chungso ûi taehan chôngch'aek kwa i e ttarûn taech'aek [Soviet and Chinese policies toward the ROK and the response], file 721.3CP 1974, Foreign Ministry Archive, Seoul.

34. Summary of a meeting between U.S. assistant secretary of state Richard Holbrooke and South Korean foreign minister Park Tong-jin, September 23, 1978, DDRS.

35. Don Oberdorfer, *The Two Koreas: A Contemporary History* (New York, Basic Books, 2002), 158–59.

36. "Secretary's Meeting with Romanian Special Emissary, August 26, 1974," Kissinger Transcripts, Digital National Security Archive (hereafter DNSA).

37. David Rockefeller's Meeting with North Koreans, May 16, 1975, Kissinger Telephone Conversations, DNSA.

38. "Meeting with Anwar Sadat, April 30, 1974," Kissinger Transcripts, DNSA.

39. Brazinsky, *Nation Building in South Korea,* 149.

40. On this phenomenon, see Susan George, *A Fate Worse Than Debt: The World Financial Crisis and the Poor* (New York: Grove Press, 1988).

41. Odd Arne Westad, *The Global Cold War: Third World Interventions and the Making of Our Times* (Cambridge: Cambridge University Press, 2005), 157.

42. Woo, *Race to the Swift,* 148–75.

43. Martin, *Under the Loving Care of the Fatherly Leader,* 154–55.

44. "Stenographic Record of a Conversation between Erich Honecker and Kim Il Sung, May 30, 1984," *Cold War International History Project Bulletin,* issue 14–15.

45. Martin, *Under the Loving Care of the Fatherly Leader,* 154–55.

46. Brazinsky, *Nation Building in South Korea,* 140.

47. China's Policy in North Asia, CIA Research Tool (CREST), National Archives.

48. Jinzhi Liu, *Dangdai Zhonghan guanxi* [Contemporary Sino-Korean relations] (Beijing: Zhongguo she hui ke xue chu ban she, 1998), 148–49.

49. Liu, *Dangdai Zhonghan guanxi,* 156–57.

50. Yan Jingzhe, *Chushi Hanguo* [Stationed in Korea] (Shandong: Shandong daxue chubanshe, 2004), 13–14.

51. Qichen Qian, *Ten Episodes in Chinese Diplomacy* (New York: HarperCollins, 2005), 115–16.

52. Paz Estrella E. Tolentino, *Multinational Corporations: Emergence and Evolution* (New York: Routledge, 2000), 238–56.

53. Andrea Matles Savada and William Shaw, eds., *South Korea: A Country Study* (Washington, D.C.: U.S. Government Printing Office for the Library of Congress, 1990), online version, http://countrystudies.us/south-korea/50.htm.

54. Woo, *Race to the Swift,* 138.

55. Savada and Shaw, *South Korea,* http://countrystudies.us/south-korea/45.htm.

56. Joseph Nye, *The Paradox of American Power* (New York: Oxford University Press, 2002), 8–9.

57. Westad, *Global Cold War,* 335.

58. Bruce Cumings, *Korea's Place in the Sun: A Modern History* (New York: W. W. Norton, 1996), 325.

10. Gorbachev's Policy toward East Asia, 1985–1991

Vladislav Zubok

The end of the Cold War in East Asia occupies a very modest place in the standard histories of Mikhail Gorbachev's foreign policy. Even the Beijing summit of Gorbachev and Deng Xiaoping in May 1989, which put an end to two and half decades of rivalry between the Soviet Union and the People's Republic of China (PRC), was overshadowed by the CNN broadcasts from Tiananmen Square and the suppression of the students' revolt, then by the fall of Communist regimes in Eastern Europe, and finally by the growing chaos and collapse in the Soviet Union. In fact, the perceptions of the media reflected realities. This chapter argues that East Asia always played a secondary role in Gorbachev's ideas of how to end the Cold War. Soviet foreign policy toward East Asia remained much more gradualist and inertial than was suggested by the rhetoric of the "new thinking" on relations with the West. And the most successful of Gorbachev's achievements in East Asia, the reconciliation with the PRC, had only in part to do with the "new thinking" and the grandiose schemes of a new global order. The changes in East Asia in the period 1986–91 were not so much the result of Gorbachev's initiatives and diplomatic engagement; the attitudes and engagement of Gorbachev's negotiating partners played a crucial, perhaps even greater role. Specifically, China's growing flexibility in negotiations with the Kremlin and Japan's continuing rigidity defined the limits of positive international changes in East Asia at the end of the Cold War.

Evaluating the Cold War Legacy

When Gorbachev came to power in March 1985, Soviet foreign policy suffered from a fundamental imbalance. In Europe, the Soviet Union had consolidated its positions in Central and Eastern Europe. These positions, which had been legitimized by the Yalta and Potsdam agreements, seemed to be internationally sanctioned by the treaties of the détente of the 1970s. In Asia, in contrast, the Soviet Union wasted the benefits of the Yalta-Potsdam framework in favor of rapprochement with Communist China and the support of Kim Il Sung during the Korean War. The Sino-Soviet alliance became the centerpiece of Soviet foreign policy toward Asia during the 1950s. Pleasing the Chinese Communist leadership, Moscow froze and sacrificed relations with other countries in East Asia, above all with Japan.

In the 1960s, however, China defected from the Sino-Soviet alliance; instead of following the Soviet example, Mao Zedong wanted to become the world's revolutionary leader. North Korea, alarmed by Khrushchev's de-Stalinization, distanced itself from the Soviet Union. When in 1969 Sino-Soviet friction escalated into the armed clashes on Damanskii/Zhenbao Island, the long border of the Soviet Union from Pamir to Vladivostok became dangerously exposed. Gradually the Soviet Far East, just as during the preparations for a war against Japan in 1932–45, became a heavily militarized frontier area. These Soviet preparations also triggered a Chinese security dilemma. In the years 1971–72, China made a remarkable shift from isolation to a partnership with the United States; and in 1978–79, this partnership began to acquire distinctly military dimensions directed against the USSR. Also, in 1978, Japanese and Chinese leaders signed a treaty with the "anti-hegemonism" clause—apparently directed against the Soviet Union.

Although, in Europe, the détente of the 1970s seemed to alleviate the self-propelling cycle of arms race and mutual fear, in Asia this cycle was in full swing. Vietnam's occupation of Cambodia in 1978 and the Soviet invasion of Afghanistan in 1979 contributed to the vicious circle of war tension in the region. Most Soviet investments in the Far East were linked to military-industrial construction: naval bases in Vladivostok and Petropavlovsk, expensive submarine and longer-range monitoring systems along the Kuril Islands and on Sakhalin Island, directed against the United States but also against China and Japan. China felt encircled by the USSR and its clients, and it advanced three conditions for the normalization of relations: the withdrawal of Soviet troops from Afghanistan; the withdrawal of Vietnamese forces, viewed in Beijing as the Soviet proxy, from Cambodia; and the demilitarization of Mongolia.

In the years 1981–82, Leonid Brezhnev made the first attempts to improve the USSR's relations with China and Japan. These attempts stemmed from Brezhnev's anguish over the collapse of détente and his concerns for security in the Soviet Far East. Yet the other senior Politburo leaders who were managing Soviet foreign affairs under the debilitated Brezhnev had no will for admitting their past mistakes and making diplomatic concessions. Many of their advisers, especially on China and Japan, shared the dug-in-trenches mentality of the Cold War.[1] The passing of the Kremlin's Old Guard and Gorbachev's election as the new general secretary of the Communist Party of the Soviet Union in March 1985 created hopes among the "enlightened" party apparatchiks and sophisticated experts that there would be further and vigorous changes in Soviet policies toward China and Japan. Gorbachev, however, preferred to move cautiously and gradually toward East Asia. Instead, he chose to focus on two other priorities: repairing the détente with Western Europe; and lessening the extremely high level of tension, fueled by the arms race and mutual military posturing, in Soviet-American relations. Gorbachev's first strategic initiative was to cancel further deployment of the SS-20 missiles aimed at Western Europe. In January 1986, two months after the first and inconclusive summit with Ronald Reagan in Geneva, Gorbachev announced a program to achieve a nuclear-free world within fifteen years. The content and propagandist tone of this program indicated that its main target was public opinion in the NATO countries and the U.S. leadership. China's role as a nuclear state was not even mentioned in the program.[2]

In the period 1986–89, Gorbachev remained personally focused primarily on relations with the United States and key Western European countries, with the goal of stopping the dangerous nuclear-strategic arms race. The Kremlin's leader, like Brezhnev, feared nuclear war. Gorbachev and Soviet foreign minister Eduard Shevardnadze attempted to find common ground with Reagan through the "personal diplomacy" of summit meetings, back-channel correspondence, and the like. The available documents reveal no trace of similar energetic engagement by Gorbachev in policymaking toward the East Asian countries. Meanwhile, under Gorbachev, Soviet foreign policy, for all its new spirit and ideas, became even more highly personalized, that is, dependent on personal attention from the general secretary. Gorbachev established good personal relations with Western European leaders (Margaret Thatcher, François Mitterrand, et al.). This personalized European diplomacy helped him to reach out to Reagan. After a few failures, especially after the dramatic summit in Reykjavik in October 1986, Gorbachev succeeded in turning Reagan into his negotiating partner. Both believed in a "nuclear-free world," and the melting of the Cold War ice began. But such personal diplomacy could not be practiced in East Asia. There, in contrast to the West, Gorbachev's dramatic vision, such as a "nuclear-free world," made little impact, and the Kremlin leader faced a long, arduous road in cultivating the leadership of China and Japan.[3]

This did not mean that East Asia was of no concern for Gorbachev. He spoke about it at a closed meeting with Soviet diplomats in late May 1986 at the

Foreign Ministry, where he reminded the diplomats that East Asia and the whole Asia-Pacific region were as vital for the Soviet Union's security as was Europe. He promised to define "a principled line" toward East Asia. Consultations, meetings, and trips should follow.[4] This promise, however, was not backed by any specific plan or progress map for this region. In the absence of anything specific to say, Gorbachev announced: "We consider our [nuclear-free] program as our contribution to the joint search, together with all countries of Asia, of a general aggregate approach to building a system of secure and lasting peace on this continent."[5]

While Gorbachev was busy mending fences with the West, Soviet diplomacy in East Asia proceeded initially as the continuation of the past policy. Still, incremental changes did occur in the decisionmaking cadres and climate. Gone were some senior officials and advisers who had been making Soviet foreign policy in the region, especially toward China. Most important, in 1985 Andrei Gromyko left the Foreign Ministry to become the ceremonial chair of the Supreme Soviet. Oleg Rakhmanin, the top authority on Chinese affairs in the International Department, who for years had treated China as a strategic enemy of the USSR, was criticized and demoted in 1985. In March 1986, Gorbachev sent into retirement Andrei Aleksandrov-Agentov, a foreign policy adviser to the general secretary. New people in the decisionmaking circle included Shevardnadze, who was not constrained by long experience with Cold War battles; and Aleksandr Yakovlev, an innovative thinker and advocate of a multipolar worldview, where Japan and China figured as separate poles of power, along with Western Europe and the United States. Gorbachev's new foreign policy assistant, Anatolii Cherniaev, was an ardent supporter of Soviet openness to the world and a friend of many liberal-minded Moscow think-tankers. With Cherniaev's help, these think-tankers—including Georgii Arbatov, Georgii Shakhnazarov, and Vladislav Dunaev—had access to the general secretary, sharing with Gorbachev their antidogmatic proposals.[6] Equally important were the nominations of new Soviet ambassadors to Japan and China. In May 1986, Oleg Troianovskii—one of the most experienced Soviet diplomats, as a former ambassador in Tokyo and at the United Nations—was sent as the new ambassador to Beijing. And in July 1986, Nikolai N. Soloviev, a professional Japanologist, became the Soviet ambassador in Tokyo. These nominations indicated the Kremlin's desire to learn more about the possible normalization of relations with these countries.

Another new feature in Moscow was Gorbachev's "new thinking," a security philosophy that emphasized human values and common interests, rather than the ideology of class warfare and military preparedness.[7] Gorbachev's views on East Asia went beyond the concerns of his predecessors about security. He admired and envied the economic achievements of Japan, South Korea, and Taiwan that had enabled these nations to make their rapid transitions from industrial to postindustrial economies. He looked at East Asian countries in the context of his own reformist designs, which counted heavily on the scientific-technical revolution and the transformation of Soviet economy in a post-industrial direction. Also, for him—as well as for other Soviet politicians and economists still conditioned by the notions about the historic superiority of socialism over capitalism—these young, dynamic economies presented a challenge, an opportunity to question the old dogmas.[8] In April 1986, Gorbachev said at the Politburo that "the center of development of civilization is shifting toward the Pacific Ocean."[9] In July 1986, after recovering somewhat from the shock and anguish of the Chernobyl nuclear reactor disaster, Gorbachev urged the Politburo again "to focus on Asia." "If the direction of the processes that are going there, especially in great countries, is positive, this would decide the future of the world," he said, adding that Soviet foreign policy should apply new "higher priorities" to the relationships with China, India, and Japan.[10]

The Chernobyl tragedy encouraged Gorbachev to intensify his "peace offensive" toward the United States, and this led to the summit in Reykjavik with Reagan. Also, preparations accelerated for his first trip to the Soviet Far East, for which his advisers prepared a major foreign policy address aimed at the countries of the Asia-Pacific region. On July 29, 1986, he gave an important policy speech in Vladivostok that was notable for its elements of continuity as well as its novel aspects. The continuity was, above all, in the vision of collective security system for the Asia-Pacific area, which had been proclaimed by Brezhnev in 1969 and revived by him in his Tashkent speech in 1982. Unlike Brezhnev, however, Gorbachev acknowledged that the United States should be a major, if not decisive, player in the construction of Asian-Pacific security. This led Tsuyoshi Hasegawa to observe that Gorbachev's speech was "a major departure from the traditional Soviet foreign policy orientation," the first embodiment of the "new-thinking-guided foreign policy in Asia."[11]

All keen observers noticed that the Vladivostok speech contained a major difference in how Gorbachev referred to China. He directly addressed some of the "three conditions" that the Chinese leadership had long linked to the prospect of normalizing relations between the two countries. First, Gorbachev declared that the USSR would reduce troops in Asia by 200,000. Second, he announced a reduction of the Soviet military contingent in Mongolia. And third, he declared a partial withdrawal of Soviet troops (six regiments) from Afghanistan. The speech also contained an important correction in the Soviet position on the Sino-Soviet border dispute, in particular along the River Amur (which opened the way for border negotiations). In contrast, however, Gorbachev's speech contained nothing specific on Japan. He chose not to revive Khrushchev's declaration of 1956 on the possibility of returning two (out of four) disputed islands to Japan. Moreover, Gorbachev did not even mention the problem of the "Northern Territories." It is fair to say that Gorbachev's speech on Japan represented more continuity than change. Not surprisingly, the Vladivostok speech energized Sino-Soviet talks, but it caused widespread disappointment among the foreign policy elite of Japan.

Preferring Beijing to Tokyo

Hiroshi Kimura argues that it was much easier for Gorbachev to fulfill the Chinese "conditions" and to reach compromises with the United States on arms control than to make concessions to Japan.[12] In 1986, however, one could have argued the opposite. Sino-Soviet relations, aside from the territorial dispute, were saddled by other conditions requiring major Soviet military rearrangements, above all the withdrawal of troops from Afghanistan. Soviet-Japanese relations, in comparison, appeared to be all pegged on the single issue of the disputed four islands, and the potential rewards of their return to Japan seemed to be appealing, including the benefits of trade and of the transfer of modern technologies from Japan to the struggling Soviet economy.

There was no lack of proposals to Gorbachev to make a bold move toward Japan by recognizing the territorial dispute. In 1985 Georgii Arbatov, director of the Institute for USA and Canadian Studies, sent him policy memoranda suggesting that the disputed islands should be returned to Japan.[13] Gorbachev's foreign policy assistant, Cherniaev, thought along similar lines. Cherniaev also brought to Gorbachev's attention Vladislav Dunaev, who ardently advocated rapprochement with Japan.[14] Yet in the years 1985–86, Gorbachev did not act on this advice. Nor did he act in 1987–89, when Soviet diplomacy toward the United States and Western Europe was at the peak of flexibility and engagement. The disputed islands remained a taboo topic, and Gorbachev, the only man who could have lifted this taboo, did not do it. Even the boldest "new thinkers" avoided this issue. Aleksandr Yakovlev, Gorbachev's most influential reformist companion at that time, also avoided any discussion of the disputed territories when he met with a high Japanese official in March 1986.[15]

So why was the USSR engaging China but not Japan? Did Gorbachev consider security on the borders with China a more important issue than the issue of economic cooperation with Japan? Or did the advisers who prepared his policies toward East Asia convince him that it would be easier to settle disputes with China than to settle the territorial issue with Japan? It is not easy to answer these questions with certainty. The minutes of Politburo discussions, which are available in the archives of the Gorbachev Foundation, and the memoirs of Soviet officials, which provide an incomplete record, are often vague and garbled because of editing and self-editing. Some tentative answers, however, can be deduced about Gorbachev's vision of the Cold War, as well as about his political manner and personality.

In the world as seen by Gorbachev from the Kremlin, the United States was an absolute focus, and American partners and allies had lesser priorities in Soviet foreign policy. Japan, in the eyes of Gorbachev and other Soviet policymakers, was a permanent and stable ally of the United States, dependent on the U.S. nuclear umbrella and never quite independent from its foreign and security policies. Could there be any guarantees, even if Moscow ceded the disputed islands to Japan, that the Japanese leadership would be able to "pay back" for this act with increased trade and technological transfers, while the Cold War lasted? A scandal flared up in 1987 when the Toshiba Machine Company was blamed for selling the Soviets computer technology in violation of a Western agreement not to sell high-technology equipment to the USSR. This scandal left a very bad impression on the Soviet leadership. Above all, it fed the suspicions that Tokyo was not in control of its own economic and foreign policies.

Also in this light, the idea of "purchasing" Japan's goodwill and hoping that Tokyo would become another intermediary between Moscow and Washington, like London and Paris, was not particularly convincing inside the Kremlin. Japanese opinion on security matters mattered in Washington even less than the opinion of the British, French, and West Germans. Japan eagerly joined the United States–sponsored Strategic Defense Initiative in 1987. The hostility of the Reagan administration toward the USSR in 1986, along with American suspiciousness about Soviet peace approaches to American allies in the West and the East, made it logical for Gorbachev to focus on improving relations directly with Reagan. He could only hope that the thaw in Soviet-American relations would make it easier to later negotiate with Japan, and hope that the Japanese policymakers would not look constantly over their shoulders to see the U.S. reaction.

In contrast, it became increasingly apparent to the "new thinkers" in the Kremlin, including Gorbachev, that China had become the United States' partner only conditionally and only in response to the perceived Soviet military threat during the 1970s. Addressing China's concerns, and thus reducing the tension along 4,000 kilometers of Sino-Soviet borders, not only responded to the USSR's immediate security interests but also promised the future neutrality of the PRC. In fact, Sino-Soviet cross-border trade and economic relations began to revive as early as 1981, and kept growing throughout Gorbachev's first years in power. In 1985, visits by Soviet political emissaries to China (among them was Arbatov) became more frequent. They brought news that the "Middle Kingdom" was changing in a promising direction, leaving behind Mao's legacy of ideological hostility to the USSR.[16] It became obvious for Gorbachev that, with energetic engagement, one could normalize Sino-Soviet relations within a few years, and therefore dramatically change the international environment in East Asia even without U.S. involvement and consent. On the eve of his trip to Vladivostok in July 1986, Gorbachev told a group of advisers (Vadim Medvedev, Yakovlev, Valerii Boldin, and Cherniaev) that "China is a huge problem [for the Soviet Union]. And we should understand the Chinese. They have made a justifiable decision to become one of great powers, and we should not assess this as chauvinism. We feel sympathy for China's plans and are ready to support them on the basis of mutual understanding."[17]

Gorbachev's experience and personality mattered in his foreign policy preferences and moves. His youth coincided with a time of great Sino-Soviet friendship and cooperation, when an entire generation of educated Russians, including Gorbachev, came to view the Chinese as their best friends, as partners forever. Thus the rift between the two Communist giants was a traumatic experience for Gorbachev. He had also personal connections in China: many Chinese students, who were classmates of Gorbachev at Moscow State University in the years 1950–55, began to make careers in the PRC's party and state bureaucracy. Gorbachev, therefore, became gradually personally engaged in restoring relations with China, in repairing the historic links between the two formerly fraternal peoples. In March 1987, he suggested to the Politburo that one should "lure Deng Xiaoping to Moscow," because he believed that a summit meeting would achieve a breakthrough in Sino-Soviet relations.[18] Also, China's search for a new economic model, apparently still within the Communist framework, was resonant with Gorbachev's own dreams of transforming the Soviet model, and this made him even more sympathetic and attentive to the Chinese. In July 1987, he said at the Politburo: "The Chinese road during recent years deserves serious analysis." A few days later, he compared the Chinese reforms to the Soviet New Economic Policy of the 1920s. He noticed, with a touch of envy, that the Chinese leadership had successfully liberated the productive energies of the nation's peasants.[19] All these sentiments translated into a more result-oriented and energetic policy toward China in 1986 and 1987.

In contrast, Gorbachev's generational experience did not spark similar impulses about Japan. The "Northern Territories" raised other emotional undercurrents in Gorbachev, as in many people in his age group: the memories of World War II and the terrible price it exacted from the Russian people. Russian nationalist feelings definitely played a role in Gorbachev's reluctance to cede the disputed islands, even before this issue became public. Gorbachev was, thanks to Dunaev and other "enlightened" advisers, impressed by Japan's economic and technological achievements. Yet, curiously, these impressions did not resonate with him as much as China's economic experiments.

Gorbachev's personality features also may explain his lack of will to approach the Japanese leadership. He could be focused on a few issues in which he strongly believed, such as the need to stop the nuclear arms race and start nuclear disarmament. Yet he was known for delaying and dodging many other decisions on controversial issues. Quite often, as a human being, he revealed a bizarre combination of remarkable optimism and a congenital lack of long-range strategic planning. He was convinced that somehow, in time, "the course of history" would cut the Gordian knots of the past. Domestically, as well as on many foreign policy issues, his actions reflected a drifting, ad hoc approach rather than a well-thought-out strategy and tactics. His favorite phrases included "let the process develop" and "the process of events is on the run." All this led to vague and noncommittal rhetoric that was not followed by actions, and this puzzled and frustrated his Politburo colleagues, his assistants, and his foreign negotiators and guests. Psychologically, his inconsistency and ad-hocism were linked to his extraordinary optimism and naïveté in foreign affairs.[20]

Examples of this ad-hocism and lack of resolve in Gorbachev's foreign policy toward Asia are numerous. Most famously, despite his early realization of the fatal deadlock for the Soviet army in Afghanistan, he allowed the Afghan war to drag on, until the necessities of improving relations with the United States and China, along with growing pressure for domestic reforms and return of the troops, made him set a deadline for withdrawal. The Geneva Agreement for withdrawal was reached in April 1988, and the Soviets began pulling out of Afghanistan in May 1988. A lesser-known example of Gorbachev's ad-hocism in East Asia was Soviet support for Vietnam, despite the evidence of the growing wastefulness of Soviet assistance to that country and the fact that Vietnam's occupation of Cambodia had created one of the "obstacles" for Sino-Soviet relations. Even in his Vladivostok speech, Gorbachev failed to mention the Cambodian question, despite the fact that Deng Xiaoping had made this issue a central question for the normalization of relations. Gorbachev did not want to use Soviet economic leverage to pressure Hanoi to withdraw troops from Cambodia, even though, in 1986–87, the Democratic Republic of Vietnam's leadership kept demanding more economic assistance from Moscow. At the Politburo, Gorbachev was indignant about the Vietnamese policies (just as he was about the situation in Afghanistan), yet his rhetorical outbursts produced no policy decisions.[21] Finally, in May 1988, the leadership in Hanoi decided—presumably on its own, without Soviet pressure—to end the occupation of Cambodia.[22] In July 1988, during talks in Moscow with Nguyen Van Linh, the general secretary of the Communist Party of Vietnam, Gorbachev approved of this move; yet this was not the policy he made.[23]

There was also inconsistency between Gorbachev's increasingly alarmist rhetoric on the Soviet financial difficulties and his policies. In 1987, he came to realize that the USSR might soon slip into a financial crisis. This was at the same time that the price of oil, the main Soviet source of hard currency, fell drastically, and the Soviet trade deficit began to rise steeply.[24] It is tempting to interpret Soviet initiatives, such as reductions of troops in Mongolia and in Afghanistan, as responses to this crisis, yet the existing records do not supply any definitive linkages. Domestically, Gorbachev never developed a consistent plan to deal with the financial crisis, and the Kremlin's lack of imagination and action led later to the financial meltdown.

This ad-hocism and inconsistency contributed to Gorbachev's lack of action on Japan. They were revealed in particular in his discussion of the future of the Soviet Far East, a potential area for economic cooperation with Japan. In June 1986, he told the Politburo on the eve of his trip to Vladivostok that the Soviet economy was "moving to Siberia, to the Far East"—pure wishful thinking. In August 1986, after returning from Vladivostok, he offered at the Politburo to open up this port city to foreign tourism, including Japanese tourists. His colleagues reminded him of many obstacles: the city and the area around it, as well as Sakhalin Island, were a giant complex of military bases, with a high concentration of secret installations.[25] Opening the area to foreign trade would have required major inconveniences for this military-industrial complex, and a possible relocation of naval and military bases, which would have been impossible as long as the USSR and the United States remained engaged in the Cold War. Even in the condition of the Soviet-American détente, the demilitarization and opening of the Soviet Far East could have been done only very gradually, and with a great investment of money, human resources, and attention from the Kremlin.[26] In 1986, however, Gorbachev dropped the issue without making any decisions. In 1988, Gorbachev again raised at the Politburo the possibility (referring to his conversations with Japanese prime minister Nakasone Yasuhiro in Moscow the previous year) of building a tourist infrastructure in the Far East, thereby creating an area of overlapping human and economic interests with Japan.[27] And again, no specific measures were discussed, and no policy decisions were made. Vladivostok and Sakhalin Island remained forbidden zones until the end of Gorbachev's tenure, when the Soviet Union collapsed.

Gorbachev's main interests in working toward a breakthrough in relations with Japan were economic and financial. His dreams of perestroika, driven by new technologies and the scientific-technical revolutions, nourished his interest in the Japanese "economic miracle." For instance, in the spring of 1986, at the Politburo, he cited Japanese automated plants in his conversations with Soviet managers: "The Japanese have built a plant to produce underwear, and it is an automated plant. A total of 600 workers produce 600 million items. And in our industry, we need 900,000 workers to produce the same amount."[28] But yet again, his rhetoric in this case was not matched with consistent thinking, planning, and actions. His awareness of the Japanese economic miracle failed to push him in the years 1986–88 to reenergize Soviet foreign policy toward Japan. The issue of Soviet-Japanese relations was never linked to discussions of Soviet domestic economic and financial issues. And there is no specific evidence, including in the reminiscences of Cherniaev, that the USSR's financial crisis activated Gorbachev's thinking about how to use the "Northern Territories" as a bargaining chip with a possibility of getting Japanese loans and economic assistance.

Normalization of the USSR's Relations with China

Ambiguity, and a lack of consistency between the Politburo-level rhetoric of Gorbachev and his practical policymaking, could be found in the years 1986–87 even with regard to China. Speaking to his advisers in September 1986, during the preparations for the Reykjavik summit with Reagan, he referred to China's "obstacles" to the normalization of Sino-Soviet relations as "artificially conceived." Repeating the "old thinking" line, he said that it was simply in China's interest to remain in conflict with the Soviet Union and receive American assistance, including the military and other technology that remained off limits for the Warsaw Pact countries. Gorbachev mentioned with irritation that the East German leader, Erich Honecker, had established separate and quite successful diplomatic and economic relations with the PRC. Yet, at the same time, the USSR's border negotiations with the PRC resumed in October 1986.[29] This inconsistency was not warranted by any conceivable need to maneuver between "the hawks" and "the doves"; there was a consensus on improving relations with China.

The crucial factor that neutralized Gorbachev's inconsistency was the growing political consensus in Beijing to shift from the ideologically driven anti-Soviet stance to a pragmatic foreign policy. In the years 1987–88, Soviet diplomats found a gradual change of opinions, more and more favoring the normalization of Sino-Soviet relations. Ambassador Troianovskii's reports from Beijing to Moscow are still classified, and we cannot analyze them. His memoirs, however, suggest that he was quick to discover that there was a potential for reaching out to the Chinese leadership; many of them had studied in the Soviet Union in the 1950s and respected Russian culture.[30] At that time, the Chinese leadership, with Deng Xiaoping in the position of senior leader, began to reassess its previous policy of rapprochement with the United States against the Soviet Union in favor of a balance-of-power approach. Although the Chinese continued to adhere to their "conditions," their pragmatic interests dictated an unfreezing of Soviet-Chinese relations.

This thaw in Sino-Soviet relations created an unmistakable positive momentum, and Gorbachev responded to this by investing more attention and political capital. In September 1988, he made another programmatic speech in Krasnoyarsk in which he addressed, among other issues, Chinese territorial concerns. By that time, the withdrawal of Vietnamese troops from Cambodia had cleared the obstacles for the normalization of Sino-Soviet relations. At the end of 1988, China's foreign minister, Jiang Xicheng, met Gorbachev in Moscow. Jiang was the first Chinese foreign minister to visit Moscow since Zhou Enlai in November 1964, and he prepared the ground for the Beijing summit. Jiang officially invited the Soviet leader to visit Beijing. He emphasized that Gorbachev's meeting with Deng Xiaoping would seal the formal process of normalizing Sino-Soviet relations. Then, to continue preparation for the summit, in February 1989 Foreign Minister Shevardnadze went to Beijing, where he and other Soviet visitors were greatly impressed by Deng's personality.

At the time of preparations for the Beijing summit, Gorbachev was moving toward the peak of his international reputation. The Sino-Soviet talks proceeded against the background of the impressive successes of Gorbachev's foreign policy toward the United States and Western Europe. At the end of 1988, Gorbachev addressed the United Nations, outlining his dramatic vision of the "common European house," the convergence of opposing political blocs, and disarmament and the renunciation of force in international relations. All these developments set the stage for truly revolutionary foreign policy departures in relations with Western powers, and the peaceful democratic revolutions in Central and Eastern Europe.[31] Gorbachev, acting from the vantage point of his growing global fame, decided that he would pay homage to the Chinese leader's seniority and come to see him as a junior politician. This gesture, of course, had a tremendous meaning against the background of previous Sino-Soviet relations—first the personal jockeying between Stalin and Mao, and then between Mao and Khrushchev. This time, however, it was not about seniority in the Communist camp or the international Communist movement. As Troianovskii recalled, the agreement on the date for Gorbachev's visit to Beijing to see Deng, May 1989, was reached only after the Chinese negotiators became convinced that no further concessions could be gained, above all on the issue of Cambodia.[32]

An important aspect of the Sino-Soviet talks was the territorial issue, which was especially sensitive given the memories of the bloody border conflicts of 1969. The Chinese raised it as one of their "conditions" for the normalization of relations. At the Politburo meeting after Shevardnadze's visit to Beijing in February 1989, the Soviet foreign minister explained that the Chinese had presented him with more conditions and proposed to have a trade-off: The Soviet Union would concede to the PRC a territory in the Khabarovsk region in exchange for 27,000 square miles in the Pamir region. Gorbachev responded that the Chinese had noted about "five obstacles" to the summit: "Let them. We will not make any excuses."[33] In the subsequent negotiations, the Chinese side continued to bargain very hard on the border issue. The official Chinese position included a thesis that in the nineteenth century, when China was weak, Tsarist Russia seized 1.5 million square kilometers of Chinese land under the "unequal treaties" of 1858–60. At the same time, the Chinese were flexible enough to grant some, rather symbolic, territorial concessions to the Soviets in exchange. Later, in 1989, when the Soviet Union withdrew from Afghanistan and began to lose its outer empire in Central Europe, and when the Baltic states and Georgia threatened secession, the very discussion of making territorial concessions became increasingly sensitive. Gorbachev's foreign policy assistant, Cherniaev, recalled that in October 1989, Gorbachev emotionally raised "the Russian question" at the Politburo in light of the directives to the deputy foreign minister, Igor Rogachev, who had conducted the border talks with the Chinese.[34] By that time, however, the talks with the PRC had already resolved major territorial disagreements, and had acquired a positive momentum of their own.

Gorbachev's visit to the PRC on May 15–18, 1989, took place at a dramatic moment in the internal politics of both countries. Gorbachev was getting ready for the decisive Congress of People's Deputies, in the context of the increasingly radicalized and fractured political situation in the Soviet Union. There were secessionist movements in the Baltic republics, the anti-Russian uprising in Georgia, and the escalating conflict between the Azeris and Armenians in Nagornyi Karabakh. At that moment, Gorbachev's foreign policy assistant, Cherniaev, felt that Gorbachev was losing control over the situation, and that his reforms would result in the collapse of the state and chaos. Cherniaev wrote about the disintegration of the economy, the Communist Party, and the Soviet "empire" itself.[35] And then, to everybody's surprise, Gorbachev's visit to China coincided with the most acute political crisis in China's history since the Great Proletarian Cultural Revolution. The students' demonstrations, culminating in the sit-ins on Tiananmen Square, embarrassed both the Chinese leadership and the Soviet visitors. Troianovskii recalled that there were "extremists" among Gorbachev's advisers who wanted him to go to meet the students. The stakes of the summit, however, were too high to jeopardize it with populist gestures.[36]

One can even speculate that the fixation of both leaders, Gorbachev and Deng, on domestic instability and reforms might have facilitated the summit, by distracting them from past disagreements and making them focus on the present and future. Both leaders had a big personal stake in bringing the summit to a successful conclusion. At the summit, Deng raised the issue of the "unequal treaties," but he graciously discounted them, suggesting that they should look into the future and not to be hobbled by the past.

The normalization of Sino-Soviet relations was a lasting achievement of Gorbachev's foreign policy, the outcome of many years of painstaking diplomatic efforts that had begun in 1981–82 under Brezhnev. The roles of Gorbachev's leadership and his "new thinking" were important, but more crucial were the end of the power struggle in the Chinese leadership and the consolidation of power in the hands of Deng, who decided to embark on pragmatic economic reforms and on an equally pragmatic foreign policy. This new course resulted in the rapid decline of the ideological anti-Soviet motive in China's foreign policy. Both sides negotiated from a position of state interests, but with the political will to settle the existing disputes. In the opinion of Troianovskii, Gorbachev and Shevardnadze were justifiably criticized for making concessions to the United States and West Germany in the years 1989–90. At the same time, he maintains, in their policy toward China, they "made no serious mistakes, and achieved an obvious success." The breakthrough in Beijing began the process of dismantling the second Cold War front line. And it removed the possibility and temptation for other great powers to regard the PRC as a card to be played in geopolitical combinations, primarily against the Soviet Union and then Russia.[37]

Anybody who wondered, then and later, why Gorbachev did not support the students seeking democratic reforms on Tiananmen Square misunderstood the nature of his leadership—which combined the evolving principles of the "new thinking" with vacillation and ad-hocism as far as specific decisionmaking, and especially the implementation of controversial policies, was concerned. His line with regard to the controversial developments in the Eastern European countries, the members of the Warsaw Pact Organization, was complete noninterference. Seen in this light, his refusal to meet the Chinese students should not be surprising. At the same time, though the Tiananmen events helped Gorbachev in his talks with the Chinese leadership, they also affected the developments in Eastern Europe and the Soviet Union itself. Until July and August

1989 many, especially in Poland, feared that the Soviets could repeat the "Tiananmen bloodbath." President George H. W. Bush was especially concerned, and he repeatedly warned Polish and Hungarian dissidents not to push the envelope too much. Yet Gorbachev's behavior, especially his triumphal tour of Europe and speech in Strasbourg, convinced everyone that he would never spill blood to save the Soviet empire and state. This conviction led to a succession of peaceful (with the exception of Romania) revolutions in Eastern Europe, created a wave of secessionist nationalism in the Baltics and the South Caucasus, and produced labor unrest and mass demonstrations in Russia, the core republic of the Soviet Union.

Deadlock with Japan

Gorbachev's trip to Japan was planned, but then postponed, for years. One reason for these delays was his inability to focus on the reappraisal of Soviet-Japanese relations. His personal inhibitions and reluctance to address the issue of the "Northern Territories" indicated the limits of the "new thinking." Fragmentary minutes of the Politburo discussions reveal that Gorbachev periodically returned to the deadlock in Soviet-Japanese relations, as if regretting it. At the meeting of the Politburo on August 6, 1987, he acknowledged that the impasse was "to the satisfaction of China and the USA." At the same time, he did not want to go to Tokyo without guarantees for a productive summit. He was thinking aloud that "any Japanese government would raise the territorial issue." And he did not want to make the first symbolic step of allowing the Japanese to visit the disputed islands: "They would see our missiles there! We cannot admit any equal rights over there. And we also have our national interests." He ended by inviting everybody to "keep thinking" on the issue and promised "to return to this problem in the light of future developments."[38] This quotation demonstrates that his thinking about Japan vacillated. He respected Japan as an economic power, and he listened to Cherniaev and Dunaev, who expressed admiration for Japanese culture and achievements. Yet, as long as the Cold War lasted, he continued to regard Japan as a loyal U.S. ally, through the prism of Soviet security concerns. He seemed to wait for the changes in the international environment, and above all for a rapprochement with the United States, before dealing with the issue of the disputed islands.

The Japanese political leadership, and especially Japan's Foreign Ministry, also decided to wait, seemingly under the impression that their negotiating position would grow stronger, as Soviet domestic problems and political turmoil were growing more visible. In Japan, the issue of the disputed islands was linked for years to domestic politics and nationalistic propaganda. And so, instead of the quid pro quo mode and back-channel diplomacy, the Foreign Ministry bureaucracy persisted in its all-or-nothing approach.[39]

The factor of timing turned out to be crucial. The best time for changing the climate and content of Soviet-Japanese relations was missed in the years 1986–88. If Japanese politicians at that time had made a principled decision to decouple the territorial dispute from the issue of normalizing relations, Gorbachev might have obtained the incentive—which otherwise was lacking—to proceed with the gradual demilitarization of the Russian Far East, including Sakhalin Island and the disputed islands. Then visits by the Japanese to the "Northern Territories" could have taken place, and options of "free economic zones" for Japanese businesses could have been discussed. Starting in the summer of 1988, however, an avalanche of rapid and unforeseen developments changed the international world system and began to diminish Gorbachev's power. Above all, the Communist regimes in Eastern Europe began to collapse one by one, and the Soviet Union lost its dominant geopolitical position in Central Europe. Gorbachev's expectations that he would have more time to reach an agreement with the administration of George H. W. Bush were shattered. Instead of working with Gorbachev on global security arrangements to end the Cold War, the Americans took a long "pause," watching with apprehension, but also satisfaction, as the ramparts of Soviet power crumbled. And meanwhile, inside the Soviet Union, Gorbachev launched radical political reforms, eroding the Communist Party's monopoly on political and economic power. This led to ethnic violence in the South Caucasus, the secession movement in the Baltic republics, economic chaos, and then the disintegration of economic life. The state's financial crisis escalated tremendously, because of a number of erroneous policies and often a lack of drastic austerity measures. The trickle of concealed criticism of Gorbachev's leadership in Soviet politics and society became a raging storm.

At the end of 1989, various political forces—including nationalists, an impatient intelligentsia, disgruntled miners and workers, environmental movements, the military, and Russo-centric Soviet conservatives within the Communist Party—began to attack Gorbachev and call for his resignation. He still retained complete control over foreign policy decisionmaking, but the domestic crisis increasingly distracted him, delaying important deliberations and decisions. Although he assumed the new title of president of the USSR, his freedom in foreign policymaking shrank, reflecting both the weakness of the Soviet Union abroad and the increasing criticism at home.

Gorbachev's visit to Japan in April 1991 took place at just the time when his power and prestige were in steep decline inside the Soviet Union, and visibly on the wane internationally. In January, his authority had been badly bruised when Soviet paratroopers used force in the Baltics, which led to civilian casualties. His plans to chair the transition from the USSR to the confederation of sovereign states were dashed by the growing ambitions of Boris Yeltsin, who in March was elected president of the Russian Federation. And one by one, the members of Gorbachev's team, including Yakovlev and Arbatov, defected, resigned, or even joined the chorus of his critics. Shevardnadze left the team in the most dramatically public way, at the session of the Congress of People's Deputies, in the presence of television cameras. In the international arena, the outbreak of war in Iraq, where the United States had ignored the advice of its "best friend" Gorbachev and acted in its own interests, left the Soviet leader under the impression that his pet project, the common European house, had in reality turned out to be an American-dominated world.[40]

Thus, in the spring of 1991, Gorbachev was no longer as omnipotent a foreign policy decisionmaker as he had been in 1989. He had spent most of his political capital at home in the debates on the political transformation of the Soviet Union. Above all, he desperately needed an international financial package to postpone the bankruptcy of the Soviet state. Since early 1990, he had become the world's most prominent beggar, arguing that urgent financial assistance to the Soviet Union was imperative for international peace. His big gamble, conceived in April 1991, was that the World Bank and the International Monetary Fund, along with the leaders of the wealthy great powers, would provide an analogue of the Marshall Plan for the USSR, in an amount up to $150 billion. Japan, along with West Germany, was the most important creditor nation at this time, and its position was crucial to ensure the success of this project.[41]

At that time, Japan was in a better position to show generosity to the USSR and delink the issue of loans and assistance from the territorial question. At a meeting in Moscow in March 1991, an immediate prequel to the Soviet-Japanese summit, Gorbachev hinted in vague but understandable terms to the powerful leader of Japan's Liberal Democratic Party, Ozawa Ichiro, that there should be a mutual effort to overcome the deadlock: "My time will soon be up. Yet I have not done anything for Soviet-Japanese relations." Then Gorbachev made an intriguing comparison of the Japanese-Soviet case with Soviet-German relations in 1989–90. The solution of the disputes, he said, should emerge in "the course of historical development." In other words, first there would be a new "atmosphere"—human contacts, exchanges, and economic and technological cooperation. Then a compromise would emerge "naturally." Gorbachev did not mention it, but it was obvious in the context of the "Soviet-German scenario," that at the end of this "course of historical development," it would be conceivable to return the four disputed islands to Japan. The Japanese politician, however, insisted on the articulation of Gorbachev's intentions before or during his visit to Japan. Gorbachev patiently repeated his "philosophy" and refused to talk about the territorial dispute. When Ozawa, rather crudely, hinted at a quid pro quo (you would give us the islands; we would provide economic assistance), the Soviet leader refused to take the bait. Gorbachev told Cherniaev privately: "I am not convinced if we should return the islands or not."[42]

Despite the efforts of his "enlightened" advisers, including Cherniaev and Dunaev, Gorbachev approached the summit without a "concept" of normalizing Soviet-Japanese relations. On March 24, 1991, he held a meeting on Japan with his "inner circle," which included Yakovlev and Boldin; the new foreign minister, Alexander Bessmertnykh, and his deputy, Igor Rogachev; Evgenii Primakov; Valentin Falin; and Cherniaev. The position of the Foreign Ministry was to return to the formula of 1956, that is, the concession of two islands. Cherniaev, according to his own notes, was against half measures: "The islands should be returned, sooner or later. Timing is the only issue." Cherniaev admitted that, in contrast to Yeltsin, any territorial concession made by Gorbachev would invoke a protest as signifying "the destruction of the empire." Still, he hoped that Gorbachev would bite the bullet. To his frustration, Gorbachev's response was: "I would be glad to concede this mission to Yeltsin." According to Cherniaev, Gorbachev was no longer in the saddle of history; he had "decided against ceding the islands and [was prepared] to beat around the bush at the summit."[43] The Japanese side also seemed to have had no concept of normalization, and preferred to haggle interminably over minutiae rather than offer ways out of the impasse. In the absence of a principled understanding on the nature of the compromise on either Gorbachev's or the Japanese side, the summit in April 1991 failed to break the old impasse and was fruitless. During the lengthy talks with Prime Minister Kaifu Toshiki in Tokyo, the negotiations never got beyond a conversation about the recognition or nonrecognition of the 1956 declaration about two islands.

Most Japanese scholars point the finger at Moscow as the main cause of the summit's failure. Tsuyoshi Hasegawa disagrees. He believes that the main reason for the failure was Japanese inflexibility, not Gorbachev's inability to accept the compromise.[44] Cherniaev, who provides most of the specific evidence on the Soviet side, argues that both sides should be reproached. Though recognizing Gorbachev's lack of resolve, he also believes that Japan's linkage between the disputed islands issue and the normalization of relations was the main cause of the deadlock. He hints that the Japanese missed several opportunities to make a compromise deal with Gorbachev. And he believes that April

1991 was a missed chance because of the lack of resolve and imagination on both sides.[45]

It is instructive to return to the comparison between the cases of Japan and Germany made by Gorbachev during the talks with Ozawa. A scholar of Chinese politics, Lowell Dittmer, wonders: "It is ironic that at the time when Moscow was prepared to tolerate the defection of Eastern Europe, the reunification of Russia's historical nemesis Germany, the collapse of the Warsaw Pact and the disintegration of the Soviet Union, it would be unable to countenance the loss of four tiny, sparsely inhabited islands."[46] However, it seems that Gorbachev and the Japanese politicians understood the lessons of the end of the Cold War in the West, including German reunification, from opposite perspectives. For the Japanese policymakers and diplomats, as well as Dittmer, Gorbachev's indecision was a great surprise. They assumed that the Soviet Union had clearly "lost" the Cold War in Europe. They also assumed that Gorbachev desperately needed international loans. On the basis of these two assumptions, they expected the linkage between international assistance and territorial concessions to work. But from Gorbachev's perspective, he was under attack from Yeltsin and the Russian nationalists, and thus could not "give away" the islands obtained during World War II. In Gorbachev's view, Eastern Europe and East Germany belonged to the Eastern Europeans and Germans, and the disputed territories belonged to the Russians. The dogged insistence of the Japanese that the USSR come up with a specific timetable for the solution of the "territorial dispute" put Gorbachev on guard. It reminded him of West German chancellor Helmut Kohl's "ten points" at the end of 1989—the U.S.-backed West German policy that took advantage of the Soviets' weakening hand to accelerate the dismantling of East Germany.[47]

Gorbachev's lack of consistency, his penchant for procrastination, and his adhocism contributed to the lost opportunities of the 1986–91 period in Soviet-Japanese relations. At the same time, the history of those years contains remarkable instances when Gorbachev's partners heeded the same qualities of the Soviet leader and thus obtained what they wanted and reached mutual understandings with him. For instance, Kohl was initially wrong in assessing Gorbachev and the meaning of his policies, and thus Soviet–West German relations remained frozen in the years 1985–88. At the end of 1988, however, Kohl realized his error and adroitly took advantage of the revolutionary changes. He took the initiative to establish friendly personal relations with Gorbachev, offering support to the Soviet leader's European project and promising economic and financial assistance. During the Soviet–West German talks of 1988–90, Kohl successfully managed Gorbachev's insecurity and fears, awakened by the rapid changes in East Germany and by its rapid takeover by West Germany. Kohl understood very well Gorbachev's ability to change his positions ad hoc and admit "new realities," and he made good use of this factor.

In another notable case, the leadership of South Korea took advantage of Gorbachev's style of statesmanship to normalize relations with the Soviet Union and gain UN membership. At the time, South Korea acted energetically to activate nondiplomatic exchanges and contacts with the Soviet Union, while Japan waited on the sidelines. South Korea opened its trade office in Moscow in July 1989, shortly after the Soviet trade office opened in Seoul. South Korean businessmen were quick to come to Moscow and explore the new opportunities opening in the chaotic climate of perestroika. Representatives of the big companies (Daewoo, Sunkyond, and Lucky-Goldstar) found a common language with Soviet economic bureaucrats and managers. And the South Korean president, Roh Tae Woo, like Kohl, realized that he had a unique opportunity to strike a deal with Gorbachev. He used various informal means and messengers to signal to the Kremlin his intention to achieve a breakthrough in Soviet-Korean relations.[48] Initially, Gorbachev and Shevardnadze were reluctant to grant recognition to South Korea, because it meant a "betrayal" of North Korea. Yet the growing Soviet–South Korean economic engagement and, above all, the South Koreans' unflagging activism won the day. In June 1990, as a result of an informal prearrangement, Roh Tae Woo and Gorbachev met informally in San Francisco, during Gorbachev's official visit to the United States. This paved the way for an official restoration of relations between the two countries during Gorbachev's visit to South Korea in April 1991, coming in the wake of his visit to Japan. Roh Tae Woo, who was later indicted for corruption, approached Gorbachev as a car dealer approaches his best client. The Soviet leader, dispirited by the petty haggling and lack of results in Tokyo, was pleased by Roh Tae Woo's sweeping promises of future cooperation, including a $3 billion immediate financial loan, no strings attached. During the negotiations among representatives of various industries, there was talk about "grandiose projects on gas and oil." These sweeping projects never materialized, but the South Korean leader got what he wanted, and Gorbachev could report back home about a rare foreign policy success. In the process, Gorbachev ignored the interests of North Korea and dismissed the strident objections of North Korean diplomats. It was, in a word, another instance of Gorbachev's ad-hocism and his ability to acknowledge "new realities," when they were generated by the energy from the other side.[49]

Returning to Japan, it is obvious that the Japanese policymakers failed where the West Germans and South Koreans had succeeded. Japan's intransigence made it impossible for Gorbachev (and later Yeltsin) to come up with a gradual demilitarization and opening of the disputed islands for the Japanese, an indispensable precondition for later territorial concessions. In the years 1988–91, it was quite possible to visualize, as a counterfactual, a gradual development in this direction, simultaneous with the ending of the Cold War in the West. But the Japanese tactics of waiting in 1988–91, instead of engaging Gorbachev with generous promises of cooperation and assistance, were wrong. And Japan's expectation that it could wring territorial concessions from the politically weakened Gorbachev in the spring of 1991 was insensitive psychologically. These tactics contrasted with China's flexible policy of not making the territorial resolution a precondition for normalizing relations. Only in March and April 1991 could Gorbachev and the new leadership of the Foreign Ministry come up with the midway concessions to Japan based on the 1956 declaration. But this was too little too late. Even these concessions made Gorbachev vulnerable to Yeltsin's criticism, and the two islands were not enough for the Japanese side.[50] The territorial dispute was passed on to Gorbachev's successors, who never gained the power and freedom of action that he had possessed as the last general secretary of the Soviet Union's Communist Party.

Conclusion

In East Asia, Gorbachev's lasting achievement and contribution to Soviet (now Russian) security and international peace were the rapprochement with China, solidified by the successful summit in Beijing in May 1989 and by border negotiations. The rest of the record is less cheerful. Gorbachev's procrastination contributed to Russia's lasting tension with Japan. And his last-minute, ad hoc recognition of South Korea failed to contribute to overall stability and peace on the Korean Peninsula. This recognition, one might argue, only embittered North Korea, which had now been isolated and "betrayed" by its northern ally. Gorbachev also failed to achieve a basic understanding with the United States on Asian security.

As this chapter has explained, Gorbachev and Shevardnadze could not be held as the only parties responsible for these singular failures. The lack of interest from the Reagan and Bush administrations and Japan's lack of flexibility should be regarded as equally important, if not more important, causes for the continuing tensions and impasses. At the same time, the new archival evidence and greater focus on the Soviet side given here allow us to better understand the extent of Soviet responsibility. First of all, and contrary to Gorbachev's general declarations of the years 1986–87, East Asia and the larger Asia-Pacific region did not turn into the focus of Soviet foreign policy—with the significant exception of China. The lion's share of the time, discussions, and practical efforts of Gorbachev, Shevardnadze, and other Soviet foreign policy actors were focused on the West, especially the arms control negotiations with the United States. Second, as with his foreign policy in Europe, Gorbachev lacked a consistent and comprehensive concept for his foreign policy in East Asia. In Europe, while active in engaging the NATO countries, he was remarkably inertial and inactive with regard to the Eastern European countries that belonged to the Warsaw Pact. In a similar manner, in East Asia his foreign policy was active with regard to China, while procrastinating on Japan and the larger regional security context. His foreign policy thus remained to the end a mixture of a grand vision of the "new thinking," procrastination and inertia, and miscalculation on the timing and tempo of changes.

Overall, the outcomes of Soviet foreign policy in East Asia point more to continuity than to a decisive break with the previous years of "stagnation." The "new thinking" had a marginal practical effect on the negotiations in East Asia, while security concerns and ad hoc arrangements, strongly linked to Gorbachev's personal predilections, mattered more than ideas and concepts. All this provides material for a critical reappraisal of the motives and dynamics of Gorbachev's foreign policy at the end of the Cold War.

Notes

1. See, e.g., the discussion at the Politburo initiated by Brezhnev on September 11, 1982 recounted by A. Cherniaev, *Sovmestnyi iskhod: Dnevnik dvukh epoch, 1972–1991 gody* [A joint exodus: A diary of two epochs] (Moscow: Rosspen, 2008), 503.
2. M. S. Gorbachev, *Gody trudnykh reshenii: Izbrannoe, 1985–1992* [The years of difficult decisions: Selected works, 1985–1992] (Moscow: Alfa-Print, 1993), 36–42.
3. Tsuyoshi Hasegawa, *The Northern Territories Dispute and Russo-Japanese Relations,* vol. 1, *Between War and Peace, 1697–1985* (Berkeley: International and Area Studies, University of California, 1998), 247–48; Anatolii S. Cherniaev, *Shest' let s Gorbachevym: Po dnevnikovym zapisiam* [Six years with Gorbachev: From the diary] (Moscow: Progress-Kul'tura, 1993), 92.
4. Gorbachev, *Gody trudnykh reshenii,* 48–9.
5. Ibid, 42.
6. On the circumstances of Rakhmanin's demotion, see Cherniaev, *Shest' let,* 49–51.
7. See more as given by Robert D. English, *Russia and the Idea of the West: Gorbachev, Intellectuals and the End of the Cold War* (New York: Columbia University Press, 2000).
8. Hasegawa, *Northern Territories Dispute;* Hiroshi Kimura, *Japanese-Russian Relations under Gorbachev and Yeltsin* (Armonk, N.Y.: M. E. Sharpe, 2000), vol. 2, 59–64.
9. *V Politbiuro TsK KPSS: Po zapisiam Anatolia Cherniaeva, Vadima Medvedeva, Georgiia Shakhnazarova (1985–1991)* [Inside the Politburo: Notes by Anatoly Cherniaev, Vadim Medvedev, and Georgy Shakhnazarov (1985–1991)] (Moscow: Alpina Biznes Books, 2006), 37, 54.

10. Ibid., 72.
11. Hasegawa, *Northern Territories Dispute,* 246.
12. Kimura, *Japanese-Russian Relations,* 98.
13. On Arbatov's memorandum, see Cherniaev, *Sovmestnyi iskhod,* 619.
14. On Gorbachev's interest in Arbatov's memorandum, see Cherniaev's notes of Gorbachev, "O ramkakh vystupleniia vo Vladivostoke" [About the framework of the Vladivostok speech], Gorbachev Fond, opis' 2, delo 1, leto 1986, listy 2–9.
15. "Zapis besedy A. N. Iakovleva s otvetstvennym sekretarem Soveta po problemam natsional'noi bezopasnosti Iaponii I. Suetsugu, 28 marta 1986 g." [Memorandum of conversation of A. N. Yakovlev with Secretary of the National Security Council of Japan I. Suetsugu], in *Aleksandr Iakovlev: Perestroika: 1985–1991—Neizdannoie, maloizvestnoe, zabytoe* [Aleksandr Yakovlev: Perestroika, 1985–1991—Unpublished, little known, and forgotten works], ed. A. A.Iakovlev (Moscow: Mezhdunarodnyi fond Demokratiia, 2008), 38–41.
16. Cherniaev's diary for November 9, 1985, in *Sovmestnyi iskhod,* 653.
17. Cherniaev's diary for July 16, 1985, in ibid., 694.
18. *V Politbiuro,* 152.
19. The minutes from the session of Politburo on July 16 and July 23, 1987, in *V Politbiuro,* 208, 211. Cherniaev's diary for November 12, 1987 in *Sovmestnyi iskhod,* 734.
20. See Vladislav Zubok, "Gorbachev and the End of the Cold War: Perspectives on History and Personality," *Cold War History* 2, no. 2 (January 2002): 61–100; and Vladislav Zubok, *A Failed Empire: The Soviet Union in the Cold War from Stalin to Gorbachev* (Chapel Hill: University of North Carolina Press, 2008), 311–15.
21. The minutes from the session of the Politburo on March 26, 1987, *V Politbiuro,* 161–62.
22. Oleg Troianovskii, *Cherez gody i rasstoniania: Istoria odnoi sem'i* [Across years and distances: A story of a family] (Moscow: Vagrius, 1997), 362.
23. The minutes of Gorbachev's talks with Nguyen Van Linh, taken by Vadim Medvedev, July 20, 1988, on file at the National Security Archive and in the personal archive of the author.
24. The Politbiuro meeting on July 24, 1986, *V Politbiuro,* 75.
25. On the Politburo discussion regarding Vladivostok, see V. I. Vorotnikov, *A bylo eto tak . . . Iz dnevnika chlena Politbiuro TsK KPSS* [And so it happened . . . From the Diary of a Politburo member], 2nd ed. (Moscow: Kniga i biznes, 2003), 128.
26. Hasegawa, *Northern Territories Dispute,* 269–70.
27. From Anatolii Cherniaev, "Poslednii zarubezhnyi ofitsial'nyi vizit M. S.Gorbacheva v kachestve prezidenta SSSR" [The last official foreign trip of M. S. Gorbachev in his capacity as the president of the USSR], the chapter written for the Japanese edition of Cherniaev's *Six Years with Gorbachev.* The Russian version of this chapter was graciously provided by Cherniaev to David Wolff and Vladislav Zubok.
28. *V Politbiuro,* 37, 54.
29. The diary of Anatolii Cherniaev, September 29, 1986, the copy on file at the National Security Archive, Washington, and in the personal archive of the author.
30. Troianovskii, *Cherez gody,* 344–45.
31. See Zubok, *Failed Empire,* chap. 9; Egor Gaidar, *Gibel Imperii: Uroki dlia sovremennoi Rossii* [The collapse of the Empire: Lessons for contemporary Russia]

(Moscow: Rosspen, 2006), and English version, *Collapse of an Empire: Lessons for Modern Russia* (Washington, D.C.: Brookings Institution Press, 2007); and Archie Brown, *Seven Years That Changed the World: Perestroika in Perspective* (New York: Oxford University Press, 2007).

32. Troianovskii, *Cherez gody,* 357, 369.

33. The minutes of the Politburo for February 16, 1989, *V Politburo,* 451.

34. Cherniaev's diary, October 15, 1989, on file at the National Security Archive.

35. Anatolii Cherniaev, *1991 goda: Dnevnik pomoshnika prezidenta SSSR* [The year 1991: The diary of an assistant of the president of the USSR] (Moscow: Terra, 1997), 16–17.

36. Troianovskii, *Cherez gody,* 372, 373.

37. Ibid., 376.

38. *V Politbiuro,* 217; the phase on the visits and the missiles is absent in the published version and can be found in the diary of Cherniaev, August 6, 1987, on file at the National Security Archive.

39. Hasegawa, *Northern Territories Dispute;* Semyon Verbitsky, "Perceptions of Japan in the USSR during the Cold War and Perestroika," and G. Rozman, "Russia and Japan: Mutual Misperceptions, 1992–1999," in *Misperceptions Between Japan and Russia,* Carl Beck Paper 1503, ed. S. Verbitsky, Ts. Hasegawa, and G. Rozman (Pittsburgh: Center for Russian and East European Studies, University of Pittsburgh, 2000), 5–41, 42–69, 70–86.

40. Cherniaev, *Shest' let,* 420–22; telephone conversation of Gorbachev with G. W. Bush, January 18, 1991, in *V Politbiuro,* 644–648; Timothy J. Colton, *Yeltsin. A Life* (New York: Basic Books, 2008), chap. 8.

41. Cherniaev, *1991 god,* 139; Graham Allison and Grigori Yavlinsky, *Window of Opportunity: The Grand Bargain for Democracy in the Soviet Union* (New York: Pantheon, 1991).

42. Cherniaev, "Poslednii zarubezhnyi ofitsial'nyi vizit."

43. Cherniaev's diary, March 20 and 24, 1991, in *Sovmestnyi iskhod,* 930.

44. Kimura, *Japanese-Russian Relations,* 87, 96; Hasegawa, *Northern Territories Dispute,* 538–39.

45. Cherniaev, "Poslednii zarubezhnyi ofitsial'nyi vizit."

46. Lowell Dittmer, "The Sino-Japanese-Russian Triangle," http://jcps.sfsu.edu/past%20issues/ JCPS2005a/2%20JRC_Dittmer.pdf.

47. Ibid.

48. See chapter 11 in this volume, by Sergey Radchenko.

49. Cherniaev, *1991 god,* 131; Gorbachev, on March 30, 1991, *V Politbiuro,* 655–56.

50. See Hasegawa, *Northern Territories Dispute;* Kimura, *Japanese-Russian Relations,* 95.

11. Inertia and Change: Soviet Policy toward Korea, 1985–1991

Sergey Radchenko

On May 23, 1984, Soviet party and government functionaries assembled at the Iaroslavskii Train Station in Moscow for a long-overdue visitor. Comrade Kim Il Sung emerged from his armored train; in his mid-seventies, Kim appeared aged but vigorous, more than a match for the Soviet general secretary, Konstantin Chernenko, who was so feeble that he could not come to the train station to personally greet his dear guest. The ailing Chernenko welcomed the North Korean patriarch at the Kremlin. He spoke first, stumbling with difficulty through a prepared text with proclamations of proletarian solidarity. Kim, for his part, presented his Soviet hosts with a list of requests for military equipment: airplanes, ships, tanks, surface-to-air missiles, and spare parts.[1] Chernenko promised to deliver. Extensive aid seemed like a small price to pay for having North Korea on friendly terms after a decade of strained relations when Pyongyang had visibly tilted in the Chinese direction. "The North Korean leader's visit," concluded the *New York Times,* "offered the Russians an opportunity to recover some of the influence lost to China in the last decade."[2]

Kim Il Sung's appearance in Moscow was an outcome of a skillful foreign policy maneuver. On the one hand, the visit signaled his dissatisfaction with Beijing, which, it was rumored at the time, not only coveted South Korean markets but also had the insolence to urge the North Koreans to adopt Chinese-style reforms. On the other hand, Kim needed Soviet economic and military aid. The hermit kingdom's economy was in dire straits. Pyongyang could not pay back its foreign loans or get new ones—not from the West. In 1985, *Institutional Investor* magazine listed North Korea as 109th—the last position—in a rating of nations' creditworthiness.[3] Soviet–North Korean trade declined 10 percent in 1983. Inter-Korean relations were in deep trouble, all the more so after Pyongyang's ill-considered attempt to assassinate the president of the Republic of Korea (ROK; South Korea), Chun Doo Hwan, when he was in Rangoon in October 1983. Under these circumstances, it was of course highly advantageous for Kim to play the Soviet card, as he had done several times in the past, from his perspective always to a good effect.

Kim was welcomed with open arms (according to the North Korean radio, with "endless reverence and admiration"), not least because the Soviets needed his services to strengthen their very vulnerable political and military position in the Far East.[4] The Second Cold War aggravated already nasty tensions in Northeast Asia, where the Soviet Union not only confronted the United States and its allies—the armed and menacing "Washington-Tokyo-Seoul axis"—but also faced an unfriendly China at a time when Sino-Soviet relations had just barely begun to thaw after nearly three decades of bitter conflict. North Korea had strategic importance in the Soviet political-military calculations as a gaping hole in the staunchly anti-Soviet Far Eastern front. In view of their mutually compatible interests, the Soviet Union and North Korea rapidly moved toward rapprochement.

Between 1984 and 1986, Soviet–North Korean relations were as good as they had ever been. Military cooperation expanded at a breathtaking pace. If, for example, Soviet military supplies to North Korea averaged 64.6 million rubles in the period 1981–85, the corresponding figure for 1986–90 was 322.6 million rubles.[5] In May 1985, a Soviet air force squadron flew into Pyongyang on a mission of goodwill. In July 1986, a detachment of the Soviet Pacific Fleet made a rare visit to the North Korean port of Wonsan.[6] It was said that the USSR obtained emergency docking rights for its navy at Nampo (a port on North Korea's west coast, facing China) and that Pyongyang allowed the overflight of Soviet military planes en route from Siberia to the Soviet Union's naval base in Vietnam. In October 1986, the Soviet Union and North Korea reportedly held an unheard-of joint naval exercise in the Sea of Japan.[7]

At the same time, the Soviet Union widened the scope of its economic aid to the troubled North Korean regime, not only increasing oil supplies[8] but also agreeing, after years of Pyongyang's prodding, to build North Korea's first nuclear power plant.[9] On December 24, 1985, the two countries signed a protocol on the development of their bilateral trade, with an eye to doubling it in the 1986–90 period compared with the preceding five-year period.[10] Not that all of this satisfied Kim's appetite; when Soviet foreign minister Eduard Shevardnadze visited Pyongyang in January 1986, he was given a new list of requests for economic and military aid. "Kim's aim is obvious," noted Shevardnadze's aide, Teimuraz Stepanov, on that occasion, "by flattering, promises, and inventing horror [scenarios] to squeeze as much aid as possible from us."[11] The ploy was at least partially successful. In any case, Shevardnadze came back to Moscow with "a firm conviction that we can and must work successfully with Kim Il Sung and Kim Jong Il."[12] To build on his success, Kim Il Sung made another trip to Moscow in October 1986 for a meeting with Mikhail Gorbachev, which revealed (at least in public statements) an identity of views on key international issues.

By contrast, Soviet relations with South Korea were not just bad—they were nonexistent. Having been vilified by Soviet propaganda as a reactionary puppet of U.S. imperialism, South Korea existed, for all intents and purposes, only as a theoretical concept, a bogeyman of Asia. The significance of South Korea's economic strides in the 1970s and the 1980s was deliberately overlooked. The only thing that was said of the ROK in the Soviet press was that it was suffering from a "deep economic crisis" and, with raging unemployment and heavy foreign debt, was in fact "on the edge of financial-economic bankruptcy."[13] There was no direct trade between South Korea and the Soviet Union, and there were no contacts between them, save for sporadic encounters of athletes or academics (every time, over bitter complaints from Pyongyang). In 1983 even these little straws snapped amid bouts of mutual hostility after the Soviet air defense force shot down a civilian South Korean airliner off the coast of Sakhalin Island.

If, in 1986, anyone had predicted that in only a few years the Soviet Union and South Korea would establish official relations, that their political contacts and economic exchange would by far outstrip the extent of Soviet dealings with Pyongyang, and that Soviet relations with North Korea would plummet nearly to the point of rupture, this sort of predictions would likely have been dismissed in circles of informed observers as the result of mild insanity. And yet it happened—a complete and profound transformation of Soviet policy toward the Korean Peninsula. But of course it happened in the context of great changes elsewhere in the world as Cold War logic succumbed to the hope of the "new thinking" in Soviet foreign policy that Moscow was implementing in its relations with the West. The Cold War ended in Europe; tensions receded in Asia as well. In retrospect, it is almost too easy to say: "It could have not been any different with Soviet-Korean relations."

A closer examination of facts reveals that the process of Soviet–South Korean rapprochement and, conversely, Soviet–North Korean estrangement was neither as simple nor, indeed, as profitable to all parties involved as it may have appeared at first sight. "New thinking" had remarkably little practical significance for the orientation of Soviet policy in Korea—in fact, much less significance than the promise of South Korean credits. Soviet recognition of South Korea came too late to make a positive contribution to peace on the Korean

Peninsula. This untimely foreign policy move, and the drastic deterioration of Soviet–North Korean relations that followed it, had most undesirable consequences for the overall situation in Korea—consequences felt to this day. The North Korean nuclear crisis as we know it is in effect one of these consequences. In the late 1980s and early 1990s, Soviet policy toward Korea suffered from inconsistencies and unexpected reversals, leading to Moscow's effective loss of leverage on the peninsula by the end of Gorbachev's tenure in power.

The Economic Promise of South Korea

The late 1980s were marked by a sudden and substantial increase in the Soviet interest in Seoul's economic performance. "Sudden" does not mean that the ROK's economy was of no interest to the Soviet experts up to that time. There were—admittedly, very infrequent—publications on South Korea's economic dependence on, and exploitation by, U.S. and Japanese neocolonialists.[14] But by and large, the meager Soviet interest in South Korea had a distinct political-strategic tint in line with the notion that the ROK offered the U.S military an anti-Soviet "platform" in the Far East. Most of what the reading Soviet public heard of South Korea up to the late 1980s was tied, in one way or another, to the imperative of countering this strategic menace to the Soviet Union. Two problems combined to draw Soviet attention to South Korea's economic situation in 1987–88.

The first problem had to do with Gorbachev's efforts to jump-start the lagging economy of the Soviet Far East. This was not a new issue; the chronic underdevelopment of this sparsely populated frontier had been a cause of headaches for earlier Soviet governments, above all for security reasons. Gorbachev was less concerned about security than about the fact that the Soviet Union was losing out on the East Asian "miracle" because of the hopeless backwardness of its Asian provinces. "The development of civilization is shifting to the Pacific Ocean," Gorbachev argued at the Politburo in April 1986. "Our economy is also shifting to Siberia, to the Far East." And again in December: "The civilization will move to the East in the 21st century. Asia has huge forces, huge potential of a future civilization." In July, Gorbachev made a widely publicized trip to Vladivostok and promised to "quickly transform this region and put its riches at the service of the Soviet people."[15]

In line with these instructions, in August 1987 the Central Committee and the Council of Ministers approved the "Long-Term State Program of Complex Development of the Productive Forces of the Far Eastern Economic Region, the Buriat ASSR [Autonomous Soviet Socialist Republic], and Chita Oblast until the year 2000." Yet in spite of this impressive-sounding document, the

Far Eastern economy went from bad to worse. Faced with the grim situation, the Economic Department of the Central Committee dispatched a task force to the Far East to find out what was going wrong. The experts, headed by the head of the Chamber of Commerce and Industry, Vladislav Mal'kevich, toured the region in March 1988. Their conclusion was that the "Long-Term State Program" put too much emphasis on self-reliance and did not pay adequate attention to the task of developing foreign economic relations of the Soviet Far East.[16] The task force prepared a report recommending the expansion of Soviet economic ties with the Asia-Pacific region, the development of "special economic zones," and efforts to attract East Asian capital—especially Japanese capital—to long-term projects in the Soviet Far East.

But the Japanese were not at all in a rush to invest in the Soviet Far East—and this was the second problem. There were several reasons for this reluctance, not least the state of Soviet infrastructure and the legal framework, neither of which inspired much confidence among Japanese businessmen.[17] But there was also a political reason: Tokyo's insistence on the "inseparability of economics and politics." For as long as the Soviet Union refused to return to Japan the four islands of the Kuril chain, which it had occupied since the end of World War II, the Japanese government was unwilling to develop close economic ties.[18] To make matters worse, Soviet-Japanese relations, after a brief thaw in 1986, stagnated and even worsened after a series of spy scandals in 1987 and a row over the sale of sensitive Japanese technology to the USSR. It was only in mid-1988 that there was a renewed sense of mild forward movement with Tokyo—but there were no breakthroughs even as the Soviet Union leaped to better relations with the West.

Under these circumstances, South Korea was seen as a possible substitute for reluctant Japan—not a full substitute, but an acceptable one. Indeed, Mal'kevich's report, praising South Korea's economic development in the 1980s, specifically listed it as one of the most promising Soviet partners in the Far East, recommending the establishment of trade relations with the country through nongovernment channels. The ROK was not only important as a "counterweight to Japan's economic influence" in the region, but its closer relations with the Soviet Union would also hopefully "stimulate the activities of its [Japanese] firms in developing contacts with the USSR." In other words, the idea was to spur a competitive scramble for the Soviet Far East between Japan and South Korea.[19] The unspoken assumption of such an approach was that the Japanese were in reality very interested in doing business in the Far East but, seeing that they were the only claimants upon the Soviet riches, were biding their time to make greater political gains.

This kind of an unspoken assumption came out very clearly in another report—prepared by the KGB in March 1989—to assist in the implementation of the "Long-Term Program." KGB sources in Hokkaido disclosed that the island's socialist governor, Yokomichi Takahiro, was very worried by the prospects of Soviet–South Korean economic relations. The reason for this was allegedly that Hokkaido's economy, already in deep trouble, would lose out if the South Koreans reaped the benefits of cooperation with the Soviet Far East. After his visit to South Korea in November 1988, Yokomichi was said to have ordered a study on Soviet–South Korean relations with an eye to amending Hokkaido's own policy toward the Soviet Far East.[20] If this intelligence was correct, the Mal'kevich task force was not so far off the mark.

In the meantime, the KGB used every opportunity to impress upon the South Koreans the benefits of investing in the Far East. For example, in January 1989, the agency approached Choi Cheol-joo, a South Korean journalist who had come to visit Sakhalin Island, with the information that the Soviets could soon open up the Southern Kuril Islands as a "zone of free entrepreneurship" and that the South Koreans would be welcome to invest. Choi Cheol-joo responded that it was likely that the Japanese government would put South Korean businessmen under all kinds of pressure to keep out of the Southern Kurils on account of the unresolved territorial problem but that he thought that some businessmen would not mind participating if they could make a profit. The KGB cited Choi's response as evidence that Yokomichi had good reason to be worried.[21]

Not all assessments were as optimistic or necessarily put emphasis on Japanese–South Korean competition for a share of profits from the Soviet Far East. For instance, in a separate memorandum to Gorbachev from mid-1988, the head of the Institute for USA and Canadian Studies, Georgii Arbatov, claimed that the Soviet Union needed South Korea precisely because Japan was no longer interested in what the Soviets could offer. South Korea, he wrote, "is now at the stage of development when it requires our traditional export goods: ore, coal, oil, timber (Japan has passed this stage already, which explains the decrease of Japanese interest in economic cooperation with us)."[22] This was not a big problem, however, because, in the absence of the Japanese, "the South Koreans could help us substantially in the development of the Far East, as well as other areas (in the construction of ports, car and electronics factories, electronics, in the establishment of joint ventures in fishing, etc.)"[23] Thus, by mid-1988, more and more experts eyed prosperous South Korea as the pressure built up within the Soviet policy community to tap into its economic potential in an effort to develop the Soviet Far East. Initial Soviet interest in developing ties with Seoul was therefore a product of crude economic calculations rather than the lofty ideas of the "new thinking"; with Japan obstinately clinging to the "Northern Territories" question, South Korea was the only substantial source of cash to pay for Gorbachev's dream of integrating the ailing Far Eastern economy into the greater "miracle" of East Asia.

The 1988 Seoul Summer Olympics

The Seoul Summer Olympic Games of 1988 was another important development that encouraged Soviet rethinking of South Korea. The Soviets protested bitterly when the International Olympic Committee (IOC) voted to award the 1988 summer games to Seoul, but there was no going back on that decision once it had been made—the IOC stood firm in the face of Soviet threats. The choice was therefore between participating in the Olympics and staging a boycott. Olympic boycotts had recent precedents; many Western countries had boycotted the 1980 Moscow Olympics after the Soviet invasion of Afghanistan. In 1984, the Soviets (and a few allies) declared a boycott of the Los Angeles Olympics. A boycott of the Seoul games was obviously a distinct possibility. From the Soviet perspective, however, this course of action had a number of serious disadvantages. First, it denied the Soviet athletes a chance to compete in the most prestigious international sports event. It could also lead to IOC sanctions against the Soviet Union. Finally, in general terms, an Olympic boycott could take a serious toll on Gorbachev's efforts to advertise his foreign policy as a positive contribution to world peace.

The ROK had to do everything possible to lure the Soviets to Seoul, for a socialist boycott of the Olympic Games would deal a major blow to South Korea's international image. The chairman of the Seoul Organizing Committee (and later South Korean president), Roh Tae Woo, even secretly approached Soviet representatives with a promise to "neutralize" the 1983 airplane incident: "If the Soviet Union takes part in the Seoul Olympic Games, all questions connected to the destruction of the Korean airplane will be taken off the agenda, because he [Roh Tae Woo] sees it as not only a mistake on the part of the USSR but a fault of another great power."[24] This jab in the U.S. direction was meant to impress upon the Soviets that South Korea had an independent posture upon the world stage.

To lessen the chances of a Soviet boycott, Seoul agreed to talks with North Korea about sharing the Olympic Games. Several rounds of talks were held in Lausanne, beginning in October 1986. There is no doubt that Seoul and the IOC agreed to the talks only to be able to blame their failure on North Korea's intransigence. As the IOC's head, Juan Antonio Samaranch, put it to South Korean president Chun Doo Hwan, the idea was "to leave North Korea with the responsibility of saying 'no.'"[25] The North Korean tactic, by contrast, had to show to the Soviets, the Chinese, and other allies that they had made a reasonable proposal about co-hosting the games, only to face ill will on the part of the reactionary puppets. Pyongyang's failure to secure a half (or, later, a third) of the Seoul Olympics would therefore give good ground to the Soviet Union to stage a boycott and ruin the games.

To Kim's disappointment, Gorbachev's endorsement of this ploy was lukewarm at best. When the two met in October 1986, the Soviet leader said that in principle he did not mind having Olympic Games in both South Korea and North Korea, and would support that eventuality. However, there should be no boycotting the games, even if Pyongyang were not allowed to host half the sporting events. "I will tell you frankly," Gorbachev added, "that the issue is in the principle, and not in the arithmetic."[26] Because the Soviet leadership generally backed the rigid foreign policy schemes of the Democratic People's Republic of Korea (DPRK, North Korea) at this time, Gorbachev had to explain just why he could not support Kim Il Sung on this particular point. The problem was in Kim's suggestion that the USSR threaten to boycott the Olympic Games: "This [the Olympiad] is an enormous channel for cooperation, for influencing [the West] in the needed direction. . . . If we were to take this road [boycotting the Games], we would hurt ourselves, our policies. This is the interconnection of these elements." This was the first time, perhaps, that Gorbachev discovered "interconnection" of Moscow's policy toward the Korean Peninsula and the broader Soviet "peace offensive." Kim Il Sung, according to Gorbachev's later account, "understood us. But he hopes for our firm position, and I promised that we will have a meeting, I promised that we will talk about this."[27]

And so they "talked about this"—for the better part of two years. The Soviet Union voiced public support for the DPRK's position but did not go out of its way to pressure the IOC. As Aleksandr Yakovlev, Gorbachev's close associate and a liberal-minded reformer, put it to a visiting North Korean functionary in May 1986, the IOC was a "reality, which we must take into account. . . . On the international stage we come up against tendencies to isolate socialist countries, and there are efforts to prevent their participation the 1988 Olympic Games in Seoul. This is the long-term strategy of the USA in the athletic movement. We must carefully weigh our steps in the IOC."[28] At the same time, the Soviets were privately telling the IOC that their chief concern was not with North Korea's obstinate position but with Cuba's staunch support for Pyongyang.[29] Under these circumstances—given Fidel Castro's great prestige—Soviet participation in the games could cause considerable friction in the socialist world and possibly undermine Soviet positions in the developing world. These were all good reasons to encourage the North Koreans to compromise. Pyongyang, realizing that it had maneuvered itself into a corner, offered one concession after another. In January 1988, Soviet foreign minister Eduard Shevardnadze had enough confidence to tell Samaranch that the gap had narrowed and the problem of North Korea's participation would soon be resolved.[30] But the South Koreans dug in their heels. Perhaps they had offered too little to allow Kim Il Sung to maintain a dignified appearance, or perhaps, as Samaranch had thought all along, the North Koreans never intended to take part in the games. There was no agreement. The Olympics were to be held only in South Korea. On January 11, 1988, the Soviet Union signaled its acceptance.[31]

The Seoul Olympics, held in September and October 1988, offered the Soviet Union an unprecedented window into daily life in South Korea, while many ordinary South Koreans had their first personal encounters with the dreaded Soviet foe. The Soviet delegation featured more than five hundred athletes, not counting officials, coaches, interpreters, and journalists. The Soviet cruise liner *Mikhail Sholokhov* brought a group of tourists to the Korean shores, including a number of Sakhalin Island Koreans, some of whom had tearful family reunions with long-lost relatives in South Korea. The Russians came with their own cultural program, drawing audiences of thousands to packed concert halls.

The Olympic broadcasts in the Soviet Union averaged fourteen to sixteen hours daily, while the opening ceremony commanded the attention of about 200 million Soviet television viewers.[32] Of course, only sports-related facilities were shown on television, but it was enough to give the Soviet audiences an indirect experience of Seoul—an experience that did not square with the image of South Korea cultivated for years by Soviet propaganda. In the end, however, it was not the common man in the living room who mattered but the elites—Soviet athletes, officials, journalists, performers, and scholars—those who had seen South Korea firsthand and now came back to share their experiences with friends and colleagues in Moscow. Many would agree with an assessment offered by the head of the Soviet press delegation Vitalii Ignatenko: "Everything I had read before turned out to be outdated; I arrived in the 21st century."[33]

Nordpolitik

Although by 1988 Soviet experts slowly but surely came around to appreciate South Korea's importance in Northeast Asia and the benefits of developing Soviet ties with it, most of the impetus for improved Soviet–South Korean relations came from South Korea in the form of *Nordpolitik,* a kind of a South Korean version of West Germany's *Ostpolitik* once championed by Willy Brandt.

Nordpolitik served several purposes. First, it improved South Korea's international standing (simultaneously undercutting that of its rival in the north). Second, it gave Seoul extra leverage for dealing with Pyongyang on its own terms. Last but not least, it was of immense personal significance to President Roh Tae Woo in the uncertain political climate of the late 1980s; mending fences with Moscow was one way of defending his credentials as a statesman and peacemaker from the vocal opposition.

Roh Tae Woo's close confidant Pak Ch'ŏl-ŏn, who was put in charge of developing contacts with the Soviets, worked primarily through Soviet academics. In May and June 1988, he first held meetings with the experts of the Oriental Institute—Nikolai Vasiliev and Konstantin Sarkisov—who arrived in South Korea on an exploratory mission. Encouraged by these contacts, Park visited Moscow in August and September, hoping to meet Gorbachev. Although the Soviet leader did not receive him, Park made important contacts in Moscow, both at the Oriental Institute and the Institute for USA and Canadian Studies, and he explored options for Soviet–South Korean economic cooperation, whetting the Soviet appetite.[34] In the meantime, the leaders of the South Korean opposition, in particular Kim Young Sam and Kim Dae Jung (both future presidents), used their own channels to contact the Russians. Kim Young Sam took the opportunity offered by the presence in Seoul of the Soviet press corps head, Vitalii Ignatenko, for the Olympic Games to get himself invited to Moscow; the invitation was issued through the Institute of World Economy and International Relations (IMEMO), whose director, Evgenii Primakov, was a friend of Ignatenko's.[35] Kim Dae Jung obtained his invitation in October from Georgii Arbatov of the Institute for USA and Canadian Studies, although that invitation was later rescinded, apparently because of Primakov's insistence that his Kim (Kim Young Sam) was the more important of the two.[36] The significance of these first contacts was that they resulted from South Korea's—not the USSR's—prodding. Although it can be said that by 1988 the Soviet Union and South Korea were moving in each other's direction, the intensity of movement and the distance covered were by far greater on the South Korean side.

Nevertheless, Gorbachev's attitude toward South Korea changed at a quickening pace. Thus, in May 1988, while recognizing that there were "signals coming from Seoul," Gorbachev still cautioned against any gesture in South Korea's direction "so that they [probably the North Koreans] don't accuse us of agreeing to the concept of two Koreas."[37] But by the fall of 1988, he was himself making such gestures, most strongly in his speech in Krasnoyarsk on September 16, when for the first time he openly called for developing trade relations with South Korea in the context, as he put it, of "a general amelioration of the situation on the Korean Peninsula."[38] This speech was a product of a build-up of Soviet interest in South Korea over the previous months, and of course its emphasis on trade relations reflected the specific nature of this interest: an interest rooted in mercantile considerations rather than lofty ideas.

Conversely, Soviet patience with North Korea was wearing thin by 1988, not least because of Gorbachev's unwillingness to subsidize "fraternal" regimes to the detriment of Soviet political and economic interests. One example of this was the practice of exporting weapons—something that Gorbachev's aides Anatolii Cherniaev and Georgii Shakhnazarov bitterly criticized in a memorandum to the Soviet leader on September 30, 1988. Exporting weapons, they argued, was incompatible with the "new thinking" in Moscow's foreign policy toward the West: "Our almost unfailing readiness to respond to these requests and even demands [for weapons] is not harmless . . . from the point of view of our relations with the West." This was because the use of these weapons by militant regimes was "in the eyes of the world community identified . . . with our intentions in this or that region."[39] Providing military aid to Soviet clients was not only prohibitively expensive but also altogether unrewarding. The memorandum concluded that the time had come for the Soviet Union to cut off the weapons lifeline, "provided by a kind of inertia, as a result of promises given in the past, or mainly in response to unending requests of those who speculate on our internationalism contrary to the interests of peace, about which they generally do not care."[40] In another memo to Gorbachev on December 13, 1988, Cherniaev argued against uncritical support of militant clients by what he called "inertia of proletarian internationalism."[41] In other words, if the economic promise of South Korea produced a positive inducement for rethinking Soviet strategy in Korea, the new priorities of the liberal wing of Gorbachev's entourage—the fabled "new thinking"—helped to widen the gap with North Korea.

This interesting interplay can be seen in the sequence of events leading up to the Soviet decision to expedite trade ties with South Korea. The catalyst was Gorbachev's aforementioned Krasnoyarsk speech, which triggered an angry reaction from Pyongyang. The Central Committee secretary, Hwang Jang Yop, was promptly dispatched to Moscow to register a strong protest. He delivered a nastily worded memorandum to Aleksandr Yakovlev, who had just been appointed the Central Committee secretary in charge of international affairs. The memorandum said that "for the amelioration of the situation on the Korean Peninsula, one must first and foremost evacuate the American troops from South Korea and put an end to the anti-people, treacherous actions of the South Korean regime."[42]

Hwang's memorandum was politely accepted, but there was no turning back the clock. The North Korean protests only made matters worse for Kim Il Sung.

In fact, Yakovlev was so upset about his meeting with Hwang that the next day, October 19, he wrote to the deputy head of the International Department, Karen Brutents: "Probably, the first proposal that we will introduce [to the Politburo] will be on South Korea."[43] That instruction apparently led Valentin Falin, the head of the International Department at the Central Committee, to call a meeting on October 22 with participation from leading Korea specialists in academia. The meeting produced a draft policy paper, "On Our Policy in South Korea," which recommended dramatic changes for Soviet policy on the Korean Peninsula. The paper criticized Moscow's tendency to "unequivocally orient itself toward our friends in the DPRK, adjusting our policy to their dogmatic line, frequently contrary to our own long-term interests." In the meantime, "without South Korea and at odds with this dynamically developing country, it is more difficult to push forward our initiatives concerning the Asia-Pacific region, and it is more difficult to develop stable and mutually beneficial relations with many countries of [that] region." The paper concluded that "due to political, military-strategic and current economic reasons, it is a ripe and necessary time to turn from demonstratively ignoring South Korea to accepting the de facto existing realities. Soviet policy must not be a hostage to the policy of the DPRK."[44]

This document—signed by Yakovlev, Foreign Minister Eduard Shevardnadze, Deputy Premier Vladimir Kamentsev, and KGB chief Vladimir Kriuchkov—was discussed at the Politburo meeting on November 10, 1988.[45] "If we don't act now," Gorbachev commented, "we will be late." Being "late" in this context meant missing out on the economic opportunities offered by rapprochement with South Korea. Of course, Gorbachev framed his economic interest by references to the political context: "A channel is being opened to our influence on the entire Korean situation. Contact with South Korea will be our response to North Korea, and a signal to the USA."[46] By "response to North Korea," he meant Soviet disapproval of Pyongyang's hard-line policies, while the "signal to the USA" would show Soviet willingness to overcome the two-camp mentality and convey an invitation to the Americans to do the same. Yet these were only secondary considerations, which couched pragmatic economic interests in the theoretical framework of the "new thinking."[47]

One interesting aspect of the policy paper was that it included Shevardnadze among its authors. The Foreign Ministry by and large remained outside early policy discussions concerning Korea, and in fact it maintained a generally conservative position based on a long-standing commitment to a relationship with North Korea. As the Politburo came around to rethinking relations with Seoul, the Foreign Ministry produced recommendations of unwavering Soviet support for Pyongyang. In October 1988, in response to reports by the Soviet

Embassy in Pyongyang about the North Korean leaders' unhappiness with increasing Soviet–South Korean contacts (probably with the exchange of memoranda on Soviet–South Korean economic cooperation on October 15), the Foreign Ministry proposed reassuring Pyongyang that there was no real intention of rapprochement with Seoul. This proposal reached Shakhnazarov, who forwarded it to Gorbachev with a damning indictment:

> The Soviet Foreign Ministry's proposal . . . raises certain doubts. The way we have it is, every time when Pyongyang sounds an angry "warning," we begin assuring them that everything will be as it was and we don't have any serious intentions of having contacts with South Korea. In reality, now we are talking precisely about the intention of acting in that direction, which is entirely in accordance with the interests of the Soviet Union, and generally speaking, will contribute to a favorable development of events in Asia. Why should we mollify Kim Il Sung and assure [him] that we will not change anything? Wouldn't it be more correct and honest to say directly that further implementation of this line is unreasonable, that everything had shifted in the world, and one should look for new approaches to the settling of the situation also on the Korean Peninsula? Otherwise, if we do not show initiative here, the West will win.[48]

Shakhnazarov's memorandum is a good example of the kinds of contradictions that permeated Soviet foreign policy at the time. The note had three layers. The first was the "West will win" proposition. This line of argument suggested that the Soviet opening to South Korea was a part of the struggle against imperialism, a kind of a tricky maneuver aimed at undermining the Western position on the Korean Peninsula. The second layer—"contributing to a favorable development of events in Asia"—was lip service to the ideas of the "new thinking." Both of these layers created a kind of an ideological curtain that obscured the real reasons for the change of policy, that is—that such a change would be "entirely in accordance with the interests of the Soviet Union," the third layer.

Shakhnazarov proposed to send a special envoy to Pyongyang to "explain these new aspects in our Asian policy." He thought that Kim Il Sung might turn out to be "very unhappy, but in the end he would have to reconcile himself" to these changes.[49] In other words, Shakhnazarov, like many others in the Soviet policymaking establishment, held the view that Kim Il Sung was first and foremost a realist who would recognize the inevitability of Soviet–South Korean rapprochement and would only protest to save face; a rupture of relations with

Moscow was certainly not in his interests under any circumstances. Gorbachev picked up on this theme at the meeting on November 10. He urged against using the "shock method" with North Korea and proposed that Shevardnadze travel to North Korea to calm Kim Il Sung.[50] Shevardnadze visited Pyongyang in December. Though records of these talks are not yet available, the foreign minister reportedly gave Kim his "Communist's word" that Moscow would not have any dealings with Seoul detrimental to the interests of the North Korean regime.[51]

It is interesting that the role of Kim Il Sung's appeaser fell to Shevardnadze, whose own institutional base—the Foreign Ministry—had a markedly conservative attitude toward the Korean question. It appears that Shevardnadze was at best unenthusiastic about Soviet signals to Seoul, despite supposedly being the soul of the "new thinking" in foreign policy.[52] As the head of the Central Committee International Department, Valentin Falin, recalled, he and Yakovlev had to "break [*sic*] Shevardnadze" to make him endorse a change of policy in Korea.[53] Falin himself, incidentally, was thoroughly dissatisfied with the pace of rapprochement with Seoul: "We have already lost economic opportunities in South Korea. The Koreans are disappointed with us," he argued on one occasion.[54]

But unlike Falin, who headed one of the most "liberal" departments in the Central Committee, Shevardnadze was in a more complicated position. Although he supported Gorbachev in many of his foreign policy initiatives, Shevardnadze also had the weight of the conservative—or, better put, "moderate" (for the true conservatives were entrenched in the military)—Foreign Ministry establishment on his back. So to some extent he had to sit between the chairs, juggling ideas from both camps. It also cannot be ruled out that Shevardnadze was jealous that Korea policy had been effectively hijacked by Yakovlev and his supporters.[55] The pro–South Korean camp (the liberals in Gorbachev's circle) had to get Shevardnadze on board for their proposals on normalizing relations with Seoul, in order to present a broader front in the Politburo discussion. It helped that although Yakovlev and Shevardnadze were talking about the same thing, they attached different meanings to Soviet initiatives on South Korea. Yakovlev clearly saw the establishment of trade relations as only the first step toward political normalization, but this idea was never clearly formulated, and the diplomats could justly claim that it was also the last step for the foreseeable future. Gorbachev, with characteristic ambiguity, trod the middle ground.

Despite Shevardnadze's promises to Kim, Soviet relations with South Korea developed dramatically in 1989. In January, the two countries exchanged trade representatives and established direct air routes. In June 1989, the leader of the

South Korean opposition, Kim Young Sam, visited Moscow unofficially, on the earlier invitation of IMEMO, whose director and candidate Politburo member Evgenii Primakov was one of the early advocates of a rapprochement with South Korea in the Soviet leadership. He held far-ranging talks with the academic experts but also with Brutents of the International Department, requesting his assistance in the repatriation of approximately two hundred elderly Sakhalin Island Koreans. The North Koreans eyed these developments with increasing anxiety but, with a display of realism earlier predicted by Shakhnazarov, Kim Il Sung abstained from a violent propaganda barrage. Instead, he dispatched a ranking Politburo member, Ho Dam, for talks with Kim Young Sam in Moscow regarding the prospects of inter-Korean dialogue. The "great leader" obviously recognized that some improvement in Soviet–South Korean relations was inevitable and decided that he could accommodate it for the time being. One would suspect that fears of diplomatic isolation, as well as the necessity of maintaining Soviet aid, added to Kim's sense of realism.[56]

In the meantime, Soviet public opinion, never before of serious consequence for Moscow's foreign relations, began to play an increasingly independent and assertive role in policy discourse. An important turning point in this respect was an article in the newspaper *Izvestiia* by a Soviet Korea specialist, Fania Shabshina, who openly called for the establishment of diplomatic relations with the ROK.[57] The diplomatic establishment was predictably unhappy; deputy minister Igor Rogachev called a special briefing at his ministry to disclaim any role in the article. The North Koreans even sent Shabshina a letter of protest, complaining bitterly of her subversion of Soviet relations with Pyongyang.[58] But the floodgates were already open. Soviet–South Korean contacts intensified, especially in the academic sphere. Soviet scholars, freed from the iron hand of party discipline, had none of the inhibitions of the diplomats in developing closer ties with South Korea. On the contrary, it was hard to resist Seoul's charm offensive—the endless invitations, the VIP treatment, and the presents. As a prominent Soviet specialist on Korea explained to this author, "The South Koreans were very generous. Presents were pouring like a river to all (even the most junior) people."[59]

But the scholars, important as their opinions were in the final calculations of Soviet policy toward South Korea, were in a different category than policymakers. Gorbachev had to balance Soviet approaches to South Korea with maintenance of a client relationship with North Korea. Indeed, opening trade relations with Seoul in late 1988 set a threshold that the Soviet leader was unwilling to pass for months, whatever the "new thinking" may have dictated. Thus, in meetings with Chinese premier Li Peng in May 1989 during his visit to Beijing, he said: "Kim Il Sung and the North Korean leadership are probably afraid that we can go from trade contacts to political ties with South Korea. This, however, is out of the question. We are not going to agree on cross-recognition. At least for today, this is not our policy."[60] What was this supposed to mean? This statement could be interpreted as Gorbachev's unwillingness to recognize Seoul, but it could also mean that the Soviet leader considered such recognition possible after "today." Of course, "today" was a stretchable concept. With his penchant for compromise solutions and halfway measures, Gorbachev deliberately maintained a sense of ambiguity with regard to his policy in Korea, expecting, much as he did with regard to Soviet-Japanese relations, that at some stage all Gordian knots would be untangled and all problems would resolve themselves.

Breakthrough

In the meantime, unofficial political contacts between Moscow and Seoul continued. In March 1990, Pak Ch'ŏl-ŏn and Kim Young Sam, each wanting to be the first achieve a breakthrough with the Russians, arrived in Moscow in a joint delegation. Park Ch'ŏl-ŏn carried Roh Tae Woo's personal letter to Gorbachev. He requested a confidential meeting with Shevardnadze, but the foreign minister had left on a tour of Africa and instructed his deputy, Igor Rogachev, not to receive the South Korean envoy. Cherniaev had to interfere with a note to Gorbachev on March 19:

> It seems to me that this is after all a question of state policy, and not of institutional-personal sympathies and calculations. Rogachev talked about stage-by-stage process. But isn't the Korean asking for a purely confidential meeting? And one can probably reconcile oneself with hurt feelings of Kim Il Sung and his heir apparent, taking into consideration the irreversible course of events.[61]

This time, however, Cherniaev did not mention a word about the "new thinking" in Soviet foreign policy. Cherniaev noted that Pak Ch'ŏl-ŏn's inclusion in Kim Young Sam's delegation was "another proof of serious intentions of President Roh Tae Woo" and that Pak Ch'ŏl-ŏn would likely use his time in Moscow "for practical and, for us, very profitable economic aims." The shift of emphasis is revealing. In the previous months, economic cooperation with South Korea was clearly on the agenda of Soviet policymakers, but it was occasionally obscured by the imperatives of the "new thinking": building up confidence in the Asia-Pacific region, stemming the militant ambitions of North Korea, reconciling Soviet propaganda about the "new thinking" with actual foreign policy priorities in Asia. But now, as the economic situation in the USSR deteriorated rapidly and Gorbachev sought funds from all possible outside sources, the recognition of South Korea suddenly acquired unexpected urgency.

Because of the Foreign Ministry's intransigence, Cherniaev recommended that Gorbachev appoint a person from the Central Committee to meet with Pak Ch'ŏl-ŏn. The task fell to Brutents, who was instructed to receive Roh Tae Woo's envoy on March 22. In the meantime, Kim Young Sam had met with Primakov. During that meeting, Gorbachev staged an "unintentional" encounter with the South Korean visitor: He walked into Primakov's office at the time of the latter's meeting with Kim. Gorbachev and Kim Young Sam exchanged a few remarks, with the Soviet leader reportedly saying that he saw no obstacles to the establishment of diplomatic relations between Moscow and Seoul in the near future.[62]

Unbeknownst to the Russians, the fact that Gorbachev met with Kim Young Sam, when it was Pak Ch'ŏl-ŏn who was Roh Tae Woo's personal envoy, deeply offended Park. As Brutents later wrote, "Sometimes our one hand does not know what the other is doing."[63] The incident also reveals the ad hoc nature of Soviet policymaking at this critical moment. Shevardnadze explicitly instructed his staff at the Foreign Ministry not to receive the South Korean delegation, because any meeting with them at the official level could not be construed in any other way than as a major upgrade of political contacts. However, Shevardnadze's instructions counted for little, because the key proponents of improving relations with South Korea—Brutents, Yakovlev, and Primakov—met with the delegation, probably with Gorbachev's blessing. Finally, Kim Young Sam, relying on his previous contacts with Primakov, managed to bypass both the Foreign Ministry and the Central Committee, securing a direct face-to-face meeting with the Soviet leader. One cannot help but be struck by the degree to which Soviet policy at the time depended on chance encounters and ad hoc decisions.

During his meeting with Brutents, Park delivered Roh Tae Woo's message to Gorbachev calling for the "speediest normalization of Soviet–South Korean relations in the name of stability and peace on the Korean Peninsula." The real message, however, was not on paper; Pak Ch'ŏl-ŏn conveyed Roh's assurances of South Korea's interest in investment projects in the Soviet Far East and Siberia. But this could come about only if Moscow offered suitable guarantees to South Korea by establishing diplomatic relations. Roh also hoped that the Soviet leadership would apply leverage on North Korea to bring about Pyongyang's cooperation in lessening inter-Korean tensions.[64]

Political strings that came with a promise of economic aid from Seoul did not discourage Gorbachev's advisers. Shortly after Kim Young Sam's visit, Cherniaev and Brutents prepared a memorandum for the Soviet leader, in which they argued that the gradual escalation of contacts with Seoul with continued gestures of commitment to North Korea was a policy of fence-sitting that neither endeared Roh Tae Woo nor really fooled Kim Il Sung. Cherniaev and Brutents therefore recommended a radical approach: immediate recognition of South Korea in return for Seoul's agreement to initiate large-scale economic projects in the USSR. Such a trade-off would be by far preferable to piecemeal efforts of normalization, because it would allow the Soviet leadership to "test the seriousness of South Korean intentions."

Perhaps recognizing that their far-reaching recommendations might upset Gorbachev as an explicit profit-making scheme, Cherniaev and Brutents paid lip service to the ideas of the "new thinking." The memorandum said that both Koreas had still not renounced the idea of using force for reunification, and therefore "normalization of relations between the USSR and South Korea will lead to a turn from a confrontation on the Korean Peninsula to creation of conditions for peaceful reunification." As for Pyongyang's reaction to this scenario, Cherniaev and Brutents warned not to overdramatize it. Kim Il Sung would do fine as long as Moscow remained "fairly loyal to the North Korean regime." In any case, "our intentions with regard to Seoul must not be unexpected for the leadership of the DPRK."[65] Obviously, the ideas of being "fairly loyal" to North Korea and not doing anything "unexpected" with Seoul ran right against the substance of the memorandum. This contradiction addressed Gorbachev's lingering uncertainties about Korea. The escape clause on "loyalty" to North Korea allowed Gorbachev to approve the memorandum, which he did shortly thereafter.

In May 1990, Gorbachev was still unsure about the best course of action. Roh Tae Woo pushed for a personal meeting. The idea was supported and championed by Cherniaev, but Gorbachev also had an open ear for Shevardnadze's complaints. The foreign minister urged caution.[66] But the Soviet leadership was running out of time. In May, Anatolii Dobrynin, the longtime Soviet ambassador in the United States and now Gorbachev's foreign policy adviser, was invited to Seoul for an unofficial meeting of former senior diplomats. He was to be received by Roh Tae Woo. On May 17, Cherniaev wrote to Gorbachev that "having no answer about his [Roh Tae Woo's] meeting with you implies a negative answer." Cherniaev proposed to schedule a meeting with Roh in San Francisco, which Gorbachev would visit shortly during his summit meeting with President George H. W. Bush. He also warned against reliance on Shevardnadze for advice:

> Shevardnadze is not a helper in search of a solution. He was offended that you met with the Korean [Kim Young Sam] despite his

> opinion, which he left with the Foreign Ministry, before leaving for Namibia. . . . We are letting billions [of dollars] slip out of hand.[67]

Financial considerations prevailed with Gorbachev at the last moment. He called in Dobrynin before his departure for Seoul and instructed him to pass on to Roh his agreement for a personal meeting in San Francisco. Gorbachev reportedly told Dobrynin that "we need some money."[68] Facing a deepening economic crisis, Gorbachev shed his ideological second thoughts about North Korea and decided to commit his efforts to rapprochement with Seoul for down-to-earth financial reasons. Unsurprisingly, the meeting in San Francisco was to be prepared secretly from Shevardnadze and the Foreign Ministry; only Gorbachev's closest confidants were aware of the plan.[69]

Roh and Gorbachev met in San Francisco on June 4, in Gorbachev's hotel suite. The site of the meeting was a special subject of discussion because the Soviet leader did not want to be seen as Roh's guest. He was also unhappy with Roh's request to pose for a joint photograph, displaying characteristic uncertainty. The Soviet leader finally gave in when Dobrynin assured him that the photo would not reach the Soviet public. Gorbachev's agreement to meet with Roh Tae Woo signified a turning point in the Soviet relationship with South Korea, but this was a reluctant turn for the Soviet leader, not so much because of Pyongyang's likely wrath or Shevardnadze's complaints but because he did not want to admit—above all to himself—that he had surrended another "principled position." The two sides also agreed to move toward normalization "step after step."[70]

Three days later, Gorbachev hosted a summit of the Warsaw Pact leaders in Moscow. In his speech, he mentioned his meeting with Roh Tae Woo in passing. Roh once again was chacterized as an American puppet. The South Korean president allegedly sought Washington's agreement to the meeting ahead of time, and he even asked President Bush's "permission" before meeting with Gorbachev. Nevertheless, the Soviet leader welcomed the results of the meeting, naturally not because of a promise of future credits from Seoul but because "this undertaking of ours will in the end contribute to positive changes in Korea and in the region as a whole."[71] Departing from his prepared text, he added: "Roh Tae Woo, naturally, endevoured to achieve agreement on diplomatic recognition as soon as possible. We linked that with the general process on the Korean Peninsula and pushed to find a constructive solution to the problem."[72] By putting the Korean problem into a wider context of the "new thinking," Gorbachev tried to justify an improvement of relations with Seoul (which was by that time increasingly a matter of Soviet national interest) to his colleagues from Eastern Europe and—above all—to himself.

Crisis

Gorbachev's contradictory approach toward South Korea worried Cherniaev, who wanted to preserve the momentum of Moscow-Seoul contacts after the San Francisco meeting. On June 23 he wrote to Gorbachev: "It seems to me that we must not leave your meeting with Roh Tae Woo without consequences. E. A. [Shevardnadze] is still 'griping,' and, probably, he is bound up by some kind of promises to Kim Il Sung. But the business must be done."[73] Roh Tae Woo was a better businessman; he had already followed up on the San Francisco meeting with a personal message to Gorbachev, proposing an official meeting of the foreign ministers of the two countries. Having Shevardnadze on board was still in question, but Cherniaev cautioned not to ignore Roh's letter. He prepared a draft response for Gorbachev, which in general terms expressed satisfaction with the San Francisco encounter and called for a lower-level meeting of economic experts as the next "step" toward the normalization of relations.

In the meantime, bitter tensions plagued Soviet relations with North Korea. As expected, Kim Il Sung was unhappy with the Gorbachev-Roh talks. It was now important to convince him that the impending Soviet recognition of South Korea (planned for January 1, 1991) would not be detrimental to Pyongyang. Shevardnadze took up the unthankful task, although he was personally unhappy with the pace of rapprochedment with Seoul. On September 2, he arrived in North Korea for a two-day visit, which ended in one of the most dramatic confrontations in his diplomatic career. In an unprecended affront, Kim Il Sung refused to see Shevardnadze. In Kim's place, the Soviet foreign minister met with Kim Yŏng-nam, his DPRK counterpart.

Kim Yŏng-nam produced a memorandum outlining the North Korean response to the Soviet decision. Kim declared that Soviet recognition of South Korea would put an end to the Soviet–North Korean Treaty of Alliance. Because the Soviet "umbrella" afforded by this treaty would no longer protect North Korea, Pyongyang would be free to develop its own defense against the U.S. nuclear weapons in South Korea by pulling out of the Nuclear Non-Proliferation Treaty. This would have terrible consequences for regional and global stability. Kim Yŏng-nam then told Shevardnadze: "You know better, which fate awaits the Treaty of Nuclear Non-Proliferation if we are forced to renounce this treaty."

The memorandum accused the Soviet Union of joining ranks with the United States and South Korea in the attempt to force the DPRK to open to the outside. The normalization of relations with Seoul meant that the South Koreans would become more arrogant in pressuring Pyongyang into opening up with an eye to "overthrowing the socialist regime in our country" and swallowing up North Korea along the lines of the German scenario. Kim Yŏng-nam warned

Shevardnadze not to count on North Korea's capitulation, à la that of Eastern Europe: "Frankly speaking, the USSR actively inspired perestroika politics in the GDR [East Germany], as a result of which the situation changed sharply and she was annexed by the FRG [West Germany]. . . . The situation in Korea will not turn out the way the USA and South Korea want it, and it will not develop the way you [the Soviet leadership] expect."[74] Here, Kim Yŏng-nam claimed, the Soviets' actions could only lead to the breakdown of the North-South dialogue.

Finally, Shevardnadze was told that as the Soviet Union abandoned North Korea like "worn-out shoes," Pyongyang would also make changes to its Soviet policy; these would entail recognition of the independence of Soviet republics. In Asia, the North Koreans now planned to improve relations with Japan, substituting race-based for class-based alignments and necessitating Pyongyang's recognition of Japan's territorial claims to the Soviet-held Southern Kurils.[75] This was a remarkable slap in the face for the Moscow. Not that North Korea carried much weight internationally; its "revenge" was at most a minor nuissance for the Soviets, who were beleaguered by a host of other problems. But Pyongyang's threats marked an unprecedented collapse of the Soviet–North Korean relationship. Overnight, Moscow's positions in North Korea were reduced to nothing. Moreover, this formerly difficult but on occasion amenable quasi-ally of the USSR now became a stray bullet with unclear trajectory. Kim Yŏng-nam's promise to go nuclear was an important indication of troubles still to come.

Pyongyang's nuclear ambitions derived from a complicated set of factors. Kim Il Sung's interest in nuclear research went back to the 1950s. North Korea's expertise in the field progressed by leaps and bounds in the 1960s, not least because of extensive Soviet aid. But a theoretical intention to have a nuclear bomb—certainly documentable from the 1960s—did not square with the Great Leader's capabilities. It is fair to say that North Korea's nuclear exploits had a primarily peaceful character, aiming, especially in the 1970s and the 1980s, at the solution of the country's persistent energy deficits. It may well be that the Soviets sometimes closed their eyes when the North Koreans used their peaceful nuclear research to gain insights into weapons production. But if so, by the late 1980s, this kind of complacency was clearly out of place.

In fact, in the memorandum cited above, which was drawn up as a policy alternative to the Foreign Ministry's mellow attitude toward North Korea, Cherniaev and Brutents strongly warned about Pyongyang's nuclear ambitions as another reason for taking a tougher line on Kim Il Sung: "One is particularly alarmed by the nuclear program, secretly carried out in the DPRK with our aid. . . . The DPRK's access to nuclear weapons will have irreversible consequences for the entire security system, which developed in the Asia Pacific after the Second World War. Decisive steps are necessary on our part to prevent such a development of events."[76] The memorandum coincided with a report by the KGB head, Vladimir Kriuchkov, stating that, according to Soviet intelligence information, North Korea had already developed a nuclear bomb, although it did not test it "in the interest of hiding from the world community and control organizations the very fact of production of atomic weapons in the DPRK."[77] Whether or not Kriuchkov's memorandum was accurate (later Western estimates suggest that North Korea was not yet as far advanced in its weapons program), the Soviets had reasons to worry—not only because a nuclear-armed North Korea would be a cause of great instability in Northeast Asia, as detrimental to Soviet interests as to those of other countries, but also because Moscow had greatly contributed to Pyongyang's nuclear program. And now the Soviets were told that it was all their fault that North Korea would seek a nuclear deterrent. The situation was not without its irony.

Turned off by the open hostility, Shevardnadze packed up and left Pyongyang hours before his scheduled departure. By the end of that month, Seoul and Moscow had established diplomatic relations, three months ahead of schedule. The initiative to expedite recognition came from the Soviet side. The Soviet leaders thought that they had nothing else to lose after the last bridge to North Korea had been burned. Shevardnadze voiced his gloom about the prospects of the Soviet relationship with Pyongyang in a conversation with Aleksandr Kapto, who was appointed the new Soviet ambassador in Pyongyang in December 1990: "At the end of the . . . conversation with me, Shevardnadze put a special emphasis on the fact that one may expect the worst outcome in relations with the DPRK. I asked directly: What does this mean? Without waiting for an answer, I continued—break of diplomatic relations? Lowering his head, he muttered: 'Anything can be expected.'"[78]

Kapto, who had previously served as the Soviet ambassador to Cuba and later worked in the ideology department of the Central Committee, was charged with the difficult task of saving what he could from the crumbling Soviet–North Korean alliance. Gorbachev's hope was that once all the cards were on the table, Kim Il Sung would recognize the inevitable and agree to coexistence with a changed Soviet Union. Kapto was given a special personal message for Kim from Gorbachev. "Dear Comrade Kim Il Sung"—began the letter (in what must have been one of the last instances when Gorbachev used the word "comrade" in his correspondence with foreign officials)—

> We suppose that the accumulated experience and all of the positive things, which developed and proved itself in relations with friendly

> states, must not be lost in the process of turbulent changes in the world as a whole. On the contrary, it must be used in a wider context. We consider this realistic approach of ours appropriate and useful for the further development of relations with your country. The Soviet leadership stands for the improvement and deepening of mutually useful cooperation with the DPRK.

Then Gorbachev's letter also praised Kim Il Sung for his peaceful initiatives —"confidence building" on the Korean Peninsula and proposals for a confederation of two Koreas. These ideas had been on Kim's agenda for years; in fact, Gorbachev's letter sounded like what he would have told the North Korean leader in 1986. It was as if Gorbachev had suddenly turned the clock five years back, crossing out all the bitterness that had built up in the Soviets' relationship with Pyongyang over the previous months. Gorbachev's letter was a striking reminder of his uncertainties; he had burned the bridges to Pyongyang, and yet he continued to pretend that nothing had happened. Unsurprisingly, Kim Il Sung did not receive Kapto, when he arrived in Pyongyang with "comradely greetings" from Gorbachev, nor did he ever reply to the Soviet leader's letter.[79]

The Soviet Union and South Korea after Normalization

There is some irony in the fact that, although Gorbachev finally agreed to his meeting with Roh Tae Woo in San Francisco with the hope of getting the South Korean credits, he did not get anything—or at least not right away. Roh had high expectations for the summit, even though the odds were against immediate recognition. Just in case Gorbachev decided to act on the spur of the moment, the South Korean delegation had prepared protocols on opening diplomatic relations with the USSR, as well as a memorandum of understanding on economic cooperation, should it come to it.[80] But the Soviet leader merely promised recognition at some future date and suggested that the two sides "proceed gradually, working step by step until the process was completed." He then offered an analogy—"the fruit will be sweet when it ripens"—to which Roh replied that he was "well known for his patience."[81]

But what about Gorbachev? Did he agree to meet with Roh Tae Woo, knowing full well North Korea's reaction to such a meeting, to exchange pleasantries and talk about peace in the world? When Gorbachev gave a green light to the meeting, he did so with a specific purpose in mind: money. The Soviet economy needed South Korean credits. Gorbachev's own political survival depended on foreign credits. He had traveled from coast to coast, calling on U.S. businessmen to invest in the USSR. Yet Gorbachev did not ask Roh for credits.

Furthermore, he postponed diplomatic recognition, though the South Koreans had stated explicitly that credits would come only *after* recognition, not the other way around. Gorbachev did just what his aides had warned he should not: He failed to reap the benefits of a prompt recognition of South Korea, but he did enough to ruin the Soviet relationship with North Korea. The reason for his uncertainty in San Francisco was probably psychological; as a great world leader, he felt it beneath his dignity to beg for credits from yesterday's "puppet" of the United States, to show to Roh Tae Woo that he was interested in South Korea for financial reasons rather than the noble imperative of peace and stability in Northeast Asia.

Concerns about being manipulated by the South Koreans were raised before Gorbachev by the unraveling conservative establishment. On January 3, 1991, the KGB, Ministry of Defense, and Ministry of Foreign Affairs prepared a joint memorandum for the Soviet leader admitting that Seoul had tried to use the Soviet Union to help bring about a German-style scenario on the Korean Peninsula. But the key was for the Soviet Union to make use of its relationship with South Korea in order to take a leading role in the multilateral dialogue on the peninsula's future. It was recognized that the Soviet Union was most interested in stability in Korea; the fate of Korean reunification was a question of secondary importance. The main thing was to avoid war. The authors of the memorandum saw it as the Soviet task to influence both North *and* South Korea in the direction of achieving stability on the peninsula. On April 2, Gorbachev officially approved this memorandum. It was another indication that Gorbachev was trying to formulate a different Korea policy—one that would preserve a special Soviet role in Northeast Asia irrespective of Seoul's coffers.[82]

The trouble was that, as always, Gorbachev was outpaced by events. Grand diplomatic strategy was of course a good thing, but there was a more pressing agenda in early 1991—survival: the survival of a country amid the economic collapse and survival of Gorbachev as a leader. On March 30, Gorbachev held a meeting of the recently formed Security Council to discuss finances. Cherniaev scribbled in his diary:

> Scraped the closets to find foreign exchange and credits and buy [food] from abroad. But we are already insolvent. Nobody is giving credits; the hope is that Roh Tae Woo will.[83]

The stakes were high. Gorbachev had to meet with Roh to see how far South Korea was willing to go. The Soviet Foreign Ministry recommended either traveling to both Seoul and Pyongyang on the way back from Gorbachev's scheduled trip to Japan, or skipping both capitals. Gorbachev himself remained uncertain, apparently as late as March 29, when Cherniaev sent him a note:

> There are requests through different channels, including personally from Roh Tae Woo, for you to stop by Korea on the way back [from Japan]. The last option: to stop at Cheju Island (this is 300 kilometers from Nagasaki) and meet with Roh Tae Woo. This will take only a few hours. Maybe, it's worth it, in order to avoid a separate trip to South Korea later?[84]

Gorbachev agreed. After his failed mission to Tokyo, on April 19 and 20 he met with Roh Tae Woo on Cheju Island, where, according to Cherniaev's later recollections, the Soviet leader achieved "mutual understanding with President Roh Tae Woo and in fact agreed to full-scale and even to some extent 'most favored' bilateral relations."[85] Roh agreed to offer credits and even talked of Korean aid to oil and gas projects in Siberia. Even Cherniaev skeptically marked in his diary: "It's hard to believe in this."[86]

Conclusion

"Most-favored relations" did not quite work well with the more balanced strategy that Gorbachev approved in his directive on April 2, but such a contradiction was anything but new. From the mid-1980s until his fall from power, Gorbachev's Korea policy suffered from frequent reversals and a divergence between proclaimed objectives and actual outcomes. I stated at the beginning of the chapter that in one sense the change of Soviet policy toward Korea in the 1980s was a predictable outcome of the "new thinking." The Soviet–South Korean rapprochement went a long way toward ending the Cold War in Asia. Surely Gorbachev deserves credit, alongside Roh Tae Woo, for his willingness to go beyond bloc logic and to embrace a former foe—something none of his predecessors even came close to considering. But although the "new thinking" may offer a convenient explanation for Soviet foreign policy in the 1980s—in Korea as, for instance, in Europe—a closer examination of the decisionmaking process (something that is only now becoming possible with the declassification of archival materials) reveals that key decisions were often taken for reasons that had nothing to do with the "new thinking."

Gorbachev's first years in power saw continuous improvement in Soviet–North Korean relations. Indeed, while there is no doubt that Pyongyang acted with belligerence here and there, the general direction of North Korean propaganda (withdrawal of U.S. nuclear weapons from Korea, reunification without foreign interference) in no way undermined Gorbachev's "new thinking" for Asia—the Soviet leader even cited Pyongyang's initiatives in his own key policy speech in Vladivostok. Conversely, North Korea's domestic rigidity increasingly became a cause of irritation for Gorbachev in 1987–88. The ups and downs of Soviet–North Korean relations, however, did not trigger a Soviet search for a different partner in Korea. It is also not true that, as Gorbachev claimed in another key speech in Krasnoyarsk, Soviet contacts with South Korea were prompted by his interest in promoting peace on the Korean Peninsula. As we have seen, Soviet interest in South Korea was originally aroused and continually maintained by the prospect of tapping into the country's economic potential. It is important to note that increasing Soviet interest in South Korea was indirectly a product of a stalemate in Soviet-Japanese relations.

Gorbachev's Korea policy was susceptible to half measures. There were voices in his immediate circle (most prominently, Cherniaev, but also Yakovlev, Primakov, Shakhnazarov, Brutents, and others) who warned that "step-by-step" rapprochement with South Korea was counterproductive and that a rapid normalization was in the Soviet interest. Conversely, the Foreign Ministry, conservative military circles, and the KGB cautioned against sharp turns in South Korea policy for fear of provoking North Korea. Gorbachev listened to both, and agreed with both. The result was a dysfunctional policy, which failed to secure the benefits of a rapid normalization for the USSR and yet antagonized North Korea. If Gorbachev had been more decisive and moved, in 1988, toward full normalization with South Korea—as, for example, Hungary did—he could have achieved this normalization on Soviet terms and, with Soviet aid to North Korea at its historic height, he would have had far more leverage with Pyongyang than he did two years later, when the flow of aid had shrunk to a mere trickle. Most important, he could have presented the breakthrough with Seoul as a historic victory for peace and a direct outcome of the "new thinking"—something he could not do in 1990 or 1991, when it was all too clear to all observers that Gorbachev had swapped recognition for credits.

Or, taking the second route, Gorbachev could have sided more firmly with the Foreign Ministry and the conservatives who cautioned against rapid rapprochement with the South. This would have allowed him to preserve Kim Il Sung's allegiance in some shape or form, and so, once again, to have more leverage over North Korea. China opted for this second scenario. Barely behind the Soviet Union in developing ties with Seoul, Beijing somehow managed to avoid the Soviet blunder of alienating Pyongyang. Russia, conversely, had to rebuild its relations with North Korea over subsequent years, after realizing the importance of "standing on two legs" on the Korean Peninsula. Perhaps an avoidance of the sharp turns in Gorbachev's Korea policy would have helped reduce the North Koreans' sense of insecurity. There is ground to suppose, as we have seen, that the rapid change in Soviet policy in Korea was one of the factors that precipitated the DPRK's efforts to obtain nuclear weapons.

North Korea's diplomatic performance in the same period was far from spectacular. Kim Il Sung overreacted to what in effect were inevitable Soviet moves and thwarted himself by slamming the door in Moscow's face. In the 1990s, he worked hard to regain some of the ground that he had lost with the Russians, this time facing a much more critical audience among liberal-minded Russian policymakers, at least until Russian "liberalism" began to wear off in the mid-1990s. Clearly Kim Il Sung learned from his mistakes, for China's recognition of South Korea in 1992 did not cause anything like the crisis occasioned by the same Soviet step two years earlier. The Great Leader bowed to the inevitable. Had he been more flexible in the late 1980s, North Korea could have avoided diplomatic isolation. Kim sought to minimize South Korea's pressure on his regime, but by the early 1990s North Korea was under pressure from nearly all sides, increasingly a besieged fortress in intensely hostile territory.

The greatest beneficiary of changes in Soviet policy toward Korea was South Korea. It was able to assert an independent posture in foreign policy and negotiate with North Korea from a position of strength. Roh Tae Woo's personal prestige and legitimacy were greatly improved by the impressive success of his *Nordpolitik.* Unlike the Japanese government, which could not go beyond the territorial issue and thus failed to achieve a substantial breakthrough in its relations with Moscow, the South Koreans overcame serious hurdles and not only secured Soviet diplomatic recognition but also replaced North Korea as Moscow's key partner on the Korean Peninsula. If it took $3 billion in credit to do that, the price was not very high. Indeed, South Korea benefited at least as much as the Soviets from the economic cooperation between the two countries. South Korean companies planted deep roots on Soviet soil, as curiously symbolized today by the Samsung billboards overlooking the Kremlin. This success is all the more remarkable in that it was attained by a country that was poorly positioned to deal with the Soviet Union; it did not have the expertise or leverage—or, in any important sense, the encouragement—of its allies. The success of South Korea's *Nordpolitik* is a testament to the importance of understanding the motives and actions of regional players in the multilayered and complicated setting of the East Asian Cold War.

Notes

1. For an account of the 1984 Kim Il Sung–Chernenko talks, see Mikhail Kapitsa, *Na raznykh paralleliakh: Zapiski diplomata* [On various parallels: Notes of a diplomat] (Moscow: Kniga i biznes, 1996); and Dmitrii Volkogonov, *Sem' vozhdei: Gallereiia liderov SSSR* [Seven leaders: Gallery of Soviet leaders], 2 vols. (Moscow: Novosti, 1995), vol. 2, 253–54.

2. John F. Burns, "Moscow Talks End for North Korean," *New York Times,* May 26, 1984.

3. John Burgess, "Prospering North Shrouded in Myth," *Washington Post,* August 19, 1986.

4. "North Korea; USSR's 'Exceptional Welcome' for Kim Il-Sung," BBC Summary of World Broadcasts, July 6, 1984.

5. "Spravki po torgovo-ekonomicheskomu sotrudnichestvu s soprovoditel'noi" [Information about trade-economic cooperation, with an accompanying memo], July 15, 1991. Gorbachev Fond Archive (hereafter GFA), Moscow, fond (f.) 2, document 8997.

6. "Soviet Pacific Fleet Flotilla Arrives in North Korea," BBC Summary of News Broadcasts, July 5, 1986.

7. "N. Korean-Soviet Naval Exercise?" BBC Summary of News Broadcasts, October 24, 1986.

8. "North Korea Believed to Have Secured Additional Soviet Oil Supplies," *Platt's Oilgram News,* February 3, 1986.

9. Balázs Szalontai and Sergey Radchenko, *North Korea's Efforts to Acquire Nuclear Technology and Nuclear Weapons: Evidence from Russian and Hungarian Archives,* Cold War International History Project Working Paper 53 (Washington, D.C.: Cold War International History Project, Woodrow Wilson International Center for Scholars, 2006), 73.

10. Iu. S. Stoliarov, "Torgovo-ekonomicheskie otnosheniia SSSR so stranami Aziatsko-Tikhookeanskogo regiona" [Trade-economic relations of the USSR with the countries of the Asia-Pacific region], Analytical Report, July 15, 1986, Archive of the Institute of World Economy and International Relations (IMEMO Archive), Moscow. There is no further information available because the IMEMO Archive is not properly organized.

11. "Bezzhiznennaia strana: O iadernoi voine v Severnoi Koree dumali eshche pri Kim Ir Sene" [A lifeless country: They thought about nuclear war under Kim Il Sung in North Korea], *Izvestiia,* March 3, 2003. The original diary entry was provided to the author by G. Stepanov, the son of Teimuraz Stepanov.

12. "Zasedanie Politbiuro TsK KPSS" [Meeting of the Politburo of the Central Committee of the CPSU], January 30, 1986, Library of Congress, Volkogonov Collection, reel 17, containers 24–26.

13. S. Agafonov, "Iuzhnaia Koreia–SShA: Plody partnerstva" [South Korea–USA: Fruits of partnership], *Izvestiia,* January 13, 1983.

14. See, e.g., Viktor Shipaev, *Iuzhnaia Koreia v sisteme mirovogo kapitalisticheskogo khoziaistva* [South Korea in the system of the world capitalist economy] (Moscow: Nauka, 1986); and Viktor Shipaev, *Ioponiia i Iuzhnaia Koreia: "Pomoshch razvitiiu" i ee posledstviia* [Japan and South Korea: "Development aid" and its results] (Moscow: Nauka, 1981).

15. "Speech on Development of Soviet Far East and Asia Pacific Affairs," BBC Summary of World Broadcasts, July 28, 1986.

16. "K voprosu ob intensifikatsii vneshneekonomicheskikh sviazei dal'nevostochnogo ekonomicheskogo raiona so stranami aziatsko-tikhookeanskogo regiona" [On the problem of intensification of external economic relations in the Far Eastern Economic District with the countries in the Asia-Pacific region], n.d. (probably 1988), IMEMO Archive.

17. See, e.g., "Otchet o vizite delegatsii Verkhovnogo Soveta SSSR v Iaponiiu" [Report on the visit of the delegation of the Supreme Soviet of the USSR to Japan], n.d. (probably November 1989), Gosudarstvennyi Arkhiv Rossiiskoi Federatsii (hereafter GARF; State Archive of the Russian Federation, Moscow), fond (f.) 10063, opis' (op.) 2, delo (d.) 198, list (l.) 20.

18. For a much more detailed account, see Tsuyoshi Hasegawa, *The Northern Territories Dispute and Russo-Japanese Relations,* vol. 2, *Neither War nor Peace, 1985–1998* (Berkeley: International and Area Studies, University of California, 1998).

19. "K voprosu ob intensifikatsii vneshneekonomicheskikh sviazei dal'nevostochnogo ekonomicheskogo raiona so stranami aziatsko-tikhookeanskogo regiona," 7.

20. "O merakh po sodeistviiu realizatsii programmy razvitiia dal'nevostochnogo ekonomicheskogo raiona" [About the measures for assistance to realize the program of development of the Far Eastern economic region], March 7, 1989, Sakhalinskii Tsentr Khraneniia Sovremennoi Dokumentatsii, f. P4, op. 152, d. 67, ll. 1–4.

21. Ibid.

22. Memorandum from Georgii Arbatov to Anatolii Cherniaev (for Mikhail Gorbachev), mid-May 1988, GFA, f. 2, document 1168.

23. Ibid.

24. Mikhail Prozumenshchikov, *Bol'shoi sport i bol'shaia politika* [Big Sport and Big Politics] (Moscow: Rosspen, 2004), 131.

25. "Entrevue entre le Président Chun Doo Hwan et le Président Samaranch" [Interview between President Chun Doo Hwan and President Samaranch], Seoul, April 25, 1986. IOC Archive, Lausanne, Seoul 88 / political matters, de 1982 a mai 1986.

26. Vadim Medvedev, *Raspad: Kak on nazreval v "Mirovoi Sisteme Sotsializma"* [Disintegration: How It Came About in the "World Socialist System"] (Moscow: Mezhdunarodnye Otnosheniia, 1994), 326.

27. "Vystuplenie M. S. Gorbacheva: Ozdorovlenie mezhdunarodnoi obstanovki, ukreplenie mira (po vtoromu voprosu)" [Speech of M. S. Gorbachev: Revivifying the international environment, strengthening peace (to the second question)], November 11, 1986, GFA, f. 5, op. 1, document 20669, ll. 31–32.

28. Conversation between Yakovlev and Hwang Jang Yop, May 16, 1986; GARF, f. 10063, op. 2, d. 55, ll. 1–8.

29. Report on a meeting with Soviet IOC officials and with Kim Yu Sun, n.d. (probably late summer 1986), IOC Archive, Seoul 88 / political matters, de 1982 a mai 1986.

30. Memorandum by Juan Antonio Samaranch on his meeting with Eduard Shevardnadze, January 20, 1988, IOC Archive, Seoul 88 / Politique, Janvier-Juillet.

31. Richard Pound, *Five Rings Over Korea* (Boston: Little, Brown, 1994), 270.

32. Don Oberdorfer, *The Two Koreas: a Contemporary History* (New York: Basic Books, 2002), 200–201.

33. Cited by ibid., 200.

34. See the detailed account of Park's exploits given by Pak Ch'ŏr-ŏn, Parŭn yŏksa rŭl wihan chŭng'ŏn [Testimony for the Historical Truth], vol. 2 (Seoul: Daeil Munhwasa, 2005).

35. Letter from Vladimir Ovsiannikov to the author, December 12, 2007.

36. Author's interview with Georgii Arbatov, Moscow, March 24, 2008.

37. Record of a Politburo meeting, May 5, 1988, shared with the author by Anatolii Cherniaev.

38. "Speech in Krasnoyarsk," BBC Summary of World Broadcasts, September 19, 1988.

39. Memorandum from Anatolii Cherniaev and Georgii Shakhnazarov to Mikhail Gorbachev, September 30, 1988, GFA, f. 2, op. 1, document 1547, ll. 1–3. This document is also reprinted by Anatolii Cherniaev, *Shest' let s Gorbachevym: Po dnevnikovym zapisiam* [Seven years with Gorbachev: According to the diary notes] (Moscow: Progress, 1993), 259–60.

40. Ibid.

41. "O vizite na Kubu," December 13, 1988, GFA, f. 2, op. 1, document 1592, l. 1. This document is also reprinted by Cherniaev, *Shest' let s Gorbachevym,* 196–97.

42. "Conversation between Aleksandr Yakovlev and Hwang Jang Yop," October 18, 1988, GARF, f. 10063, op. 2, d. 126, ll. 1–13.

43. Karen Brutents, *Nesbyvsheesia: Neravnodushnye zametki o perestroike* [What did not come to pass: Heartfelt remarks about perestroika] (Moscow: Mezhdunarodnye Otnosheniia, 2005), 216.

44. Cited by Vladimir Li, *Rossiia i Koreia v geopolitike Evraziiskogo Vostoka (XX vek)* [Russia and Korea in the geopolitics of the Eurasian East] (Moscow: Nauchnaia Kniga, 2000), 235.

45. Li gives the names of Falin, Georgii Kim, and Evgenii Primakov as the authors of the memorandum cited above. He also writes that the memorandum was approved by the Politburo on November 18; see Li, *Rossiia i Koreia,* 235. However, the Politburo meeting actually took place on November 10.

46. Record of a Politburo meeting, November 10, 1988, shared with the author by Anatolii Cherniaev.

47. "Rossiia i mezhkoreiskie otnosheniia" [Russia and inter-Korean relations], April 17, 2003, http://www.gorbi.ru/rubrs.asp?rubr_id=124&art_id=13119.

48. "Dokladnaia zapiska M. S. Gorbachevu k Spets N. 696 iz Pkhen'iana" [Note on a speech by M. S. Gorbachev to Spets N. 696 from Pyongyang], October 26, 1988, GFA, f. 5, op. 1, document 18169, l. 1.

49. Ibid.

50. Record of a Politburo meeting, November 10, 1988, shared with the author by Anatolii Cherniaev.

51. The story about Shevardnadze's "Communist's word" comes up in several versions in several sources, though it is yet to be documentarily confirmed. See, e.g., Evgenii Bazhanov, "Soviet Policy towards South Korea under Gorbachev," in *Korea and Russia: Toward the 21st Century,* ed. Il Yung Chung (Seoul: Sejong Institute, 1992), 100; Oberdorfer, *The Two Koreas,* 213; and Aleksandr Kapto, *Na perekrestkakh zhizni: Politicheskie memuary* [On the crossroads of life: Political memoirs] (Moscow: Sotsial'no-Politicheskii zhurnal, 1996), 434.

52. By contrast, Shevardnadze would later claim that he was at the forefront of developing relations with South Korea. Author's interview with Eduard Shevardnadze, Tbilisi, May 7, 2008.

53. "Reagan provotsiroval nas khlopnut' dver'iu" [Reagan provoked us to slam the door], *Vlast',* March 11, 2005.

54. Cited by Bazhanov, "Soviet Policy towards South Korea," 98.

55. Author's interview with Anatolii Cherniaev, Moscow, April 1, 2008.

56. Kim Young Sam, *Taet'ongnyŏng hoegorog: Minjujuŭi rul wihan naŭi t'ujaeng*

[President's memoirs: Struggle for democracy], vol. 3 (Seoul: Joseon Ilbosa, 2001), 187–91.

57. "Soviet Relations with South Korea," BBC Summary of World Broadcasts, September 18, 1989.

58. Author's interview with senior researcher at the Oriental Institute Iurii Vanin, Moscow, March 28, 2008.

59. Author's interview with Aleksandr Vorontsov, the head of the Korea and Mongolia section of the Oriental Institute, Moscow, March 21, 2008.

60. Cited by Bazhanov, "Soviet Policy towards South Korea," 98.

61. Memorandum from Anatolii Cherniaev to Mikhail Gorbachev, March 19, 1990, GFA, f. 2, op. 1, document 8240, l. 1.

62. Kim Hakjoon, "The Process Leading to the Establishment of Diplomatic Relations between South Korea and the Soviet Union," *Asian Survey* 37, no. 7 (July 1997): 645.

63. Brutents, *Nezbyvsheesia,* 217.

64. Ibid., 218.

65. Ibid., 220.

66. Oberdorfer, *Two Koreas,* 214.

67. Memorandum from Anatolii Cherniaev to Mikhail Gorbachev, May 17, 1990, GFA, f. 2, op. 1, document 8315, l. 1.

68. Cited by Oberdorfer, *Two Koreas,* 209.

69. Ibid., 209–10.

70. Ibid., 211–12; "Dokladnaia zapiska Cherniaeva i proekt pis'ma Ro De U" [Notes of speech of Cherniaev and draft letter to Roh Dae Woo], June 23, 1990, GFA, f. 2, op. 1, document 8346, l. 2.

71. "Materialy k zasedaniiu Politicheskogo Konsul'tativnogo Komiteta gosudarstv-uchastnikov Varshavskogo Dogovora (PKK) v Moskve" [Materials for the meeting of the Political Consultative Committee of the Warsaw Pact Government in Moscow], June 7, 1990, GFA, f. 5, op. 1, document 15354, l. 2.

72. "Rede des Prasidenten der Union der Sozialistischen Sowjetrepubliken M. S. Gorbatschow" [Speech of the President of USSR M. S. Gorbachev], June 7, 1990, SAPMO, Berlin, DC20/I/3/3000, s. 125. Available at the Web site of the Parallel History Project on NATO and the Warsaw Pact (PHP), www.isn.ethz.ch/php, by permission of the Center for Security Studies at ETH Zurich and the National Security Archive at the George Washington University on behalf of the PHP network, http://www.isn.ethz.ch/php/documents/collection_3/PCC_meetings/coll_3_PCC_1990.htm.

73. "Dokladnaia zapiska Cherniaeva i proekt pis'ma Ro De U," June 23, 1990, GFA, f. 2, op. 1, document 8346, l. 1.

74. Ibid.

75. Cited by Kapto, *Na perekrestkakh,* 432–36.

76. Cited by Brutents, *Nesbyvsheesia,* 217.

77. Evgeniia Albats, "Eshche v 1990 godu KGB SSSR dokladyval: V KNDR zavershena razrabotka atomnogo vzryvnogo ustroistva" [Already in 1990 the USSR KGB reported: The DPRK completed the working of the atomic explosive device], *Izvestiia,* June 24, 1994. It is worthwhile to note that the above source reprints what it claims to have been a KGB report. The authenticity of this report cannot be taken for granted.

78. Kapto, *Na perekrestkakh,* 436.

79. Cited in ibid., 438–39.

80. Embassy in Seoul to the Secretary of State, June 2, 1990 (Seoul 06215), Don Oberdorfer Files, National Security Archive, Washington; Interview with Sun Joun-yung, Seoul, July 27, 2007.

81. Embassy in Seoul to the Secretary of State, June 2, 1990 (Seoul 06215), Don Oberdorfer Files, National Security Archive, Washington.

82. Cited by Kapto, *Na perekrestkakh,* 448–53.

83. Anatolii Cherniaev, *Sovmetsnyi iskhod: Dnevnik epokh, 1972–1991* [A joint exodus: A diary of two epochs] (Moscow: Rosspen, 2008), 933–34.

84. Memorandum from Anatolii Cherniaev to Mikhail Gorbachev, March 29, 1991, GFA, f. 2, op. 1, document 8845, l. 1.

85. Cherniaev, *Shest' let Gorbachevym,* 440.

86. Cherniaev, *Sovmetsnyi Iskhod,* 937.

Contributors

Gregg Brazinsky is an associate professor of history at George Washington University. He is the author of *Nation Building in South Korea: Koreans, Americans, and the Making of a Democracy* (University of North Carolina Press, 2007).

Chen Jian is the Michael J. Zak Professor of History for U.S.-China Relations at Cornell University. He is the author of *China's Road to the Korean War: The Making of the Chinese-American Confrontation* (Columbia University Press, 1994); *The China Challenge in the 21st Century: Implications for U.S. Foreign Policy* (U.S. Institute of Peace, 1998); and *Mao's China and the Cold War* (University of North Carolina Press, 2001).

Ilya V. Gaiduk is a senior research fellow at the Institute of World History of the Russian Academy of Sciences in Moscow. He is the author of *The Soviet Union and the Vietnam War* (Ivan Dee, 1996) and *Confronting Vietnam: Soviet Policy toward the Indochina Conflict, 1954–1963* (Stanford University Press, 2003).

Tsuyoshi Hasegawa is a professor of history at the University of California, Santa Barbara. He was the organizer of a three-year conference on the Cold War in Asia. His major publications include *The Northern Territories Dispute and Russo-Japanese Relations,* two volumes (International and Area Studies, University of California, 1998); and the prize-winning book *Racing the Enemy: Stalin, Truman, and the Surrender of Japan* (Harvard University Press, 2005). The revised and translated edition of *Racing the Enemy* in Japanese received the Yomiuri-Yoshino Sakuzo Prize in 2006 and the Shiba Ryotato Prize in 2007.

Steven Hugh Lee is an associate professor of history at the University of British Columbia. He is a specialist in American and Canadian diplomatic history and in Korean-American relations, and is the author of *Outposts of Empire: Korea, Vietnam, and the Origins of the Cold War in Asia, 1949–1954* (McGill–Queen's University Press, 1995); and *The Korean War* (Longman, 2001).

Lorenz Lüthi is an assistant professor of history at McGill University. He is the author of *The Sino-Soviet Split: Cold War in the Communist World* (Princeton University Press, 2008), which won the Edgar S. Furniss and the Marshal Shulman awards.

Sergey Radchenko is a fellow in international history at the London School of Economics and Political Science. He is the author of *Two Suns in the Heavens: The Sino-Soviet Struggle for Supremacy,* 1962–1967 (Woodrow Wilson Center Press and Stanford University Press, 2009); and the coauthor (with Campbell Craig) of *The Atomic Bomb and the Origins of the Cold War* (Yale University Press, 2008).

Nobuo Shimotomai is a professor at Hosei University. His recent publications include *A History of the Cold War in Asia* (in Japanese, 2004) and *Moscow and Kim Il Sung* (in Japanese, 2006; in Russian, 2009).

Kazuhiko Togo is a professor at Kyoto Sangyo University. He joined the Foreign Ministry of Japan in 1968, and worked extensively on Soviet/Russian affairs. He served as ambassador of Japan to the Netherlands and retired in 2002. He is the author of *Japan's Foreign Policy 1945–2003: The Quest for a Proactive Policy* (Brill, 2005) and *The Inside Story of the Negotiations on the Northern Territory: Five Lost Windows of Opportunity* (in Japanese, 2007).

Odd Arne Westad is professor of international history at the London School of Economics and Political Science and codirector of LSE IDEAS, a center for the study of diplomacy and international strategy. His recent books include *Decisive Encounters: The Chinese Civil War, 1946–1950* (Stanford University Press, 2003) and *The Global Cold War: Third World Interventions and the Making of Our Time* (Cambridge University Press, 2005), which won the Bancroft Prize in 2006. He is the coeditor (with Melvin Leffler) of the three-volume *Cambridge History of the Cold War* (Cambridge University Press, 2010).

Vladislav Zubok is a professor of history at Temple University. He is the co-author (with Constantine Pleshakov) of the prize-winning book *Inside the Kremlin's Cold War: From Stalin to Khrushchev* (Harvard University Press, 1996) and the author of *A Failed Empire: The Soviet Union in the Cold War from Stalin to Gorbachev* (University of North Carolina Press, 2008), which received the Marshall Shulman Award. His most recent book is *Zhivago's Children: The Last Russian Intelligentsia* (Harvard University Press, 2009).

Index

(*continued from p. ii*)

Confronting Vietnam
Soviet Policy toward the Indochina Conflict, 1954–1963
By Ilya V. Gaiduk

Economic Cold War
America's Embargo against China and the Sino-Soviet Alliance, 1949–1963
By Shu Guang Zhang

Brothers in Arms
The Rise and Fall of the Sino-Soviet Alliance, 1945–1963
Edited by Odd Arne Westad